SIGNERS
OF THE
Mayflower Compact

BY

ANNIE ARNOUX HAXTUN.

THREE PARTS IN ONE

CLEARFIELD

Originally Published
New York, 1897-1899

Reprinted
Genealogical Publishing Company
Baltimore, 1968

Reprinted for
Clearfield Company, Inc. by
Genealogical Publishing Co., Inc.
Baltimore, Maryland
1998, 2004

Library of Congress Catalogue Card Number 67-28609
International Standard Book Number: 0-8063-0173-2

Made in the United States of America

INDEX TO CONTENTS

	Page
Adams, John	103
Alden, John	24
Allerton, Isaac	19
Allerton, John	85
Bassett, William	103
Billington, John	73
Bradford, William	9
Brewster, Jonathan, on the Fortune	111
Brewster, Rev. Nathaniel, of Brookhaven, L. I.	115
Brewster, William	15
Brewster Records	89, 117, 127
Britteridge, Richard	84
Brown, Peter	75
Carver, John	7
Chilton, James	72
Clarke, Richard	79
Cook, Francis	51
Cooke, Pilgrim Francis, Will of	109
Cooke, John, Will of	109
Crackston, John	69
Doty, Edward	80
Eaton, Francis	71
English, Thomas	85
Fletcher, Moses	70
Forefather Ships: Fortune, Ann, and Little James	102
Fuller, Benjamin	128
Fuller, Edward	67
Fuller, Samuel	27
Gardiner, Richard	85

	Page
Goodman, John	71
Hickes, Robert	104
Hicks, Robert, of the Fortune	105
Hopkins, John, Will of	109
Hopkins, Stephen	36
Howland, John	33
Leister, Edward	85
Margeson, Edward	78
Martin, Christopher	28
Mayflower Log	86
Morton, George, of the Ann	106
Mullins, William	29
Priest, Degory	72
Ridgdale, John	66
Rogers, Thomas	58
Soule, George	77
Standish, Myles	21
Tilley, Edward	50
Tilley, John	49
Tinker, Thomas	66
Turner, John	70
Warren, Richard	32
White, William	30
Williams, Thomas	74
Winslow, Edward	12
Winslow, Gilbert	78
Winslow, John, of the Fortune	123

THE MAYFLOWER COMPACT.

On the 11th day of November, 1620 (old style), there was drawn on the lid of a chest on board of the Mayflower in Plymouth harbor, and signed by forty-one of the principal men of the first band of Pilgrims, a platform of government known as the Compact, and which gave to these people the claim of being the first "signers" of this great and free United States of America.

THE COMPACT.

The following is the full text of the compact:

IN YE NAME OF GOD, AMEN.

We whofe names are underwritten, the loyall fubjects of our dread fovereigne Lord, King James, by ye grace of God, of Great Britaine, France and Ireland, King, defender of ye faith, etc., haveing undertaken for ye glory of God and advancemente of ye Chriftian faith, and honour of our King and countrie, a voyage to plant ye firft colonie in ye Northerne parts of Virginia, doe by thefe prefentf folemnly, and mutualy, in ye prefence of God, and of one another, covenant and combine ourfelves togeather into a civill body politik for our better ordering and prefervation and furtherance of ye end aforefaid, and by vertue hearof to enacte, conftitute and frame fuch juft and equall lawes, ordinances, acts, conftitutions and offices from time to time, as fhall be thought moft meete and convenient for ye generall good of ye Colonie, unto which we promife all due fubmiffion and obedience. In Witnef whereof we have hereunder fubfcribed our names at Cap-Codd ye 11 of November, in ye year of ye raigne of our fovereigne Lord, King James of England, France and Ireland, ye eighteenth, and of Scotland ye fiftie-fourth, Ano Dom. 1620.

John Carver,	Edward Tilley,	Degory Priest,
William Bradford,	John Tilley,	Thomas Williams,
Edward Winslow,	Francis Cooke,	Gilbert Winslow,
William Brewster,	Thomas Rogers,	Edmund Margeson,
Isaac Allerton,	Thomas Tinker,	Peter Brown,
Myles Standish,	John Rigdale,	Richard Britteridge,
John Alden,	Edward Fuller,	George Soule,
Samuel Fuller,	John Turner,	Richard Clarke,
Christopher Martin,	Francis Eaton,	Richard Gardiner,
William Mullins,	James Chilton,	John Allerton,
William White,	John Crackston,	Thomas English,
Richard Warren,	John Billington,	Edward Dotey,
John Howland,	Moses Fletcher,	Edward Lister,
Stephen Hopkins,	John Goodman,	

PART I.

Signers of the Mayflower Compact.

JOHN CARVER. First Signer.

There seems something strange and elusive about the fact that so little is known of Gov. Carver, and yet from the outset he held the most important places of trust and authority among the Leyden Pilgrims.

One of the oldest of this little band, he must have acquired the traits of character that inspired confidence in his ability, in some broad field, where education and the friction of intercourse had developed him until he became a ruler of men.

"John Carver, Sonne of James Carver. Lincolnshire, Yeoman, called by ye grace of God Governor of our Colony, Dec. ye 10th, 1620, for one year," came to the Leyden Colony unannounced, so far as the records place him; still, when it was necessary to send as envoy to England and the West Indian Company one who would make their interests his own, he was the unanimous choice, and the sequence showed that, for the means at his command, he had requited their trust to the fullest extent.

The die was cast. The Pilgrims, weary with the well-doing that could not secure them peace either of conscience or of mind, surrounded by foreshadowings of war in Holland, the derogatory intercourse with the people from many lands thrust upon their children, must make for themselves a new home.

For this there was but a small fund, and only by contract with some company, who would surely claim their pound of flesh in return, could it be made a possibility.

So John Carver and Robert Cushman went forth armed with the authority to make terms, seek of the King "freedom to worship their God unmolested in the New World, and of the Virginia Company, which was established 1606, a patent on which they might settle."

THE KING.

That the King should turn a deaf ear to their petition seemed a matter of course. Any liberty, even that of thought, if it had been in his power, would have been denied them. Through 1618-19 Carver and Cushman were active in London. The patent was not issued directly to the separatists, but it ran in the name of John Wincob (or Winkop), a member of the Earl of Lincoln's household, who intended to join the emigration in the future, but never did, and the patent was never issued.

The Virginia Company, torn by internal dissensions, the King only playing with their request, never willing to give them terms "under his hand and seal," the poor Pilgrims, weary and discouraged, were driven to bay.

They next pleaded their cause with the Dutch traders to Manhattan, but, as the result shows, all they did was to acquaint them with both plans and hopes, and as a return reap their reward in deceit and double dealing. What wonder that, discouraged on all sides, they turned to one Weston, who appeared on the scene expressing kind sympathy with the situation, offering his services and means for their benefit, that they should, as the result of his counsels, place themselves in the hands of some seventy English merchants, known as the "Merchant Adventurers," and accept, though they did it very unwillingly, their terms.

Robert Cushman was the one appointed for the negotiations, and John Carver saw to fitting the ship out.

The little all of the colony was intrusted to their care. The money, so priceless from its scarcity, they disbursed. "Seven hundred pounds was expended in the provisions and stores, and seventeen hundred pounds was the value of the trading venture they carried."

The failure or success of the enterprise devolved wholly upon John Carver and Robert Cushman. No word of criticism has ever been given of Carver's conduct, but, when the Mayflower was finally fitted out and the requirements of the adventurers were known, a strong but impotent spirit of rebellion was aroused.

Pastor Robinson had never approved of Cushman's connection with Carver, and proclaimed that "he was unfit to deal for other men by reason of his singularity, and as a man more facile in talk than faithful in service."

His strictures seemed borne out by the terms, which hardly left the Pilgrims any personal control; still, there is something to be said in extenuation, when Cushman claims that it "was one thing to settle matters among themselves in Leyden, and quite another to make terms with the other side in London."

Robinson, writing at the time of the agreement between Cushman and Weston, was very conscious of the extortions agreed upon, and says: "He also claimed it to be unfit for such men as Deacon Carver to serve a new apprenticeship of seven years and not a day's freedom."

Showing, as this does, a knowledge of Carver's previous life, there seems some hope that the present search and writing up of the English guilds may evolve a reliable record concerning Gov. Carver.

So, with the proceeds of their own estates and the assistance of the merchants to whom they mortgaged their labor and trade for seven years in return for their venture, two vessels were provided, one in Holland of sixty tons, called the Speedwell, which was intended to transport some of them to America, and there remain for one year in their service for fishing and the natural uses of a new settlement; another, of 180 tons, called the Mayflower, chartered by Mr. Cushman in London, and sent to Southampton, where Mr. Carver was waiting to superintend the equipment.

"A Governor and two or three assistants were chosen from each ship to order the people by the way and see to the dispensing of their possessions and such like affairs."

THE START.

All preparations being made, the vessels pronounced ready for sea, they sailed August 5, 1620. Before the start was fairly made the Speedwell was reported leaky. This seemed but a trifle, and both vessels returned, the Speedwell was repaired, and again, August 21, they put to sea. Their troubles were not over; the history of the Speedwell was repeated, and, though no defects were revealed on the second search, the whole thing was attributed to general weakness, and she was condemned as unfit for use.

"Twenty of the passengers were put on shore, the others, with their worldly possessions, transferred to the Mayflower," and the start for the colony they were to found made, with the knowledge that there must be no turning back.

Upon the defection of the Speedwell office sought John Carver, and he was made Governor of the whole colony.

The day of the signing of the compact off Cape Cod John Carver was confirmed in his office of Governor, though both Young and Belknap state that no oath of office was required, and he entered upon his official duties without ceremony or parade. His term of office as chief magistrate, a position he held without an assistant, was of short duration.

In four months and twenty days the little colony, April 5, 1621, was called upon to part with one who had endeared himself by every act to all surrounding him. The "good estate he had in England was spent in his migration to Holland and America."

He had gone hand in hand with the Pilgrims in all their sorrows, borne the heat and burden of the day when the necessities of the situation called him from affairs of state to work in the field for the means to sustain life.

The Governor must set an example, lead, not follow, in the emergencies which were pressing so hard upon them.

The fatal first sickness, so much as he was part of it, was telling seriously upon his strength. Work must be done, but the hands to do it were lessening, and those left were weak and nerveless.

Whatever Gov. Carver's physical condition, "he was one of the foremost in action, and bore a large share of the sufferings of the colony." True to his life record, his death was caused by overwork and exposure in the fields, where, side by side with the humblest of them all, the Governor bore his part, asking no exemption by virtue of his office and age, and when the end came, stricken at his post, "he was seized with that species of apoplexy which in advanced life is superinduced by great bodily fatigue and exertion."

HIS BURIAL.

"Gov. Carver's remains were consigned to the earth with all the affectionate solemnity which circumstances at that time would permit, and with the discharge of all their firearms."

Unknelled, perhaps uncoffined and unmarked, the rude winds of winter chanting his requiem, John Carver, always the Governor, rested from his labors.

How they mourned and missed him history has not failed to record. He had suffered all the privations uncomplainingly, never too weary to listen to their confidences and give of his abundant sympathy in all times of trial. Perhaps he realized from the first of his arrival that the privations which were inevitable would prove beyond his powers of endurance, and he endeavored to make his impress of character and unselfishness as potent as possible to buoy up their flagging spirits.

Their testimony as to his worth was unceasing, telling that Gov. Carver was a "gentleman of singular piety and rare for humility, as appeared by his great condescendancy when, as this poor people were in great sickness and weakness, he shunned not to do very mean service for them, yea, the meanest of them."

No one appreciated Gov. Carver's worth more than Gov. Bradford; he recognized his true character and upheld his every act.

WESTON.

The trust placed in Weston as principal in their final contract with the adventurers was of short duration.

He was speedily tired of the slow returns he received from his investment, and complained that the colonists represented by Gov. Carver had not exerted themselves to send back in their cargo just tribute money to the adventurers.

Gov. Bradford, cognizant of all that had gone before, realizing that the sick and dying had required their care, answered Weston, telling him, with touching pathos, "He is departed this life and is now at rest in the Lord from all these troubles and encumbrances with which we are yet to strive. He needs not my apology, he who, for the common good, oppressed himself."

Gov. Carter gave his life to his country and poor Catherine Robinson Carver, who was supposed to be a sister of Pastor Robinson, of Leyden, and wife of the first Governor of Plymouth Colony, mourned her dead and would not be comforted.

Frail of constitution, her great sorrow upon her, the struggle for life was more than she could bear. The future had no hope strong enough to rouse her failing faculties. The other world made a better claim; there she would not be alone; her isolation was only on earth; so, without a struggle, she, "weary with the march of life," simply lingered until the summer, and then lay down beside her husband in that "eternal sleep which knows no waking."

CHILDREN.

Bradford's journal, if accepted without any search into a possible meaning, would dispose of the hope that Gov. Carver left descendants, still the power of tradition, the universal statements of early historians are so strong that, while there are not the absolute record proofs, the conviction which no one will part with lightly seems reasonable that Gov. Bradford only meant descendants bearing the name of Carver.

The presence of other Carvers in the colony, who perhaps made some obnoxious claim of relationship and consequent rights, may have induced the assertion that Gov. Carver's family died with him. Little Elizabeth Tilley's future was fixed, her mother had long since departed this life and was never a part of the Pilgrim company, Bradford was cognizant of.

This view unites all; there are no conflicting statements, simply the fact that Bradford never analytically spoke to those of the same knowledge of affairs as himself and looked no further.

WILLIAM BRADFORD, Second Signer.

William Bradford is one of the few Pilgrims of whom much can be written without conjecture. He started his life with a record, and left one which admits of pride on the part of his descendants. Even those who have no blood relation to claim can enjoy with those who have without the slightest desire to repudiate any of his actions. From the day of his advent into the world where he was eventually to become so important a factor, he associated himself with William Brewster.

The tie so started was a very trifling one, but the oak grew from the little acorn of omen, and the man who was appointed Post of Scrooby the year of William Bradford's birth became his dearest friend and wisest guide.

Two miles and a half north of Scrooby, the home of Elder Brewster, lies the Yorkshire village of Austerfield, near Bawtry, which is a historical Pilgrim connection. The place was of small moment, only two laymen in the subsidy of 1575 owning sufficient property to be rated, William Bradford and John Hanson, two of those small landholders called yoemen, a class in Elizabeth's reign ranking next to the gentry, and entitled to use coat armor, who formed the strong sinew of England. With local property interests easily identified, the great people of their section, William Bradford, Jr., and Alice Hanson, married naturally from a propinquity of residence and interest.

March 29, 1590, the young parents welcomed to their home a third William Bradford, destined to become one of the great of the land—the future Governor of Plymouth Republic.

Bred to agriculture, a serious youth who held communion with nature's visible forms; an orphan thus apart from many home ties, he took to his heart the living truths, and early in life identified himself with Scrooby and the teachings of William Brewster. What their friendship was to them can only be revealed to us at "that great day, when the secrets of all hearts are open."

They could look before themselves to the life they hoped to and did spend together, and to the hereafter, which held the same promises for each. "Bradford, if not a thoroughly educated man, was certainly one of cultivation." Brewster, with his special gift of teaching, and intense humanity, would hardly neglect the opportunity of directing the studies of this young aspirant for knowledge. Self-reliance, forced upon Bradford as it was in early life, tended much to his development. When only 18 years of age, he suffered imprisonment in Boston, in Lincolnshire, for his religious beliefs, and perhaps for his identity of association. His youth pleaded for him, but he was only successful in his effort to reach Holland after being again arrested and escaping.

From the time of Bradford's arrival in Holland until his departure for New England, he seems to have gone on his way slowly, steadily, gaining strength in the march.

His first step on arriving at Amsterdam was to apprentice himself to a Frenchman, who taught him the art of silk weaving. On reaching his majority he invested his little property, about which there are many estimates as to its value, in starting in business for himself.

HIS MARRIAGE.

His second important venture is gathered from the municipal records of Leyden, which the wise consideration of Hon. Henry C. Murphy has secured to us, that "William Bradford, of Austerfield, England, married November 13, 1613, Dorothy May, of Witezbuts, England." Another account gives more complete history of the marriage in Leyden. "November 15, 1613, William Bradford, fustian maker, young man (i. e., before unmarried), from Osterfeldt in England, affianced to Dorothy May, from Witezbuts, England." "The banns were again published November 20 and 30, but the marriage took place elsewhere."

At Amsterdam is found the following record: "December, 1613, William Bradford, from Osterwelde, fustian maker, 23 years of age, being at Leyden, where he is betrothed, married Dorothy May, aged 16 years, from Witezbuts." To this is appended their signatures, the "maiden fair to see" spelling her name "Dority."

They had one son, John, born in Leyden, left there with his grandfather, Elder May, a man for whom Bradford must have entertained very kindly feelings, as he wrote him confidentially for years. John Bradford's record so far as any continuous history is concerned, soon ended, for he arrived in America in 1627, married Martha, daughter of Thomas Bourne, and dying childless in 1678, closed the page of connection with William Bradford's early marriage.

Though the Mayflower seemed singled out for discomfort from the start, there must have been times of enjoyment from the very makeup of the passengers. Walks on deck, where they planned the history dear to all. The "pipe of peace" smoked after the nameless dinner, the beer drank, though it was doled out in stinted measure with a due regard to its lasting the voyage through and more. Perhaps toasts drank, when they threw off the anxieties of their venture, and were "themselves again." Then, too, Bradford tells us there were many good singers among the Pilgrims. Instructed by Ainsworth, no doubt. Thrust upon their own resources, how natural to imagine them bursting forth in song on the slightest provocation. Standish, holding a little aloof, even though Rose is by his side, a guarantee of future comfort and happiness, but when the melody proved too much for him joining in his full deep bass. No one for a moment could doubt the quality of his voice, or that Brewster and Alden would need no urging to chime in with their sweet tenors. Surely baritone for Bradford, and for leader Priscilla, with her pure, clear soprano, emotional, but the true spirit of song which leads to prayer.

Brewster's hand had long been taken from Bradford's head as he knelt within his reach. The coming man was demanding more outward respect, but the elder prayed better, the words rangs out truer, when he could feel that Bradford was beside him, and their hearts were pouring out in unison the same, thanks for blessings received, and desire for their continuance. Dorothy May Bradford was but a name in the history of the expedition, she married, had one child from which she had to part, and then, to complete her personal record, was drowned in Cape Cod Harbor, December 7, 1620, while her husband was away on an exploration expedition, not even landing to locate for herself a home, and by accident being deprived of a resting place in Mother Earth. Poor young wife and mother! The privations she was spared were no compensation for the love she lost! To doubt Bradford's sorrow would be to deny him the character he had shown, but days of toil brought nights of sleep, and Dorothy's name, of necessity, grew fainter and fainter on his lips. The remedy for his loneliness was soon on its way to him, and shortly after the arrival of the Ann he, the Governor, was married to Alice, daughter of Alexander Carpenter, of Wrenton (Wrington), England (August 14, 1623), and widow of "Edward Southworth, son of Thomas and Jane Mynne Southworth, a man of long and honorable lineage."

LINEAGE.

The fact that Bradford belonged to the two best families in his section explodes the theory, or romance, of the supposition that the Carpenters, from their superior position, had looked with disfavor on Bradford's suit. The results were eventually to his liking, for she became very willingly his second wife, coming out to America with her sister who married George Morton, on the Ann in 1623, at Bradford's request, perhaps, worded in such a manner that resistance was impossible, and when his death took from her the emoluments and precedence of his position, clung to his memory with the same love she bestowed on his living self.

Drawn more and more together by the privations of the situation, their responsive hearts felt it all lessened by the fact that they were together, that their affinity of desire had united them, though the way to the result was over the broad ocean, from luxury to poverty.

From the time Bradford put foot ashore at New England his strength and power grew rapidly. His youth was merged in experience; circumstances were developing him to fill the places that came to him. He had shown his worth, his goodness of heart, his integrity of purpose in the first sickness, in the explorations, in his conduct to the Indians. And though he was weary and worn, sick almost unto death, he was appointed when only 33 years old to succeed Carver as Governor and Isaac Allerton placed as his assistant.

There is a fine touch of human nature all through Bradford's life. The Southworth boys, who came with their mother, were welcomed and treated as his own children, there being only the difference of name to place them apart. In future years, when Mary Carpenter, the "Godly old maid who never married," was left alone in England after her mother's death, Bradford invited her to come to them, "though they had grown old," and would pay her passage (about £5), if she needed it. The natural conclusion from this offer of Bradford's is that the Carpenters were people in moderate circumstances. Gov. Bradford, no doubt, was willing to do all in his power, even seeking opportunity among his kin by birth or marriage, but he required all detail attended to, no overdrawing the bank account.

THE JOURNAL.

The debt of gratitude owed Bradford for his journal is not appreciable; its value is limitless. The "History of Plymouth Plantations" is all we have to place us in accord with the Pilgrims' early lives, so quaintly told that the records are word pictures, bringing events before us in a very tangible way. He, of all others, was best fitted to write it, not only from his special literary capacity, but because he, being at all times in public office, knew better than any one else the occurrences of the times, and, in common with all busy men, so regulated matters that he could avail of every opportunity to commit to paper these valuable records.

There is something about Bradford which gives one the feeling that he had a special touch with little personalities, and, like all people who appreciate that their pen is powerful for description, the work of recording was second nature.

In a not pushing way Bradford liked, as was his right, to be in evidence. The mystery connected with the disappearance of this valuable manuscript is easily solved by the conjecture that some British officer, recognizing its value, carried it as a trophy of war to England, where, intentionally or otherwise, it remained unknown until found in Fulham Palace, London.

Not having the gift of eternal life, what benefit accrued to this officer is untold, unless he shared his secret with some one who could give him military preferment as a reward. "It has been said by the Bishop of London that in his opinion a special act of Parliament would be required to secure the return of the original manuscript."

To-day, thanks to the kind offices of Senator George Frisbie Hoar and our Ambassador to the Court of St. James, Mr. Bayard, this book is to return to us. It has nothing more to tell, duplicates being in every library, but our English ancestors will be nearer and dearer to us from this act of kindness and international courtesy.

Bradford had very few repinings, though he says of himself that "he was unused to trade and traffique of any kind." "He was a good writer compared with others of those times, though his style may seem uncouth to modern ears. He understood several languages, Greek and Hebrew; French and Dutch he spake, and was conversant with theology." Popular acceptance assures us he had property, but that, being put in the common fund, what he left was the result of the various allotments he received and his own special thrift. Given the opportunity, he did not fail them; always Governor or assistant, his mark was upon everything. Carver, from the situation, could merely plan from day to day, so upon Bradford devolved the organization and carrying out of laws for the benefit of all.

The early condition of the colonists was pathetic indeed. Winter was approaching. They had tilled the land, which was the only thing they had in quantity, so far as there was seed to plant. But the greed of hunger was too much for them and the little store appropriated for that purpose went, oftentimes, to sustain life. Game was abundant at the start, but there was no leisure for hunting, and the ammunition must be kept for times of peril from the ever-present Indians. Starvation stared them in the face. Appointing a day of fasting and prayer was irony indeed. Hope was at its lowest ebb. Their envoy, Mr. Prince, who had gone to Ireland, to procure stores, had not been heard from, and fear grew almost to a certainty that the vessel had met with some disaster, and, sharing the fate of many vessels of the times, had fallen into the hands of pirates.

THANKSGIVING DAY.

Fasting and prayer came without appointment. But shortly their sorrow was turned to rejoicing, the vessel was sighted and its stores soon theirs. Lamentations turned to praise; the dear ones in the far distant lands were heard from, and Gov. Bradford, needing no inciting, appointed with prophetic choice of day February 22, 1631, as the first Thanksgiving in the colony.

Not to have New England left out of the count, it is interesting to know that "Gov. Bradford, of Plymouth Colony, about 1630 was offered manorial privileges by the 'Council of New England,' whose president was the Earl of Warwick; the patent ran to William Bradford and his heirs forever, who were given the right to hold the present counties of Barnstable and Plymouth as a manor, and the other colonists as their tenants and subordinates. Gov. Bradford would have been well fitted to have become Lord of the Manor, had he so chosen, for, although poor, he came of an ancient and good family."

Between Alice Carpenter and Gov. Bradford was the love that lived, true once, true always. Morton claims for her that "she was well educated and brought considerable property into the country." This, and her will signed with a cross! Elder Faunce "eulogizes her for her exertions in promoting the literary improvement and the deportment of the rising generation, according to the accounts he had received from her contemporaries."

ALICE CARPENETR BRADFORD.

How easy to picture Dame Bradford happy in her popularity, interspersing her lectures on "current topics" with little asides when the "court courtesy" demanded her attention, while the Governor, instinct with love and admiration, stole a position where he could witness her grace and render the applause he felt to be her due. He was not left to see the contrast, the sad lesson which has been so long as time gives knowledge. As the Old Colony records state: "She was a godly matron, and much loved while she lived, and lamented, though aged, when she died." Alice Carpenter Bradford had outlived her usefulness, and required explanation of her rising superior to the span of life allotted to mankind, so that at her great age she was lamented.

Mrs. Bradford, feeble from age and illness, died March 26, 1670, aged 80, and her wish to lie beside her husband was gratified.

Of their children, William, born June 17, 1624; Mercy, born 1627, and Joseph, who, Winsor says, was a twin with Mercy. Mercy married Ben Vermayes, who attained no prominence; Joseph married Jael, daughter of Rev. Peter Hobart, of Hingham, a famous minister, May 15, 1664.

THE DEPUTY GOVERNOR.

Willam Bradford, the oldest son, married Alice Richards, daughter of Thomas Richards, of Weymouth, Mass.; second, Widow Wiswall—(In his will Major Bradford gives to his son Joseph, the only child by his second marriage, "the lands that were his mother's, at Norwich, Conn.," which leads to the belief that she came from that region)—and for his third wife took Mary, widow of John Holmes, pastor of Duxbury, and daughter of John Atwood. Bacon says: "The only difference between polygamy in New England and Utah is that in Utah they have their wives at once, in New England in succession."

From his position, which certainly brought with it some privileges, William Bradford, second, may have been exempt from the trials and discomfitures attending many marriages. Judge Sewall surely depicted them as not a very satisfactory part of life. At the start, when women were in the minority, to be three times successful was quite a tribute to a man's wealth and worth—even if he depleted the family treasury by the inevitable courting. Oliver Wendell Holmes was in full sympathy with the position when he wrote:

"Of my billings and my cooings I do not now complain,
But my dollars and my shillings, they will never come again."

No wonder that Bradford had so many descendants, with William's nine sons and six daughters, and Elisha, son of Joseph, who had fifteen children.

Major William Bradford, also Deputy Governor, early obtained high distinction in the colonies, having been elected assistant and chief military commander early in his career. Other honors rapidly pressed upon him, and in 1692, when the Colonial Government terminated, he was elected Deputy Governor, and soon Councilor, of Massachusetts. All through the Indian wars he was a strong power. To doubt his valor and judgment would be to question the general statements of history, growing stronger and stronger with each repetition. Hubbard and Church will give the searcher all that is wanted of the Indian wars, too comprehensive to grasp in a short story.

No criticism, even in the light of renewed search, detracts from the position held by Deputy Gov. William Bradford; his dignities and responsibilities he bore meekly, knowing he held all positions on his merits. He had followed in his father's footsteps, of whom it was said, "This year it pleased God to put a period to the life of His precious servant, Mr. William Bradford, who was the second Governor of the jurisdiction of Plymouth." "This worthy gentleman was interred with the greatest solemnities that the jurisdiction to which he belonged was in a capacity to perform, many deep sighs as well as loud volleys of shot declaring that the people were no less sensible of their own loss, who were surviving, than mindful of the worth and honor of him that was deceased."

Gov. Bradford died May 9, 1657, aged 68, a serious loss for the colonies, but a kind Providence let the mantle of his worth fall on his son, and gave him the greater "length of days," he dying February 20, 1704, at the age of 79. His "epitaph from Burying Hill" gives to the world on his tombstone:

He lived long, but still was doing good,
And his country's service lost much blood;
After a life well spent, he's now at rest,
His very name and memory is blessed.

Had his will been made with a prophetic outlook for the needs of the present day, he could not have better touched the wants of a time when every relic would be valuable beyond expression.

HIS WILL.

In leaving his property to his sons, he enjoins upon them "to sell it to none who do not bear the name of Bradford, and be not descended from him." This feeling in regard to himself and the name of Bradford as strongly personal, seems inherited evidence of the tenacity his father, the Governor, may have felt in the same respect where Governor Carver was concerned. No usurpers would be allowed. To David "he bequeaths a silver bowl, not to be alienated from the family of the Bradfords." "My father's manuscript," which he left to his son John, is the one so long supposed to be destroyed with other papers in the belfry of the Old South Church, Boston.

Each family has its claim, traditions help to the appreciation, but the record that tells of William Bradford, second Governor of Plymouth, need never be closed against the reader.

GOV. WM. BRADFORD (PLYMOUTH).

"The last will and testament nunckupative of Mr. William Bradford, Sr., deceased May the 9th, 1657, and exhibited to the court held at Plymouth, June 3, 1657.

"Mr. William Bradford, Sr., being weake in body, but in perfect memory, having deferred the forming of his will in hopes of having the healp of Mr. Thomas Prince therein, feeling himself very weake and drawing on to the conclusion of his mortall life, spake as followeth: 'I could have desired abler than myself in the disposing of that I have, how my estate none knows better than yourselfe,' said he to Lieftenant Southworth. I have deposed to John and William alreddy theire proportions of land which they are possessed of.

"My will is that what I stand engaged to prforme to my children and others, may bee made good out of my estate, that my name suffer not. Further, my will is that my son Joseph bee made in some sort equall to his brethren out of my estate.

"My further will is that my dear and loving wife Alice Bradford shell be the sole exequtrix of my estate, and for her future maintenance my will is that my stocke in the Kennebecke trad bee reserved for her comfortable subsistence as farr as it will extend, and soe further in any such way as may be judged best for her.

"I further request and appoint my much beloved Christian ffriends Mr. Thomas Prince, Capt. Thomas Willet and Lieftenant Thomas Southworth, to be the suppervissors of the desposing of my estate according to the prmises, confiding much in theire faithfullness.

"I commend to youer wisdome some small bookes written by my owne hand to be improved as you shall see meet. In speciall I commend to you a little booke with a blacke cover, wherein there is a word to Plymouth, a word to Boston, and a word to New England, with sundry useful verses.

"These ptculars were expressed by the said William Bradford, Gov'r, the 9th of May, 1657, in the presence of us:

Thomas Cushman,
Thomas Southworth,
Nathaniel Morton."

The inventory of his estate was taken by Thomas Cushman and John Dunham. There is an account contained in it of articles "in ye old parlor, in the great room, in the kitchen, in the new chamber, in the studdie."

Exact copy of Bradford's will, from abstract of earliest wills in probate office of Plymouth, N. E., Gen. and Biog. Register, Vol. V., p. 385.

Mistress Alice Bradford (Plymouth).

Will.—"Wishes to be interred as near to her deceased husband, Mr. William Bradford, as conveniently may be." To sister Mary Carpenter; to sons Constant Southworth, Joseph Bradford; to grandchild, Elizabeth Howland, da of my dec'd son, Capt. Tho. Southworth: to servant maid, Mary Smith.
Her mark.

Inventory, March 31, 1670, on oath of Mistress Carpenter, £162 17s.

By Geo. Watson, Eph. Morton, Wm. Harlow.

All proper names in the will in italics.

EDWARD WINSLOW, Third Signer.

Edward Winslow, the third Governor of Plymouth Colony, was born at Droitwich, in Worcestershire, the ancestral home of the Winslows, son of Edward and Magdalen Ollyver Winslow, and grandson of the first Kenelm. His birth is thus rendered in old St. Peter's Church at Droitwich: "1595, Edward, son of Edward Winslow, born the previous Friday, which was the 19th."

This old church is fast losing its identity, the ravages of time and the changes incident to progression have left only enough to admit of the continuance of the sentiment attached to it.

The registers, however, have been valued and carefully preserved. The texts of the church illuminate the walls, bidding "peace on earth and good will to man," and on the arch in this edifice, where the Pilgrim Winslows were held at the baptismal font, and were wont to worship, are the creed, commandments and Lord's prayer.

History's connections are passing strange. To reach Droitwich from London, one must pass through Worcester, the place where. in "battle array," Charles I. marched his forces against the very Cromwell who in after years was the warm and appreciative friend. of Edward Winslow, Governor of Plymouth Colony. The booming cannons which told those at Droitwich of war and carnage were, to be sure, a thing of the past in that section; only a change of place and participants, however, when Winslow was to the front.

Edward Winslow, the diplomat of the Plymouth Colony, went to Leyden simply as a traveler seeing the world; a man of leisure, education and wealth—one who had behind him the ancestry of many generations, which had placed their impress on character and manner, commanding for him, what he was always credited with being, "of higher social position than the rest."

To confine him in a narrow sphere would be to lose the best of the man. Small methods were not matters of his knowledge. He required contact with people and affairs for his development, and a wise Providence guided his steps toward Leyden, where he was received, not as a refugee from religious persecution, but as a strong man, of moral character, whose subtle conception of the high integrity of word and deed required to keep the little community at Leyden together, made him from his arrival to his death such an important factor for the good of the whole.

The debt, however, was not all on the Pilgrim's side. Edward Winslow, in other situations, might only have been the good comrade and welcome guest. The serious part of his nature found its maturity under the influences surrounding him, and Edward Winslow, the man of the world, with the simple faith of a child, accepted the religion of his fathers as the motive power of his future life.

Many attribute his conversion to Pastor Robinson, but one glance at Weir's picture of the "Embarkation," where as the bride Elizabeth Winslow is portrayed, gives the thought that perhaps her weak woman's hand may have led him with loving care to "choose that better part that cannot be taken away."

Edward Winslow's first wife was Elizabeth Barker, of Leyden, born in Chetsum, England, to whom he was married according to Leyden's records, by Pastor Robinson, May 16, 1618, Isaac Allerton for Winslow, his wife for the bride acting as witnesses. The first thought of colonization in far-off America, where the field was large enough to satisfy his desires, was in Winslow's mind. His instincts as a traveler were roused, and the preparations were developing his hitherto dormant powers for the diplomatic life so truly in the future a part of the man's very being. For him there was no struggle, his whole make-up was in favor of the start. Elizabeth, his wife, strong in her love, shared his anticipations. The home her husband described as to be their's the other side of the great ocean she looked forward to with eagerness, seeing everything with his eyes.

The dreaded ship life, with its close quarters and many discomforts, was safely over. Bleak New England was not responsive to her expectations; but she was strong in her love and determination to bear her part in the arranging which needed a woman's hand to secure to the husband of her choice even a semblance to the home which was part of her life.

THE FIRST SICKNESS.

But all this was of no avail. The unaccustomed privations on their long voyage, the desolation of the situation, with so little prospect of its betterment, and the keen winds of the Cape Cod coast, made sad ravages among them. Poor Elizabeth Barker Winslow, weary with the struggle, was "gathered to her fathers" March 21, 1621. Even the comfort of a grave bearing her name, which should tell her young husband and others that she had once been with them, was denied her. The Indians were keeping watch; the little colony was surrounded by fears worse than death. So the graves were leveled and planted, that the Indians might not know of their depleted numbers and attack them unawares and secure victory from the situation.

Let us hope that the English daisy Winthrop is said to have brought out with him may have sought that unknown grave and marked it with its beauty and piety.

Edward Winslow, called in history "the head of the emigration as Myles Standish was the right hand," was only twenty-six when he arrived at Plymouth, young, ambitious, with strong ideals for his future life, one of the gentry in the land of his birth and who, from the start shared with Bradford the main burdens of the government, owning a position to which the world yields ready homage, second in wealth in the colonies, a fact never registered against a man, found himself, notwithstanding these material benefits, alone in the world. Why should he thus remain, when a remedy was close at hand?

Elizabeth, so recently his companion, was "sleeping the sleep that knows no waking." A fellow-sufferer needed comfort, who so fitting to give it as himself?

His mind being fully made up, he sought advice of Bradford, and the surprise he evinced in no way affected his action. Wise Winslow made an appearance of consultation at least, prepared with arguments only on one side, however. All wavering was a thing of the past, so May 12, 1621, "was ye first marriage in this place, which according to ye laudable custom of ye low countries, in which they had lived, was thought most requisite to be performed by the magistrate, as being a civill thing upon which many questions aboute inheritances doe depende," and Edward Winslow welcomed to his home, perhaps heart, Susannah Tilley White.

She hardly had time to realize the tie which bound her to William White before it was a thing of the past. "Only a dream at the best."

No one could doubt the benefits accruing to her from this second marrage. Susannah Tilley Winslow held the first place in everything, the first mother, the first bride, and then her son, Josiah Winslow, was the first native born Governor of Plymouth Colony. A husband, who had precedence always, what mattered the claims of his birthright, when the rank which was of the soul was his, and for which in honesty of purpose, he knew he must give much in return, having received much?

He made his professions, and lived up to them.

WHAT HE WANTED.

His reasons for coming to America showed him to be a loyal Englishman at heart. "He wanted the protection and language of his own country, the benefits of an equal education for his children, and to secure them in another country the right to live without being surrounded by the profanation of the Sabbath they saw on all sides in Holland."

The records tell us that Winslow was associated with Brewster in Leyden as a printer, and another statement is to the effect that "Winslow, Bradford and Winthrop, blessed be their names, and their descendants, were journalists."

At all events, Edward Winslow started on his diplomatic career early in his Pilgrim life. When it was necessary to visit and confer with Massasoit, the Indian chief, to sound his intentions, and, so far as possible, make some plan of action in regard to their intercourse, this delicate mission, carrying the olive branch, with due care to convey sense of power, was intrusted June, 1621, to Edward Winslow and Stephen Hopkins.

With that tact which never deserted him, Winslow secured a friend in the Indian chief, accomplished his mission, "and with the tribe they hold friendly intercourse and 'eat oysters.'"

"He was a man of great activity and resolution, hence qualified to conduct enterprises." This treaty with Massasoit, "the work of only one day, being honestly intended on both sides, was kept with fidelity as long as Massasoit lived," but was afterward broken in 1675 by Philip, his successor.

Considering the courtesy and justice of both men, it is highly probable that the account of this interview and treaty was written by Edward Winslow. The precedence always given Stephen Hopkins establishes it, as they were the only persons engaged in the mission.

Squanto, the ever faithful, was their guide and interpreter.

The arrival of the Ann in 1623, followed closely by the Little James, the last of the "forefathers' ships," brought them personal and physical comfort. Still, the growing needs of the colonies and their inadequate supplies forced the conviction on them that the strongest and best fitted of their number, to cope with English experience and so place affairs before the Adventurers and Merchants, as to secure for the colonies both supplies and credit, must be sent back in her.

That Winslow should be chosen for delicate diplomatic service was without doubt, so he sailed with the ship, nothing loth for the journey, to be sure, that should so soon return him to the scenes with which he was in such strong personal touch.

ANOTHER TRIP TO ENGLAND.

Again, in 1635, he made a voyage to England to seek protection against the incursions of their too intrusive neighbors.

The French in the East, the Dutch in the West, were too much for them. Disaffected people were venting their spleen on the already overwhelmed people, broken by privations, sorely wounded, without any power of redress, with full knowledge that their enemies at home were placing matters to their injury before the powers that be and endangering their chance of relief from abroad.

Particularly was this spirit maintained by Thomas Morton, of Merry Mount, a man who, by his own action, was debarred from citizenship and forced to return to his native land, where he had a larger sphere, and they were rid of his little pleasantries in the way of supplying the Indians first with the rum which made them wild for deeds of murder and destruction, then putting in their hands the weapons with which to follow out the course of their wild passions.

For all of this Winslow must make excuses, as well as answer the charge against him "of officiating in church and the celebration of marriages without being in holy orders."

To suffer imprisonment for a continuance of these offices as established in Holland, where a civil contract constituted marriage, was hard indeed. Anything would serve for a cause; it was truth crushed to earth, but it would rise again, and the vindication of Edward Winslow's intentions only a matter of time, placed him on a securer platform than before.

"This decree, or law, about marriage, was published by ye Stats of ye Low Countries, Ano. 1590.

"That those of any religion, after lawfull and open publication, coming before ye Magistrates, in ye Town, or Stathouse, were to be orderly (by them) married one to another."

If ever he had the austere manners attributed to the Pilgrims, which is surely doubtful, association with the world and the best society of England must have tempered both conversation and conduct.

The sentiment connected with their life at Leyden was very dear to him; no length of absence or the silence of lessening memory could obliterate the feeling which it recalled. "I persuade myself never people on earth lived more lovingly together and parted more sweetly than we the church at Leyden."

Dear as he was to his own section Winslow's fame was not confined to Plymouth. The Massachusetts Bay colony had deep and abiding faith in him in their dissensions; they recognized him as "a fit man to be employed in our troubles in England, both in regard to his abilities of presence, speech, courage and understanding, as also being well known to the commissioners."

They had not counted without their host, for "by his prudent management and the credit and esteem he was in with many of the members of Parliament, and principal persons then in power, prevented any prejudice to the colony from either of these applications."

All of his work in London was held in high esteem, and records of it kept in a book entitled "Calendar of State Papers."

While he was in England as agent to the colonies in 1623 he published a work which, fortunately for his aspirations, was considered quite an advancement upon the literary standard of the day. It was entitled "Good News from New England; or, a Relation of Things Remarkable in That Plantation."

With characteristic modesty he signed it simply "E. Winslow."

Edward Winslow was several times Governor, and he was the first person to hold that office by election, which was recorded in 1633.

MARSHFIELD.

Some prophetic feeling seems to have actuated Gov. Winslow in preparing during one of his stays in this country, his beautiful home at Marshfield, called "Careswell," where his wife kept watch and guard for the husband who never came—a place further, and worthily, celebrated in history, for near it, on the estate of Wm. Thomas, an early settler of Marshfield, the one who gave a site for the first meeting house and burying ground, lived Daniel Webster. The great statesman had a very natural "ambition to own every acre of the original grants to Wm. Thomas and Edward Winslow in Marshfield." His wish was mainly gratified, and he built on the "Careswell" estate a house for his son Fletcher, which has since been called "Careswell House," and where, in the burying ground sacred to those of Winslow blood, his dust mingles with many generations owning that claim. A pretty bit of sentiment comes to history in the fact that Admiral Winslow, of Kearsarge fame, received his commission in the navy from Daniel Webster.

The name of Marshfield first appears in the records on the 1st of March, 1641-2. It was represented in the colonial government in 1644, and its earliest list of freemen, taken in 1644, with only a representation of eleven people, had on it Mr. Edward Winslow, Josiah Winslow, "Kanelme" Winslow.

Only two of Winslow's children lived to grow up—Josias, born in 1627, afterward Governor, and Elizabeth, their daughter, who married first Robert Brooks, of Scituate, and second Capt. George Curwen, a prominent merchant of Salem. The two sons Edward and John did not reach maturity.

Gilbert Winslow, third brother of the Governor, who was also on the Mayflower, went to Piscataqua after the settlement was commenced there, and the tradition is that he sailed to England and never returned.

John Winslow came in the Fortune, one of those left behind by the Speedwell, and married Mary Chilton, of historic fame, known as the Pilgrim Orphan, and for whom is claimed the honor, if such it is, of being the first to place foot on Plymouth Rock.

Kenelm and Josias, the other brothers, came before 1632 and settled at Marshfield.

Our Winslow had many gifts and did not suffer the privations of the Pilgrims, being always their envoy to other shores, where he picked up from time to time the broken thread of his former life, and won for himself honor and renown.

He was a man to take comfort in any evidences of cultivation, and says: "We refreshed ourselves with singing psalms, making joyful melody in our hearts, as well as with the voice, there being many in our congregation very expert in music, and indeed it was the sweetest music that mine ears ever heard."

Winslow had an artistic appreciation of all the elegancies and showed strong sentiment always to the events that had made impression upon him and touched his heart. His high-bred consideration for others and their wants marked him as the Christian gentleman, and it was not unnatural that on this platform he and Bradford should have affiliated.

Winslow recognized the office as well as the man, and yielded ready, prompt obedience. Adaptative himself, he had the great gift of drawing from those he was surrounded by the best of themselves, wisely recognizing that he need put forth no claim of precedence. If talent existed, it would speak for itself, and the strength of results prove his capacity to wield the power vested in him.

INTERCOURSE WITH BRADFORD.

Bradford yielded Winslow all honor. He could do so cheerfully, free from the aggressiveness that sometimes tinctured his speech of those whom he could only indorse in part, and yet struggled with his fine nature to render justice to.

He calls "Edward Winslow the most accomplished of the 'old-comers,' distinguished for the important services he rendered the colony both at home and abroad, and for the eminent abilities which he displayed as the representative of the sister colony to the English Government."

Fortunately a fine portrait of Gov. Winslow, painted while on a mission to London in 1651, is in the possession of the Massachusetts Historical Society. It represents him when about 57 years of age, in the pride of his certain maturity, strong of purpose, rich in experience.

Strange to say at this late date an authentic miniature of the third Governor has been found, taken when he was a child of four years, and yet bearing such striking likeness to the future man as to insure its acceptance without the proof which accompanies it.

With no assertion, he takes his place in the foremost rank always, and while his recognized position is that of a diplomat, he shows in other places, which, in the light of the world's opinion, seem of minor consideration; still, the bearing upon the colony was even greater than his successful missions.

Winslow "searching for food" appeals warmly to our affection, installs the man where neither literary nor diplomatic strength has placed him, and all feel a common sorrow that on his return from this voyage he should have "found the colony much weaker than when he left it. The want of bread had abated the strength and flesh of some, and swelled others, and had they not been where are diverse sorts of shellfish, they must have perished."

OLIVER CROMWELL.

Edward Winslow was a great favorite of Oliver Cromwell and his officers, and yielded to the pressure brought to bear upon him to accept employment under the Protector.

No greater proof could be given of his touch with the world, intelligent feeling of the public pulse, than the appointment he received in 1654 as first commissioner on the part of the Commonwealth to arbitrate and determine the value of English ships seized and detained by the King of Denmark.

The original commission from the Protector is now in Plymouth.

Such a preferment to a man who for thirty-four years had been a resident in the American colony with the Pilgrims and Puritans, governed by their small, narrow habits, is convincing as to the value of the desires of the colonists, even if the carrying out was restricted by their necessities, though in Winslow's case his life in Plymouth was interspersed by various trips to the old world.

From the start of his official intercourse with Europe, the spiritual welfare of the Indians was dear to the heart of the Christian Edward Winslow. He was a zealous advocate of their civilization and conversion, and it was from his unwearied efforts and strong influence came the "Society for Propagating the Gospel in New England," which was formed in England in 1647, the act of corporation bearing date July 27, 1649.

In 1650 President Steele, of this society, wrote to the Colonial Commissioners that "Winslow was unwilling longer to be kept from his family, but his great influence with and acquaintance with members of Parliament required longer stay." I was very glad to find this record; there seemed so little account of Winslow's personal relations to his family that the question might naturally arise as to whether he had merged all his life into his foreign relations.

Both countries needed him, but there was always a "good and sufficient reason for his remaining in England."

Cromwell's pleadings were too strong for the ties that were pulling him to home, wife and children. His confidence in him was unbounded, many commissions at various times had been assigned to him, and when the Protector planned an expedition to the West Indies, with the object of attacking St. Domingo, 1655, secure in this trust, he placed Edward Winslow at the head, with Richard Holdrop and Edward Bragge as assistants.

The whole was under Admiral Penn and Gen. Venables.

Only this one man of those in authority in whom Cromwell could place absolute dependence, knowing that most were really against him, and attached to the House of Stuart. Disagreements arose. They were men of different minds and tempers, their hearts not in the work. The troops ill appointed and badly provided for. Then, to add to their troubles, they were landed a long way from the city, and lost their way in the woods.

The army, composed of raw material, without the training which rendered them subordinate to a leader, devoid of proper nourishment, the first instincts of a soldier unknown to them, it was hardly a great military achievement to defeat these troops.

Overcome, not by army tactics, but the stern depression of "hunger, thirst, heat and fatigue," they were routed, six hundred killed, and the rest, without cowardice, took refuge in the vessels, started to Jamaica, and the army, which really never existed, except on the roll call, surrendered.

WINSLOW'S DEATH.

All this wore sadly upon high-spirited Winslow, the chagrin of defeat—for he did not live to enjoy the after victory—told on his constitution, worn by heat, fatigue and anxiety, threw him into a fever, and the sacrificed life of Edward Winslow, third Governor of Plymouth Colony, always its diplomatic head, ended the 8th day of May, 1655, in his 60th year, on the ship in which he was going from Hispaniola to Jamaica.

What mattered it that he was buried with funeral honors; that the booming guns told to all the position of the man consigned to the great deep?

The country of his love and adoption will never cease to regret this valued life thrown away to satisfy a man's ambition.

GOV. WINSLOW'S SON.

Gov. Josias Winslow, the first native-born Governor of the colonies, married in 1657 Penelope Pelham, daughter of Herbert Pelham, Esq., of England.

Her fate met her in an unusual way, as there were few temptations for a beautiful woman to make a pleasure trip to America. The father, always interested in the colonies, with a desire to see and assist, if possible, their struggles for advancement, made them his personal care, and, with his young daughter for a companion, sought New England.

The result was the old, old story, and Penelope Pelham, for love of Josias Winslow, said to be the handsomest and most courtly man in New England, gave up the refinements of her English home and remained in the country. Were the story all told, there were less than forty years of improvement and comfort as a compensation.

But it was not always thus. Everything being valued by contrast, she had the future pleasure, as first lady of the land, of welcoming to her beautiful home in Marshfield the great and good of all nations who visited the home of her adoption.

The courtesy of her dispensing, the cordiality and dignity of her hospitality, form the record of the times. Her personal beauty fortunately is perpetuated, and if reproduction in descendants is an evidence of strength, that existing, Mrs. Winslow must be credited with force of character.

There were four children by this marriage, two sons and two daughters, but only one son lived to manhood, Isaac, who married Sarah, daughter of John and Elizabeth Paddy Wensley, of Boston, July 11, 1700, and through her their descendants were related to both Elder Brewster and Gov. Prince.

Sad to relate, Gov. Edward Winslow has no one bearing the name who can claim lineal descent from him.

Josiah Winslow stood on a pinnacle from any point of view, diplomatic, social or military, and the fact that his physical condition was far from robust, shows strongly the metal of the man, who, under soch odds, could do so much.

He filled many offices, was magistrate, Governor, and in 1675 commander-in-chief of all the colonies of New England in the war against the Indians, known as "Philip's War." Being the bright and shining mark he suffered severely through no fault of his own from the animosity of the red man. The encroachments they made upon him rendered him virtually homeless, his wife and children forced to seek a place of safety.

And in one sense what made it harder to bear was that this persecution was a retaliation without foundation, the Indians themselves alleging no cause of discontent except the execution of three murderers (Saccamons), who, it is asserted, acknowledged the fairness of their trial, and one confessed his crime.

THE QUAKERS.

By contrast of thought and life the Quakers were always a source of contention, and Gov. Josias (as he always wrote his name), strong in his sense of justice, resented the treatment they received.

Gov. Prince spent much of his time in reducing their rights and privileges to a minimum, and even suspended from the claims of citizenship those who showed sympathy with that sect.

These Winslow reinstated immediately on his accession, and during his administration managed to infuse an outward semblance at least of regard for their creed, where there was no overt action against the government.

Hardly a martyr, but certainly a sufferer from the cause he espoused, which, in his case meant every line that had a touch of prevention, of humanity and Christian charity. Josiah Winslow died December 18, 1680.

He was "buried at the expense of the colony in testimony of its endeared love and affection for him," his tombstone bearing the inscription: "The Hon'ble Josiah Winslow, Gov'r of New Plymouth, Dyed December ye 18th, 1680, Aetatis, 52."

Being in England with his father on one of his missions, Gov. Josias Winslow's portrait was painted there.

Mrs. Winslow survived her husband twenty-three years, dying December 7, 1703, in the 74th year of her age. Her portrait, too, exists, and is a very representative type of the high-bred Puritan face history has handed down to us.

The Winslow descent has made fine history by sea and land—the "living present" gives us many bearing the name—but the sorrow must always exist that not one comes in a direct line from Edward Winslow, third signer of the compact on the Mayflower off Cape Cod, 1620, and third Governor of New Plymouth, the first by elective voice of the people.

WILLIAM BREWSTER, Fourth Signer.

The history of the separatists and their exodus to Leyden is written the length and breadth of the Northern post road of England, starting from London, and going north to Berwick, the last stopping place in England, though its real end is Edinburgh.

Passing through the counties of Middlesex, Hertford, Cambridge, Huntingdon, Rutland, Lincoln, Nottingham, York, the Bishopric of Durham and Northumberland, the student of this early history easily makes connection with the places and peopeople that have put their stamp on the early colonies of New England.

In view of the fact that leaving their country for cause, they chose to lose their identity of residence and personal record, it is rather pathetic to think that they are in evidence from the very naming of the villages of their new residence, after the always dear homes of their birth and early life.

Much more than two centuries have passed, and yet these very local names are the guides searchers take as a foundation of fact. They make their records very rapidly, as you start from London, through Newington, now a parish of London, famous for the ancient archery butts placed at the ends of the fields for targets.

Guilford, Enfield and Waltham on the road, Chelmsford and Thomas Hooker near at hand, St. Albans, where William Wilcoxson, of Stratford, Conn., came from, with his rector's certificate; Hatfield, too, in close proximity.

There on the direct route, Hertford, the shire town, "Governed by Mayor, 9 Burgesses, etc. Electing Parliament men," and for a crowning glory having a market on Saturday. In its prosperity the place could boast of five churches, but the diverting of this great road from it reduced it to three. Still the familiar names pursue us, telling that the little colony who left Hartford, Conn., located in Stamford, so called from England's Stamford, on this road, a large, flourishing town (within easy access of Coventry, Derby, Oxford, etc., in Linconshire, only eighty-nine miles north from London.

"It was originally named Steanforde, derived from the Saxon stean, a stone, and forde from a passage across the river Welland being paved with stones." Next it was Stanford; but ultimately reached its present spelling. The town is charmingly situated on the side of a hill, rising in a beautiful terrace from the northern bank of the river Welland, "across which a stone bridge of five arches connects it with Stamford Baron, or St. Martin's, in Northamptonshire."

All that locality seems to be of great antiquity, "Stamford being ascribed by tradition to a period long before the Christian era."

From here to Rutland, and then our resting place Scrooby, a living interest, sufficient in the present day to take out a band of history seekers, in the hope, not a vain one I trust, of bringing back to us much that their present increased knowledge will enable them to appropriate and place in position.

SCROOBY.

Small as Scrooby was, a village of only two furlongs, it was accessible on all sides to many of the important places, and from it you were brought to a kill, where together you enter Yorkshire and Bawtry, "a town of three furlongs extent with a market on Saturdays, and chiefly noted for its trade in millstones."

William Brewster, son of the William Brewster who was appointed by Archbishop Sandys in January, 1575-6, receiver of Scrooby, and all its liberties in Nottinghamshire, and also bailiff of the Manor House, to hold both offices for life, had from his advent into the world the abundance consequent upon his father's position.

The family were there "even earlier, for on the administration of the estate of William Brewster, of Scrooby, being granted to William Brewster, his son, in 1590, it is noted that the widow Prudence held the office of post when he died, and that the father of the deceased man held it before him."

This places two generations previous to the William Brewster all have a legendary affection for, and renders it almost certain that our elder William was born at Scrooby.

BREWSTER ARMS.

The original grant for the Brewster arms (given with the crest to Humphrey Brewster, of Rushmore, 1561) is in the possession of the family of Cardinal Brewster, of Greenstead Hall, Halstead, Essex.

Burke says: "But that other branch with which we are now concerned was established in the United States of America by William Brewster, the ruling elder and spiritual guide of the Pilgrim Fathers, who, 1620, went out to America and were founders of New England."

Brewster's birth, according to the records, was about 1560, and, happily for him, his educational advantages were the best of his time. He was a scholar at the University of Cambridge, as a pensioner of Peter House College, where, though his attainments were not great enough to make any special mark, his subsequent career showed that he availed himself of everything that came within his grasp.

"He was a fluent Latin scholar, with an insight into Greek."

Life at Scrooby was not vegetation for William Brewster. The place was full of historic interest. The Manor House had domiciled royalty in the height of its power, and misfortune when Cardinal Wolsey became an inmate after his fall. Realizing, as he said, that he had served his King better than his God, the few weeks he passed at Scrooby, if meant as expiation, left the record of that time as well spent in service for the good of others.

DAVISON.

Undoubtedly it was at Scrooby, when he was traveling to Scotland on affairs of state, that Brewster met William Davison, one of Queen Elizabeth's Ambassadors, and Secretary of State, who did more than any other toward forming his character.

A man of whom Bradford writes as "a religions and godly gentleman." Becoming Davison's secretary, an office he was singularly fitted for, all the religious and diplomatic benefits followed him. The best of Secretary Davison's life was his connection with Brewster, who then, young and impressionable, absorbed and retained the influence he was surrounded by.

He shared some of Davison's glory, for when it was Elizabeth's pleasure to make league with the States of Holland, through her Ambassador, Davison, he attended him as secretary, and while there "the keys of Flushing were committed to his care, as the safest possible repository, pending the negotiations.

"As a recognition of his valuable services, the States presented Brewster with a gold chain."

QUEEN ELIZABETH.

Elizabeth's favor was only a question of time. Mary, the unfortunate Queen of Scotland, had been tried and condemned after the manner of Queen Elizabeth's reign, under a law devised to suit the occasion, and the Parliament of England had petitioned for her execution.

The Queen privately ordered Davison to draw up a death warrant, which she signed. Even if the ever-present precedent had warned him of the fickle mistress he was serving, it would have been of no avail.

Her uneasy head, which wore a crown, held nothing higher than her own caprices. His consulting her appointed counselors was a deed written on the sand. She charged him, Mary having suffered the death penalty, with too much haste.

The consummation she devoutly wished for at the moment, in the face of the inevitable, perhaps, aroused some womanly feeling for the head she had laid low. Still, Davison's doom was sealed. Davison's appointment was because he was easily imposed upon, so, "the better to appease James, whose concern for his mother was sincere and cordial, she committed Davison to prison, and ordered him to be tried in the star chamber for misdemeanor."

Davison suffered keenly from the railing of the very men who, in the eagerness for the final act, had induced him to carry out Elizabeth's plans with indecent haste, promising him their countenance and support if harm should reach him. Even with all this to his credit, the sentence of imprisonment during the Queen's pleasure, and to pay a fine of a thousand pounds, was not abated one iota.

It makes another colonial connection to recall that when "Elizabeth appointed a commission of forty noblemen and privy councilors, and empowered them to pass sentence on Mary," they should have sent to her at Fotheringay Castle (in the county of Northumberland) Sir Walter Mildmay as one of those to inform her of the commission and her approaching trial.

Davison's fall was a change of career for Brewster. He had made a successful start in a mode of life he seemed eminently fitted for, and subsequently followed one as a result of this deposition from office of his chief on conviction, the very contrast of his past. True to the man's instincts of life, he stood by his patron till the last, and Davison in the same spirit remained Brewster's benefactor always.

Every surrounding circumstance of Brewster's official life seemed to be weaving for him a strong leading to what made his power for the future.

Even among Davison's assistants there was a George Cranmer, who, from being a pupil of Hooker's and a helper in his work of ecclesiastical piety, had grown fond of theological studies, and his knowledge on these subjects naturally gave him a strong influence on Brewster, always susceptible to such convictions.

Cranmer did not retire from public life, so, "less fortunate than Brewster, was slain in Ireland as early as 1600."

Then, too, he lived with Sir Edwin Sandys, whom King James afterward disliked because he was one of the leaders of the people's party in the House of Commons, and who, by birth and inclination, took a foremost rank among the ecclesiastical reformers of the day.

ELDER WILLIAM BREWSTER.

Upon William Brewster's death, Davison suggested that his son, the future Elder, should be successor. Sir John Stanhope, who was appointed to the office of "Post master-General by letters patent, bearing date at Westminster June 30th, in the thirty-second year of Elizabeth" (1590), wrote, August 22, 1590: "Regrets he cannot comply with his request, on the death of old Bruster." One Samuel Bevercotes had written to him for the place of Postmaster at Scrooby, with which he complied.

States the reason for not conferring it on young Bruster, who had served in that place for his father, old Bruster.

This proved to be a personal grievance that Stanhope had against William Brewster for neglect of courtesy toward himself, yet he left a loophole for any explanation on the part of Brewster in case his applicant failed to present himself.

"All this while, and to this hour, I never heard a word from young Brewster; he never came to me being in town, nor sent to me being absent, but as though I was to be overruled by others, made his way according to his liking. I know my interest, such as whether he had the place or no, I can displace him, and I think him worthily displaced for contempt of me, in not seyking me at all."

The change of mind came, and Brewster was appointed. Whatever records or desires of his personal life history is obliged to do without, his "ordinary wages" are fully explained, commencing with "20d. per diem," and closing with 2s., when he resigned the office on September 30, 1607.

The posts were emphatically the royal roads, and were always spoken of as "Journeys of the Court." Still the Northern road, which to us represents "Scrooby" as the great stopping place, was the most important in the United Kingdom. It is recorded that "though none of the best Way for after the first 20 or 30 miles 'tis so generally bad that there was a certain late imposition upon Travellers during three years at Stilton, and a place or two on this side, of about a Penny for a Horse, etc., toward the Repair of that part of it, yet it is well accommodated for Entertainment, and at moderate rates."

Great responsibilities were attached to the office. Brewster was an innkeeper, obliged to provide for distant deliveries, there being no cross posts on the great highway to the north. The nature of his occupation is easily understood, in the record of expenses of Sir Timothy Hatton, the Archbishop's son, on a journey to and from London in 1605.

"He paid the 'post' at Scrooby, who must have been Brewster, for a conveyance (post chaise) and guide to Taxford, 10 shillings, and for a candle, supper and breakfast, 7 shillings and tenpence—so that he slept under Brewster's roof. On his return he paid 8 shillings to the post of Scrooby, for conveying him to Doncaster, then recorded 7 miles, and 2 shillings for burnt sack, bread, beer and sugar to wine, and three pence to the 'ostler."

Relays of horses were always kept at stated distances, and over this great road journeyed the kings and queens of the times.

The mail matter was largely in the hands of envoys or private individuals, and the reading of Winthrop's letters gives us assurance that many a hamper of home made delicacies, "cappons and cheese," found their way along the line.

Retrospection brings William Brewster before us speeding the parting guest, blessing by "the word in season" those he came in contact with, and placing himself and his teachings on never-to-be-forgotten record.

SEPARATISTS.

"The communities of persons who separated themselves were called Separatists, Congregationalists or Independents, until the time of the civil wars.

"The Separatist was a Puritan, but the Puritan was not necessarily a Separatist." The latter felt with the Nonconformists, but did not act with them. They sought relief from the ceremonies, made special pleas for their discontinuance, but while entering into their church unions, lacked the "courage of their convictions" when they required their taking the decisive step and leaving England.

Robinson and Brewster were gathering around them from the neighboring villages converts who were ready to take their lives in their hands for the church. Young Bradford had joined them, and the persecutions on all sides were warning them that the Manor House at Scrooby must be left and a congregation gathered across the sea.

The people at Scrooby needed a central figure upon which they could lean, a man to be their conscience, and the choice fell like an unwritten election from the voice of the people on William Brewster.

Whither he went "they would go, his God should be their God," so, with teh consent of the multitude of counselors they decided to seek Amsterdam, in Holland. They pinned their faith on him—a sure foundation.

The best argument for a belief in God was Brewster's own existence and manner of life. "Separation, the full blossom of the bud of Puritanism," was the impelling power for their departure. There were no half way measures for them.

The arrangements for Holland were made with the greatest privacy; the company divided into two parts, one to go to Boston, on the southeastern coast of Lincolnshire, the other by the Humber, flowing between Lincolnshire on the north and Yorkshire.

All their foresight could suggest was done, but of no avail; the captain, for cause unknown, in both cases betrayed their plans. The hope that had pulsed their start was flighted by the reality. The Boston company, seized by officials, with a total disregard of any rights on their part, were sent divers ways, Brewster, Bradford and others being thrown into prison.

Brewster was the chief among the nonconformists who were taken to Boston, one of the seven kept the longest in prison, and who, as a penalty of their beliefs, suffered the greatest loss.

His position at Scrooby gone, other punishments awaited Brewster; a fine of £20 was imposed upon him for his failure to appear before the Ecclesiastical Commission, and this "contempt of court" secured for him a further fine of £20, the payment of which he wisely postponed by his flight to Holland.

CAPT. EDWARD BREWSTER.

While affairs at Scrooby were assuming proportions the Virginia Company in London was gaining strength. The two really claimed a community of interest from the fact that Sandys was an important factor in each.

Kink James declared that the "Virginia Company was a seminary for a seditious Parliament." After a variety of namings and the usual changes in the plans, on the 23d of May, 1609, a new charter was granted authorizing "the use of the corporate name of the Treasurer and Company of Adventurers and Planters of the City of London, for the first colony in Virginia." This charter was seized with avidity. The outlook was exactly to their minds, the list of Adventurers was soon full, among them Edward Brewster and his son, Edward.

At the date of the charter Brewster was doubtless in Amsterdam. Staunton says of him about that date "that he was frightened back into the Low Countries." A man "hunted by Sir Dudley Carleton, the English Lord Ambassador in Holland, and Sir Robert Naunton, the Secretary of State in London," could hardly feel at peace with a situation which might unite at any moment and deprive him not only of personal liberty, but the life work he was looking forward to.

His son, Capt. Edward Brewster, however, went to Virginia "as Lord De la Warre, Captain-General of Virginia, to whom he appears to have been attached in some official or military capacity, sailed from England the spring of 1610. It is probable that young Brewster emigrated at that time."

Elder Brewster, however, was borne on their books, for in the list of Adventurers, with the amount of their ventures, appear "William Brewster 20 li. and Capt. Edward Brewster, his son, 20 li.

All through the Pilgrim life in Holland Edward Brewster remained in Virginia, leaving there in the early part of 1619.

His return to England, however, was hardly voluntary. On the 15th of October, 1618, he was "court-martialed by Gen. Samuel Argalls on the charge of having complained of the unlawful use of Lord Delaware's servants by Argalls, and condemned to death." Lord Delaware had died the previous spring on the passage from England to Virginia.

A pretty item of history is found in the record of that day.

While those already in Virginia were waiting for the expedition headed by Sir Thomas Gates and Sir George Somers, the colonists elected Mr. West, brother of Lord Delaware, "temporary president." To-day this family name (West) of the Delawares, who were also of the English Temple blood, unites both continents in Dr. Charles E. West, of Brooklyn, and "that grand old man—Gladstone."

Edward Brewster's punishment was afterward commuted to banishment, and he returned to England.

Of course such a trial was a farce, and thus was recognized by the Virginia Company in London. They reviewed the proceedings and findings, and declared they were "unjust and unlawful, and not warrantable either in matter of form by the laws of the realm, or by any power or authority derived from his Majesty."

There is a world of supposition in this claimant to the Brewster's blood, rendering other children possible, not yet accounted for, and helps to explain the constant reference to the earliest times to Brewster's large family.

EDWORD BREWSTER CONFORMS.

Capt. Brewster, after his return, conforms to the church, and settles down in London. His relations with the Virginia Company were always cordial. In 1623 he is mentioned among the members present at the meetings.

"He and Henry Seile, in 1635, were booksellers near the north door of St. Paul's, and at a later period he was treasurer of the Stationers' Company.

HOLLAND.

Life in Holland was their period of probation and assimilation; they had put behind them all thought of their life in England, made common cause of their labor and their necessities, cast aside class feeling and became one in anticipation and appreciation.

Brewster wrote with Robinson from Holland to Sir Edwin Sandys: "We are knit together as a body in a most strict and sacred bond and covenant of the Lord, of the violation whereof we make great conscience and by virtue whereof we hold ourselves strictly tied to all care of each other's goods and of the whole."

The aid of every individual member of the little settlement was required and cheerfully given; small feelings had no place in their busy lives. The Leyden records account for another child of the Elder's, who died in 1609.

"Brewster was enabled to set up printing by the help of some friends," and so had employment enough. The life was congenial to him so far as the necessity which knows no law required labor as a means of livelihood. The possibilities of doing good he saw before him as a result of the dissemination of the truths his books contained, were sadly destroyed by the restrictions put upon their circulation.

His opinions were not popular according to the desires of the official powers, and the field he had laid out for himself was curtailed, if not entirely destroyed, by force of law. "In 1619 the English Government complained that Brewster's books were 'vented underhand' in their country, and asked that he be given up for trial in their country." Proud of their detective system, they arrested the wrong man, and one Brewer (who was also a member of the Leyden company) suffered imprisonment for the crimes imputed to Brewster.

When the churches with their pastors had removed to Holland, William Brewster was chosen Ruling Elder, an office he held worthily through all the mutations of time and change, until the close of his life. Peculiarly gifted with power of expression, and the ability to convey to others all that was truest of himself, this life with but one purpose made its impress on every surrounding, gathering to him the worthy and unworthy that they might benefit by his precepts and example.

His teachings were magnetic, from his abundance all must gain in knowledge, and the fame that went forth when he became, as he was, a teacher in Leyden University for years, brought students to him from all quarters; sons of great men attracted by his superior methods. Danes and Germans who craved what he alone seemed capable of giving. Latin served him in good stead; the "confusion of tongues" he was surrounded by required that time-honored classic as an interpreter.

Prosperity attended Brewster's efforts; he ceased to be an object of sympathy, so that toward the close of his twelve years in Holland his "outward condition" was greatly improved. "He lived well and plentifully."

Leyden, the place of many privations and uncertainty, was wearing upon their courage; the mouths to feed were increasing out of all proportion to their ability to fill them; the baneful influences surrounding their children were a cause of great anxiety and thought for themselves. "Their desires were set on the ways of God, and to enjoy his ordinances" they realized they needed physical and moral strength to make their praises avail.

A time of at least partial prosperity must have come to the Pilgrims during their early residence in Holland, for in 1611 they were able to buy a large tract of land, with a spacious house on it, for which they paid $3,000. "The site of this house is now indicated by a stone in the front wall of the building, which records that on this spot lived and died John Robinson."

The Leyden band were not rigid separatists. Brewster and Robinson accepted the members of their church from those who were willing to "renounce the pomps and vanities of this wicked world" and join with them in keeping pure and uncontaminated from the wickedness which surrounded them.

So their thoughts turned to the far away new world, where these tenets could be well carried out, free from the supervision of church and state, where their God spoke from every quarter and had written His plan of creation for the animate and inanimate, on the broad expanse of land, sea and sky.

They wanted a church without a bishop, a country without a distant sovereign; so long as Brewster was with them other desires could be passed over, and from the start at Scrooby, the life of Leyden, and broader, stronger needs of Plymouth Colony, he never failed them.

In the nature of things it would have seemed that on reaching New England Brewster should have been made Governor, but as he was "ruling elder," it was not "compatible with that office to vest a civil and ecclesiastical office in one person."

In Plymouth he usually preached to them twice every Sunday for nine years. What a sweet intercourse a prayer meeting under his guidance must have been, as in his need he called upon the brethren to lead in prayer and exhort. "The chief were Bradford, Edward Winslow, Thomas Southworth and Secretary Nathaniel Morton—men of superior talents and parts and good learning."

Elder Brewster, true to his instincts of the best possible good, wanted short but frequent prayers, only sufficient to give a text for the self-communion he hoped would follow—a thought to carry with them to their humble labors.

Circumstances had aided the Pilgrims in carrying out their simplicity of desire, as regarded church connection in Plymouth, Robinson to the day of his death holding the same pastoral relations to them, they continued to be his people without thought of change, until when they were called upon to part with him, giving their pastor back to the God who gave him. they desired to confer the office of pastor or teaching elder on Brewster. He, however, "while declining the office, performed the duties."

BREWSTER'S CHARACTER.

Thatcher says "he was too diffident for the position," and Baylies rather verifies this statement by recording that the "submissive piety of Brewster, indeed, produced a moral effect as important in its consequences as the active virtues of others." But he was "as bold in defending the colony against the Indians as he was meek and humble in diffusing the truth."

Ready of sympathy, his high-toned temperament made the personal response such as only a broad, true nature could give, working during the heat and burden of the day side by side with any member of the little community, cheering them by the example of his unwearied efforts in their behalf.

And when the time of physical exhaustion and death came to them without respect to person, "their Reverend Elder and Standish, their Captain," did with sorrowful, tender hearts all that could comfort or benefit those thus thrown upon their humanity; the strong men and brave, who took the first rank as soldiers, watched over the sick with woman's ways and woman's care.

"The good Elder fought as he prays, and although he would far rather convert an enemy than hurt one, he would not dream of allowing him the first fire."

Human nature went with the little band to even desolate Cape Cod, taking class distinctions to the colonies, for Morton speaks of Brewster's sympathies "for those who had been of good estate and rank, and were fallen into want and poverty, and none did more offend and displease him than such as would haughtily and proudly carry and lift up themselves, being risen from nothing."

This in the wilderness, surrounded by red men, food not only at the lowest point, but every outlook for the continuance of their privations.

ON THE MAYFLOWER.

Elder Brewster's family on the Mayflower consisted of the Elder Dame Brewster, the gentle guide of the young people on the ship; Lucretia, wife of Jonathan, a son who came out in the Fortune in 1621, and two sons, Westling and Love.

Patience and Fear, the daughters the mother's heart yearned over, were on the Ann, reaching the colony in 1621.

This union was not for long. The delicate, wearied mother was slowly but surely turning her feet toward the Eternal City. Pastor Robinson writes to the Elder from Leyden, December 20, 1623: "I hope Mistress Brewster's weak and decayed state of body will have some repairing by the coming of her daughters, and the provisions in this and other ships sent." Poor Mary Brewster! At least, she had the plain, unvarnished truth set before her; no temporizing to spare her the shock.

All prophecies were fulfilled when she closed her mortal eyes on this life of rigid exactions and unavoidable want in 1627.

Love married March 15, 1634, "Miss Sarah," daughter of William Collier, a very prominent citizen of Plymouth. He moved to Duxbury and had four children, three sons and one daughter.

Jonathan became a member of the early secession to Duxbury in 1632—an active, progressive man. Frequently deputy, a power in the settlement, and with true Pilgrim spirit he gave his best endeavors to building up the church. He is styled gentleman, a title of importance in those days. The change to the new colony of New London seemed a matter of benefit to the place of his settlement and himself. He was Associate Judge, and established by appointment a trading post on lands purchase of Uncas, chief of the Mohegans, and afterward called Brewster's Neck. Fortunately, for the world likes to perpetuate honor, he had three sons and one daughter. Patience Brewster married Gov. Prince in 1624, and died in 1634. Fear became Isaac Allerton's second wife in 1626, and she died in 1633.

Brewster's library gave evidence of his cultivation and continued interest in learning. Out of the three hundred volumes sixty-four were classics.

The spirit that guided Elder Brewster through the vicissitudes of his life remained with him until his closing hours; the content which had made him accept whatever came to him was his rest in the Almighty's will. Death stole upon him unawares; the sorrow was more to those who loved him than himself, and after one day's sickness he closed his mortal account "nere four skore years of age (if not all out) when he dyed," his spirit going to the God who gave it April 16, 1644. Brewster "died as simply and grandly as he had lived; the apostolic benediction on his lips, the last they knew of life, and the rest was silence until the end, and then the transfiguration, which made him grander in death than even he ever was in the life he had lived for humanity in America and for his God."

Elder Brewster left no will, but letters of administration were granted to his sons Jonathan and Love, June 5, 1644.

Wearing apparel, household utensils, &c., appraised by Capt. Standish and John Done, May 10, 1644..... 28.08.10
Articles at his house in Duxbury, by Standish and Pearce, May 18....107.00.08
His Latin Books, by Mr. Bradford, Mr. Prence and Mr. Reyner, May 18, sixty-three volumes 15.19.04
His English Books, by Mr. Bradford and Mr. Prence, Between three and four hundred volumes 27.00.07
Latin and English books, 42.19.11.

Total sum of goods 150.00.07

Some discussion has been caused by the fact that the Elder's estate was inventoried separately, in Plymouth and Duxbury. This created doubt as to the possible place of his death. However, that seems decided as Plymouth, though he was one of the pioneer residents of Duxbury, and his home was there.

"The part of his inventory which was accredited to Plymouth was as follows:

4 paire stockings,	2 paire of shoes,
3 waiscoats and a paire of drawers,	2 sherts, 26 handkerchiefs,
1 old goune,	1 fine handkerchief,
2 gridles,	3 handkerchers,
2 paire of thin stockings,	1 wrought capp, 1 laced capp,
1 knit capp,	1 quilted capp,
1 blew cloth suite,	2 old capps,
1 old suite, turned,	1 ruffe band,
1 black coate,	1 ruffe sift out,
Old cloaths,	6 bands,
1 black cloth suite,	1 red cap,
1 paire of greene drawers,	1 paire garters, 1 knife,
1 list wascoate,	1 pistoll,
1 trusse,	1 combe,
1 black coate,	2 brushes,
1 black stuffe coate,	1 paire of black silk stockings,
1 black suite & cloake	
1 doublett,	A dagger and knife,
1 paire of stockings,	Tobaccoe case,
1 blacke goune,	1 rapier,
1 black hat,	Tobaccoe & some pipes,
1 old hat,	
2 paire of gloves,	A tobacco box and tongs.
1 paire of shoes,	

"His Duxbury inventory, which included his wardrobe, contained:

1 sword,	1 violet color cloth coate,
1 sword,	
White capp,	1 coslett.
A trusse,	

"His estate, divided between his two sons, consisted of his house and appointments in Duxbury, with one hundred and eleven acres of upland, besides marsh lands belonging to him, as well as his share in the undivided lands as one of the purchasers of the patent and plantation of New Plymouth."

The brothers not fully agreeing in the disposition of the effects, a meeting of the men most likely to judge of the Elder's wishes in the matter was called at the Governor's house, where the differences were fully discussed on all sides, and an amicable settlement was made.

Miss Louise Winthrop Koues, the student of personal history, and a professional worker, gives from this naming, suggestions which are certainly very convincing, and any future Brewster historian will be very glad of the guide which opens wonderful possible history.

"The name of Robert Love occurs with that of Roger Mompesson, in partial list of 'Justices of Quorum.' "

Edward Love, married Elizabeth, daughter of —— Moody, of Garsden.

Edward Love, Jr., of Aynho, married Mary, daughter to —— Harecourt.

Elder William Brewster had much to do with this Dudley circle, which embraced the Mompessons and others of greater distinction.

See note at end of Part I.

ISAAC ALLERTON, Fifth Signer.

Mr. Isaac Allerton was born too soon. He is wanted to-day for the syndicates, the trust companies, the mining interests, the corporations, where power and capacity have their place, and every man, from the highest to the lowest, is subordinate to by-laws and the changes consequent upon the majority vote. He could place his household goods at a moment's notice, and transfer them in the same space of time to the antipodes.

The New England people had an arbitrary way of arranging the fate of man. Every action, almost thought, was open to the public, the judgment of them being in the hands of those who had no shirking sense of their duty, as they waited upon the so-called delinquent to administer the needed rebuke.

One place required freemen to be members of the church, according to the lights prescribed by the ruling elders and deacons, who held other men's consciences in their hands. Another, like the Pilgrim Colony, claiming only a certificate of good behavior and intention.

In early days Allerton had imbibed the spirit of the London Company he came from. There a man, be he a duke's son or merely "one of the people," until 1635, was obliged to purchase his freedom, his right to citizenship, by identifying himself according to the requirements of law, with one of the "Livery Companies or Craft Guilds." A younger son was himself, nothing more. To be sure, the knowledge that only primogeniture stood between him and the coronet did not tend to lessen the resentment of the fate too hard for him. To have the privilege of voting for the Lord Mayor of London was something, and to know that for 800 years the office was filled by a man who had earned his right of office by virtue of being a freeman of one of the twelve great livery companies of the city, was a slight compensation. Nevertheless, one's birthright is hardly sold with willingness for a "mess of pottage."

He knew when he started on his career what the possibilities were. To be a freeman from the "Merchant Tailor Company of London" did not beget ignorance. If he appeared inexperienced he belied himself.

INDEPENDENT.

Isaac Allerton was a power; he carried his citizenship with him to Leyden, and acquired the same rights there, February 7, 1614, in common with William Bradford and his brother-in-law, Degery Priest. Confining him to general rules and regulations was beyond the possibilities of any one. He wanted everything of his own constructing; even his religious beliefs were in an evolutionary state; what the cause he never thought to inquire. Why should he? These changes were part of his daily life, and he was willing to stand or fall by them.

There is a difference of opinion in regard to his age. Those who said they knew placed his time of birth at 1585; still it was claimed that he was 31 when he reached Plymouth. At all events, he married first November 4, 1611 (O. S.), at Leyden, Mary Norris, of Newbury, England. This is verified by the records in the Staathuis, or City Hall, of that place, and no one disputes his right to put himself on record as from London. The witnesses to this marriage were Edward Southworth, Richard Masterson and Randolph Tickens; for the bride Anna Fuller and Dillon Carpenter.

No one in the whole Leyden colony was more efficient and eminently useful in all the preparations for their departure. He was hoping to find in America a sort of Bohemian life that would fit with his desires, being in a hurry to emancipate himself from his surroundings. That he had great powers of organization goes without saying; he knew the way and showed the will.

IN THE COLONY.

The cloud, "no bigger than a man's hand," that grew and wrecked him in after years, was then only the calmly blue atmosphere that could shine upon his every action. There is little account of their life on shipboard. One only judges of it by a combination of circumstances, but when they reached Plymouth, Allerton was in the height of his glory. By virtue of necessity he soon occupied a false position. Carver had gone from them to the realms of light, Bradford, the people's choice for Governor, was ill unto death, and Allerton, the active, stirring citizen, the man of great resources, was placed as the power behind the incapacitated throne. The opportunity was his; now was the chance to try how he could work out his own advancement, and when the time was fitting, step into the shoes he felt were none too large for him. He was hardly the victim of circumstances; his own pleasure must count for something. Only the combination had much to do with his future life. Bradford was ill, the affairs of State beyond his weak physical condition, so Allerton, the reins of government in his hands, did fine work for the colonies, never being a gentleman forgetting himself.

He was looked up to, sought advice from, and gained power day by day. To be sure, the office he temporarily held was not his own, and Bradford could hardly expect that when, with returning strength he assumed the duties which were his, Allerton would efface himself, forgetting he ever had an opinion on affairs of state. This jealousy of his power was perfectly natural, but "trifles light as air" assume great proportions when seen through the green glasses.

HARD WORK.

Allerton's work had counted in the colony; he had cast self aside, tilled the ground, when plowing the sea and waves was his desire. The barns and houses which grew by magic power he viewed only as temporary habitations; the churches, from his abhorrence of their narrow faith, were almost repugnant to him, yet he onward "plod his weary way," while Bradford was laid low, and when he recovered wanting all or nothing, he constituted himself a "committee of ways and means," looked around for a change of local habitation, almost name, a matter agreeable to all concerned.

His organization was a not unusual one— fine possibilities, great capacity for work, yet always needing a guiding hand over him. He brought experience, and soon got his bearings, whatever the situation, but a man who is smart for others would naturally count himself in when opportunity presented itself. Chafing under restraint, unwilling to be guided by Bradford's slow, conservative policy, wanting to strike while the iron was hot, there is little wonder the Governor should hardly understand a man whose disposition must always be recorded in extenuation of his action. Honest Bradford wanted integrity in the spirit of the word, requiring no special pleading to convince.

In the fall of 1626 Allerton went to England in the interests of the colonists. Their terms with the Adventurers who advanced the money for their start pressed heavily upon them. It was all outgo and no income. Those who had assumed the debt wanted to see 'if a composition could be made by which the claims should be discharged and their rights be conveyed to the actual planters at Plymouth. This was accomplished, and the instrument of conveyance, dated November 15, 1626, which is preserved in Gov. Bradford's letter book, has forty-two names attached.'

VOYAGE TO ENGLAND.

The wish being father to the thought, Allerton, desiring to enlarge his borders at all times, undoubtedly "took a hand" in any scheme for his own advancement. Up to a certain restricted point, his offices were all for the benefit of his mission; after that himself always. The third voyage to England, which was principally for the procurement of the patents, became very disheartening, and he was obliged to return August, 1629, without accomplishing the object of his journey. If his ways were not their ways, why the colonists should have sent him out again on the same business in the autumn of 1629 is a mystery. By assiduous application this trip was a success, and January 29, 1630, the patent was obtained. Shirley, his associate, in his letter, written March 19 following, expresses his high sense of the services performed by the agent. "Till our main business of the patent was granted, I could not set my mind or pen to writing, and Mr. Allerton was so turmoiled about it, and found so many difficulties and oppositions, as verily I would not, nay, could not have undergone it, if I might have had a thousand pounds." Mr. Allerton's return to England to accomplish this object was strongly urged by Shirley, who was cordially appreciative of his conduct, and always putting his pen to paper to give expression of these feelings.

He says to Gov. Bradford: "Give me leave to put you in mind of one thing. Here are many of your Leyden people now come over, and, though I have ever had good thought of them, yet believe not every one what they shall report of Mr. Allerton. He hath been a trusty, honest friend to you all, either there or here." This man could not have slumbered in inactivity, so with Shirley as a boon companion he acted on the market quotations of one day, and, being without the telephone with which to remind himself, the next forgot, and used the same methods as the opposition.

MISFORTUNE.

Shirley's flattery, or what Allerton considered merited commendation, did not fit him for depreciation at the other end of the line. One or the other opinion must be wrong, and for him there was but one choice. Misfortune soon followed misfortune; he was down and the kick was ready for him, but there is no attempt to question his ability. Point Allerton, at the entrance of Boston Harbor, took its name from Isaac Allerton, as Morton says, "perpetuating the memory of a man of the greatest commercial enterprise in those early times." More honors were his, for the history of Duxbury tells us: "An early mention is made of Allerton Hall, which was probably called after Isaac Allerton, one of the first pilgrims, though there is no notice of his being a resident of Duxbury at any time."

With Allerton and his wife in the Mayflower came three children, Bartholomew, born in Holland about 1612, who, however, returned to England, marrying, making his home and dying there. Remember, born in Holland, has a very short record, not being heard of after 1627, about which time she probably died. Mary, also of the Mary Norris marriage, born before the start, married, in 1636, Thomas Cushman. Isaac Allerton may look down proudly on this descent; there is no trouble in following their records. Mary, his first wife, died February 25, 1621; Sarah, the youngest child, remained, by virtue of her tender years, with her aunt, the wife of Degery Priest, coming out in the noted forefather ship Ann, and in 1637 married Moses Maverick, of Marblehead, giving her father a son-in-law whom he must have liked, else why their business connection.

SECOND MARRIAGE.

In 1626 the good angel of his life came to Isaac Allerton in the shape of his second wife Fear Brewster, daughter of the elder. She often stood between him and harsh judgment, even overt act. The good elder must be spared. Fear Allerton had a short life; let us hope that her husband appreciated what she had been to him and dropped more than a passing tear over her grave. No doubt he did; a man of his stamp would make an unreliable, erratic, but affectionate, husband, in his good times compensating for previous shortcomings.

The religious life of the pilgrims was not all peaceful. The adventurers brought in a new element, and there was a division among the supporters of the Plymouth Colony in England, part of whom considered the religious policy of the Pilgrims too narrow and unfavorable to the operation of trade. It was very easy for those who were the diplomats spending much time abroad to keep in touch with the times, enlarging their views with occasion, but the ones at home, working and denying, fearful of the future, could not grasp the varying methods.

"As an agent Mr. Allerton appears to have been indefatigable in his attempts to promote the interests of his employers. He was a man of uncommon activity, address and enterprise." Still, he was not a success. In 1633 Bradford continues the narrative of his losses by noticing the failure of a trading wigwam "at Machias, which Mr. Allerton, of Plymouth, and some others had set up." "In 1634 the wreck of his pinnace from Port Royal is mentioned, and in 1635 the loss of his bark at Cape Ann is noted." Whatever the results, he was the first merchant of New England, the true founder of all the large enterprizes. The coasting trade he delighted in, and the fishing interest was the emanation of his leisure hours. He believed in competition if he could get ahead, and when his trading stations on the Kenebec and Penobscot were broken up—the latter by the French in 1634—he simply "appealed," asking no permission to locate in another place.

History always accords to him the honor of being the founder of Marblehead, aided by his son-in-law, Moses Maverick. The impulse he gave to trade was never lost, and the "first building in Marblehead for business purposes is Allerton Block, the history of which is almost unknown." All his honors did not deter him from the expression of his opinion in his own peculiar manner, antagonizing the authorities by his too liberal views to such a degree that, with the law as a propelling power, he was forced to "leave between two days."

QUAKERS OPPOSED.

All the desire to extenuate Allerton's faults, allowing for the difference of the times, would only permit one opinion of his conduct in bringing back as his clerk and familiar friend Thomas Morton, of Merry Mount, a man expelled from the country for constant wrongs to the colony, with nothing to recommend and everything to condemn. Allerton, seeing Morton when "he a monk would be," may, if such a thing were possible, have been imposed upon, but it was a very short-sighted policy, and only served to accentuate other acts.

It is, however, to be recorded in his favor that during the excitement against the Quakers Allerton and some others appeared in opposition to the measures pursued; in consequence, he and they became so unpopular that they were left out of their offices of magistrates. A Quaker to Gov. Prence was like a red cloth to a bull in the arena, and if the question in regard to them had two sides, he could only see one.

Of course, he was generous, that goes without saying, even if he was not always just. Old colony records (December 2, 1673), speaking of "Godbert Godbertson's" debts, tells that "whereas the greater part of his debts are owing to Isaack Allerton, of Plymouth, merchant, the said Isaack hath given free leave to all other creditors to be fully discharged before he receive anything of his particular debts to himself, desiring rather to lose all than that they should lose any."

The happiest time of Isaac Allerton's life was when he was in partnership with Govert Loockermans, in New Amsterdam, where he settled soon after the death of his second wife. They were kindred spirits, and went into the trading business with great zest. Allerton sold his yacht Hope to Loockermans, and, having one of his own, each held equal office as commodores of their private squadron. There was water, water everywhere and plenty of beer to drink, while his great tobacco warehouse, which stood on the shore of the East River near the present Maiden lane, furnished the fragrant weed for their confidential hours.

IN PARTNERSHIP.

Being in partnership, with the same pursuits and returns, there was no rivalry. Perhaps they knew each other in Holland. At all events, Govert Loockermans was not a stranger he could "take in." Together they raised the chickens for their "home market," and if any one of the breed had fighting instincts they would not be above watching the encounter, even making a pool with some of the Dutchman to hold the stakes.

Their butter, over the making of which they cracked their little jokes, was the gilt-edged commodity of the period. The interest in it being so great, it served for table talk as they regaled each other with the favorable opinions passed upon it, while making their quick sales. Presumably they dealt in everything that was marketable, and one thing begat another as those wise heads revolved how to turn an honest penny in the speediest possible manner.

Some of Allerton's actions to-day would not cause a passing thought—simply be recorded in the newspapers of one day (with a portrait), and the next only remembered by reference to the file. So much for fame.

He was a resident of New York for some time, and in 1643 was one of the representatives of the citizens in the council called the "eight men," and held other offices under the Dutch administration. He owned the William and John, a "ketch" trading with Virginia. Going on most of the voyages himself, he acquired property there, and as his family were constantly with him it is highly probable that Isaac, Jr.—his son by his second wife, Fear Brewster—who was born in Plymouth, 1630, and graduated at Harvard College in 1650, formed his love for Virginia by this intercourse. He took up his residence in Northumberland County, Virginia, in 1660, and resided there until 1683.

A daughter of his became the second wife of Hancock Lee, seventh son of Col. Richard Lee, the "head of that distinguished family, who was a Roundhead, and allied himself with the Cromwellian party."

THIRD MARRIAGE.

The balmy South records Isaac Allerton, of the Mayflower, as the progenitor of the Lees, of Ditchley, Va., and through them his lineal blood flows in the veins of the Traverses, Cookes, Colstons, Corbins, Willoughbys, etc., of Virginia. If they inherit his strength, unswerving hope, always sanguine of success, they have a rich heritage indeed.

His third and last wife, Joanna, only a name to the world, is first noticed about 1644. True, she made no history, but she managed to secure the love of her stepson, and, fitting into her husband's declining years—for he was about 60 at the time of their marriage—accomplished much toward giving Mr. Allerton's perturbed spirit rest and peace. His last home, if he ever truly had one, was at New Haven. To it he applied the knowledge he had acquired in New Amsterdam, and a "grand house on the creek with four porches" was the result. When the house was demolished the workmen reported that the woodwork was all of the finest oak, and the "best of joiners" had placed it in position. On paper he left a fine estate, though the result was nothing. The debts and the assets hardly balanced.

But the good son, Isaac, mindful of his worthy stepmother's interests, purchased the house where the regicide Judges Whalley and Goff had been harbored; where restless, nervous Mr. Isaac Allerton, as he is always called, closed his eyes on the world to which he had contributed so much, and presented it to his stepmother to "have and to hold" during her life. There can be no difference of opinion as to the esteem in which this man is held by his descendants. Averaging his character, they have so much more to respect than to condemn that they apply this law, and strive bravely to prove themselves worthy of him.

MYLES STANDISH, Sixth Signer.

For the benefit of the Pilgrim Company at Leyden, there came among them, sword in hand, one Myles Standish, of whom the first known is that while a youth he received from Queen Elizabeth a commission in the English Army in Holland, then aiding the Dutch against Spain.

Myles, an old Roman name for soldier, was short of stature, but he made his record according to his inches, not feet, his energetic nature and military training fitting him for the endurance and indomitable self-control demanded by the many duties thrust upon him. His life in Leyden seems to have been wholly a military one, but he was taking notes, maturing his judgment for the colony's benefit in that future of mark. Stalwart as he was, a kind Providence had gifted him with a contrasting sweetness, deep sense of justice that made him a ruler among men, all the more powerful that his reticent nature had a personal holy of holies, into which few were admitted.

A scion of a distinguished house, stung by his wrongs, he never forgot this circumstance, and all through his life recognized that he must so comport himself that the truth of his claim would show without saying.

The lowly surroundings of the Pilgrims were not to his taste; still through all times he bore himself with that unmistakable dignity which placed him where he belonged.

ON THE MAYFLOWER.

With him came on the Mayflower his gentle wife Rose, unrecorded, save that with sweet confidence and anticipation she placed her hand in the strong grasp of Myles Standish, and went forth to do battle with the world, which for her held but short time of trial—only the landing and accompanying doubts in the choice of residence, and Myles Standish was alone with his grief, "a hero in the strife."

A born soldier, the music of fife and drum his birthright, he was heart and soul with the colonists in all their vicissitudes, stern want, sickness and death. The hand which naturally sought the sword hilt, when the loved ones were laid low, served them deftly with the gentleness of a woman. His strong arms were so restful in their security, his abundant love rendering the ministrations welcome indeed to those who in their hour of need turned to this self-contained soldier to hold them firm for the change awaiting them.

Thrown upon his care, Bradford learned to know this man, who felt no weariness in well doing, performing the most menial service with gladness, considering nothing too much that would save to them their beloved Bradford.

Wise Bradford and wise Standish, this tie was never broken; to each the other's faults were lost in the balance of virtues.

Stern of purpose, a disciplinarian in the broadest sense of the word, always a leader as trouble confronted them, a man bristling with danger signals when aroused, he yet has given to history the most romantic side of all the colonists.

High of station, free from care, holding a military position he was fully in accord with, his joining the little band was a mystery, but he was a zealous, devoted citizen, one with them in all thought and deed, save the very purpose which made their exile bearable.

The freedom to worship their God according to their individual desires was at the start nothing to him. Many historians declare him of the Catholic faith of his fathers. From this he certainly changed, as events proved, but when it is known that he was not actively of the Pilgrims' faith, all the more credit to his strength of character that he was able to force the conviction in those he was surrounded by that he must be left alone, answerable only to his own conscience for his method of religious service.

As his personal history makes itself, there seems no possibility but that, from whatever leading, he became an earnest though unrecorded member of the Pilgrim faith.

THE START IN PLYMOUTH.

The mishaps of their start, the deceit of their landing chafed Myles Standish sorely; he wanted something to overcome—this was his metal, so the impatient few, against the better judgment of the majority, to the number of sixteen, under Capt. Standish, always by virtue of his service in the Netherlands their military leader, started out to view the land and report.

Justice compels the statement that he was accompanied by William Bradford, Stephen Hopkins and Edward Tilley.

The Indians they expected, they met, but the foes they deemed unworthy of their steel, with the power of rendering their lives miserable, brought themselves to their notice. Wolves were not attractive guests, roaming at will; they were the unknown evil. This expedition was not successful, and with kindly thought of the anxiety of those left behind they returned, only the better for their experience.

Hope came with the morning, the ship's shallop they had wearied of waiting for was put together, the start for the end made, and before long they safely anchored in Cape Cod harbor, with foot on Plymouth Rock; the real life of Myles Standish, the first officer to hold a military commission in the United States, began, and only ended "when his eyelids closed in death."

MILITARY CLAIMS.

This Cincinnatus of the colony, strong and true, too brave and single of purpose to have suited the ill-disposed, made for himself hosts of friends. They knew he meant what he said, and they judged him according to his own temperament and character.

Born, as it is asserted, in 1584, Myles Standish, it was found by the association formed in 1846 to endeavor to regain the estate belonging to him in England, held the commission of a lieutenant, given him by Queen Elizabeth. As he is first mentioned as captain, that is probably the rank he bore when he left Leyden; indeed, as such he continued till his death.

The lack of promotion may have been the result of insufficient military organization, also of their unwillingness to follow English precedent in the way of army arrangements.

When John Winthrop was Governor of Massachusetts, and the "Ancient and Honorable Artillery" were brought up for consideration, the Governor greatly feared that such a body would tend to overthrow the civil government. Second thought decided him in its favor, and his own sons, as soon as they attained a proper age, became members. It is natural to suppose this was the spirit of the times, and needed a showing of military want to convince.

SECOND MARRIAGE.

Rose was dead, and, true to the Biblical conviction, which deemed it "not well for man to live alone," Standish, as events confirm, sent for Barbara, who naturally must have been at least an old friend, and who is generally credited with being his first wife's sister.

She came over in good company on the Ann, and the reflective hours of sea life, with Alice Southworth as chaperon, made the prospects of the new home and worthy lover very attractive.

To the romance connected with Myles Standish and Priscilla Molines, told by writer and poet, stern-appearing Myles Standish may have given the keynote and a poet's license the imaginative story young and old are cognizant of. If all the tales familiar as household words are true, he had a long look ahead, in preparing for his refusal, by having a wife to his liking in readiness for him. The study of his character, which makes a high claim in the search, renders this view impossible.

The man who dictated such a will as his could do no wrong to any woman. He, a woman's protector, would guard her by the strong arm of the law and the loving care of the man without fear or reproach where his family ties were concerned.

This very fact has made the record. No neglect has been shown him in the statements of events. The poet has sung of him, and not only of love, as Oliver Wendell Holmes, in his "Lending a Punch Bowl," says:

" 'Twas on a dreary winter's eve; the night was closing dim,
When brave Myles Standish took the bowl and filled it to the brim.
The little captain stood and stirred the posset with his sword,
And all his sturdy men-at-arms were ranged about the board."

Equal to the occasion, the same sword would carve the Christmas turkey, if the box arrived too late for conventional dispensing, and sharing with his knights of no table enjoy it while following out the hasty order of march.

So like Myles Standish, our hero.

THE SWORD.

This sword, with its Arabic inscription, of which he was so justly proud, was fit for all occasions, and now that we have an interpretation of the characters on the sword, acquired no doubt by Standish "when he was fighting the battles of Christendom against the Turk, in what is now Austria," before the Captain went to Flanders, studded with deeds, not gems, all are sure could be put to no base uses.

Safe at Plymouth, a token of the past which honors the living, rests the sword. Some Arabs traveling in this country who saw it there say "it is one of the oldest arms in existence, and very valuable."

The translation tells us quaintly that "With peace God ruled His slaves" (meaning creatures), "and with the judgment of His arm He troubled the mighty of the wicked" (meaning the most powerful and evil of the wicked).

The jealousy of John Alden, attributed to Standish, he certainly held well in hand, welcoming to his home in after years Sarah, daughter of "Pilgrim John," and the lovely Priscilla Alden, as wife of his eldest son, Alexander, the one who to him always represented the heir apparent to those lost estates at "Duxbury Hall."

Being the leader, any acts not fully understood, if they were failures, reflected on Standish.

The Indians, without civilization and its consequent tempering, made wholesale assaults against their enemy the white man, and some have censured the worthy commander for his violence in his treatment of this foe. Others, whose opinion was of value, felt that his conduct needed no apology.

Upon his foresight, grasp of the situation and decisive action, depended the very existence of the colony. Prompt measures alone would serve as an example. He simply obeyed orders, was true to his oath of office, conforming to the "blue book" of that day, which then, as now, left no alternative of action.

Even Pastor Robinson, who knew him well, and always loved him, was really too severe, considering the distance that separated them and his own cloth, with hearsay evidence only to guide him, when he wrote for the people "to consider the disposition of their captain, who was warm of temper," and more that must have wounded the spirit of brave Standish, but he was stanch of faith, stood by his trust in his friend, in his will remembering "Mayre Robinson, in consideration of the love he bore her grandfather."

Faith without works would hardly do for the Indians. They knew he had a marvelous knowledge of them, understood intuitively when they were intending bloodshed; then with the strictest secrecy thwarted their designs, leaving the Indians astonished at his divination.

One Indian, who, with the cunning of his nation, made a trade in furs his cause of interview, returned to his tribe not deceived by the calm demeanor of the captain, and informed them that "he saw by his eye that he (Standish) was angry in his heart."

How it happened that so many offices were merged in one man can only be explained by his superior adaptation, and the circumstances of the new colony. The practical side of the captain's character always stood out in bold relief. He arranged for trading depots, saw to the fishing, laid out the roads and surveyed the new towns.

There is no evidence, not even an insinuation, that the colony was ever dissatisfied with his management. He was trusted with their money as treasurer, and in 1625 went out as agent to England in a mercantile position, to sell and purchase for the colony. Not one ray of brightness greeted him on this trip. London, the place of his sojourn, was visited by plague and pestilence, when all "mourned their dead and would not be comforted." No hope awaited him on any side. The state of the country was far from conducive to business transactions, trade of whatever kind was the exception, not the rule, and Standish had little showing for his five months' stay.

The rates of interest were simply ruinous, and yet his mission was not only satisfactory, but acceptable. The colonists never wavered in their faith, accepting as inevitable the fact that circumstances were too much for him. The news he brought back was more than dispiriting. The King had died, and his son, Charles I., was already well on in the career which ended his life in an untimely manner. The non-conformists had no possible chance with Charles, he being a warm advocate of their great enemy, Bishop Laud. Cushman and Robinson had passed the Rubicon, their landmarks were destroyed, and they were already a thing of the past. "Sorrow's cup of sorrow was full for them; the overflowing drop could not intensify where feeling had ceased."

CHURCH INTERESTS.

"Myles Standish was not a church member, and sometimes was a little rough and strong in his ways, but he could be a voter and a magistrate," under the lenient Plymouth system.

The need of room, perhaps desire for a change of privileges, about 1630 sent the Pilgrims to Duxbury "close by," which was so named after the English home of the Standish family. Duxbury Hall, where Hugh Standish was living as early as 1306, and the same domain in England was held in 1812 by Sir Frank Standish.

Whatever the cause of the change, it is evident by the following record:

"Ano 1632, April 2.—The names of those which promise to remove their fam(ilies) to live in the towne in the winter time, that they m(ay) the better repair to the worship of God.

John Alden,
Capt. Standish,
Jonathan Brewster,
Thomas Prence."

that Myles Standish had to do with the church arrangement, and when, the distance being great, they were obliged to have a meeting house of their own, in due course of age, Alexander Standish always the heir apparent, was deacon.

Attendance upon church was a compulsory requisite of position in those days, and while some of the fines were unintelligible to modern ears, all can appreciate the consensus of opinion in Duxbury when, in 1666, Edward Land, John Cooper and John Simmons were fined ten shillings each for "prophane and abusive carriages, each towards the other, on Lord's day at the meeting house." Could they have been written in the hymn book? Matters in regard to this church had a progressive scale, for in 1690 Deacon Wadsworth had "ten shillings" for sweeping the meeting house, and in 1693 the same deacon increased to "fifteen shillings" for performing the same offices.

Capt. Standish showed his strength of character, by using, not abusing his power, and, strange to say, though his intercourse with the Indians was of the law and order style, they appreciated the position he took that he was their just friend in reverses, and rendered him affection and even homage in many instances.

The Indian, Hobomok, who was a friend of the English, early adopted the Christian religion, and became an inmate of Capt. Standish's house, endearing himself to all by his loyalty, going with Standish, as his guide and interpreter. According him the spirit and power of a ruler, the quick resentment that had a code of honor where wrongs were inflicted, the records of Plymouth and Duxbury hold no cleaner pages than those which bore his name, telling that he only twice appeared before the court, and then simply to punish offenders for cruelty to his animals, once his dog!

"Though small of stature he had an active genius, a sanguine temper and a strong constitution," affording us "an instance not only of the nerve of the Pilgrims, but a type of their hearts."

Thomas Morton, of Merry Mount, and Standish were born antagonists; there could be no favors between them; only a repulsion of character, and yet readily understood from the get-up of the men. During one of the fights, when Morton was making common cause with the Indians, selling them guns and ammunition, rousing them by "firewater" to deeds of violence, he hurt Standish more than he could by a gun, when he derisively called him "their great leader, Capt. Shrimpe."

Active to the last, he commanded the Plymouth quota in the Pequot war, and even as late as 1653, when age, his only conqueror, was upon him, he was given command of the colony forces when trouble seemed imminent with the Dutch at Manhattan.

HIS LIBRARY.

His library is in evidence for his literary tastes. The people of that epoch were not collectors, but students. His possessions, simple and homely though they were, were very large for the times; the stress laid in the inventory on his pewter dishes was not uncalled for; they ranked with the sevres of to-day, and everything being by comparison gave importance to his will. More would have come of his inheritance could the claim he put forth have been authenticated, but on visiting the Isle of Man, where his first marriage is said to have been consummated, no register of the event could be found to substantiate the assertion, and they were obliged to abandon their efforts, the legality being not proven.

STANDISH'S WILL.

"An inventory of the goods and chattels that Capt. Myles Standish, gent, was possessed of at his decease, as they were showed to us whose names are underwritten, the 2d of December, 1657, and exhibited att the court held att Plymouth the 4 May, 1657, on the oath of Miss Barbara Standish.

£. s. d.
It. one dwelling house and outhouse, with the land thereunto belonging. 140 00 00
It. 4 oxen 24 00 00
It. 2 mares, two colts, one young horse 48 00 00
It. 6 cows, 3 heifers and one calf.. 29 00 00
It. 8 ewe sheep, two rams and one wether 15 00 00
It. 14 swine, great and small........ 3 15 00
It. one fowling piece, 3 musketts, 4 carbines, 2 small guns, one old barrell 8 01 00
It. one sword, one cutles, 3 belts.... 2 07 00

It. a cronicle of England and the country ffarmer	8 00
It. the history of the world and the Turkish history	1 10 00
It. ye history of Queen Elizabeth, the state of Europe	1 10 00
It. Doctor Hale's works, Calvin's institutions	1 04 00
It. Wilcock's workers and mayors	1 00 00
It. Rogers' seven treatises and the ffrench akademy	12 00
It. 3 old bibles	14 00
It. Ceser's comentaryes, Bariff's artillery	20 00
It. Preston's sermons, Burroughes' Christ in contentment, gospel conversation, passions of the mind, the phisisions' practise, Burroughes' Earthly mindedness, Burroughes' discovery	1 04 00
It. Ball on faith, Brinsley's watch, dod on the Lord's supper, Sparke against herisye, davenporte apologye	15 00
It. A reply to Doctor Cotten on baptisme, The Garman History, the Sweden Intelligencer, reasons discued	10 00
It. one testament, one psalme booke, Nature and grace in conflict, a law book, The meaning in mourning allegation against B. P. of Durham, Johnson against hearing	6 00
It. a pcell of old bookes of divers subjects in quarto	14 00
It. Wilson's dixonary, homers Illiad, a commentary on James Ball cattukesmer	12 00
It. another pcell in octavo	4 00
It. half a young heifer	1 00 00
It. one feather bed, bolster and two pillows	4 00 00
It. one blankett, a coverlid and a rugg	1 05 00
It. 1 feather bed, blanket and great pillow	2 15 00
It. 1 old feather bed	4 00 00
It. 1 blanket and 2 ruggs	1 15 00
It. 1 feather bolster and old rugg	14 00
It. 4 paire sheets	3 00 00
It. 1 paire fine sheets	1 04 00
It. 1 table cloth, 4 napkins	10 00
It. his wearing clothes	10 00 00
It. 16 pieces of pewter	1 08 00
It. Earthen ware	5 00
It. 3 brasse Kettles, one skillett	2 00 00
It. 4 iron potts	1 08 00
It. a warming pan, a frying pan and a cullender	9 00
It. one paire stillyards	10 00
It. 2 bedsteads, one table, 1 forme chaires, 1 chist and 2 boxes	2 13 00
It. 1 bedstead, one settle bed, one box, 3 casks	1 07 00
It. 1 bedstead, 3 chists, 3 vases with sense bottles, 1 box, 4 casks	2 06 00
It. 1 still	12 00
It. 1 old setter, 1 chaise, one kneading trough, 2 pailes, 2 traies	16 00
It. 2 beer casks, 1 chun, 2 spinning wheels, one powdering tubb, 2 old casks, one old flaskett	15 00
It. 1 mault mill	2 00 00
It. 2 sawes, with divers carpenters tooles	1 19 00
It. a timber chaire, with plow chaires	1 06 00
It. 2 saddles, a pillion, one bridle	1 00 00
It. old iron	1 00 00
It. 1 chist and a husking table	8 00
It. 1 hatchett, 2 tramells, 2 iron doggs, 1 spitt, one fier forke, 1 lamp, 2 gars (?), one lanthorn, with other old lumber	2 01 00
It. in woole	15 00
It. in hemp and flax	6 00
It. eleven bushells of wheat	2 05 00
It. 14 bushells of rye	2 02 00
It. 30 bushells of pease	5 05 00
It. 25 bushells of indian corn	3 15 00
It. cast and peakes, and plow irons and 1 brake	2 05 00
It. axes, sickles, hookes and other tooles	1 00 00
It. eight iron hookes, 1 spinning wheel, with other lumber	14 00
	358 07 00

John Alden.
James Cudworth.

The whole will, even the inventory, speaks for itself. The library would hardly come under the tenets of the Roman Catholic Church.

No, Capt. Myles Standish, perhaps, with much self-communion, left his religious record; a dying testimony. It is all very tender history.

Write him down conqueror!

The cabinet of the Plymouth Society is rich in treasures of the Standish family. The veritable sword used by the "doughty captain" is there, one of the celebrated pewter dishes, and as well a piece of embroidery in a frame executed by Lora Standish.

THE CHILDREN.

Myles and Barbara Standish had six children. Alexander, who married, first, Sarah Alden; second, Desire Doty, widow of Israel Holmes; Myles, who removed to Boston and married a daughter of John Winslow, July 19, 1660; Capt. Josiah, of North Bridgewater, and Norwich, Conn., married Mary, daughter of John Dingley, who died the same year; then he married Sarah, Daughter of Samuel Allen, of Braintree; Charles, died young; Lora, who died before her father, and John, died young.

Capt. Myles Standish, the hero, a man who demands and receives one's love, and respect, as they read and write of him, "died October 31, 1656, aged 72," a man full of years, and honored by his generation. His last moments were full of suffering so intense that death was a relief, and in his agony, when the hero's prayer for strength went up, his friend, Dr. Fuller, who had been with him in all his joys and sorrows, was away without possibility of recall. His friendly offices could bring no healing or mitigation of the pain that was consuming him. Even the medical knowledge he had himself acquired for the physical benefit of others was of no avail when quivering with pain; he could only endure.

Secretary Morton, another stalwart of the colony, in recording his death, gives evidence of his Christian faith when he says: "He growing very ancient became sick of the stone, or stanguillon, whereof, after suffering of much dolorous pain, he fell asleep in the Lord, and was honorably buried at Duxbury."

All doubts about the place of his interment being solved, it was agreed to place natural bowlders on the graves of Myles Standish, his daughter and daughter-in-law.

"The one on the Captain's grave weighed about five tons, and is marked on its face with the name of Myles Standish, in three-inch block sunken letters. The bowlders marking the graves of Lora and Mary Dingley Standish are smaller, and were obtained from the Captain's old farm at South Duxbury. Cannon and shell, the gift of the Navy Department, are placed in position around the three graves."

The Daughters of the Revolution, on Monday, September 30, 1895, erected a cairn of stones to commemorate the landing of Myles Standish at Squantum Head, September 30, 1621, a promontory which juts out into the water of Boston Bay. It is ten feet in height, and is composed of cobblestones, each participant in the historic occasion contributing a stone.

There should be no sorrow in leaving this man to the verdict of public opinion. He has won on his merits; still, it is a case where one wants to know how all feel and think, whether his true value has been conveyed, and he has found his real place in the hearts of the American people.

Capt. Myles Standish, of Duxbury Hall, England, of Duxbury, Plymouth Colony, made his mark on the history of the country he sought of his own free will; the rest must be done by his descendants. To them he has left a name so grand, broad and true that he has a right to claim, even allowing for the intervening time which is recorded, that they should so order their lives as to perpetuate it intact, as it went from him to them.

JOHN ALDEN, Seventh Signer.

Pilgrim John, that "young enthusiast," had a place of his own among the colonists. Youngest of those who signed the Compact, buoyant and sanguine of disposition, he went forward always with the anticipation that much would come from his desires, and the lamp of the genii in his hands needed but a slight turn to secure to him the best in the power of those he was surrounded by to bestow.

In this one must agree with his own unspoken expectation, as they watch the consummation of affairs. When he is mentioned the voice even changes to a petting tone, and though one celebrated historian wrote me that he was "a very overestimated young man," the harm was done before this knowledge, and the inspiration for this opinion remains.

If he had faults, his sweet personality condones them, and this "tall and handsome" Pilgrim keeps his position always as a prime favorite. No need for him to have asked anything as a favor; before the wish was formulated, some one stood ready to grant him all their intuitions could foresee.

MARY CHILTON.

With this knowledge can one for an instant believe that, except as a boyish prank, he would even desire to take precedence of Mary Chilton as the first to put foot on "Plymouth Rock"? Why argue the case, she the first woman, he the first man? And when she afterward, as the result of the terrible first sickness, became the "Pilgrim Orphan," surely John Alden never denied her anything until her graces of mind and person won for her the love of John Winslow, a prominent merchant and large ship owner of Boston, brother of Gov. Winslow, who, knowing her lonely early life, sought to make up to her for all she had lost by his manly care.

John Alden was born in 1599, having, as I make history, finished his guild apprenticeship, proud of the citizenship he had thus gained, was out seeing the world, when fate led him to the docks where the Mayflower was preparing for its voyage, and with the sanguine feeling of untried youth, that his certificate rendered him an expert, gave his offices, in all probability advice, as to the "fitting out."

Here his personality was strong upon all. They wanted his companionship, youthful energy and experienced services, so "John Alden was hired for a cooper at Southampton, where the ship victualed, and being a hopeful young man was much desired, but left to his own liking to go or stay, when he came here; but he stayed and married here."

Fortunately for the colony there were no modern laws to contend with, or he would have been returned as a "contract laborer."

POSITION.

Nothing was against this man at the start, and it would seem strange if such men as formed that Plymouth Colony should have taken him into immediate consultation, office and dependence of judgment, with his youth against experience, if he were not a man of at least equal birth and breeding. He had a strong grip upon everything of a public nature, and his repetition of office is an evidence of his wearing well in their estimation.

The wooing of our Pilgrim is the tale told from generation to generation, ever new, always acceptable where young people with an affinity of desire realize that the world holds nothing good which separates them.

Priscilla had her record well defined, one of the loveliest of the lovely, a favorite of all on her merits. Daughter of William and Alice Molines, of the Walloon Huguenot contingent, she brought with her not only all that makes woman attractive, but that deft knowledge of household matters, love for art which could utilize very lowly surrounding and make of the wilderness a paradise of beauty.

True, her life shadows fell very early, but she was not alone in her grief, and while it was none the less personal, the fellow-feeling of sorrow roused her to deeds of sympathy and comforting, where self was soon forgotten.

Still, life was not all an effort when John Alden, the well-beloved, was always at the trysting place, and ready at any time to single her out for his attentions.

Their love grew apace, and human nature forbids my believing of him as ambassador for Capt. Standish, unless he was so certain of his own innings that he could appear generous with no fear of the result. Longfellow, with the mental telepathy of lineal descent, may have felt his right to take any liberty he chose with their history, and certainly all would wish to believe the story as he tells it of John Alden in those early nuptials, when perforce the "coach and four" of fairly lore being out of the count, he "covered his bull with handsome broadcloth and on it rode to the wedding," but when the words had been pronounced which recorded Priscilla his wife, and they were about to start for the home his love and care had provided, he tenderly put the bride in her place and walked in conscious pride beside her, leading the bull by the ring in its nose.

Why must stern facts and a regard for historical truths destroy this beautiful story, and take even one gallant act from Pilgrim John's list? But fate is too hard for us, and "John and Priscilla," as one calls them naturally in the intimate relations assumed toward them, were married in 1621, and "in 1624 Edward Winslow returned in the Charity, bringing besides a good supply, three heifers and a bull, the first beginning of any cattle of that kind in the land."

How hard to imagine John Alden doing his wooing through a "courting stick." It would be simply impossible. The matter was to be attended to, and he must go the whole figure, with only his own prescribing as to the manner.

Whispering his words of love with a fixed distance between himself and the object would not be at all to his fancy. Neither was Priscilla conventional. She knew the road to a man's heart, and, with a certain consciousness of her attractions, added to them by the means nature dictated.

PRISCILLA'S HOUSEKEEPING.

Could John Alden resist her "partritch stew'd," prepared from an inherited formula, where you "take marrow bones of beef or mutton, boil them well, strayn the broth, and put it into an earthen pot; then add a good quantity of wyne thereto; then stuffe the partritch with whole pepyr and marrow, and sow up all the vents of the burd; then take cloves, mace and whole pepyr, and let them boil together with the partritch; when it is enough cast into the pot powder of gingyer, salt and saffron, and serve it up in broth," when he returned from an exploration for the inner man, the "vacuum nature abhors?"

Perhaps if they were ready he would prefer "Hennes in Brette." "Take the hennes and scald them, cut them into gibbetts and seethe them with pork, pepyr, gingyer and bread; temper it up with the same broth or ale; color it with saffron, seethe it together and serve it forth."

Priscilla would never be a woman with only one resource, and John, in those early days, was enough of a boy to want a "sweet," so she gave him "Apple Muse" for a change, carefully writing down the components for the children to use when they had homes of their own. Thus she told it to them: "Take apples, seethe them and searse through a sieve; then add almond, milk, honey, grated bread, sanders and salt; let them all seethe together; stir it well and serve it." There were no regrets when "John and Priscilla" gave a party.

PILGRIM JOHN'S CHARACTER.

The strong side to this pilgrim's character was always kept before the people. It was not from habit that he served for forty years as assistant to every Governor but Carver; thirteen years their treasurer, and, to keep himself out of mischief from idle hands, eight times deputy from Duxbury. The man had a place that could only be filled by himself.

He and Capt. Standish were the best of friends, and Barbara never knew any cause for jealousy of the "good wife" at whose hospitable, attractive board she was always a welcome guest. They grew in beauty side by side, and when in the course of events each was to give a child to the other, they were more than gratified at this perfecting of their union.

Plymouth soon became too close quarters for its inhabitants, so Duxbury took the overflow; but, with wise foresight, when the church seceded from the parent church "care was taken to enact that Plymouth should always be the capital of the colony."

This first church of Plymouth, organized in Scrooby, England, by these Pilgrim Fathers, for sixteen years between there and Holland, their earthly paradise, continued in "New Plimouth," the meetings being held in the "Common House," in Leyden street, the historic first street laid out by the Pilgrim colony.

Its first meeting house was built on the north side of Town Square in 1637; then came the one of 1683, and the third in 1744; the fourth, built in 1831, was the one destroyed November 22, 1892, by fire, and where, sad to relate, the town bell, cast in 1801 by "Paul Revere and Son," met a fate all would have desired to avert, being broken in its fall from the tower. Wisely, however, it has been voted to recast it, and the same bell will ring out the welcome to church. The Duxbury church was second to none in its position. History must accord precedence to the original first church as to time of start; but under the other roof was gathered much of the power, religious strength and best personal representation of the time.

CHURCH MEMBERSHIP.

"In Massachusetts not one man in four was a church member, but there and in New Haven only church members were allowed to vote. No such restriction was ever adopted in Plymouth or Connecticut, but in Plymouth the offices held much more responsibility than dignity or emolument, hence many people avoided citizenship through a desire of escaping petty offices and court duties which a freeman might not decline without suffering a fine."

Alden had a poor return for his devotion to public interest. Private affairs were lost sight of, and though he was "crowned with that competence which is vital to content," republics not being in his case ungrateful, he ultimately found his private treasury so depleted that the voting of aid for him by the town was very acceptable. His will gave evidence of the situation. He left but £50 and there was not hope for the debts due the estate, "most of which are desperate."

The pioneer settlers of Duxbury had much to contend with. Their cottages, hastily built for immediate occupancy, were hardly sufficient protection against the winter's storms and the Indians, a little too neighborly, were still a source of dread.

The church, too, caused agitation and discussion. Alden was "always a firm supporter of the clergy and the church, and everything of an innovating nature received his determined opposition."

The beliefs he joined the church with must serve him to life's close. Age narrowed him, sad to relate, and he became "a Puritan in theory and practice," "stern, austere and unyielding," "an iron-nerved Puritan who could hew down forests and live on crumbs."

This is the pilgrim I do not know; my lines with him have been cast in pleasanter places. Even going with him to Josias Winslow's funeral, when "he had Priscilla on his arm," a venerable couple, the last time recorded together, was better. Our mind's eye shows us Priscilla on that occasion compactly gowned with Puritan kerchief crossed meekly across her breast, no "silken whispers of full best skirt" to disturb the assemblage as she entered; John and herself of one mind, one step, as they sought the seats apportioned them.

Narrow as the life of that period was, there was a slight vent in attending the "annual fair which was allowed in Duxbury in 1638." A very natural place for "Pilgrim John," wending his way through the various wares, and sampling the best of everything to his heart's content; ready to give a Bunsby opinion to any committee, the fact that he was ignorant being no drawback, when much that was attractive had been prepared under his own roof, Priscilla, his wife, giving the finishing touches which had rendered the articles artistic and attractive. The toothsome dainties were part of the daily providing of his own table, why hesitate to judge when he was an expert from habit? As treasurer of the town, who so fitting to do duty in winding up affairs and seeing the accounts came out straight? A living example of figures as an exact science, philanthropy with him meaning that the proceeds should reach the object they were intended for, without any diminution in transit.

This was the old-fashioned man, who knew of these fairs before he started on the journey that was to end in New England. They originated in Coventry, where they were first "Wakes," held in the churchyard on St. John's day, and then the "hawkers" of "small wares," soon evolved into merchants with a full stock, and in their progress became fairs, with booths, and large mercantile interests.

HOME LIFE.

"John and Priscilla" were people whose journey of life was with one thought. The children, the care of each, no matter which heard their catechism, in either's hands it required perfect, attentive response. The sermon, long and tedious, must be analyzed and the truths applied, no one forgetting they were sinners, and every punishment meted out to mankind was theirs by virtue of wrongdoing. Being the greatest of delinquents, they must kiss the rod and bow in submission to Divine will, regardless of the counteracting mercy which would come to them for the asking.

John lived for Priscilla, Priscilla for John, the children, their joys and comforts, still a very secondary consideration. Even the old Dutch doll Priscilla brought from Holland, reminder of the days when the parents, now in their rude graves, watched her innocent play, was dear to him from the association, as part of the life of his dear wife.

If it at all resembled those in the "New Haven Colony Historical Collection," Priscilla never left it in its stolid appearance; surely some tri-colored ribbon added to its charms.

The death of Capt. Myles Standish was a great loss to John Alden; he was his balance wheel, the friend to whose counsels he would not only listen, but render obedience.

Had he lived, Gov. Prence and William Collier would never have let him go far astray in his treatment of the Quakers.

How his nature became so warped is a mystery; but the fact exists, and all would ask forgetfulness of this "blot on his 'scutcheon." His rounded character, not so strong, perhaps, as some of the other colonists, but so loving and dear, is the view to take of him; it is what he deserves.

"Number of days" are considered a blessing, so if number of children fit into the same category, our Pilgrims were singled out for privileges, for they had eleven.

Elizabeth, born 1622, or 3, "the first white woman born in New England," though, with the modesty of her sex, she never competed for any share in the tangible benefits which came to "Peregrine White, as the first-born Englishman," married William Pabodie, December 26, 1644, "a man much employed in public affairs, and of much respectability."

In 1684 they moved to Little Compton, R. I., making a new home for themselves on this "stern and rock-bound coast."

Until 1745 this place was in Massachusetts, but then the boundary was changed. The people there, with Betty Alden's cottage in sight, only allow that it was altered as to State, but claim that the habits and habitations now, as of yore, partake of the Massachusetts methods.

The Boston "News Letter" of June, 1717, Little Compton, May 31, records that "This morning died here Mrs. Elizabeth Paybody, late wife of Mr. Will Paybody, in the 93d year of her age."

Little Compton has made her death local possession by placing a tablet to her memory.

Then came John, the mariner, born in 1624, who married twice, his last wife being the widow of Abial Everitt. Next, Joseph, born in 1627, who settled in Bridgewater. Sarah, wife of Alexander Standish; Ruth, probably born in 1631, who married John Bass, of Braintree, son of Samuel Bass, the first deacon of that place, a prominent law-abiding citizen, always classed in history with John Adams.

This is a descent to linger over; a claim for every American citizen to rise up in his might and proclaim it a nation's pride and blessing.

John Adams, John Quincy Adams, and Samuel Adams are names written with a firm foundation, for all the world to honor; the part of American history that, even with more than a century between the present and their living selves, rouses the blood and deeds of every patriot, came to us through this branch.

Capt. Jonathan, the son, like his father, the one who fitted so into his life and happiness, married Abigail Hallett, of Barnstable, and to the end of his days perpetuated the Pilgrims' traits.

Then Zachariah, whose daughter Anna married Jonah Snell, and welcomed nature's poet, William Cullen Bryant, into their descent.

Rebecca, Mary, wife of Thomas Delano; David, a resident of Duxbury, and a prominent member of the church, who married Mary Southworth. Still another Priscilla, though "perhaps" is attached to her name. A few more or less won't count with such a "full hand."

POSSESSIONS.

"One John Alden, of the Middle Temple," is mentioned as having a coat of arms assigned him in 1607. He belonged in Hertfordshire, and from the similarity of names, and the location along the Scrooby Post Road, it seems natural to place Pilgrim John Alden as of the same family.

The possessions of the Aldens, which remain as relics, are as imposing as any, until we reach the members of the Winthrop Fleet. One descendant has a table made of English oak which came over in the Mayflower, and seems to be authentically placed as belonging to Priscilla's mother.

If it were not for the minuteness of detail entered into in the wills and inventories of the early settlers, much could be believed, which this fact casts doubt upon. I have never heard it questioned that John Alden brought a Bible with him, which is well known as of Robert Barker, printer to the King, 1620, and one treasures the bit of romance "Goodwin" attributes to it, as being a parting gift, or the purchase dear to the man's heart, preparatory to his leaving England, his native land. This, with a few official papers, are placed in Plymouth Hall as landmarks of association with John Alden.

Dr. Samuel Alden, of Bridgewater, had

in his possession a deed that belonged to the emigrant Alden, and there is said to be in Cambridge, Mass., a silver tankard once owned, as a descendant repudiatingly said, by that Cooper!

The paper cannot speak, but the "hall marks" are indignation.

This may be a confusion of terms, and mean the same pitcher which on the 4th of August, 1896, was in the loan exhibition at Plymouth, Mass.

Fine old mahogany furniture is said to have come out in the Ann. I have seen around Boston more chairs reputed to have been on the ship than the Mayflower could have held, with only chairs for her cargo. In the Connecticut Historical Society, at Hartford, there is Elder Brewster's chest, and recently in Connecticut I was shown a mahogany low boy that had its pedigree to the Mayflower, 1620.

Another heirloom connects history, for Miss Mary A. Alden, of Duxbury, Mass., who lived in the home of her father, Major Judah Alden, some eighty years ago, by inheritance, had a Southworth pewter platter.

Whatever his beginnings, Pilgrim Alden grew fast, and before me is a letter, saying, on the authority of a learned professor in Boston, an Englishman by birth, that Prof. Haldane, of St. Andrew's, Scotland, claimed relationship to the Aldens of the north of England.

Our Pilgrim planted well. The Adams family belong to him, and further honor lies in the Trumbulls and that descent which gives the learned men of earth.

Then the Seaburys—Samuel, the first Episcopal Bishop of America, being so near the Pilgrim, could nearly place his hand on his head—are his worthy representatives.

Honoring Pilgrim John Alden is out of our power. The man only comes to his own.

SAMUEL FULLER, Eighth Signer.

This Luke, the beloved first physician of Plymouth colony, was well fitted to be an example to guide the people on the road he trod, though ofttimes weary and sore with the march. His marked career began in Leyden. Early one of the deacons of that church, his usefulness increased as time went on. This office was not an empty one, for the deacons of the church, though laymen, were as carefully selected and formally ordained as the clergymen. The man's life invested the position with the power of his own force of character.

Unswerving regard for the precepts he was teaching gave to his words a meaning all recognized as the man himself attuned to the work in his Master's vineyard, wherever it might be located. Before his start for the new world he had taken a deep draught of the cup of sorrow, which came to him in the death of his first wife, Elsie Glascock, whom he probably married in England, and who left him so young he felt it hard to kiss the rod Providence had laid heavily upon him. Then he married, according to Leyden records, in 1613, Agnes, daughter of Alexander Carpenter.

It is opportune here to mention that very shortly after this marriage Edward Southworth married Alice, her sister, though only this fact is recorded at Leyden, without any reference to his birthplace. Soon, Agnes Fuller was gathered to her fathers, and in 1617 Deacon Fuller married Bridget, daughter of Mrs. Joseph Lee. The famous overflow ship, the Ann. in 1623 brought this third and last wife to Dr. Fuller, with their child, who, however, died soon after their arrival. Two children were born to them in Plymouth, Samuel and Mary, who married Ralph James, and he is only recorded from that fact. Honor enough, surely, to have for wife a daughter of Dr. Fuller.

HIS REPUTATION.

What he was to the colonists can be imagined without any limit as to the extent of his power. This great Christian healer brought with him to their sick and dying beds, in addition to his medical skill, the love of his God, which should be theirs but for the asking, that endless gift, if accepted, which would last through eternity.

The faith to feel that death, which comes to all, is only a difference of time, the transition but the opening of the pearly gates, then the rest and blessing of a place in his Father's kingdom.

Although he gave bonds, with others, to the company of adventurers in England, the deacon was not concerned in the bargain for gaining the trade of the colony—a matter agreed to in their despair, and which had much to do with the trials of their start.

They had freedom to worship their God as they desired, but there it ended.

The cast iron demands of the bonds executed by those in authority left them without personality, and, for a time, redress. They performed their tasks with weary hearts; no buoyant hope for the future to light them on the way. But one comfort all experienced—they were sure of the sympathy and advice of this man they could go to with every sorrow, knowing his faith and offices would strengthen them if only for endurance.

Our "medical deacon" added to his many attributes a love for theology, hardly disputation, but the rigid, narrow beliefs of the Puritans, on matters both spiritual and temporal, irritated him sorely, and he warred against Gov. Endicott, whose views were more than antagonistic to him, as strongly as against disease.

ENDICOTT'S CHANGE OF OPINION.

Though "with patience he stood waiting," the time came when Gov. Endicott, realizing the sore straits of his people, surrounded by sickness, sent to Gov. Bradford, begging that he might have the services of their physician, so dear to all.

This was Dr. Fuller's opportunity, and he availed himself of it, relieving his vigils beside the sick bed by learned discourse with the Governor, and not almost but wholly persuading him to look upon the error of his ways.

To this Endicott bore open testimony, visiting Gov. Bradford to thank him for sending Dr. Fuller to him in his need, and saying: "I acknowledge myselfe much bound to you for your kind love and care in sending Mr. Fuller among us, and rejoyce much yt. I am by him satisfied touching your judgment, of ye outward forme of God's worshipe."

The views of the Pilgrims and Puritans were so diametrically opposite that such a change of opinion must of necessity have had a bearing on the whole colony, and Dr. Fuller, whose services were always held in special request, both for the souls and bodies of the people, a man high in their esteem for his unfeigned piety, realized that his visits to Salem were very satisfactory.

Queer times, surely, as Dr. Fuller in a letter to Bradford, June, 1630, says: "I have been to Matapan (now Dorchester) and let some twenty people blood." This told with self-congratulation when the people were suffering from scurvy and other low diseases produced by want, the middle of summer, and the anxiety about the replenishing of their stores, a subject of serious thought and prolonged prayer. A remedy was at hand. During this sickness of 1630 all hope had fled, despair reduced them to prostration and inertness, when "in the middle of winter Pierce arrived once more in the Lion, and fortunately brought with him a large supply of lemon juice, by the aid of which the deaths were confined to the discouraged."

MORTON, OF MERRY MOUNT.

Dear as Dr. Fuller was to all, he could not escape the ridicule of Morton, truly the clown of the colony, who, when the deacon was "spending and being spent" for the common good, said that "Dr. Noddy had a great cure for Capt. Littleworth—he cured him of a disease called a wife."

Deacon Fuller in his office had some very modern methods. At one church service in Plymouth, when Gov. Winthrop had been their guest, giving his aid in the exhorting, assisting the others in prayer, "Dr. Fuller put the congregation in mind of their duty of contribution, upon which the Governor and all the rest went down to the deacon's seat and put into the bag and then returned."

When he had time he was assistant, but not having solved the problem of being in two places at once, he could not conform to the general wish, though he always did his duty and more. Friend and foe alike were secure of his offices, even in the war, when the life of an Indian was a matter of little moment, the "good physician" took charge of the Namaskets at Plymouth, and, regardless of the possibility that they might prove the vipers to "turn and rend him" after he had warmed them in his bosom, he used all his healing and sent them forth cured.

History is one oft-repeated tale of his goodness, a man of spirit, guarded and controlled by the promises he had accepted.

HIS DEATH.

Dr. Fuller died in 1633. "When it pleased ye Lord to visit them this year with an infectious fevoure, of which many fell very sicke, among those who died were Samuel Fuller, who was their surgeon and physician, and had been a great help and comforte unto them as in his faculties so otherwise being a deacon of ye church, a man godly and forward to doe good, being much missed after his death."

His library contained only twenty-seven books; it is very supposable they were medical works, which must have been scarce in early times. However, we would not require many authorities if "letting blood" and "lemon juice" were the remedies which cured every disease, and prevented "every evil under the sun." Dr. Fuller's reputation would surely have accorded him the use of anything that could have contributed to his pleasure and well being, if contained in the libraries of Brewster and Bradford.

One historian wrote me, though I cannot give authority for it from history, that those libraries were for public use.

The physical endurance required for the day's labors hardly fitted the poor Pilgrims to desire anything beyond their night's rest when the shades of evening gathered round them. Balmy sleep needed no wooing in their behalf.

The will of the deacon proves that in addition to his many other attributes he had been a teacher of youth, as he mentions: "Elizabeth Cowles, who was submitted to my education by her father and mother at Charlestown, to be returned to her parents."

True to his religious instincts, showing himself always ready to contribute to any upbuilding of his faith for the benefit of others, in 1633 Deacon Fuller, "the phisition," wrote in his will, "I will give to the church of God at Plymouth the first cow calf that my brown cow shall have."

His widow and son, feeling sure they were carrying out the Doctor's wishes, gave in 1644 a lot in Leyden street, Plymouth, for a parsonage. Working well together their whole desire was to continue the plan they recognized might have been intended by the one each cared to honor.

Samuel Fuller, the son, became a clergyman, and was the first minister of the church at Middleboro, Mass., but had preached there for sixteen years before being ordained, when the "first church was gathered," December 26, 1694; dying there August 27, 1695 (N. S.), in the seventy-first year of his age. He married Elizabeth, daughter of Jonathan Brewster, and granddaughter of the "Elder."

For some reason he refused a call to the church at Rhibboth, July 3, 1663, although, knowing his devotion to his mother, the town invited her residence there, giving her an office which secured her independence.

The end of this saint was peace, and his record places him, where all would wish to be when the last hour comes, which shows how valueless everything in life is that does not tend to preparation for the close.

CHRISTOPHER MARTIN, Ninth Signer.

Looking back upon the Pilgrims, their start from home and its cause, there is a natural feeling that they were at peace with all men and themselves, aiming only at the results which should settle them forever in the content of well doing.

After all, our forefathers had all the strong traits of humanity at the bottom, and the "Old Adam" reigned in force, the same as it did before their organization, and has since they taught us the lessons of their fidelity and implicit faith in Christianity.

"Several friends in England were to join the emigrants, and one of their number, Christopher Martin, of Billerica (Essex), was made co-agent with Carver and Cushman."

"And therefore it was thought meet and convenient by them in Holland that these strangers that were to go with them, not so much for any great need of their help, as to avoid all suspicion or jealousy of any partiality," should hold positions.

Impulsive in their integrity, they placed Christopher Martin as treasurer; they wanted to show their trust—and only realized regrets. Money was king, and a good bank deposit gave the holder a power above and beyond everything else.

Cushman felt in writing of him to "his friend, Edward Southworth, August 17, anno 1620," that he was the "beggar on horseback," inflated by his temporary possessions, and says "nearly £700 hath been bestowed (spent) at Southampton upon what I know not, and he will not, neither can he give any account."

Feeling himself the dispenser of the funds, the capitalist, and the rest his consequent inferiors, he played, as was claimed, the tyrant; he was in command, and their rebellion counted for naught.

Calling the merchants hard names, and including Cushman in his assertions, did not weaken his hold. Money in hand, he could venture on any course of action, and his was to see the funds fly, and call himself in his communions a "prince of good fellows."

PERSONAL CLAIMS.

For one thing, Mr. Christopher Martin has his own record. He is definitely placed in Billerica, also in connection with his servant, Solomon Prower, and his own son.

Then, too, he is one of the few who received the prefix Mr., which in those days stood for Master.

Cushman's opinion of him may be susceptible to a little change. They were brought in very close contact, and Cushman, feeling himself to be one of the Leyden Church, accredited from its members, hardly relished the clinking of the gold, which held him at all times in an inferior position.

History claims that Mr. Christopher Martin must have been trusty "to have satisfied such men as Warren, Hopkins and Mullin."

Everything in the arrangements was antagonistic to Cushman in his relations with Martin. The Mayflower, small as she was, rated at only 180 tons, was a fine representative vessel, according to English possessions, for in 1587 there were not more than five merchant vessels exceeding two hundred tons.

Here human nature comes in. The fine vessel could not be wholly occupied by the leaders. The claim of favoritism would thus be made, and it was rather hard lines to place Mr. Christopher Martin on the Speedwell as Governor of her passengers, identical with Gov. Carver's position on the Mayflower, and rate Cushman as assistant.

FURTHER INDIGNITIES.

Still further trials were in store. The Speedwell put back; the original ninety passengers on the Mayflower were increased to 102, and the remaining passengers were to stay behind, awaiting some more convenient time for their voyage. Mr. Martin went to the Mayflower and Cushman was left to commune with himself and chafe over his adverse fate.

MARTIN'S DEATH.

The old Pilgrim story came to their treasurer January 16, and was sent to the ship, that Mr. Martin could live but a few days, and Gov. Carver's presence was desired to settle up his accounts as treasurer.

On Sunday he arrived, the call none too soon, for Monday closed his earthly career.

The record tells us "Christopher Martin, he and his, dyed in the first infection not long after the arivall."

Young, in his "Chronicles," p. 78, says: "Mr. Christopher Martin came, with his wife and two children, in the Mayflower."

Bradford, in "Prince," p. 182, records: "January 18—This day dies Mr. Christopher Martin." He was the ninth signer of the Compact, and one of the few distinguished with the title of Mr.

He was not one of the Leyden Church, but came from Billerica, in Essex, and was associated with Cushman and Carver, to provide means for the voyage. He brought his wife and two children with him, one of whom, Solomon, died December 24.

The other child is still to be accounted for. I have seen it as two sons. If so, the name remains.

As yet I have not found this record, but that is no reason for claiming it does not exist.

There is always the hope that may prove a certainty.

WILLIAM MULLINS, Tenth Signer.

Pilgrim history varies in the spelling of this name. Many called it Molines, and continued search makes quite a legend of the possible connections.

Among others are Du Moulins and Molineux, and here history, with its strong sense of the inevitable relations of many of these people, comes to us all, making us wonder when the tangled skein will be unraveled and this family, at least, come to a knowledge of its many branches.

Using Molineux for the text, it fits into the Standish family, where "James Prescott, senior, who married —— Standish, had a son, who took to wife Alice Molineux, and for his bravery and military achievements he was created lord of the manor of Dugby, in Lincolnshire."

Again the Scrooby post road!

Two of his descendants married Standishes, and lived, died and were buried at Standish.

The half is not yet told. The Southworths married into the Molineux family, so, through the placing of one historical name, the avenue is opened for much study of at least four of the passengers on the Mayflower.

A little imagination only is required to believe it possible that William Molines and Capt. Standish knew of this relation, and the story of the confiding of Priscilla to the captain's care may have been a natural sequence of that knowledge, having so much foundation, nothing more. The instinct of blood seemed strong when the father realized that Priscilla would soon be left alone in the world.

HOLLAND.

The life of the Mullins family in Leyden was a very complete one. Their business connection with the Dutch had placed all of them in knowledge of that language. English they acquired from their church relations, and French, their dear native tongue, was the voicing of their emotions of pleasure or of pain, the tender home greeting, or the demonstrations of affection.

To be linguists was but an acknowledgment of their birthright, an equipment from which so much good was expected.

What a home Alice Molines must have made in Leyden with her French tastes and housewifely capacity. Never forgetting her great gift of cooking, which from the unknown provisions accorded her, provided the dainties so appetizing to all. Think of the "simnels, buns, biscuits, comfits, carraways and cracknels" she evolved from the ship's stores on the Mayflower. Although she could not "catch the hare," she would cook it if brought to her. For all this she was willing and deft, and when with light fingers she was preparing for the people already sickening on the ship, little did she think that soon she, her husband and the little Joseph she loved so well, would be ferried over the river of death, leaving Priscilla alone to fight the battle of life in the colonies.

HIS WILL.

The will of William Molines speaks of his wife Alice and two children who were left in England, a son William and a daughter Sarah, who married a Mr. Blunden. "The Probate Act Book supplies the English residence as Dorking, in the county of Surrey."

William Molines died February 21, 1621, "pious and well deserving, endowed also with considerable outward estate, and had it been the will of God that he had survived, might have proved a valuable instrument in his place."

HUGUENOTS.

Dr. Charles W. Baird, in his "Huguenot Emigration to America," states that Priscilla Molines was a Huguenot.

"The etymology of this word has never been satisfactorily explained. Cassaneuve and others have suggested the Flemish word Huguenon, which means Puritan. Other writers claim for the Huguenots that they were the French Calvinists.

The many gifts of the parents repeated themselves in Priscilla. She filled every position more than well. When the "common house" at Plymouth was the home of the young people, her buoyant acceptance of the economies and watchful thrift lessened the privations of all; indeed, they ceased to exist, for out of the food at her command too much was realized to admit of any discontent.

Although other people by the name of Mullins came to the colony, their identification was never with the "old comers." Priscilla made much history for them, but she was early merged into an Alden, and her numerous descendants carry with them the wide world over her traits of character.

More may come when the Huguenot Society secures all the records of the families they recognize as of themselves. In one of the early celebrations they give the name of Mollineaux as one to which they have a claim, and all know that there was a Catholic branch in the North of England, as well that Ireland records them. Working this out in the broad opportunities of the present may reveal much that has baffled the historian.

WILLIAM WHITE, Eleventh Signer.

Denied the span of life, which brings maturity of experience, William White told little of himself, and yet some possibilities make him a man of inherited prominence.

The will of Bishop John White, dated 1621, "alludes to a son, not called by name, who had left his country and church."

This tells the story, and, though William White succumbed to the "first sickness" soon after his arrival in Plymouth with his wife, whither he had gone to make the home denied them in England, to enjoy the privileges of his own form of worship, he left behind him a record his descendants must appreciate.

The bond with the Leyden people, strengthened by the very natural belief that Roger White, the brother of Pastor Robinson's wife was a kinsman of the Pilgrim White, made his stay in Holland have some touch of family interest, a connecting link between himself and the past, which must do him honor.

HIS EARLY DEATH.

All the anticipations of hardship and privation were closed by his death, only the wrench of the start and sorrow at parting from his dear ones to record. Even the wife he had so tenderly loved, and with watchful care led to a willingness to leave all behind her, that was the habit of her life, took upon herself new duties and affections, with a broad future which would have been a temptation to any woman, even if in her hours of self-communion she realized that six short weeks between the grave and the altar were hardly enough of mourning for the one who had been the chosen companion of her young life.

The circumstances were peculiar, the colony needed family ties for its very existence, and to be the wife of Edward Winslow, brought with it honors not to be ignored.

"THE OLD BIBLE."

According to Leyden records, William White married Anna Fuller February 6, 1612. In the summer of 1895 I saw the old Bible with many records on the blank pages, spaces and margins, owned by Mr. S. W. Cowles, of Hartford, Conn. It was printed in London in 1588, part in 1586, and through devious ways has reached the hands of its present owner. This Bible claims to have been originally the property of William White, of the Mayflower, and by his bequest went to Elder Brewster. There is no pretense at asserting that all the entries were made as they occurred by the participants, but there seems strong cause to believe that they were placed there by persons who, if not themselves eye-witnesses, had the records from those who were, and the fact that subsequent owners continued the book as a family Bible gives strength to the supposition of its reliability as a matter of history.

The "old Bible" is authority for William White's second marriage to Susanna Tilley "ye 3d of March, 1620."

To my mind this exactly accounts for the circumstantial evidence surrounding this family. Learned men have satisfied themselves that the after calling of Mrs. White Susanna was merely the use of the name of Anna Fuller White in full. My search, which has been great, reverses this. For the first hundred years in New England Susanna was the baptismal name and Susan the diminutive or pet name, not used by itself until the middle of the eighteenth century.

So Anna, or Annah (as the old name was), in early times had nothing whatever to do with Susanna or Susannah.

In later years the change is found during the lifetime of one person, she not dropping the Susan, but the Anna.

By baptism, and even later, when signing papers for admission to the church, the name would be Susanna, or with the final "h." But in greater maturity, showing the change which is periodical in names, the same woman used Susan in signing her will, or as a beneficiary. Naturally, when dropping the Anna and making Susan for brevity and strength the real name, Anna, secured a definite position.

DISCUSSION.

This very name was brought up for discussion in regard to Rev. Thomas Hooker's wife by Rev. William S. Porter, connected with Yale College, the one who helped Savage with his dictionary, and died some forty years ago.

With William White and his wife on the Mayflower, came one son, Resolved White, who afterward married a daughter of William Vassell, a gentleman of family and fortune, one of the early settlers of Massachusetts. The fact that very little is said of this son in connection with his mother, and that he hardly occupies the place a mother would claim for her son, seems to corroborate the appearance of her being his stepmother.

The Pilgrim Mr.   e was a wool carder, and most of the trades chosen show a bearing on the woolen industries, which proved such a component part of the commercial connection between Holland and England during Queen Elizabeth's reign. The cosmopolitan character of Amsterdam and Leyden made strong history. The French, with their attributes of art, poesy and all graceful accomplishments, combined with their unvarying industry and cheerfulness, assimilated well with the phlegmatic Dutch, and the Mayflower, in consequence, took out the elements of future greatness in all directions.

THE FIRST-BORN ENGLISHMAN.

Happily for Peregrine White, "so named in token of the pilgrimage then in process," he was the first-born English child in New England, a welcome addition to the family of William White—a fact he never forgot during his life, and which yielded him good return. Upon this accident of birth he based his claim for lands and privileges. When the patent for Plymouth Colony was surrendered to the "Body of Freemen," three tracts of land were reserved for the "Purchasers, or Old Comers."

In 1655, Prence being Governor, this grant was recorded: "In reference unto the request of the King's Commissioners in the behalf of Lieutenant Peregrine White, desiring that the Court would accommodate him with a portion of land, in respect that he was the first of the English that was born in these parts, and in answer unto his own petition preferred to this Court respecting the premises,

"The Court have granted unto him two hundred acres of land lying and being at the path that goes from Bridgewater to the bay adjoining the bay line."

Resolved had no showing, only the legal right of primogeniture, but matters were reversed without his selling his birthright.

PERSONAL APPEARANCE.

Given one claim, another came to Peregrine, of which he was fully conscious, his fine personal appearance. He was very modest, but he kept the evidence of it well under control, and, though he was "a youth unduly gay for his time and generation," his other attributes served him well in the estimate of the public.

True to the knowledge which comes with these gifts, Peregrine did all in his power to enhance them, and when he went to visit his mother at Marshfield, whom he dearly loved, "he wore a coat with buttons the size of a silver dollar," presenting himself to her ever-admiring eyes on a coal black horse, himself the objective point, a natural delight to a fond mother's eyes.

To her he was always the loving son, and the wild ways attributed to him did not tell against her estimate, when he was always dutiful and attentive.

His stepfather, Gov. Edward Winslow, was no drawback, and had he been asked his blessing on their nuptials, in view of the return to himself, would have signified his unqualified approval.

His unknown father he had never missed; he was only a name to him and had no claim upon his memory.

Peregrine White married a daughter of William Bassett, and if old age is a guarantee of a blessing, it accompanied this union.

"Saturday, August 9, 1755, died at Scituate, in the ninety-second year of her age, Mrs. Sarah Youngs, the virtuous widow of Mr. Thomas Youngs, the eldest daughter of that Peregrine White, of Marshfield, who was the first born English child in New England.

"And this his eldest Daughter was Born in Marshfield in Oct., 1663, enjoy'd her Senses and Health in good measure till towards her end, and left four sons surviving."

The warlike element was not wanting in this Pilgrim descendant. In 1636 he volunteered for the Pequod war, and in 1642 was made "ancient bearer," or ensign, of the trained band when the forces were raised to protect the colonies against the Indians of the Narragansett tribe, of which "Miantonomo" was chief. Standish being in command, even this brave warrior, with his proud bearing, could be kept within bounds.

He was in his element at the head of a band, a proper victim for concealed wells, could the Indans only have known, that in his whole line of march, even with death at the end of it, he would never abate one iota from the military tactics furnished by his manual of arms.

So with "head erect and eyes to the front," he pursued his onward march, sharing in any glory that came to the expedition.

The "pen which is mightier than the

sword" was his in his youth, and he used it in a forcible manner, but in his last days made his mark on his will.

Peregrine White "lived in great Health and Vigour to the 84th year of his age, when a fever carried him off on July 22, 1704."

True to the instincts of his surroundings, even at the advanced age of 77, he joined the church, and the Boston "News Letter" of the period completes his history. "Death of Peregrine White, Marshfield, July 22, 1704.

"Captain Peregrine White, of this town, Aged Eighty-three years and Eight months, died the 20th Instant.

"He was vigorous and of a comely Aspect to the last.

"Was the son of William White and Susanna, his wife; born on board of the Mayflower, Captain Jones Commander, in Cape Cod Harbor, November 1620, was the First Englishman born in New England. Altho' he was in the former part of his Life extravagant, yet was much reformed in his last years, and died hopefully.'

The descendants of Peregrine White inherit his martial spirit, one of them Isaac White, born in Brimfield, Mass., enlisted from North Adams, Mass., was wounded at the battle of Bennington and carried off the battlefield in a chair, which the "tradition in the family tells was brought over in the Mayflower, and is still owned by the descendants."

How the chair so opportunely reached the scene of action is a matter of no moment, the deed, the valor is worthy of the Pilgrim.

This article has been left as originally written, with the feeling that there are historical truths involved, but the following quoted from a letter which reached me recently from Mr. Thomas Bradford Drew, librarian of the Pilgrim Society, Plymouth, Mass., gives opportunity for discussion.

"I notice you are inclined to have faith in the genuineness of the entries in the 'Old Bible at Hartford.' I have never seen it, but have noticed the quotations from it in different works, and one or two dates appended to the entries have made me very suspicious of the whole.

"First, the birth of Peregrine White is there given thus: 'Sonne born to Susanna White, Dec. 19, 1620, yt six o'clock morning.' Now, according to Bradford and Winslow's Journal, that birth was between the 27th and 30th of November old style, or the 7th and 10th of December new style.

"Worse than that, however, is the record of the parents' marriage there given, which, as you quote, was on 'ye 3d of March 1620.' Now that makes (according to the old style of reckoning dates) the marriage of those parents three months after Peregrine was born, and some time after Mr. White had died, for it must be remembered that the year 1620 was not past until the 25th of March.

"Whoever wrote that, if they had wished to record an event which occurred in March previous to the child's birth, would have made it March, 1619.

"There is certain proof that the Pilgrim company did use the old style of dating, and by referring to the sixtieth page of Bradford's manuscript, or ninety-ninth of the printed copy, you will find the following: 'And being now come to ye 25th of March I shall begin ye yeare 1621.' "

For myself, while knowing myself to be in deep waters, at loss how to extricate the truth from the mass of material available, I cannot feel but that in justice to future writers on the Pilgrims, all I command should be placed at public disposal.

RICHARD WARREN, Twelfth Signer.

Stern facts must be accepted in writing history, and, willing or otherwise, the records prove that Richard Warren, the Pilgrim, cannot be placed in any certainty with regard to his family relations before his advent in the colonies, as one of the Mayflower Pilgrims.

Certain it is that he came on this ship, and was followed later on in the Ann by his wife, Elizabeth, and his daughters. The confusion in regard to him arises from the fact that there was another Warren, who was early in the colonies, and who had the honor of being a son of Christopher Warren, and the pleasure of having Elizabeth Jouatt, or Ivatt, widow of —— Marsh, for his wife. There the story, as told us of the Pilgrim, ends, their children being two sons, Richard and John, as the chart accompanying this article shows.

Yet, for all practical purposes, our Pilgrim, arguing from the family names there represented, must have his place as kin somewhere in the records.

in the short time allowed him, all bearing testimony to his value, not needing to wait until he had passed the Rubicon, and in his silent grave closed the living animosities. They described him as "a man of integrity, justice and uprightness, of piety and serious religion."

SIGNER.

Richard Warren, the twelfth Signer of the Compact, with the honorable prefix of Mr., to which he always seemed fully entitled, is mentioned by Bradford "as a most useful man during the short time he lived, bearing a deep share in the difficulties and troubles of the plantation."

For some unknown cause, through all the accounts of this banding together of the Mayflower passengers for their better government, and personal responsibility of good behavior, the place occupied by each one in the compact seems to be considered a matter of precedence of position. If so, what an argument for John Alden and John Howland and the men "called servants."

Five daughters and two sons owed filial allegiance to Richard and Elizabeth Warren.

The girls, who came with their mother in the Ann, married active men in the colonies, Mary becoming the wife of Robert Bartlett; Ann, of Thomas Little; Sarah, Joseph Cooke; Elizabeth, Richard Church, October 4, 1632, a carpenter, born in 1608, a sergeant in the Pequod war, and, best of all, they were the parents of Col. Benjamin Church, the distinguished hero of the Indian wars.

Then Abigail, to complete the list, married Anthony Snow, one of the prominent men of Marshfield.

Nathaniel and Joseph, the sons, were born in Plymouth, the first marrying Mary Walker, and Joseph, Priscilla Faunce. Both the names and marriages of this family have been greatly to their credit.

Their Norman blood flows through the veins of the patriots, the pleaders, the successful merchants of this country.

The descendants of the Pilgrim Richard Warren have largely inhabited Plymouth and the eastern part of Massachusetts, although the State of New York also puts in a claim.

BOTH BRANCHES.

The two branches of Warren unite very naturally in the fact that the Pilgrim descendant Gen. James Warren, the revolutionary officer and president of the Provincial Congress of Massachusetts, succeeded Gen. Joseph Warren, of Bunker Hill fame, a member of the other family, in office. The following record shows how naturally the mixing of the lineage occurred, and though, by reference to the chart, we can see that it was not the Mayflower Pilgrim, there are so many points in common with the record handed down to us that all would be unwilling to change their opinion without the strong substantiation of authenticated history:

John Warren of Hedbury in the p. of Ashburton.

Christopher Warren, s. & h.

William Warren = Ann d. of Tho Calston in Cornw. = Mable of Will Culling of Woodland in Devon 2d husb.

Christopher Warren s. & h. = Alice d. of Tho Webb of Riddenham. | 1. William Culling 2. John | 3. Richard 4. Thomas of London

Robert Warrren, 1 s, parson of Ronne in Corw. = Marg. d. of Peter Burgis of Peter Tavvy in Cornw. | John, 2 | Richard, 3, of Greenwich in Kent, mercht. = Eliz. d. of Ivatt & relict of —— Marsh.

Christopher Warren, 1 s. | 2. Robert 3. Thomas | 4. Peter Nathaniel, 5 | Margaret, 1. Anne, 2 | Richard Warren, 1 s | John 2.

Christopher, 4, of London. = Sarah d. of Nich. Opie of Plymouth. | Thomas ob. s. p. | William 5, of London, merchant. = Mary, d. of Will Culling of Wooland. | Ann John Richards.

Harleian Society Publication of Visitation of Devonshire in 1620.

Richard and Joseph repeat themselves in both families; then, too, there are Nathaniels.

Still, I can take, "grave Richard Warren" from his start with us, and give him hearty thanks for his descent, even if the ascent still remains unknown.

Of him, personally, there is, sad to say, an unfinished record to place in evidence. Escaping the first sickness, living to greet his wife and daughters, it seems a hard fate to relate that he only lived to 1628, and "it was not until after seven years of co-labor that any of the men who joined in that pioneer Thanksgiving festival in 1621 had been laid in his grave."

He had taken the initial step, proved himself worthy of the position he had achieved

And how strange, as you read the list, is the peculiarity of physical strength at the beginning, the early death rate being mainly from the numbers as they increase.

Richard Warren was a true Pilgrim spirit, whether of the Leyden Church or one of the converts along the Scrooby Post road, too weak of purpose to join the movement at its inception, but who grew in strength with time and conviction, until the move for bleak New England found him more than ready, waiting to record himself as of the little band.*

*Why should he not have been the Richard Warren recorded as Sheriff of Coventry, 1610? Having five daughters to come out with their mother in the Ann, fits into the necessary maturity.

Richard Warren——Elizabeth, daughter of —— Jouatt, and one of the first settlers of Plymouth, N. E. He died in 1628. | Greenwich, Co. of Kent, merchant, widow of —— Marsh. She died at Plymouth in 1673, aged 90.

The Warrens lead straight to the Mayflower, though the repetition of names in the two families makes the title a very puzzling one, but there need be no doubt of the claim if presented by those bearing the names of Otis, Winslow, Walker, Doty, Bradford and many others scattered the whole world over.

Again the matter must be left to the Society of Mayflower Descendants. Their good work is progressing, fed by the knowledge gained from each seeker for enrollment on the list of members. See notes.

JOHN HOWLAND, Thirteenth Signer.

There is no possible position that can be taken in regard to John Howland, that proof is not brought forward in exact opposition to it.

The statement that the Howlands are all traceable to Essex County, England, gives a very satisfactory point to work from.

In fact, John Howland is just where he should be, with the record we trust behind him of his youth spent with those whom, knowing all, have learned to honor.

There were five John Howlands in Essex, any one of whom might have been our Pilgrim's father. However, all of this makes very little difference, for in 1646, Humphrey Howland, "citizen and draper of London," left his brothers "Arthur, John and Henry, respectively, £8, £4, £4 out of a debt due from Mr. Ruck, of New England," which seemed sufficient proof to identify him in this relationship with those Howlands, who belonged to us from the start.

A gift of money is a crucial test of a man's connection with the donor.

I had sent my dove from the ark, content in the feeling that the branch he would secure from the receding floods, would place me safely and surely. It brought back the above history, and in a peaceful frame of mind I prepared to follow the fortunes of John Howland.

But the spirit was soon ruffled by a letter from one whose name and location entitled him, not only to a hearing, but a respectful desire to admit his claim.

He tells me that "as a matter of authentic record the above identification has never been made, and there is not the least evidence of the relationship. Much research was made to demonstrate it, and the belief survived failure to prove it and, indeed, considerable evidence that Arthur and Henry were in no way related to John the Pilgrim."

Whatever the Howlands lack, they are certainly persistent, and those who have accepted the "three brothers," will still adhere to their own opinion until the proofs are definite to the contrary.

LINCOLNSHIRE.

In writing the personal history of the Pilgrims, taking Lincoln, in Lincolnshire, for the text, does much toward proving the great centralization of interests in Leyden, and the transporting of them to the colony in New England.

Granting the truth of the record in the "Old Bible," which gives John Carver as "sonne of James Carver, Lincolnshire, Yeoman," and that in Boston in the same county Brewster and Bradford were imprisoned, then all know that the original patent to the colonists was issued in the name of John Wincob, a member of the Earl of Lincoln's household, and the strong binding together becomes a local certainty.

"The See of Lincoln comprehended certain counties, and Abbots, Aston and Winslow. John White, Prebendary, of Winchester, and Warden of Rickham's College, there was consecrated Bishop of Lincoln."

This continues the story:

Here, too, in Lincolnshire are Robinsons, one named John; and in those times the perpetuating of Christian names was part of the family history of a place.

Another point: William Fuller held this See, and here are found Turners and Warrens high in position.

QUEEN ELIZABETH.

The conviction is forced upon one by search that much of the strong history of the world was made during Queen Elizabeth's reign. She had her vagaries, but the working of them out involved the civilized nations of the earth.

One point for our purpose is that she gave the Howlands their grant of coat-armor in 1584, which is now used by that family, authenticated from the Heralds' College, London, that started with Bishop Howland.

A striking matter of consideration to which I wished to lead is that this same Bishop Howland performed the obsequies of Mary, Queen of Scots.

This proves at least a connection with Elder Brewster, for he was secretary to Ambassador Davison at that time, and perhaps they consulted together over the arrangements.

As these items narrow in to a few people a historian gathers much valuable data to work upon, and a hope of the possibilities they desire; it makes it easy to imagine Brewster in this spirit extending from love of his family much care and interest to John Howland.

CARVER'S SERVANT.

According to English law John Howland came out as Gov. Carver's servant, or indentured assistant. The use of this term has been hard for the Howlands to grasp; applied to others, they accepted it, but not for their own progenitor.

Time has solved the misconstruing of the term, and a fragment of Bradford's journal when he tells of the mishap which befell him on the journey over the Mayflower, places him as he belongs.

"In a mighty storm John Howland, a Passenger (!) a stout young man, by a keel of ye ship was thrown into ye sea. But it pleased God, He caught hold of ye Topsail Halliards we hung overboard, and run out ye length, yet He kept his hold the several Fathoms under water, till He was drawn up by ye Rope to ye surface and by a Boat Hook and other means got into ye ship: and tho' somew't ill upon it, liv'd many years, and became a useful member both in church and Commonwealth."

A needed member of Gov. Carver's household, "he was one of the leading men in the colony, and a partaker of their hazardous undertakings, and eminent for his devotion to its interests, both in civil and religious matters."

Office sought him from the first, for John Howland, in conscious dignity, never usurped another's place.

On this basis he was "Deputy and Assistant the greater part of his long and useful life."

DIFFERENCE OF OPINION.

This Pilgrim cannot be written of without much discussion and with the strong connections, the traditional history that has become part of the beliefs of every section of this land, it is very hard to give up a recognition of the statements of early writers which were received without a doubt until the finding of the lost journal of Gov. Bradford removed Gov. Carver's daughter from her position as John Howland's wife. The "old Bible in Hartford" places her more naturally as Carver's granddaughter. John Howland's marriage was in 1623 or 1624—one of the earliest weddings in the colony. The Mayflower Society gave it as in 1621. As he was 28 when he arrived in the Mayflower, 1620, and his marriage took place before the land division in 1624, making him, allowing for the unknown months, 32 or nearly so, the supposition has arisen that he might have been a widower, and by his first wife a member of Gov. Carver's family. Gov. Bradford states distinctly, and his record is accepted, that Gov. Carver left no descendants.

I feel with the descendants, and would like to prove that he meant simply none bearing the name of Carver. As early as 1638 there were Carvers in the colony who had a grant of land in Duxbury, and Gov. Bradford may have had some personal reason, perhaps prejudice, against their presuming on any supposed relationship, by virtue of their name, with Gov. Carver.

Tradition, that always has some foundation in truth, has clung with barnacle-like tenacity to every Howland descendant; in regard to this marriage nothing can shake their faith in the teachings of their childhood.

The story has been handed down from grandmother to grandmother, and facing the inevitable does not lessen their own belief; they are silenced, but not convinced. This claim comes constantly, even in the light of the acceptation of Bradford's journal.

HIS MARRIAGE.

Quietly, as he did everything, John Howland "took to wife" Elizabeth, the young daughter of John Tilley, "to have and to hold," and the histories of the times find no fault with the home he provided, or the love he bore her. If her mother could be established as the daughter of Gov. Carver no more would be asked of her, though she simply went on her way, "sorrowing, toiling, rejoicing," the births of her children recorded her daily life, of interest to no one but her own household.

John Howland came into his property at Island Creek Pond and also two small islands in Geeir's Harbor. With his possessions followed the feeling that they needed his personal supervision, so for a time he yielded to necessity, but the early love for Plymouth was upon him, and he left Duxbury, returning to his home all the better citizen for his little outing.

In the progression of the times, and a growing consciousness that Plymouth was a barren land, so far as cultivation and yield was concerned, he made his last move to Rocky Nook, in Kingston, before 1665, and remained there until the time of his departure for his final home, which took place

February 22, 1672, when he had reached fourscore years.

"A godly man, and an ancient professor of the ways of Christ, one of the first-comers, and proved a useful instrument of good in the place."

In the height of the Quaker troubles he was dropped from the General Court, probably because he was found to be too liberal for the times. Gov. Prence did not stint his evidences of disapproval when a man differed from him in his opinion with regard to the Quakers.

There is never any effort made to withdraw one word of praise from this Pilgrim; he had his convictions, and the strength of them, willing always to be placed on record for his acts.

Gov. Bradford's confidence in John Howland was implicit. He called him among the "ten principal men" for the "third exploration," and, as he is credited with having a "military turn," he, with Jonathan Brewster, was appointed to be joined with the Governor, etc.," to assess men toward the charges of soldiers."

Reference to Plymouth records shows that John Howland, in 1627, was associated with Gov. Bradford and six other of the prominent men of the colony in a compact made with London merchants in regard to the relinquishment of claims, upon certain conditions.

Alden and Howland seemed to go into all enterprises side by side, men of similar tastes up to a point, and then far apart.

CHILDREN.

His children, as given in the history of Duxbury, were John, Jabez, who married Bethiah Thatcher, and was a lieutenant in the Indian war under Church against Philip, after the conquest of Mount Hope going to Bristol, where he was allowed to "keep a house of entertainment."

In view of the Quaker interest, if not proclivities of these Howlands, it is interesting to know that his son Jabez was vestryman of St. Michael's Episcopal Parish in 1724.

Isaac, another son, was also an officer of the war settled at Middleboro, "kept an ordinary" there in 1684, and died in 1724.

Joseph remained at Plymouth, but he had no diminished head to hide; his services were at the command of his country; he became an officer, and made his mark in the home of his Pilgrim father, increasing his value in the local history by marrying Elizabeth Southworth.

Desire, named for Desire Minter, who was the kind friend of her mother's orphaned girlhood, married Capt. John Gorham in 1643, and may be proud as an ancestress of this descent.

Hope married Elder John Chipman, of Barnstable, and their large family are living through their representatives a broad life, always ready to lend a helping hand to anything that promotes the interests of others and the public good.

Elizabeth married twice, her second husband being John Dicgarson. Lydia married James Brown, of Swansey, and Ruth, Thomas Cushman, of Plymouth, November 7, 1664.

Succeeding generations of Howlands have been given to the perpetuating of the names of Desire and Jabez; the female name we can place, but Jabez must come from some ancestor, who could, if known, make one of the name records.

HOWLAND RELICS.

The intermarriages of "ye olden days" make it difficult to follow the heirlooms, even if they existed, still the very combination narrows them into fewer representatives and tells us that Joanna Howland, a great-granddaughter of the Pilgrim, married Gideon White, a great-grandson of Peregrine White, early in the last century, and her home is referred to by Buckingham in his "Travels in America" as a "remarkable depository of Mayflower relics."

Hannah and Mary White, great-great-granddaughters of "Peregrine the first born," died unmarried, the former in 1843, the latter in 1838, aged 87.

Their sister Joanna married Pelham Winslow.

"It was at the house of these 'ancient maiden sisters' that Buckingham saw the ancient Howland coat-of-arms, published in his 'America,' vol. 2, p. 483."

A long search found that it was in the possession of Rev. T. Howland White, Shelburne, N. S.

The following letter from him explains the matter exactly:

"June 1, 1885.—It was left me by my venerable aunts, Mrs. Winslow, wife of Pelham Winslow, and Miss Hannah White, of Plymouth. The copy which is in my possession is evidently a very ancient one, and the tradition is that it was brought over soon after the arrival of the Pilgrims, if not on the Mayflower herself.

"It is painted in water colors and is highly ornamented. I have no doubt from its appearance that it came from the Heralds' College, as it perfectly agrees with a printed copy since issued."

There is also an old arms in the possession of Mrs. Julia M. Barnes, perhaps copied from this (as she has kept up her intercourse with the relatives in Nova Scotia), in embroidery and water colors, so long in the family that they have no knowledge of a time, even traditionally, when they were without it.

Even the lineage of this family has a choice as to its beginning, so many for reasons unknown being willing to omit the Tilley start, which gives them one generation more to secure their papers, being recorded as descendants of John Howland.

As the line of Bishop Phillips Brooks, of Massachusetts, is not only dear to all of that kin, but goes into a variey of families, and I hope will add through the Phillipses, another claim from Long Island, I give it.

1. John Howland, of the Mayflower.
2. Capt. John Gorham, born 1620; married, 1643, Desire, eldest daughter of John Howland.
3. Col. John Gorham, his second son, born February 20, 1651-2; died, December 9, 1716; married, February 24, 1674-5; Mary Otis, daughter of John Otis and Mary Jacob. He was second in command in the expeditions against the French in 1703 and 1704, under the command of Col. Benjamin Church.
4. Stephen Gorham, eldest son of Col. John, born in Barnstable, June 23, 1683; married, December 25, 1703, Elizabeth Gardner, of Nantucket, daughter of James Gardner and Mary Starbuck.
5. Nathaniel Gorham, of Charlestown, Mass., eldest son of Stephen, born in Barnstable, May 3, 1709, died, December 24, 1761, married January 6, 1736, Mary Soley, daughter of John Soley and Dorcas Coffin,
6. Nathaniel Gorham, eldest son of Nathaniel, born in Charlestown, May 27, 1738, was a very distinguished man.

He was a member of the convention which framed the Constitution, and occupied the chair several times at the request of Gen. Washington. He married in 1763, Rebecca Call, eldest daughter of Caleb Call.

7. Lydia Gorham, the youngest child of Nathaniel Gorham, married, December 23, 1798, John Phillips, son of Samuel Phillips and Phebe Foxcraft. She died at Andover, Mass., June 3, 1856, aged 77.
8. Mary Ann Phillips, daughter of Lydia Gorham and John Phillips, born March 17, 1808, married, September 9, 1833, William Gray Brooks, of Boston, and their son, the late Bishop Phillips Brooks, was born December 13, 1835.

From another section, which will serve for many lines of Mayflower descendants, comes another.

1. John Howland, who came in the Mayflower, married Elizabeth Tilley, daughter of John and —— Tilley, about 1623.
2. Jabez Howland, son of John and Elizabeth Tilley Howland, married Bethiah Thatcher, daughter of Anthony and Elizabeth (Jones) Thatcher.
3. Jabez Howland, son of Jabez and Bethiah (Thatcher) Howland, born November 15, 1669, married Patience Stafford, daughter of Samuel and Mercy (Westcoat) Stafford, of Warwick, R. I. (date of marriage unknown). Jabez Howland died October 17, 1732. Patience, his wife, died October 23, 1721.

(Austin's Genealogical Dictionary of Rhode Island.)

(Stafford family, page 387).

4. Bethia Howland, daughter of Jabez and Patience (Stafford) Howland, born December 5, 1702; married, by Rev. John Usher, to Nicholas Bragg, son of Henry and Elizabeth (——) Bragg, of Bristol, R. I. May 19, 1725. Nicholas Bragg died at Surinam, South America, February 8, 1732.

Mrs. Bethia Bragg married a second time Simeon Davis, August 29, 1733. (Bristol records).

5. Nicholas Bragg, son of Nicholas and Bethia (Howland) Bragg, was baptized at St. Michael's Church, Bristol, R. I., June 2, 1728. He married Sarah Greene, daughter of Benjamin and Anne (Hoxsie) Greene, by Friends' ceremony, at Greenwich, R. I., June 23, 1757. (Records of Greenwich monthly meeting of Friends; also family records, the original marriage certificate still in possession of the family.)

The Benjamin Greene referred to above was a brother of Nathaniel Greene, "the preacher," who was father of Gen. Nathaniel Greene of revolutionary fame.

6. Temperance Bragg, daughter of Nicholas and Sarah (Greene) Bragg, born April 28, 1771; married Ethan Foster, son of John and Ruth (Hoxsie) Foster, of Richmond, R. I., March 12, 1801.
7. Ethan Foster, son of Ethan and Temperance (Bragg) Foster, born in Groton, Conn., June 5, 1808; married Anna A. Wilbur, daughter of John and Lydia (Collins) Wilbur, of Hopkinton, R. I., October 24, 1837.
8. John Barclay Foster, son of Ethan and Anna (Wilbur) Foster, born September 27, 1841; married Elizabeth F. Perry, daughter

of Charles and Temperance (Foster) Perry, of Westerly, R. I., September 16, 1868.

Nos. 6, 7 and 8 can all be proved by the records of South Kingstown monthly meeting of Friends.

Although many of the Howlands were Friends, they certainly were not wholly repressed under their Quaker garb. With them rhyming was an inestimable gift. My correspondent does not tell me that they burst forth in song. As yet that impulse rests with those of the name of Hopkins.

"The late Robert Howland, senior, was always ready with quaint and peculiar rhymes. He was born, I think, about 1765, and his gift has spread through several branches of the family.

"Upon the election of one of his neighbors to the office of 'field driver,' sometimes called 'hog constable,' he gave the following impromptu:

" 'It seemeth strange to our weak brains,
    The town should think it best,
To pass a vote to choose one Shoat
    To govern all the rest.'

"On another occasion he was expected to take one of three ladies to a ball, whose names were respectively Wing, Soule and House. At that time carriages were in little use, and a lady rode on a pillion behind a gentleman on the same horse.

"Upon being rallied for his want of gallantry, if he took neither lady to the ball, he said:

" 'What mortal man could think that I
Should with one Wing attempt to fly,
Or have another Soule to cross
Or carry a House upon a horse.' "

Few of the Pilgrim families seem to have retained the instincts of the original "old comers" more than the Howlands. Without the inspiration of convivial times they can always sing, "And I Have Loved the Ocean," using this attraction in shipping interests, and when rewarded by the wealth consequent upon their industry and ability they "Sail the ocean blue" in their pleasure craft, content to be "borne upon its bosom, like the bubbles, onward." They ask no more of the world, which to them has been always kind.

STEPHEN HOPKINS, Fourteenth Signer.

No signer of the Mayflower compact at Provincetown, off Cape Cod, 1620, opens more historical possibilities in his story than Mr. Stephen Hopkins. To secure what I have so eagerly sought for I will write of him in many aspects, bringing all possible circumstantial evidence to bear upon a kinship I so earnestly desire and hope to prove —that he was the father of John Hopkins, of Hartford, Conn.

Goodwin, in his "Plymouth Republic," places the possiblity of Hopkins being from Scrooby upon his apprentices (Doty and Leister), names sounding as if from that section.

To me Coventry fulfills all historical requirements and seems from every point to be the place of his forbears.

The northern post road of England, leading from London to Scrooby and Scotland through towns whose familiar names were early repeated in the colonies, connects naturally with Coventry and all the places from which sprang the Nonconformists and Separatists, to whom, under the name of Pilgrims (the passengers in the vessels called the forefather ships), Americans owe such warm allegiance.

"These wielders of mighty doctrines and tillers of the stern New England soil" were not strangers, if pilgrims, as they welcomed each vessel bearing its living freight to the "first comers."

COVENTRY.

"The city of Coventry is supposed to have been founded at a very early period, as the final syllable of its appellation is evidently the British 'tre,' a town. The prefix seems to have been from a convent erected on the spot. On excavating in 1792 there was found at the depth of five or six feet from the surface 'a regular pavement, and on the pavement a coin of Nero in middle brass.'"

Viewed in every light, it was a town of great importance. Commerce, manufactures and arts developed rapidly in its borders, while its renowned hospitality is a matter of history.

The people were even venturesome enough to entertain Queen Elizabeth, who was never above carrying away with her tangible tokens of esteem, appreciated according to their absolute value, while the pageant could never be too great for her desire and acceptance.

In 1565, when "Queen Bess" was a guest of the town, the Scarlet Coats, "yhich sate close," liveried horses, not forgetting the "purse supposed to be worth xxty marks, with one hundred pounds of Angells in it," which the Queen received, and said to her lords, "It was a good gift; I have but few such, for it was an hundred pounds in gold," were part of her welcome.

HISTORICAL NAMES.

Among the historical names of Coventry, I find Richard Hopkins in 1554, Will Hopkins, 1564; Samuel Hopkins, 1609 (mark this name connection); Sampson Hopkins, 1640; Christopher Davenport, 1641, "who gave twenty marks per ann. to maintain, and keep, one schoolmaster, for educating such poor children of this city, whose parents are not able to pay for their learning."

Then there is a Richard Warren, Sheriff in Coventry, 1610, and Mr. Richard Hopkins is recorded as Burgesse of Coventry.

When Charles II. was proclaimed (1659), Richard Hopkins, the steward, was knighted, and received a service of plate, the value of which they did not fail to record.

The Hopkins of Coventry are well and honorably mentioned with the Davenports.

Here William Hopkins was Alderman and Mayor, founding Bablake School, one of the most celebrated free schools in Coventry, giving his daughter in marriage to the son of Edward Davenport, Mayor of Coventry, and they in their turn sending to us their son John, born in Coventry 1597, educated at Oxford, of whom it is recorded that "in 1633 John Davenport (afterwards of New Haven), a preacher of London, fled to Holland and preached there two years and a half as colleague of Rev. John Paget."

With him on his journey across the water came Edward Hopkins, the future Governor of Connecticut, his cousin, one naturally supposes.

So accepting, for the sake of argument, Coventry as the place of Stephen Hopkins's nativity, almost the location he is placed by Goodwin, I come to his religious beliefs, and copy from history: "Elder Brewster and his son Edward, in 1609, became members of the Virginia family just formed, and this year Stephen Hopkins and family, and other Nonconformists, sailed in the fleet of Gates and Somers for Virginia."

This tells the tale, proves him a Nonconformist, and why, as Brewster had a son not known to us in connection with him, should not Hopkins have had other children of future birth, who were not on the Mayflower?

The shipwreck off the coast of Bermuda of the vessel destined for Virginia was the means of discovering that island and returning to his native land the man destined to become one of the most prominent of the Plymouth Pilgrims.

TEMPERAMENT.

Knowing Stephen Hopkins, as all do, in his strong character, with its perversities and partial resentment of control, it is hard to recognize him as "lay reader" to Mr. Buck, chaplain to the expedition of Sir Thomas Gates, and realize that he had "much knowledge of the Scriptures and could reason well in them."

The gift of speech, perhaps controversy, always rested with him, and the legal instinct which made him ere long one of the two Ambassadors to Plymouth Colony, the person sharing this fame with Gov. Edward Winslow, gives us ready understanding of the position he took after the wreck of two of the vessels of this fleet at Bermuda.

He claimed that the ships having sailed under contract to serve the company in Virginia, their landing in a place unknown and unprepared for released them from their bond and subordination to "the powers that be."

Perhaps Stephen Hopkins counted the cost of this act; he was hardly a man to plead ignorance in extenuation; at all events he had to face the results. A summary court-martial being convened, charging him with treason, sentence of death was passed upon him. Only the intervention of those whose favor he had won on previous good behavior saved him. Sir George Somers, the admiral and chaplain, besought his pardon, but in face of the findings of the court, the lawless disregard of human life which came with isolation and the times, it was easy to turn a deaf ear. The carrying out of the verdict was close at hand, when, under pressure, Sir Thomas Gates yielded and his pardon was secured. The life of such a man must be spared if there was any power of vindication.

VIRGINIA COMPANY.

Sir Thomas Gates had been in the service of the United Netherlands, another "wheel within the wheel," and on the 24th of April, 1608, the States General passed the following resolution:

"On the petition of Sir Thomas Gates, captain of a company of English soldiers, commissioned by the King of Great Britain to command with three other gentlemen, in the County of Virginia, in colonizing said county, the petitioner is therefore allowed to be absent from his company for the space of one year, on condition he supply his company with good officers and soldiers for the public service."

"Subsequently the State paid him for the time he was absent in Virginia." About this there is no speculation, Stephen Hopkins was a Nonconformist, of the same company as Elder Brewster, and his son, Edward, peple of like thought and convictions, which they adhered to until "Edward Brewster conformed, and returned to the church," remaining in England.

The six months spent on the island of Bermuda was an experience which told well in the Pilgrims' future life. Lack of food developed their ingenuity, and instinct with the hunger, which from its force and continuance became a greed; they brought every living thing to bear on their needs, learning to trap the deer and other animals for their daily food.

How little Hopkins thought that in his next venture this knowledge would serve a good purpose, only it was under bleak New England skies that he applied it, and Gov. Bradford was the victim to the Indian trap.

Bradford gives Stephen Hopkins as one of the Mayflower passengers from the "London section." This certainly fits in well with Coventry, only ninety-one miles from London, and everything in the man's future life shows for his energy, desire to see the world, and what may have been the part of his character, which in after years led historians to suppose from his constant connection with Standish to be the result of his military proclivities, would naturally make him seek a larger and more stirring sphere of action.

In this spirt he joined the Virginia company, and circumstances entirely beyond his control returned him to the land of his birth, which must have been about 1611 or 1612.

JOHN HOPKINS.

And here I claim came John Hopkins, of Hartford, born near 1613, and early left without a mother, for Stephen Hopkins's second marriage took place according to the records at

St. Mary's, Whitechapel, London, "Stephen Hopkins et Eliza; ffisher, March 1617."

The records of "marriages at St. Mary Le Strand, London," adds the family names of descendants to the list:

"October 25, 1610—James Hopkins and Margaret Howell.
November 23, 1612—John Hopkins and ⌐ane Marshall.
———, 1624—Samuel Hopkins and Ann Tumber.
February 15, 1616—Hughe Richardson and Mary Hopkins.
All married by "lycenc.""

It is no stretch of the imagination to place the above as brother and sister of Stephen Hopkins, of the Mayflower—one brother for whom John, of Hartford, was named; then Samuel perpetuated constantly in both families, giving us, thus called, some of the most celebrated of American divines, men never spoken of without pride and respect.

FAMILY ON THE MAYFLOWER.

On the Mayflower came "Steven Hopkins and Elizabeth, his wife, and two children called Giles (Gyles) and Constanta, a daughter, both by a former wife, and two more by this wife, called Damaris and Oceanus (the last was born at sea), and two servants, called Edward Doty and Edward Lister."

Poor Oceanus, though he, without doubt, had the advantage of being rocked in the celebrated "Fuller cradle" on the great deep, seems to have been a "waif and stray," as to his personal location, always being recorded as the one to fill the position in the number of passengers made vacant by the death during the passage of William Butten, the servant of Dr. Fuller.

Bringing with him experience and capacity, our signer started his record from the minute he put his foot on the ship, and when, land being reached, it was necessary to explore and see whether it might be fit "to seat in or no," he was one of the three sent to pass judgment. His constant connection with Standish on his missions leads to the supposition that he was either "somewhat of a military man" or that his coolness and influence might be a restraint to the captain's impetuosity. As early as 1620 he was placed in this position with regard to Standish, which seems to prove that those on the ship had former knowledge of his capacity, which rendered him acceptable, and prevented any antagonism because of his occupancy of so many trust places.

On the expedition they were much troubled with thirst, "having brought only some biscuit and Dutch cheese, with a little bottle of aqua vita." Their sufferings became intense, but nature had provided them with a guide to relief, and, led by the deer, as they went to slake their thirst at the cooling springs, they refreshed themselves, and, in their exhausted, suffering condition, they even magnified the blessing they felt it to be by chronicling that it was "as pleasant unto them as wine or beer had been in former times."

A change of opinion would hardly be registered even against a Pilgrim!

Bradford claims that "they took the original of their death here."

THIRD EXPEDITION.

The "third expedition," which tested the Pilgrims' strength to a serious degree, told sorely on those who were quietly succumbing to the "first sickness," which was upon them, and each day recorded victims to the privations surrounding all. "Ten of their principal men" had been selected from the volunteers—of course, Stephen Hopkins one of them—but they went out weary and heavy laden, to work in the service of those they loved, hardly seeing that through devious ways of His own choosing Providence was leading them slowly but surely to a home, such as it was, on the barren land of Cape Cod's shores.

News of their arrival could not be kept to themselves. So, when Samoset made his unexpected, perhaps unwelcome, visit to the colony, during the light hours of the day, when nothing hidden was unrevealed, all united in entertaining him, and true to the instinct implanted in man's heart, whether white or red, "he called for beer," which not being forthcoming, he dined with them on "strong water followed by biscuit, with butter and cheese pudding and mallard."

"All this he liked well." He would be hard to suit, indeed if not satisfied with this, when as an unbidden guest he dined "en famille."

As night's mantle, with them, was always sable, when it fell fear began to possess their souls.

The one Indian of the daytime might increase and multiply during the night. The feeling of hospitality had merged into self-defense, and what guest chamber to give Samoset was a problem not easily solved. His stay with them was by his own invitation, and the Mayflower was intended for his abiding place. However, it was found that at this time, which might be their dire need, the shallop had failed them, but there was a man of their number, Stephen Hopkins by name, a physical as well as intellectual power, and he was designated as "mine host," one who could keep a vigilant eye upon the undesired inmate of his domicile.

Morning broke, hope returned, and the speeding of the parting guest was so in keeping with their wishes that they searched their stores to give him evidence of at least the last sentiment toward him formed in a blaze of sunlight with courage to the front, and presented him, with becoming unction, with a knife, a bracelet and a ring.

DIPLOMATIC RELATIONS.

No one can doubt the relations between Bradford, Winslow and Hopkins; they were always evident, never more so than when, by the Governor's order, the diplomat Winslow and Hopkins were associated on the embassy to Massasoit, where the greatest possible tact and statesmanship were required; a false move would wreck them.

They were to adroitly ascertain the location of the Indians, elicit some knowledge of their power, discover the country and all its attributes of strength, prevent abuses and make the amende honorable for any supposed encroachments of the white man, continuing the league of friendship and peace already formed.

This, all know, they secured, Massasoit's pledge continuing through his lifetime.

They had gone for information of every kind, to acquire an idea of the Indian habits and all pertaining to them, but they had not intended results to be quite so personal, when they found they were to share the guest chamber, even the downy couch, with Massasoit, his wife, and, I am not wrong in saying, some of his braves.

That they would have preferred keeping the "midnight watch" more to themselves cannot be doubted.

SURROUNDINGS.

If there were not contrasting history, how delightful Mr. Winslow's letter to those at home, dated December 11, 1621, would sound, when he says, "The summer has been delightful, the climate lovely, the natural fruits of the earth abundant, grapes, strawberries and budding and blossoming roses in such sweetness and variety that for a little while New England looked like a paradise."

He tells them (George Morton and those coming out on the "Ann"), bring paper and linseed oil for your windows, with cotton yarn for your lamps, deploring that the company who come out in the Fortune (1621), depending wholly upon them, should have depleted their stock of corn so that they would have little enough till harvest.

Not forgetting every care for their comfort, the standard of arms required, he reminds them that the juice of lemons, which they should bring, is of good use if taken fasting, and "for hot waters, aniseed water is the best, but use it sparingly."

No one need be left out of the count when this was dispensed, even Oceanus could find his place at seven bells!

Much history hinges on the statement of Goodwin, in his "Plymouth Republic," that Constance, daughter of Stephen Hopkins, by his first wife, was over 13 years old when she arrived with her father on the Mayflower, and Giles (Gyles) by the same marriage, about 13, making Giles born 1605 or 6, and Constance probably 1608.

This places John Hopkins of later birth, about 1613; after Stephen Hopkins's shipwreck and return from Bermuda, natural.

All of this fits well into the subsequent records. John, bereft of his mother, must be provided with a home, and as it is known that he came from Coventry, England (American Ancestry, vol. 4, page 288), naturally some Hopkins kin took kindly care of him, possibly either John or Samuel Hopkins, whose marriages I have given.

It is very simple history, borne out by dates, the sequence of events, to place Damaris, the oldest child of the second marriage, which took place in March, 1617, as somewhere near 2 years of age, when the Mayflower started, and Oceanus's birth on the ship in 1620 does not admit of a doubt.

STEPHEN HOPKINS'S POSITION.

Stephen Hopkins's power and position are always shown by his being called "Mister," a title applied as Master.

"Only twelve people have the prefix Mr.

in the whole list of the passengers on the Mayflower, Fortune and Little James."

Mr. Stephen Hopkins was a man of great enterprise, and in the present day would have been a very acceptable and appreciative companion at all athletic sports, whether on sea or land. At his place, near Eel River (Plymouth), which he sold in 1637, there was a wharf which gave evidence of age, and was the first one spoken of in the colony. His yacht is not mentioned, though he was part owner of the first ship built in Plymouth, but it was on hand if he could materialize matters to his liking, and there were sure to be "chips" on board for a time of need, though he never carried a "chip on his shoulder."

Not to give precedence to his allegiance to old Neptune, he owned the first horse on record (1644), when a mare belonging to the estate of Stephen Hopkins was appraised at £6 sterling.

Its rate of speed has not come to us, but nothing slow flourished under this master.

His officeholding was continuous—of the Governor's Council from Plymouth, 1623-4-5-6; in 1637 one of the volunteers in aid of Massachusetts Bay and Connecticut in their war with the Pequods, when the colony concluded to send them assistance, and then was of the committee appointed to levy an assessment to pay the charges of the expedition; then in 1642 was chosen to the Council of War from Plymouth.

No desire could make a narrow-minded Puritan of Mr. Stephen Hopkins; he was broad enough even for the methods of the present day. It was not in the blood to live up to the requirements of that early "Vigilance Committee," who were a law unto themselves, with a "single eye" to the faults of others.

BENEFIT OF TRAVEL.

He had seen the world and profited by the knowledge gained, acquiring a certain liberty of action for himself and others, which sometimes got him into trouble, as he was "fined in 1637 for permitting servants and others to sit in his house, drinking and playing shovelboard."

Gov. Winslow need never have written, so far as he was concerned, to George Morton for the "paper and linseed oil for windows;" he would content himself with "tallow dips," if there were enough of them, so long as darkness was not made visible to the prowling white and red men, who scented mischief afar, and took, from force of habit, his house first on their beat.

The absence of glass or even paper windows to his house was not an indication of want or narrow means, so pride and inclination joined forces in his case. If, as is a matter of history, they were a luxury in the time of Henry VIII. and in Queen Elizabeth's reign were confined to the houses of the nobility, and by them considered as movable furniture, why should he, one of the sovereign people, rebel that he was not compelled by usage to have what he didn't want, and what might many times be his undoing?

Given permission, any opportunity for pleasure would lose its value to our friend Stephen; he liked to "go it alone" at the start; then "call his neighbors in," at least such as would recognize him as a "good fellow" and fall into the place he designed for them without discussion.

OPINIONS.

A note sent to me says Mr. Stephen Hopkins was a man without education, an adventurer, signing his name with a cross.

This, when he was "lay reader to Mr. Buck, chaplain to the expedition of Sir Thomas Gates," must have seen the little company at Leyden were tending, and, when necessity compelled decisive action, knowing they wanted stanch material to draw from, have turned naturally to his former companion.

They had ample opportunity for discussion, through Gov. Carter, in charge of the fitting out of the Mayflower, who was in England in 1618 and 1619, and Brewster himself had some time for intercourse.

Mr. Hopkins had married again, his life was settled to his family duties; he must forget his love for the ocean and make a home for his children, where, under his own eye, they could grow up according to his beliefs.

SIGNING WITH AN X.

Signing his name with a cross hardly needs explanation, in the present search of history, particularly when one reflects that Alice Southworth Bradford, who was eulogized by the great Elder Faunce "for her exertions in promoting the literary improvement and the deportment of the rising generation," did the same, and the well-known "first-born Englishman," Peregrine White, entitled to the best of his day, "who in his youth used his pen in a forcible manner, in his last days made his mark in his will."

PURSUIT.

A friend told me that Stephen Hopkins was a leather dealer; this I cannot find, but he was in the beaver trade with Mr. John Attwood, of Plymouth, which renders his falling in with other skins suitable for tanning purposes possible, and it may be that Doty and Leister were indentured to this trade.

The permissions of the early government seem to have been given with reservations, for though they allowed our Pilgrim to build a house and cut hay for cattle at Maltachus (now Barnstable), he was not to stay there and risk his family for the winter.

His real home was on the strip of land reaching from Leyden to Middle street, Plymouth, where, surrounded by the "first comers," he led his active, useful life.

Try as I may, there is no evading the fact that Stephen Hopkins found some of the restrictions upon which the Pilgrims set so much importance constant annoyance to him, and his coming before the court on a variety of occasions to answer some trivial charges had such cause of resentment—nothing more.

This plan of record progresses for him, and he is presented at court for "selling beer for ijd. the quart not worth jd. a quart." This dignified error of appraisement was witnessed by Kenelme Winslow.

The story continues, and two years later he was again before court for "selling a looking glass (the first record of a looking glass in the colony) at 16d., the like of which is bought at the Bay for 9d."

He kept everything up to the highest market quotations. No bargain days for him.

The signer's life was too broad and active for small feelings. What mattered his dwelling so long as all were alike, and those early settlers were as happy in their log or block houses, with a chimney erected from the center of the building through the roof, as the oldest sons in the marble halls of their progenitors.

The old houses, with their thatched roofs, are, indeed, a thing of the past, but in the colonies so important did they deem the "preservation of this material for the preservation of their log houses from the inclemency of the weather that every town was ordered to construct a house in which to secure the long beach grass for this purpose."

The "better class of these houses had their chinks filled up with mud to protect them from the cold, chilly blasts of winter."

No doubt of Stephen Hopkins having all the modern improvements, with Doty and Leister as his assistants, a pleasant relief from their "duplicate whist" played in the gloaming, on the table of hasty construction, easily dropped when the too friendly neighbors, who had no temptation to conviviality, came in unawares.

THE STEPMOTHER'S JEALOUSY.

The very natural suggestion on the part of Savage and others of the jealousy of Elizabeth Hopkins, which led her to exercise undue influence over Stephen Hopkins and make him leave her son Caleb as heir-apparent, regardless of the rights of Giles, the first-born son, makes a claim for her leaving John, of Hartford, behind when starting for their new life. Very naturally, being too young for any practical benefit, he might prove in the way—her lack of affection would not be against her, as circumstances seem in favor of his not having been under her care.

THE CHILDREN.

Giles Hopkins, his child by his first wife, born in England, married October 9, 1639, Catherine, daughter of Gabriel Wheldon, of Yarmouth and Barnstable, and died about 1690.

His first home was with his parents at Plymouth; he then removed to Mattachuse. In 1642 he was the surveyor of Yarmouth, and until 1662 a surveyor of Yarmouth and Nansett, or Eastham; 1655, one of the list of twenty-nine freemen of Eastham.

Giles Hopkins had ten children, and as history I note that the first son was named Stephen, the second John!

Constance, also the first wife's child, born in England, married in 1627 Hon. Nicholas Snow, one of the founders of Eastham, who came over in the "Ann."

They give a double claim as signers, through their descendant, Robert Treat Paine.

Then come the children of the second wife: Damaris, born in England, married in 1646 Jacob Cooke, son of Francis, of the Mayflower, and died after 1666, leaving Jacob with the privilege of marrying again, which he availed himself of—after the fashion of the day.

Oceanus, the Mayflower gift, that came to them about October, 1620, died before

1627, without attaining the age when his special birthrights would tell in his favor.

Deborah, born at Plymouth, 1622, married in 1646 Andrew Ring, of Plymouth, who was made freeman that year, and being early an orphan was left by his mother to the good Dr. Fuller's care.

Then Caleb, of Plymouth, his father's executor, who bore arms in 1643, and, true to his family instincts, followed the sea, dying at Barbados, "probably unmarried." Strange, that for all his mother's successful efforts in his behalf, gaining for him precedence over his older brother, the descent should really and only, unless John Hopkins, of Hartford, is accepted, come through Giles, the oldest son.

Then Ruth and poor Elizabeth, who, still a child, in 1647 was, by action of Capt. Miles Standish and her brother Caleb, intrusted to Richard Sparrow, but did not live to marry and have what her heart desired, a home of her own.

STEPHEN HOPKINS'S WIFE.

The unknown wife of his early days had long passed from his life, but the Pilgrim was very appreciative of the one left for his comfort, though he survived her; the separation was not for long, and his dying request was to be laid beside her in the grave where he had so lovingly placed her. The records give his death as 1644, and hers between 1640 and 1644.

She had done well by him after her own plan of action, their few and simple culinary utensils, in keeping with their homes, she used to the best advantage. Whatever the situation, Mr. Stephen Hopkins was a wiser and better man when he dined well; the early habit of two meals a day would hardly suffice for him, and Doty and Leister, being of the family, would never refuse the "rear supper" told us of by the writer of "Piers of Fulham," for fear of surfeiting, in Plymouth colony!

Elizabeth Hopkins "piped to dinner with great regularity," and no one answered the summons with more alacrity than her liege lord and master. Her experienced hand told in the preparation, and Stephen cared for the accessories.

JOHN HOPKINS, OF HARTFORD.

John Hopkins, of Hartford, the man who honors Stephen, of the Mayflower, if his son, was made freeman in 1634 (Records of Mass., vol. I., page 370, confirmed as to statement by C. R., vol. 1, page 153), the same year his son Stephen, whose name would seem to corroborate the kinship between the two, was born.

To make the above satisfactory and beyond any present doubt, as it is in evidence from all the authorities in our possession, I quote the records on which everything is founded, and leave to the public the accepting or refusing my own strong convictions.

In tracing the ancestry of Col. Archibald Hopkins, of Washington, through his father, the great Mark Hopkins, of Williams College, to John, of Hartford, "who came from Coventry, England, to Cambridge, Mass., in 1630," the above is stated without demur in "American Ancestry," vol. IV., pp. 227-228, and the book was published in 1889, when this discussion was at least in a quiescent state.

Then, in Paige's "History of Cambridge," p. 33, it is implied that John Hopkins's name first appears in the list of proprietors in 1633, while a little later on, it is stated that "perhaps many of them were here earlier than the dates would indicate."

The next confirmation (which also is applicable as to the Windsor, Conn., records) by the author is to the effect that "some whose names are given under date of 1632 were certainly in Cambridge in 1631, and some entered in the lists under 1633 and 1634 may have been residents one or two years previously."

HIS MARRIAGE.

John Hopkins married Jane ——, and furthermore history saith not, but if he came over in 1630, as "Munsell" unhesitatingly asserts, and only attained his majority which entitled him to freemanship in 1634, he must have married in America, and it is quite a natural surmise that his wooing may have detained him in Cambridge, instead of seeking his father in Plymouth or elsewhere.

In a history which I have never been able to find again, so have not even the faintest actual authority for the statement, after this marriage of John Hopkins to Jane —— there was written in pencil "Strong." The wish may have been father to the thought, still the possibilities tend naturally that way, claiming as I feel borne out in saying by constant study of their personal connections, that those who came over for twenty years after the Mayflower, were mainly relatives, only waiting for the verdict of the pioneers to make their start.

The human consignment of the "Adventurers" were not those to the "manner born," and should not be cast upon the "old comers," as of their ilk.

HIS RESIDENCE.

In Paige's early plan of Cambridge (pages 15 and 16), John Hopkins draws among the first, being only "24" on the list, his house situated on Spring or Mount Auburn street. The whole desire of placing everything I could gather before the public was not for assertion, but discussion; convictions which one must hold alone are of little value, and, fortunately, I have been spared this, but every Hopkins must have some legends or records, and if the impulse to bring them forward is not strong enough for action, they have the regrets which will always remain with them.

Figures make strong testimony, are accepted as facts. Thus John Hopkins, of Hartford, who, according to the possibility resulting from my search, was born in 1613, becomes truthfully a "freeman," as told in the records of Massachusetts, vol. I., page 370, March 4, 1634. A proud husband immediately after, and, to fill the year with blessings, welcomed Stephen, sole son of his heart and home, the same year.

He went to Hartford with Rev. Thomas Hooker's company. Location and time are in favor of this. There must have been some great attraction drawing him there, for his position in Cambridge was of the best.

However, in Hartford, he became an original proprietor, "townsman," if that were an additional honor, 1640, juror 1643, and then surrounded by all that proves life attractive, died in 1654, making him, according to his freemanship and the date of birth I have supplied, 41 years of age, his comparative youth being always in history.

A man was only required to be of age to secure "freemanship," but there was, of course, a varying rate of age after that. Time of arrival and inclination (the cause for the latter I have already explained) had much to do with claiming or accepting it.

JANE HOPKINS.

His wife, Jane Hopkins, thus early a widow, found that traditional Pilgrim comforter in Nathaniel Ward, of Hartford, afterward of Hadley, and so far as the step relations she gave the Hopkins descent, had no cause for regret.

Stephen, the first child and only son, married Dorcas Bronson, daughter of John Bronson, the emigrant ancestor of that family, a man of military fame, having served in the Pequod war.

Bethia, the only daughter, "born about 1635, married, first, May 21, 1652, Deacon Samuel Stocking, of Middletown; second, James Steele, of Hartford."

I have hoped much from this name connection, have traced it among the early settlers and thought to place it in England so directly as to be family proof. Seeking a friend on this subject, he joined the search, and we make the earliest record in the Mildmay family collaterally.

That period was such a field for "Elizabeth" in every form that it seemed possible to me among the many nicknames that followed everything in "ye olden times," Beth, Betha and Bethia might result. The lax spelling for centuries added or took away a letter without the slightest compunction.

This would be a singular confirmation of relationship if John Hopkins, of Hartford, had this purpose in naming the daughter of Bethia after his stepmother. Since writing the first edition of the Mayflower Signers, my friend, Rev. M. E. Dwight, of Plainfield, N. J., whose association with my work will always be in evidence, has written me that "both Elizabeth and Bethia have the same meaning, viz: 'Worshipper of God'." This is of some importance as the early Puritans gave Bible names to their children from this very significance. Elizabeth is the Greek for the Hebrew Elisheba, wife of Aaron. Elisheba menas literally "to whom God is the oath," i. e. consecrated to God, and therefore "a worshipper of God." The word is explained to signify "worshipping God" in Webster's Dictionary. Bethia is in Hebrew Bithyah, and means literally a daughter of Jehovah, i. e., a worshipper of Jehovah. And when one reflects on the horror of the Pilgrims at anything savoring of Popery, the force of thus naming Stephen, son of John, of Hartford, is a very powerful argument, for the relation to Stephen, of the Mayflower, as St. Stephen, would interdict such an act except for the strong family desire of perpetuating the father's and grandfather's name.

JOHN THE MILLER.

To properly bring in the various Hopkins branches necessary for the perfect whole, John Hopkins, of Waterbury, called in history "The Miller," son of Stephen, of Hartford, and grandson of John, the emigrant, is a most important factor.

I have a record before me from a Hopkins historian, who gives the wife of "John the Miller," as Hannah Rogers. I feel that this cannot be substantiated by either him or myself, but as he had it from some one, proof of it may be given by those not before interested in the search.

Still, John Hopkins, of Waterbury, Conn.,

spoke for himself, "one of the most respected and influential of the early settlers of Waterbury," a man who acquired wealth for the times, held every office, was even with other duties of a large public and private nature, "tavern keeper," and then by promotion, rose to the pinnacle of power, being "ordinary keeper," a position eagerly sought for and held by the great ones of the land.

Miller John was also much of a soldier, in a time when "military titles were in high repute among the colonists. They were preferred to civil or ecclesiastic honors. A corporal was on the road to distinction. His office was occasionally, but not usually, attached to his name. A sergeant had attained distinction, and his title was never omitted. An ensign, or lieutenant, was lifted quite above the heads of his fellows."

Our John, started with the claim to distinction, was ensign in 1715 and lieutenant in 1716. This pride of military position being his, he was from that date called "Left Hopkins." What he was himself was good, he fulfilled the inherited claim that he should do well, and his descendants have acted nobly their part in this solid family history.

John the Miller, in 1729, when the new meeting house came to be selected, was one of the revered dignitaries who were voted into the "first pew at the best end of the pulpit." Succeeding generations have been the "teachers of men," and from the pulpit itself have spoken to "those in authority."

REAR ADMIRAL RICHARD WORSAM MEADE, 3d, U. S. A.
Again death has entered the little circle of those interested in my work, and Admiral Meade, a member of the "CHOIR INVISIBLE" has no part in the living present, but speaks by the record he gave me for the place it now occupies.

1. Richard Worsam Meade, 3d, Rear Admiral United States Navy, born October 9, 1837, at No. 59 Perry street, New York City, corner of Fourth street, the residence of his maternal grandfather, Judge Henry Meigs.

2. That he is the son of Richard Worsam Meade, 2d, (who became a captain in the United States Navy), born March 21, 1807, died in Brooklyn, N. Y., April 16, 1870, and Clara Forsyth Meigs, his wife, born New York City, January 29, 1811, married, New York City, December 5, 1836, and died at Huntington, L. I., February 5, 1879.

3. That the said Clara Forsyth Meigs was the daughter of Henry Meigs (Judge and M. C. of 16th Congress, New York City), born, New Haven, Conn., October 28, 1782, died in New York City May 20, 1861, and Julia Austin, his wife, born in Philadelphia, 1784, married February 19, 1806, and died in New York City, 1842.

4. That the said Julia Austin was the daughter of Stephen Austin, of Philadelphia, gentleman, born——, died in Philadelphia ——, and Huldah Hopkins, his wife, born May 17, 1752.

5. That the said Huldah Hopkins was the daughter of Thomas Hopkins, 2d, of Hartford, Conn., born 1725, and Anna, his first wife, born ——, married 1748, and died May 27, 1759.

6. That the said Thomas Hopkins, 2d, was the son of Thomas Hopkins, 1st, of Hartford, Conn., born 1692, died 1764, and Mary Beckley, of Wethersfield, Conn., his wife, born ——, married 1717, and died ——.

7. That the said Thomas Hopkins, 1st, was the son of Stephen Hopkins, 2d, of Hartford, Conn., died 1702, and Sarah Judd, of Waterbury, Conn., his wife, born ——, married November, 1686, and died about 1693.

8. That the said Stephen Hopkins, 2d, was the son of Stephen Hopkins, 1st, of Hartford, Conn., born about 1634, died 1689, and Dorcas, daughter of John Bronson, of Farmington, Conn., his wife.

9. That the said Stephen Hopkins, 1st, of Hartford, Conn., was the son of John Hopkins, of Hartford, Conn., born about 1613, died 1654, and Jane ——, his wife, who remarried, Nathaniel Ward, of Hartford.

10. That the said John Hopkins, of Hartford, Conn., was the son (?) of Stephen Hopkins, of Coventry and London, Eng., born about 1580, died 1644, and his first wife (mother of Gyles, Constanta, and John, of Hartford (?), died about 1614.

11. That the said Stephen Hopkins, of England, emigrated to America in the ship Mayflower, 1620, and was the fourteenth signer of the Compact of the Plymouth Colonists.

Admiral Meade married, June 6, 1865, Rebecca, daughter of Admiral Paulding, U. S. N., son of John Paulding, captor of Major Andre (1780), and lineal descendant of Joost Pauldinick, who in 1700 owned the land on which the present City Hall stands. He has one son, Richard Worsam, 4th, born February 7, 1870, at present secretary to the general manager of the New York Central Railroad Company, New York.

CELEBRATED DIVINES.

Who would not claim relationship with Rev. Samuel Hopkins, D. D., of Newport, R. I., the famous divine, from whom the Hopkinsian School of Theology received its name, better known to some readers as the hero of the "Minister's Wooing?" Son of Timothy, of Waterbury, grandson of John the miller, he tells the story of his life, when writing to his cousin, Rev. Jonathan Judd, of South Hampton, November 5, 1789, he says:

"We are going into a world of light, where it will be known what truth and what errors we have imbibed, and contended for in this dark world, and then all matters will be set right, to which I feel no reluctance, hoping I sincerely love the truth, and that I am building on the sure foundation laid in Zion, whatever hay or stubble may be found with me. And as to those who are the professed friends of Christ, I desire not to judge any of them before the time," etc. "Your kinsman and old friend, S. Hopkins."

REV. MARK HOPKINS, LL. D.

Then bringing the name down to the memory of the living, that greatest of all those who have borne the name of Hopkins, treasured by every student at Williams College who had the pleasure of being under him, held inexpressibly dear in the hearts of all, this Rev. Mark Hopkins, LL. D., as they called him, who, when visiting his grave the centennial of the college, October 8, 1893, "The Sainted Hopkins" gives added value to this inheritance.

An extract from a sermon delivered by him at Plymouth, Mass., December 22, 1846, from the text Matthew xxiii., 8, "And all ye are brethren," fits prophetically into the needs of to-day.

"The term brethren indicates equality and affection, and these must form the basis of a perfect society. Let every man be at his post, never ashamed of the plain rigging of his good ship, but always hearing that voice of duty, and of the voice of the God of our fathers, which will speak above the war of every trumpet, and then if our ship must go down the will of God be done.

"But then she will not go down, then the hand which guided the Mayflower will guide her."

GOV. EDWARD HOPKINS.

Edward Hopkins, Governor of Connecticut and founder of the Hopkins Grammar Schools, of New Haven and Hartford, was born, according to the Memorial History of Hartford, at Shrewsbury, County Salop, in England, 1600, son of Edward or Edmund Hopkins, and Katherine, sister of Sir Henry Lello, and came to this country, arriving in Boston June 26, 1637.

Shrewsbury is not far from Coventry, and the places have a strong ecclesiastical connection; still, I wished it nearer, and was delighted to find from Scavea's "Hartford in the Olden Time" that he was born near Shrewsbury in 1600, which lessens the distance and increases the connection with Coventry, the home of the Hopkinses.

The history of Shrewsbury gives nothing of importance in the line of my study, while Coventry, in the same series of English works, furnishes much of interest and gives high place to those we are seeking.

"Edward Hopkins was brought up in London in handsome style," and in his manhood was a "Turkey merchant."

This identifies him from boyhood with London, and Stephen Hopkins, of the Mayflower, was called from the "London section."

The future Governor of Connecticut came out in the same vessel with a very noted Hopkins cousin, Rev. John Davenport, and as he was a preacher in London, before fleeing to Leyden, the strong, continuous family weaving of interests had every opportunity of increasing.

All of this was carried along the lines, not only to those bearing the name, but the various members of families, with a strong pulley to the American colony, where ties of blood were awaiting them.

EDWARD HOPKINS'S LIFE.

"He was exemplary for his piety, integrity and charity. He did everything to maintain peace and justice. He had to combat with many evils, not only in subduing the wilderness, but with others, which gave a wound to his spirit; an incurable dementia had seized his wife at the same time that he was subject to pulmonary complaints. The latter he could have borne with resignation, for what are the infirmities of the body compared with the trials of the heart?

I promised myself, said he, "too much content in this relation and enjoyment, and the Lord will make me to know that this world shall not afford it to me."

Gov. Hopkins married "Ann, daughter of David Yale, of Denbighshire," and step-daughter of Gov. Eaton, who was a fellow-passenger on the ship that brought him out.

Though one with the early settlers, in all respects identified fully with their interests,

Edward Hopkins never lost his connection with the London of his previous life. He placed his mark indelibly here, but returned to England and resumed his large associations at the time of the death of his brother, Henry, 1654, who had received the office of Warden of the Fleet from his uncle, Sir Henry Lello, and by his will constituted Gov. Hopkins Warden of the Fleet and Keeper of the Palace of Westminster.

"Added to this, he was agent in London for a colonizing company, the chief members of which were Lords Say and Seal, Lord Brook, Lord Rich and Sir Richard Saltonstall and others of influence, politically and socially."

Sad for our history, he died without issue in 1657, and this country, which would have been his home but for his domestic afflictions, had to be content with the results of the sum of money he left "for the breeding up of hopeful youths, both at the grammar school and the college, for the public service of the colony in future times."

The bequest has caused much trouble in the courts "on both sides of the ocean, but now in the hands of trustees the college receives part of the income from it."

The position I have taken is of great moment if I am successful in establishing it, but I am not alone in opinion. I know President Mark Hopkins, of Williams College, believed that a relationship existed, though I have never heard what degree of consanguinity he thought possible, and Dr. Park, who wrote the preface to the life of the great theologian, Dr. Samuel Hopkins, of Newport, says: "This Gov. Edward Hopkins, and Stephen, who came in the Mayflower, conjectured by some to be related, as also to John Hopkins, who came to Cambridge, etc."

Additional supposition comes from the new "History of Waterbury:"

"The mill at Hartford, from its beginning, seems to have been held in the Hopkins family, Gov. Edward Hopkins himself owning the mill, or an interest in it."

Then vol. I., page 573: "Stephen Hopkins, son of John I., who was the owner of a mill in Hartford, accepted the proposal to build the mill in Waterbury, built a mill, and sent his son John to run it, but did not come himself, or remove his family thither."

This was in 1680, several years after the death of Gov. Hopkins, and these facts regarding business relations would seem to confirm their kinship.

Thanks to Dr. Charles J. Hoadley, LL.D., State Librarian of Connecticut, my attention was called to the commission of John Winthrop as first magistrate at Namecock, now New London, dated October 27, 1647. "It has on it the oldest known seal of Connecticut. "The commission was written and signed by Edward Hopkins, doubly valuable from the fact that very little of Gov. Hopkins's writing is in existence. It was given to the library by Mr. Robert C. Winthrop, part of his family papers.

No high-minded person desires to appropriate to their family advancement a coat-of-arms not clearly and authentically their own. As regards this family there can be no doubt. The arms "may still be seen carved in oak, in what is now a machine shop, but that some centuries ago was known as the Palace Yard, because there the Hopkinses entertained so often the nobility and royalty of England."

The Americans who could claim the right to the use of arms might be counted, "perhaps," on one hand, according to English law. With them they only come by primogeniture, and as every man cannot be the "oldest son of the oldest son," the use of it is false, as a legal position, still there is no denying the propriety of placing the heraldic design of one's family wherever the taste of the owner dictates, where it simply indicates the family position.

Mr. Mortimer Delano, the heraldist, gives me the arms of the Coventry house of Hopkins as: Sable on a chevron between three pistols or three roses gules. The roses are on the gold chevron.

Every form of criticism has come to me in regard to the "arms;" my own ignorance of the subject prevents my taking it up, even as a discussion.

There is a very pretty piece of history attached to the arms, and, having dates at my command the story told will carry conviction to every one who reads and "inwardly digests" the arguments that have

preceded in regard to the Hopkins family.

It is assured to the family of John of Hartford and his descendants, and I doubt not will be acceptable, with an acknowledged kinship to all holding a title clear to "Mr. Stephen Hopkins, 14th Signer of the Mayflower Compact."

THE ARMS.

The arms given were taken from the family Bible of Reuben Hopkins, now through intermarriage in the possession of Campbell Steward, of Goshen, Orange County, New York, and by him presented to Mr. Lewis C. Hopkins, of New York, who has worked with me and for me in this search, his pleasure in the possession of the arms greatly enhanced by the knowledge that it would be available for my needs.

The signature is a fitting accompaniment and tells a long historical connection with the past, the Bible record giving us Reuben Hopkins (son of Stephen Hopkins, Esq., and Jemima Brunson Hopkins) was born in the town of Amenia, in Dutchess County, on the 1st day of June, old style, in the year 1748, and was married to Hannah Elliott, daughter of Col. Aaron Elliott and Mary Elliott, by Rev. Eliphalet Huntingdon, November 23, 1773, etc.

With the filial regard of the day, Reuben has recorded in this Bible, "My father, Stephen Hopkins, was born in Hartford, Connecticut, and married Jemima Brunson, who was born in Waterbury, in Connecticut. My father died in Amenia, in the county of Dutchess and State of New York. My mother died at Bennington, in the State of Vermont, in the 84th year of her age. They were many years and before my birth professors of religion."

Afterward in another handwriting is "Reuben Hopkins, died at Edwardsville in the State of Illinois, in the year 1819."

So this arms speaks to us, probably from the last century, and tradition says that "John, the Miller of Waterbury," had possession by right of primogeniture of coat-armor.

Found in the family Bible of a man who died in 1819, made personal, by his own old-time signature, carries ample conviction. Still, evidence of its authenticity is not wanting in other branches of the Hopkins family of close collateral descent.

Mr. Charles Hopkins kindly brought me his arms, which he had "from Timothy Hopkins, of California, by him taken from the Bible of his stepfather, the late Mark Hopkins, the great financier of Great Barrington, Mass., and California." They are the counterpart of each other. Col. Archibald Hopkins, of Washington, D. C., confirms the arms, he having visited Coventry, where he saw the family tombs at St. Michaels, and the old house of Sir Richard Hopkins.

CONVICTION.

Increased strength is found in the impossibility that Reuben Hopkins, who died in 1819, could have secured his arms from the others. So the descendants may appropriate the arms without hesitation, and feel quite secure that when "John Hopkins, of Hartford," started "in search of his father," he brought with him family proofs of his identity, at least locally.

Reuben may have been an unknown quantity to many branches, but to-day he makes his claim, and not an unworthy one—for by birth and his own marriage to Hannah Elliot (fifth in descent from "John Elliot, the Apostle"), who was born August 31, 1746, and is placed on the records as "highly educated," he gave in his turn much addition to the family inheritance of distinction.

MILITARY CONNECTION.

The military record of this branch of the family is unequaled. Stephen Hopkins, of Hartford (son of Ebenezer), then of Hawinton, afterwards of "Nine Partners" (Amenia, Dutchess County, New York), had five sons officers in the revolutionary army, two being killed by the Indians. Can a country ask more of its citizens?

"It was a wonderful family, filled with piety, good works and patriotism."

My endeavor will be to place a few genealogical lines, from various sections, that I can authenticate, so that those of the same lineage will see where they belong in this great history.

Mr. Lewis Cheesman Hopkins (starts until notice is given him of another generation), with John Hopkins, of Hartford, then Stephen, his only son, who married Dorcas Bronson; next Ebenezer Hopkins, born in 1669, resided in Hartford, married Mary, daughter of Deacon Samuel Butler, of Weathersfield.. Hezekiah P., their son, born November 21, 1702, in Hartford, afterwards of Harwinton; married Sarah Davis, June,

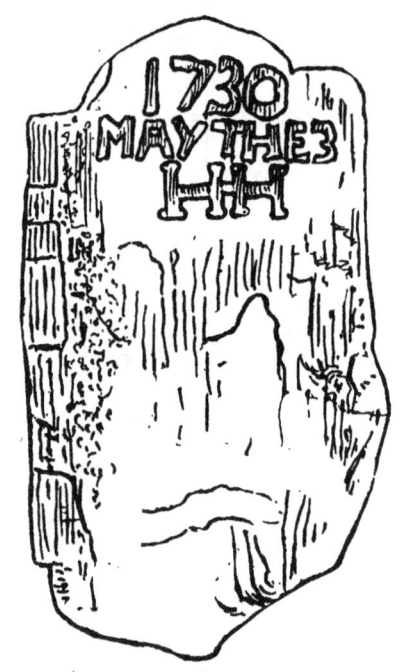

HANNAH HOPKINS'S TOMBSTONE.

1742. Hezekiah, the second, of Haminton, born in 1758, married Eunice Hubbell, June 12, 1783; their son William Milton, born August 1, 1789, married Almira Adkins, November 7, 1807.

Then Lewis C. Hopkins, who married Julia Maria Whetstone, and to their two living sons gives the inherited family patriotism, himself a son of the American revolution, a memeber of the "Founders and Patriots' Society," while the grandchildren, following in his footsteps, are learning duty to their country and flag, with the "Children's Society of 1776."

From this branch comes Major Robert Emmet Hopkins, with a fitting military record from the civil war. Captain in the 149th Regiment of New York Infantry, taken prisoner at Chancellorsville, Va., confined in Libby Prison until exchanged, when he rejoined his command. Then, after participating in the battles of Wahatchie Junction, Lookout Mountain, Missionary Ridge, and Ringgold, resigned on account of ill health, July 3, 1864.

FAMILY GIFTS.

Knowing the tradition that all the Hopkins family had as a birthright the gifts of music, and art, I took pains to search for the truth of this report, and found at every step corroboration from many branches, and different localities, and myself have added on conviction, the gift of composition.

Another branch has a large claim, running through John, of Hartford, then Stephen, and Dorcas (Bronson) Hopkins, he born 1634, "John the Miller," their son, born in 1665, his son, Stephen Hopkins, born November 19, 1689, married Susanna, daughter of John Peck, of Wallingford, 1717, died 1769. Next their son, Joseph Hopkins, of Waterbury, born in the limits of the present Naugatuck, June 6, 1730, married Hepzibah, daughter of Thomas Clark, November 28, 1754.

This Judge Joseph Hopkins is one of her sons that Waterbury is justly proud of. He died in office in New Haven, Conn., March 27, 1801, having lived through the stirring times of the revolution, a patriot, as the country then demanded and made of men. The records tell us that "Gen. Lafayette, once during the war, perhaps more than once, passed through Waterbury. He also on one occasion stopped at the house of Joseph Hopkins, Esq., then the most prominent civilian in the place."

Jesse, the son of Joseph, born May 20, 1766, married, December, 1794, Elizabeth, daughter of Nathaniel Goodwin, of Hartford.

This takes us into Jefferson County, N. Y., where, in 1813, Jesse Hopkins was appointed County Judge by De Witt Clinton, and from this line comes Goodwin Brown, of Albany, and Charles Hopkins, of Brooklyn, as well as Katherine Hopkins, the third principal of Mount Holyoke Female Seminary, whose bright career closed too early for the good of the college, but the worthy memory is still fresh in the hearts of many of the living. Born in Rutland, Jefferson County, N. Y., August 22, 1835, Heaven claimed her March 10, 1865, before she had reached her thirtieth year.

Among those from the Waterbury, Conn., section are Richard Burton, Hartford, Conn.; Capt. Milton Haxtun, U. S. N.; Dr. George G. Hopkins, Col. Woolsey R. Hopkins, Prof. G. L. Raymond, of Princeton University.

I have given John Hopkins' lines only in this paper to prevent confusion, though there are many in various parts of this country, who, having this descent, have never doubted the Mayflower at the other end, the question not having come up for consideration.

Coventry, the home of the Hopkins family, was always a place of the greatest commercial importance. Wealth came to it from its progression. Royalty, secure in the pageant of his or her reception, sought it frequently, and the people who left there for homes in the new world, being in the leading strings of heredity, no matter what garb or sect they hid it under, made citizens of note and power as a result.

The guilds with them were very numerous —"The Merchants, Trinity, St. Katherine's the Sherman and Taylor's, Corpus Christi, and many others; the chantries, almshouses, pensions and indemnities, hospitals and schools show how great and important a place the city of Coventry was during the middle ages."

The power of these guilds cannot be overrated; their influence was widespreading, so those bearing the names of Hopkins, Davenport, etc., were not "strangers to be taken in" by any one at whatever period of their own or the country's existence they reached New England. They came stamped with the best the mother country could give, and through succeeding times have left their impress on the seats of learning, the manufactures and arts.

One finds in St. Michael's (Coventry, England) Church, on the north side of the chancel, a finely executed white marble monument with three busts, and the following inscription:

Near this place, lye the remains
Of Richard Hopkins Esq. and of Mary his beloved Wife
To the pious memory of whom this monument is erected
By the order of their only Son Edward Hopkins,
With design to transmit to posterity the character of both,
Justly allowed to them, in the age they live in.
Richard was a tender husband, an indulgent father, a sincere friend
A devout Protestant, and a true loyal Patriot;
Of the latter he gave proofs, in the several Parliaments
In which for many years he represented this City.
Mary no less possessed all the virtues of her sex, she was charitable, chaste and pious; a dutiful wife and affectionate mother.
He departed this life Feb. 1, 1707, in the 68th year of his age
She Oct. 13, 1711, in the 63d year of her age.

This son Edward, who also represented Coventry in Parliament, died in 1736.
The list of the Mayors of Coventry gives us:
1498—Wm. Hopkins, dyer.
1564—Wm. Hopkins, draper.
1609—Sampson Hopkins, draper.
1640—Sampson Hopkins, merchant.

Here lyes ye body of
WILLIAM HOPKINS,
the husband of Rebecca Hopkins,
who departed his life
June ye 26, 1718.

"The family of Hopkins trace founder's kin to St. John's College, Oxford. The name was originally written Hopkyns. It was so spelt by John Hopkyns, who filled a civic office in the city of Coventry in 1567."
From the History of Waterbury, Vol. 1, page 668:
"Perhaps the stone that will interest the greatest number of readers of this History is that of Hannah Hopkins, wife of John the miller, and fore-mother of a long line of distinguished men.
"Her descendants to-day are many, and it is a matter of regret that her maiden name is unknown. She died May 3, 1730."
This tale is told. Hannah Hopkins dead, still lives with many to rise up and call her blessed. Through none is her descent stronger than her son Timothy, of Waterbury, father of Rev. Samuel Hopkins, D. D.

In memory of
Samuel Hopkins, D. D
Pastor of the
First Congregational Church
in Newport
who departed this life
Dec 20th A. D. 1803
in the 83d year of his age
Whose faithful attention to the duties
of his pastoral office and
Whose valuable writings
Will recommend his character
When this monument
Erected by his bereaved flock
Shall, with the precious dust it covers
Cease to be distinguished.

Copied from old tombstones in the Centre Church in Hartford by Dr. Charles J. Hoadley, State Librarian of Connecticut, to secure preservation:

Here lieth the
Body: Hopkins
Gorton: who died March: 27
1725: about: 20
Years: &: 11: months
of: age: Born: at
Warwick: in Rod
Island: Cols.
The Grave
of Lemuel Hopkins M. D
who died 14th April 1801
Aged 50 years.

Here lieth ye body of
JOHN HOPKINS,
Died
July ye 22d. 1727,
in ye
22d year of his age.

The above from the old graveyard in Orient, Suffolk County, L. I., New York, and being Stephen Hopkins's descendents, have the Coventry names.
Without doubt this is the William, son of Stephen Hopkins, of the Mayflower.

Also
of his eldest daughter
Rebecca the wife
of John McCrackan
who died 14th November 1803
Aged 21 years.

In memory of
Doct'r Asa Hopkins
who died Dec. 4th 1805
aged 48 years.

Also of
Edward
Son of
Asa and Abigail Hopkins
who died
April 18th, 1799
aged 13 months.

In memory of Mrs. Sally Hopkins
wife of
Mr. Samuel Hopkins
and daughter of the late
Benjamin Payne, Esq.
who died December 23d
A. D. 1796
in the 29th year
of her age.

In in Memory of of
Mrs. Rebecca Hopkins
Wife of
Mr. Asa Hopkins
and daughter of the late
Benjamin Payne Esqr
who died Sept. 17th
1791
Aged 29 years.

T. H.

Here lies the body of
TIMOTHY HOPKINS, Esq.,
Who died February ye 5th,
A. Dom. 1743,
Aged 57 years.
when this you see
then think of me.

Copp's Hill Inscriptions:
This stone is erected in memory of
Capt. Caleb Hopkins Jun'r
who died Octobr 19th
1791
in the 39th year of his age.
Here lies the body of
Betsey Hopkins
Dau'tr of Michael and Joanna Hopkins
died August 29
1783
aged 15 months and 17 days.

In memory of
Enoch Hopkins
who departed this life Dec. 27, 1778
a. 55 years.
"Tell them tho' 'tis an awful thing to die,
'Twas e'en to thee; yet the path once trod,
Heaven lifts it's everlasting portals high
And bids the pure in heart, behold their
God."

Here lies ye body of
Samuel Hopkins, son to
Mr Enoch and Mary Hopkins who died
Sept. 23d 1767
aged 1 year and 8 months.
From old cemetery, Chatham, Mass.;
Mrs. Lydia Hopkins
wife of Barzilla Hopkins
Died Jan. 5th, 1773
In her 35th year.
Mr. Elisha Hopkins
Died Feb. 1, 1741-2
Aged 53 years, 1 mo., 5 days.

(Note.—Rev. M. E. Dwight, of Plainfield, N. J., has sent me the following record: "Your statement that the name of Stephen was not often given by the early Puritans of New England, probably on account of its association with St. Stephen, has led me to consult Savage on this point. In 500 pages of Savage, taken from each one of the four volumes, I have found only ninety of this name. Fifteen of these were emigrants of whose ancestry nothing is recorded, and so may be discarded. There remain, then, seventy-five by the name of Stephen, of whose ancestry something is known, although in most instances the information is meager. Of these, however, no less than thirty-nine, or more than half, have ancestors of that name, or in a few cases uncles, by the name of Stephen. This seems to bear you out in your position that the early Puritans of New England did have a prejudice against the name of Stephen, and that when they gave it they did so as a namesake.)

The position of the descendants of John Hopkins, of Hartford, needs no indorsement from the dead or living. They are well placed at every turn, and make good all that can be said of them. Mr. Stephen Hopkins, of the Mayflower, too, records his claim, and gives us in the present day the highest State Executive in the length and breadth of the land.

The chart explains itself, but does not tell all, for the Morton line also leads back to the early colonies, to the George Morton who came out in the "Ann," and so established himself and descendants as to make it a line eagerly sought for.

"Hon. Stephen (1) and Elizabeth Hopkins
|
Deborah Hopkins (2)——Andrew Ring
|
Mary Ring (3)——John Morton
|
Captain Ebenezer Morton (4)——Mercy Foster
|
Ebenezer Morton (5)——Mrs. Sarah Cobb
|
Levy Morton (6)——Hannah Dailey
|
Rev. Daniel O. Morton (7)——Lucretia Parsons
|
Governor Levi Parsons Morton."

Many letters have come to me since the publishing of this article on Stephen Hopkins, and even with my own convictions on the subject of this relationship, I have been surprised to find how frequently the lines are carried directly from the Mayflower to the descendants of John, of Hartford, and the writers have no question but that their statements are well authenicated.

I have given before what I feel to be strong historical evidence in the repetition of the same names in both branches, and even at the risk of the tedious "twice told tale," I would like to revert to the peculiar naming of the children of Gyles Hopkins, oldest son of Stephen, of the Mayflower, the first called Stephen for his grandfather, the second John, as I call attention to, for his brother, John, of Hartford, another child, Caleb. This John names his son Stephen, his daughter Bethia, with a strong possibility of its being after his stepmother, and then Stephen in turn, calls his son Samuel. From a Mayflower descendant on Long Island comes a record which proves "Sameul's" place in both branches.

Giles Hopkins had a son, William Hopkins, who lived and died on Shelter Island, L. I., in the year of 1718. His son, Samuel Hopkins, died at Miller's Place in 1790. His son, Samuel Hopkins, of Miller's Place, died in 1807. His son, Samuel Hopkins, of Miller's Place, died in 1866, leaving a son, also Samuel (J) born in 1836, to whom I am indebted for this genealogical record.

Mr. Samuel J. Hopkins, with the kind courtesy which I have received on all sides, has hunted up for my benefit all that he could find of William Hopkins. He has an account book of William Hopkins on Shelter Island dated December, 1682, showing that he kept something like a small store, also that he made shoes for people. This book gives dates until 1710.

Mr. Hopkins also has a probate of his will, dated in 1710, which speaks of his eight children, and makes his wife, Rebecca, his sole executrix of his will. Then he has a bond dated in April, 1718, given William Hopkins (1) by his son William for the sum of $250 in place of any share in his property after his decease. The elder William died soon after he received this bond.

"In regard to the said William Hopkins, son of Giles Hopkins, born in 1660, he must have been 22 years of age when he came to Long Island and 58 when he died.

"I do not know who may be the descendants of these eight children, except Samuel Hopkins, who must have been one of the younger children.

"On the tombstone of the above Samuel Hopkins, which is in the cemetery at Mount Sinai, L. I., it is stated that he was born at Shelter Island, and was in the eightieth year of his age when he died in 1790.

"My first account of him is from deeds given him at Wading River, L. I. (then Southold), in 1743, and on to 1755; then in 1757, at Miller's Place. He was a carpenter and mason by trade.

"In this place he bought about 600 or 700 acres of land, some of which I now own.

"He had only one heir, a son, Samuel Hopkins, born in 1743, and died September, 1807. He was a deacon of our church (Congregational) and a trustee of our church society. He had two wives; two children by the first, and ten by the second, eight of whom lived to mature years and left many descendants.

"Samuel, who lived on the homestead; William, at Miller's Place (has one son living); Gilbert, lived in New York City (was a merchant, also a general in the army, and has two sons living); George, lived in New York, was a physician (one son living in New York City).

"Next Samuel Hopkins, born November 20, 1781, and died December 9, 1866. He was 85 years old, lived, died and was buried at Miller's Place. Was trustee of the church from 1807 until his death. He was a farmer, had ten children, seven of whom lived to mature years—one son and one daughter still living."

Then the Mr. Samuel J. Hopkins to whom I am a debtor, born December 3, 1836, succeeded his father as trustee of the church, and still remains as such. Married Sarah C. Hallock in 1864, and had four children—Philip H., Rupert H., Samuel Ernest and Merritt J.

This fills a blank in the lineage sent me from Cape Cod, and as it is of great value to descendants of this branch, I write it in full. It is sufficient, the history having been given, to repeat that, Giles (2), son of Stephen (1), married October 9, 1639, Katherine, daughter of Gabriel Wheldon; he died about 1690.

Their children were: Mary, born November, 1640; Stephen (3), born September 1642, married Mary Merrick; John (3), born 1643 (died an infant); Abigail (3), born 1644; Deborah (3), born 1645; Caleb (3), born 1650, died 1728; Ruth (3), born 1653; Joshua (3), born 1657, married Mary, daughter of Daniel Cole; William (3), born 1660; Elizabeth (3), born 1664.

Stephen Hopkins (3), son of Giles, and mentioned in his grandfather's will while yet an infant, born 1642, married Mary, daughter of William Merrick, of Eastham, May 22, 1667. She was admitted a member of the new church at Harwich 1700, when that place was set off from Eastham. She soon after died, and in 1701 he married Bethia Atkins. In 1665 he was allowed two kegs of powder and a grant of land on Sampson's Neck (Eastham). Removed from Eastham to what is now Brewster in 1702, on land his father gave him. He died October 10, 1718, leaving issue by first wife only.

Elizabeth, born 1668.
Stephen (4), born 1670, married Sarah Howes, died April 9, 1732.
Judah J. (4), born January, 1672.
Ruth (4), born 1674.
Nathaniel (4), born 1680.
Samuel (4), born 1682.
Joseph (4), born 1688, married Mary Mayo.
Benjamin (4), born 1689, married Rachel Lincoln.
Mary (4), born 1692, married John Maker.
Stephen Hopkins (4) (son of Stephen 3), born at Eastham, in the part now called Brewster (records in the present town of Harwich). He was of the third school division, 1725, with his brothers, Nathaniel and Joseph. He married, 1692, Sarah Howe. They had the sixteenth pew in the church. He soon turned it over to Lieut. Freeman. His wife was taken as a member of the new church about 1700. He died April 9, 1733. Their children were:
Jonathan (5), born 1693, died 1717.
Thankful (5), born April, 1700.
Elkanah (5), born August 12, 1703, died 1720.

Thomas (5), born June, 1705.
Ebenezer (5), born January, 1706, married Rebecca Crosby, 1732.
Mary (5), born 1708.
Phebe (5), born July 11, 1711.
Hannah (5), born November 4, 1714.

Ebenezer Hopkins (5), (son of Stephen 4), born 1705, married Rebecca Crosby, October 12, 1732, and recorded on the town records of Harwich, Mass., are the following:

Issue of Ebenezer and Rebecca (Crosby) Hopkins:
Mary (6), born March 20, 1732.
Eunice, born October 18, 1734.
Phebe, born April 12, 1737.
Stephen, born May 1, 1739. } Gem.
Abijah, born May 1, 1739. }

No more births occur of this line, but upon the church records of the "North parish," now in the custody of the orthodox minister of Brewster, Mass., is this entry:

"Betsy Hopkins, daughter of Ebenezer and Rebecca Hopkins, presented for baptism, November 6, 1757."

Also two more were presented, whose names do not occur in the birth records of any Cape Cod towns.

(It seems hardly possible their parents were the above Ebenezer and Rebecca.)

Caleb, son of Giles, son of Stephen (1), born 1650, died 1728, leaving issue Caleb, Nathaniel, Thomas, Thankful.

Joshua, son of Giles, son of Stephen (1), born 1657; married Mary, daughter Dan Cole. Children: John, born 1683, died 1700; Abigail, born 1686; Elisha, born 1688; Lydia, born 1692; Mary, born 1694; Joshua, born 1697; Hannah, born 1700; Phebe, born 1702.

William, son of Giles, son of Stephen, the paper says, "I have found no record of." (This, however, is the descendant of Mr. Samuel Hopkins, of Miller's Place, Long Island, so he is easily put in line.) From Stephen of the Mayflower descends Mr. Thomas S. Hopkins, of Washington; Rev. Daniel Requa Foster, of Trenton; Gov. Levi P. Morton, Mr. Charles H. Hopkins, of California; Mr. C. W. Hopkins, of Providence; Mr. E. S. Hopkins, of Providence; Mr. Philip Hopkins, of Long Island; Mr. B. C. Hopkins, of St. Albans, and, of course, a great many others, but I have given enough for those interested to make their search on.

The John Hopkins family can be readily found in many branches in both the Hartford records and the "New History of Waterbury," which has thoroughly written all that can be found in regard to this family under discussion.

Closing this article, which has been such an interesting study, I can only hope that my convictions may be authentically verified, and the descendants of father and son have the right they desire of joining the Society of Mayflower Descendants.

History certainly moves in a mysterious way, when gaining one point of knowledge opens the door for limitless additions.

With the records which accompany this article, conviction seems certainty, that Stephen Hopkins and Elder William Brewster were, if not blood relations, at least kin by marriage, and the joining the Virginia company together, afterwards the coming out on the Mayflower, were not accidents.

If Elder Brewster married, as is highly possible, Mary, daughter of Edward and —— Moody Love, the chain of circumstantial evidence to this end is strong and convincing.

Given Coventry as the starting point, the material is all before us. There lived the Dudleys, people of kindred position, like the Hopkins family, to the manor born, following in their wake were the Mompesson family, and here history enlarges, for they were relations of the Dudleys and Loves.

In the Love family there is a Gyles Love; in the Mompesson family a Constanta, the names peculiar enough to attract attention at any time; yet they were given to the children of Stephen Hopkins by his first marriage, and I never forget John, who had forbears sufficient of his name, to make the placing individually, more difficult from the number.

MORE CLAIMS.

The connection goes still further. Stephen Hopkins married for second wife Elizabeth Fisher. Into this family also married the Dudleys. Without doubt much more connection could be made by easy search into these kindred people of Coventry and that section.

The following additional Hopkins history has nothing of conjecture or search on my part in it. I have simply enjoyed the consciousness that it did not come to me until after my own article was completed and published, and I now have much that corroborates my own opinion.

I owe this to the sisters of Mr. Frederick Hopkins, of Catskill, N. Y., who died January 19, 1879, while in the midst of a very enthusiastic search for everything pertaining to his own family. In this he was greatly aided by Mr. James Usher, of No. 9 Murray street, New York, who had the only heraldry office at that time in the city, and I have to thank Rev. John Bodine Thompson for his earnest interest.

I will make no attempt at placing this as consecutive history, only take it up as records.

In 1551 Stephen Hopkins was rector of Great Wrotham and North Wrotham, in Norfolk, till 1559.

He was entered a scholar of King's College, Cambridgeshire, in 1532, afterwards became a fellow and served as provost of the college. He became a chaplain to Cardinal Pole, and was instituted March, 1556-7, to the living of East Northam, in the gift of Eton College, and he held the two benefices in unison. He resigned or was deprived of them after the accession of Queen Elizabeth, and was on account of his adherence to the Roman Catholic religion imprisoned in the Fleet, when he was released, 1561, by special order of the Queen.

Stephen Hopkins is termed Confessor to the Bishop of Aquila, the Spanish Ambassador.

"Hopkins, from Robert, through Hob and Kin (Danish). The H. R. form is Hobekyn. A family of the name have possessed a farm at Swatcliffe, County Oxon, from the thirteenth century, and thirteen successive proprietors bore the name of John. The arms of Hopkins appear to have been partly borrowed from those of Wykeham tempo John and Henry III.—From Patronymica Britannica. Stephen Hopkins was entered at King's College, Cambridge, 1532, and afterwards became a fellow, and served as vice-provost."

RESEARCHES.

"William Hopkins represented Coventry, in the 22 and 23 of Edward IV. He had sons, William, Richard, Nicholas (Sheriff of Coventry, 1561)——Burke. Nicholas married Mary (sister of Sir Giles Poole), 'Col. of Arms.' Stephen Hopkins, who came over in the Mayflower, named his oldest son Giles. He was probably the son of the above Nicholas." (F. H.)

"A Stephen Hopkins died in Warwickshire in 1611." (Usher.)

After this follows the genealogy of the Hopkins family, which, of course, is through Giles, and which has been given in this paper; only it is noticeable that Giles names one of his children after this sister, Ruth, as shown by the town records of Eastham. One branch, however, may make history, and places the beckoning of other Pilgrim descendants as to locality of settlement. James, son of Caleb and Mercy Hopkins, born at Truro, 1736, married Mahitable Freeman. They removed to Middletown, Conn., and had eight children. Caleb, their son, born at Middletown, Conn., January 2, 1780, married at Catskill, N. Y., January 18, 1811, Keturah Hill, who was born at Caleb Hopkins died at Catskill, 1852. They had twelve children, one of whom was Mr. Frederick Hopkins, who died January

19, 1879, and who made these searches.

On this same paper is a note, Mehitable Hopkins (daughter of James Hopkins, of Middletown, Conn.), said that Gov. Stephen Hopkins, of Rhode Island, was a cousin of her father, and visited her mother during her father's imprisonment in England. He was taken during the revolutionary war and sent to England and put in the prison ship, where he contracted disease, from which he died shortly after his release.

If this is true, then I make the genealogy of Stephen Hopkins, of Rhode Island, as follows:

Stephen Hopkins, of the Mayflower, 1620.
Giles Hopkins.
William Hopkins, January 9, 1660, married Abigail Whipple.
William Hopkins, married Ruth Wilkinson. Their children were Stephen (Signer and Governor) and Ezekiel, commander-in-chief of the American Navy.
Jeremiah Hopkins.
Samuel Hopkins.

All the Hopkins carried the same arms and were from the same stock.

Usher, 9 Murray st., New York,
Expert Heraldist.

The above is written on a very large sheet of stiff paper, resembling parchment. At the top there had been a seal, but little remains of it, however. The corner of the paper had a Hopkins crest stamped on it, repousee, uncolored, the burning castle with the motto "Pietas est Pax."

The pedigree of the Hopkins family, so far as traced by the papers of Mr. Frederick Hopkins, I give below:

"Stephen Hopkins was entered at Kings College, Cambridge, England, 1532.

"His son William represented Coventry, England, in the reign of Edward IV.; his son Nicholas, Sheriff of Coventry in 1561.

"Giles Hopkins, named for his uncle, son of Nicholas, probably brother of Stephen of Plymouth.

"Giles Hopkins, son of Stephen, who came over in the Mayflower, was born in 1585."

Vol. 4, page 281, for 1850 (from an abstract of the earliest wills of the probate office of Plymouth):

STEPHEN HOPKINS OF PLYMOUTH.

"His will was exhibited at court August, 1644, and dated June 6, preceding. He desires to be buried near his deceased wife. He names his son Caleb as heir apparent and executor of the will, and, together with Capt. Standish, supervisor; also another son, Gyles (and his son Stephen), daughter Constance (wife of Nicholas Snow); Deborah, Damaris, Ruth and Elizabeth.

"Witnessed by Myles Standish and William Bradford (though attached to the instrument in the record book the names of the witnesses appear to be autograph signatures).

"An inventory of his estate was taken July, 1644, by Capt. Standish. Thos. Willt and John Done. Amount, £25 14s. 5d."

Division of the estate of Stephen Hopkins: "The several portions of the children of Mr. Steven Hopkins, deceased, as they were divided equally by enumeration of the allotted portions of Deborah, Demaris and Ruth, each amounting to £9 6s. 8d. In relation to the other daughter, Elizabeth, there is a paper containing six articles, signed by Standish, Caleb Hopkins and Richard Sparrow, being an agreement by which she was 'put out' to Sparrow until she should come of the age of 19 years, or until marriage, and in consideration of the weakness of the child, and her inability to perform such service, as they acquit their charges, in bringing of her up, Sparrow was to receive into his hands her portion of the estate provided if 'Goodwife Sparrow' should die Standish and her brother might dispose of Elizabeth as they thought best."

Witnessed by William Paddy and Thos. Willet.

Next follows a paper by Sparrow, promising payment, in consideration of the above, and witnessed by Paddy, and a receipt by Standish, dated May 19, 1647

Volume 5, page 53, for 1851, contains a pedigree of Samuel Hopkins, of Newport, R. I. (descendant of Giles).

Prof. J. W. Moore, of Lafayette College, Easton, Pa., furnishes a record which finds fitting place among these people—New York Hist. and Gen. Register, Vol. XLVII., Snow Genealogy. Henry F. Waters, in his "Genealogical Gleanings in England" (Register, vol. 39, page 166), states that Joseph Walker, of St. Margaret, city of Westminister, gentleman, in his will, dated February 13, 1666, proved February 27, 1666, bequeaths "to my kinswoman, Mary Snow, wife of Nicholas Snow, citizen and armourer, of London, whom I nominate executrix." Also, the will of George Upham, Windiscombe, Somerset, dated 1653, mentions testator's brother-in-law, Nicholas Snow. This Nicholas Snow and Mary, his wife, may have been the parents of our Nicholas. He named his eldest daughter Mary. He died at Eastham November 15, 1676. He married, in Plymouth, Constance Hopkins, daughter of Mr. Stephen Hopkins and a former wife.

To continue from the papers of Mr. Frederick W. Hopkins:

"R. H. Bingham, Civil Engineer, city of Albany, Surveyor and Engineer's Office,
"Albany, 27 Dec., 1876.
"F. W. Hopkins, Esq.:

"Dear Sir—The motto above the crest, Interprimos (among the first), shows that the Hopkins family were placed in the first rank of the Commoners of England, or what was known as the untitled nobility.

"The crest, a castle or fortress in flames, was granted during the time of Louis XV. of France, a fortress of which King was taken and burned by the Queen's Royal American Rangery, commanded by a Hopkins of the Arms. In heraldry a chevron was never given for anything but military

achievement, and so is accounted the most honorable of all heraldic charges.

"The chevron, having blazoned in it the three red roses, shows that the arms were granted by one of the English kings of the house of Lancaster, whose badge was the red rose, for distinguished services during the wars of the roses, between the rival houses of York and Lancaster. How the pistols came I know not, but presume it was because the Hopkinses were a fighting race, to whom weapons of war were peculiarly applicable. The motto under the shield, 'Aut suavitate aut vi,' translates 'Either by courtesy or main force.' Truly yours,

"Portcullis, Pursuivant-at-Arms."

Another paper of Mr. Frederick Hopkins's tells its own story. The sheet is rather over unusual length, of legal paper, with accompanying arms at the head.

"The worshipfull Sampson Hopkins, of the City of Coventry, that had formerly served for Sheriff and Alderman of London, having been also Mayor of Coventry, departed this mortal life at his house, in Coventry, upon Wednesday, the XXII day of January, 1622, and his body lyeth buried in the parish church of St. Michaell, in Coventry. He married two Wives, the first was Katherine, daughter of Mr. Smart, of Essex, of kindred to Sir Ned Tracy Smart, Knight, now living; by her he had issue William, John and Sampson, and three daughters, Elyoner, the nowe wife of Mr. Thomas Vicares, of Herefordshire, by descent, and nowe Merchant of London, and hath issue, 3 daughters, married Mr. John Gayer, of London, Merchant.

"The second wife of the said Mr. Sampson Hopkins is Jane, daughter of Mr. Richard Butts, of Ham-Curt, in the County of Surrey, Gent, and by her he hath issue 2 Sonnes, Samuel and Richard, and 2 daughters, Jane and Anne. The executors of his last Will and Testament are the said Jane, his Widdowe, William Hopkins, his eldest Sonne, and Isack Walden, of Coventry; the premises is testified by the above named Thomas Vicares, who hath subscribed his name.

"Thomas Vicares."

"The above certificate is faithfully extracted from the Record of the College of Arms, London, and examined therewith, this fifth day of February, 1875.

"George Harrison,
"Windsor Herald,
"Registrar."

Too much is possible, to leave the Hopkins family as ended with any willingness. The honors they are entitled to come home to many of us, and, speaking for myself, the old people of this blood it has been my pleasure to meet and live with would have thought no language could convey more than they are worthy of; indeed, they would hardly allow that the half had been told. They never forgot to put the "cousin" before the name when speaking of President Mark Hopkins, and while I with historical eagerness long to place his ancestor, John, of Hartford, as son of Stephen, of the Mayflower, I have no modesty in feeling I am honoring the pilgrim.

The large arms given were in the possession of Capt. Caleb Hopkins, Jr., who died in 1791, and whose tombstone is in Copp's Hill Burying Ground, Boston. A niece of his, who was also an adopted child, inherited his money and possessions, taking the coat-of-arms to the old Catskill homestead, where she resided with her brother, Caleb Hopkins. To this home she brought many valuable heirlooms—such as silver tea set, tankards, porringers, brocade dresses, minatures, ornaments, jewelry, fans, etc.—all quaint evidences of the days more than a hundred years before. As she sought this brother's protection in 1823, the century accredited would place these treasures as in easy connection with the Pilgrim's children.

What these "old comers" had they kept, and it is authenticated history to tell of a ring found under the door step of James Hopkins, of Middletown, Conn., about fifty years ago, which had laid there for sixty years and was found by workmen who were tearing down the house, and forwarded to the old home on Catskill Creek, where one meets at every turn stories of the past, of generations of garrets never given out to ruthless hands, but guarded with their tales with the reverence of self respect. The ring told the story of the early loved and lost, engraved as it was in deep cut letters, "M.

Hopkins, ob. 6th February, 1749, aged 18 months."

It was made in memoriam, and passed on to the next infant girl, who was likewise named Mary.

"My prophetic soul" leads me to hope that by the time the third part of the pamphlet is written more of the Hopkins family can be given as a supplement. I leave them unwillingly, but feel that I have given much to their history. Perhaps some one else will finish the story. To whoever it may be I say "God speed."

Note—Prof. Hedge, so long of Harvard, was a descendant of Stephen Hopkins.

This tombstone, taken from the graveyard at Harwinton, Conn., may be of historical use, and certainly will give some idea of records of that period:

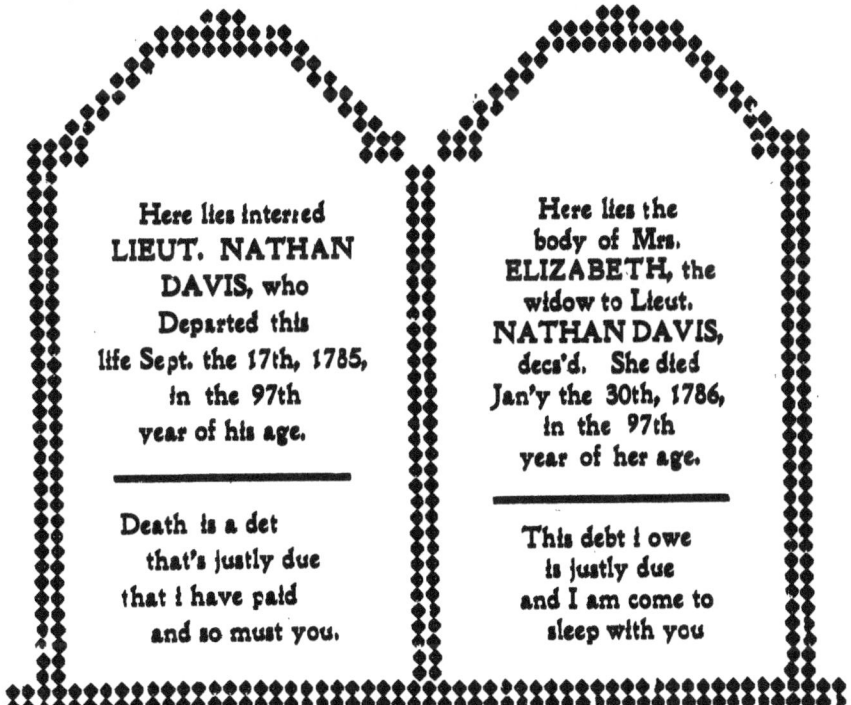

Here lies interred LIEUT. NATHAN DAVIS, who Departed this life Sept. the 17th, 1785, in the 97th year of his age.

Death is a det that's justly due that I have paid and so must you.

Here lies the body of Mrs. ELIZABETH, the widow to Lieut. NATHAN DAVIS, dec's'd. She died Jan'y the 30th, 1786, in the 97th year of her age.

This debt I owe is justly due and I am come to sleep with you

Perhaps parents of the Sarah Davis who married Hezekiah P. Hopkins, son of Ebenezer and Mary Butler Hopkins, as told in the record.

END OF PART I.

PART II.

Signers of the Mayflower Compact.

JOHN TILLEY, Sixteenth Signer.

John Tilley, for some cause unknown, does not strike the same responsive chord as John Howland, and though he would make still another ancestor on the Mayflower, the line does not generally begin with him.

True, his young daughter married John Howland, but he was not there to accord consent or watch over the welfare of the Elizabeth so dear to her father's heart.

A record sent me claims he left a son, but I have never been fortunate enough to prove this.

The very mention of Elizabeth Tilley Howland's name arouses the traditional spirit of her descendants to call out with one voice, loud enough to penetrate the mystery which seems to prevent the establishment of the records of generations—from which they have never swerved one iota, even in the face of the assertion that Bradford makes that Gov. Carver left no descendants—and claim their own.

For my part, there has never been a wavering thought; I believe the old Hartford Bible tells the tale, and my sorrow at not being able to carry the entire weight of conviction, when I wrote of Carver and Howland, was rendered doubly great, as I found in my notebook, but, sad to say, without any authority attached, that John Tilley married, in 1615, Bridget Van der Velde!

All search for the lost connection was without avail, and I began to feel that I must yield to the pressure of circumstances too strong for me.

SUCCESS.

Reluctantly I made what was to be my last effort, and the reward is before me.

There are tides in the affairs of history, as in all vital matters, and by some magnetic association, within the last few weeks, many claims to Mayflower descent have come to me, starting from John Tilley. I accept it as an omen, and put forth the authentic history, which may give to powerful, widespread, historical tradition the value I feel it deserves.

Mourt, in his "Relation of Plymouth," p. 14, note 41, tells that "Edward Tilley came with his wife Ann, and two children that were their cousins, Henry Samson and Humility Cooper."

"He was probably also elder brother of John, who brought over his wife and daughter Elizabeth. All of both families died in the first mortality except Henry Samson and Elizabeth Tilley, the former of whom married Ann Plummer, and had nine children; the latter John Howland, and had ten."

Mourt's "Relation," page 44, says: "John Tilley—I find in the Leyden MS. records: "This February, 1615, John Telley, silk worker, of Leyden, married Bridget Van der Velde,' which may be the hint of the man's occupation and affiliation. Bradford does not give his wife's Christian name."

HARTFORD BIBLE.

Again the old Hartford Bible comes to my rescue, which gives John Howland's marriage to "John Tilley's daughter, Elizabeth, granddaughter of Gov. Carver!"

As the Howland marriage took place, according to the official account of the "Society of the Mayflower Descendants," in 1621, and the Pilgrims started for Holland in 1609, John Tilley's marriage to Gov. Carver's daughter must have occurred before they left England, else Elizabeth Tilley, the child, would not have been 12 years of age in 1621, if she were born after their arrival in the Low Countries.

Then "Carver and Fuller joined the Pilgrims in Leyden," which lessens the time.

NOT TWO JOHN TILLEYS.

This entirely explodes the assumption that there were two John Tilleys, one who came to America with the colonists, and another who married Bridget Van der Velde.

Bradford wrote only after his arrival in New England, and the "Relation," edited by his brother-in-law, George Morton, who was left behind, by the unseaworthiness of the Speedwell, was sent out to him, inserting telling that the vessel was seized by the pirates, to secure the cargo of furs, etc., forwarded by the Pilgrims to the Merchant Adventurers, as an installment in payment of their bond.

The manuscript being utterly worthless to the pirates, with a little sympathy perhaps with the situation, ultimately reached its destination.

So the John Tilley who married, as Bradford put it, Van der Velde, was our Pilgrim, and she was not the mother of our Elizabeth Tilley Howland!

For my own part I am satisfied, and Bridget Van der Velde will no longer haunt me on every side as an obstacle to be overcome.

The leaf may be turned down.

JOHN TILLEY'S DEATH.

"John Tilley took the original of his death," on the expedition of the "ten principal men;" his work in the colonies was daily, hourly, until the seal of eternal rest was placed upon him, and if granted knowledge in his closing hours, died happy in the consciousness that his young daughter had a natural home with her grandfather, Gov. Carver.

Bradford was only eighteen when he left England, too young to be interested in much of the personal history of those he probably was surrounded by, even if he knew "John Carver, sonne of James Carver, Lincolnshire, Yeoman." He was fully occupied with his own troubles, repeated imprisonments, which were part of his history incidental to joining the Pilgrims in Holland.

Graver matters filled his mind than the parentage of John Tilley's daughter. She was in good hands, why heed things that in no way concerned him—the mother probably not in evidence.

John Tilley's spirit of adventure has fallen upon one, at least, of his descendants, and while the Pilgrim succumbed to the privations more than he could endure, Gen. A. W. Greely, the Arctic explorer, watched over by the God of his Pilgrim forefathers, even when the portals of heaven seemed wide open for his entrance, was saved by the naval relief expedition to do good to the country, which is his on a claim of more than two centuries.

His descent will be very important from the variety of names and many locations which after all are sectional.

I. John Tilley's first wife, Elizabeth (Carver?); second, Bridget Van der Velde, died 1621.

II. Elizabeth Tilley, born 1607, died December 21, 1687, married August 14, 1623 (?), John Howland.

III. Hope Howland married before 1646 John Chipman, born 1615, died July 8, 1684.

IV. Hope Chipman, born August 13, 1652, died July, 1728, married (1) John Huckens 1649-1678; she married (2), March 1, 1683, Jonathan Cobb (son of Henry Cobb, of Plymouth, 1629), born April 10, 1660, died at Middlesborough, Mass., October 8, 1727.

V. Samuel Cobb, born February 23 (baptized April 6), 1684, died October, 1767, married about 1708 Abigail Stewart, born 1686, died September, 1766, "aged 80."

VI. Chipman Cobb, born March 5, 1708-9, died after October, 1775, at or near Falmouth, now Portland, Me., married in 1731 Elizabeth Ingersoll (daughter of Elisha Ingersoll and ———— Mary), born July 12, 1705, died before 1765.

VII. Andrew Cobb, born March 27, 1734, at Falmouth, Maine, married 1754, Hannah Green (daughter of Daniel Green); Andrew Cobb, married (2) April 21, 1804, Hannah, widow of Moses Fowler.

VIII. Andrew Cobb, born February 7, 1764, at Gorham, Maine, died February 22, 1822, married (1) December, 1782, Betsy Irish (daughter of Joseph Irish and Hannah Doane), born about 1764, died after 1800. Andrew Cobb, married (2) December 10, 1808, Mary Cobb (widow of Ebenezer Bangs), daughter of Jedediah Cobb and Reliance Paine.

IX. Samuel Cobb, born March 11, 1785, at Gorham, Maine, died December, 1854, at Bartlett, N. H., married August 12, 1812, at Baltimore, Md., Eleanor Neale (daughter of John Neale and Mary Lona), born August 16, 1793, at Baltimore, died August 22, 1882, at Webster, Mass.

X. Frances Dunn Cobb, born April 20, 1819, in Limerich, Mass. (now Maine), yet living in 1897, married (2) October 30, 1842, at Newburyport, Mass., by Rev. Darius Forbes, John Balch Greely (son of Stephen Greely and Betsy Balch), born July, 1802, at Newburyport, Mass., died October, 1864, at Newburyport, Mass.

XI. Adolphus Washington Greely, born March 27, 1844, yet living, 1897, married June 20, 1878, at San Diego, Cal., by Rev. Mr. Camp, Henrietta Cruger Hudson Nesmith (daughter Thomas L. Nesmith and Maria Antoinette Gale.

Another line from John Tilley is in entirely different families, and makes many connections with the Nantucket early settlers:

Starting with Mrs. James L. Morgan, Jr. (Alice M. Hill Morgan).

John J. Hill, who married in Albany, N. Y., September 3, 1840, Mary Elizabeth McCurdy, born July 21, 1822, daughter of Isaac McCurdy and Mary Warner, of Albany, married April 28, 1821.

Mary Warner, daughter of William Smith Warner, and Mary Wood, of Albany, married 1798.

Mary Wood, daughter of James Wood, of Albany, and Lydia Swain, of Nantucket, married 1780.

Lydia Swain, daughter of William Swain, Nantucket, and Lydia Gorham, of Barnstable, married February 14, 1750.

Lydia Gorham, of Barnstable, daughter of Stephen Gorham, of Barnstable, and Elizabeth Gardner, of Nantucket, married December 25, 1703, Stephen Gorham.

Stephen Gorham, son of John Gorham, of Barnstable, and Mary Otis, of Hingham, married February 24, 1674.

John Gorham (2), son of Capt. John Gorham, of Plymouth, married Desire Howland, of Plymouth, 1643, daughter of John Howland.

John Howland, of Plymouth, married in 1621, Elizabeth, daughter of John Tilley, of the Mayflower.

John Tilley married (1) Elizabeth, daughter of Gov. Carver (?) (2) Bridget Vandervelde.

FIFTEENTH SIGNER.

Edward Tilley.
DIED FIRST WINTER.

Ann Tilley
His Wife.
DIED FIRST WINTER.

FRANCIS COOK, Seventeenth Signer.

With all the sentiment and history attached to Scrooby, the home of the Separatists, it was largely dependent upon the surrounding villages for its congregation and connection with the world.

The post led directly, according to its route, to Edinburgh, and the side issues were by special arrangement with those in charge. No sudden intercourse sprang up from propinquity. There were deep-laid plans for their interchange of intention, and while passengers along the road carried knowledge of what they were effecting, they were dealing with the positive.

"The first body of worshipers, to the number of one hundred or more, in 1567, occupied a hall in London, in Anchor lane, belonging to the company of the plumbers, and held service according to their own methods."

So London makes the first claim, an easy headquarters from which to disseminate their form of doctrine and worship.

Gainsborough, in the north, offered a valuable field of action, or rather quiet waiting, being in more direct communication with Holland by water, a place now spoiled by the modern iron works, and described by George Eliot, in "The Mill on the Floss," under the name of St. Oggs.

From this section came the Cookes, who give fine record in England, tangible and acceptable.

Rev. Mr. Baines, in his "History of the Parish of Blyth," York, England, gives two families of this name, and fortunately the one he records as knowing nothing about is of no importance to us, but Francis Cooke, the Mayflower Pilgrim, is announced as from Blyth, a parish adjoining Austerfield, which means Scrooby. Brewster, Bradford and Robinson, the strong components of the after history, all are searching for.

The living man may elude us, but the receptacle for the dead—the place where the silent man returns to kindred on being placed in mother earth, carries conviction—so the record gives us:

"Here lyeth body of Edward Cooke (in St. Michael's Church Belfrays), allied, and long tyme brought up at the feet of that famous and worthy learned man of his tyme, Sir Edward Coke (Cooke) Knight Lord Chief Justice of England, and of his Majesties most honorable privy counsell."

This relation is claimed by the descendants of Francis Cooke of the Mayflower, and the same church gives another testimony of one who from similarity of names, and appropriateness of time, might be our emigrant's father.

"Here lyeth Francis Cooke, late of cittye of Yorke gentleman, one of the attorneys of the common pleas at Westminister, who departed this lyfe to the memory of God, the 26th day of May, anno Dom 1583."

This is not inconsistent with the statement that the father and grandfather of Francis Cooke were silk mercers.

Always the guilds to interpret these connections, and prevent the detractions supposed to result from labor in foreign countries, though why, with the light of history before us, I cannot understand.

Among the old German nobility there was but a step from the counting room to the offices surrounding royalty, and, far stranger, from the kitchen and linen closet of the thrifty housewife to personal attendance upon queen and princess.

A person can be no better than the times in which he or she lives.

There is always a doubt to contend with when placing Francis Cooke as to the time of his espousing the doctrines of the Separatists, but he was in the list of those designated as "exiles from Scrooby," joining Brewster and Bradford in worship there, going with them to Leyden, and so on to their haven of rest on Cape Cod.

Scrooby had once been the hunting seat of the Archbishop of York. The palace it contained was a rather pretentious structure "built of timber with front of brick, approached by a broad flight of stone steps, had two court yards, and was defended by a moat."

Religion being at all times a controlling power to the fact that under Protestantism it was not needed as a hunting seat, and the well-disposed inclinations of Archbishops Grindal and Sandys, history owes that this property was put in the charge of the "senior Brewster as a man of official character."

There is a natural indication that the ancestors of the Cookes were Romanists. So it follows from all form to no form would be the leading, and the change finds Francis Cooke making choice on conviction of the simplest mode of worship, the personal communication between his Maker and himself, needing no intermediary to plead his cause.

The parish records of Blyth attest to their manorial rights; also to the ownership of the convent of Blyth as early as 1540. They furnish at the same time dates of the marriages, births and deaths of the Cookes for many generations.

Francis Cooke was born in 1577, and, following the unerring hand of Providence, fled to Holland, with Pastor Robinson, and, for some cause of affinity or favoritism, became an inmate of his family—his personal charge.

The social position of the Pilgrims has always been a matter of controversy. I bring our Pilgrim from a manor house, and cannot comprehend in these days, when the "knowledge of good and evil" seems used to break down the statements and traditions associated with the past, in which the modern majority have no part, how they can dispose of the claims of these early times, and believe that Archbishop Laud and the throne of England would have persistently followed up with their persecutions a body of unknown, unfeared men, devoid of position and power, only what in England would have placed them without the pale of consideration, members of the "lower class."

Their descendants have grown with the times; they are the best of to-day, as their ancestors, the Pilgrims and early colonists, were of theirs. Through this inheritance they have recorded themselves at the ballot box, upholding the dignity of the nation, proving their right to citizenship, backed by the Society of Mayflower Descendants, Sons of the Colonial Wars, Sons of the Revolution, of the War of 1812, and the living pride as saving their country's honor in the civil war.

The large house of Pastor Robinson, in Leyden, used also as a place of worship, under the restrictions of the Dutch Government, which required "new and unusual sects to worship in private houses, which were as large as churches," was the home of Francis Cooke, and as one of the little congregation gathered there, came Hester the Walloon, later to be his wife, and after they were of those who kept house in the twenty-one houses erected in "the large garden," which ran back 125 feet, though the width not being given, the size is left wholly to imagination.

Francis Cooke, known at Cape Cod as a carpenter, seems to have had no part in the building of these Leyden houses. In all I can find they are attributed wholly to "Wm. Jessop, who built the small houses in Bell lane, adjoining Pastor Robinson."

Why Hester, the wife of Francis Cooke, is not further recorded time may tell. She is always in evidence, yet is only known as a Walloon from the southern province of Belgium. People with a sad tale to unfold of their persecutions, loss of country, separation from kindred, all of which wore upon their spirits and strength. Thousands flocked to Holland, and there the text was the same for all, only a difference of language and sectional interests to divide them. The value of this contingent can never be doubted. They brought their references with them and proved them authentic.

Their expert knowledge of the industrial arts, quick conceptions and ability to turn their hands to anything that presented itself, willingness to economize and spend themselves in any direction that was for the general good, naturally made them welcome.

Each country gave them a different name; they denominated themselves Gaulois, the Dutch placed them as Wallecke, and the English, from their locating on the River Wall, in Holland, called them Walloons.

Their language is a dialect different from the French and German, as well as the Flemish, and is said to resemble the old French of the thirteenth century.

The fact that these are the people who applied to Carleton for permission to emigrate to Virginia, a request denied them from their determination to govern themselves without any dictation by the company, and their subsequent attainment of their object though the management of wise Jesse de Forest, shows the close connection with New Amsterdam, proves their community of interests.

Hester was not one to meet trouble with trouble. Going to Leyden was a necessity. That the "wind had been tempered" to her well being was a source of gratitude. The shadows that started with her life in Holland were all dissipated by the great good that came to her, and while the prosperity of the change was not too much for her to grasp, it certainly opened for her a new and broader sphere of action, gave a home where she reigned supreme.

As the Pilgrim Separatists reached Holland in 1609, and Francis Cooke's wife was of the Walloon contingent worshiping in Pastor Robinson's house, it is a natural supposition that they were married about ten years before seeking their new home. No one can imagine Hester a figurehead during that time. With her French proclivities it is only fair to estimate her as contributing much to the home life so necessary to man's well being, both as a matter of temper and act.

She had learned the royal road, and the receipts of the day carried out under her wise supervision would suit the educated palate of the present.

With the mutton "done to a turn," the juices reserved for man's consumption, what better could be asked than Hester's effort "To fry cucumbers for mutton sauce you must brown some butter in a pan and cut the cucumbers in thin slices, drain them from the water, then fling them into the pan, and when they are fried brown, put in a little pepper and salt, a bit of onion and gravy, and let them stew together, and squeeze in some lemon; shake them well, and put under your mutton."

The thought of this for Sunday dinner would have made the closing of the church services welcome to even Francis Cooke, and reflecting that "the poor quality of the water in Holland confined the Pilgrims almost exclusively to beer sold at a penny a quart as their daily beverage," increased the "appetite which waits on digestion."

Francis, too, was willing to provide against the physical waste sure to come from his share in the duties of the little colony there assembled before he retired to rest. He knew the "forty winks" were impossible, but whatever the nature of the exercise he was to take, wise Francis would hurry up if he knew Hester had opened her book to where it told her how "To make a Poloc."

"Take a pint of rice, boil it in as much water as will cover it; when your rice is half boiled, put in your fowl, with a small onion, a blade or two of mace, some whole pepper and some salt; when 'tis enough put the fowl in the dish and pour the rice over it."

The variety in the larder was not great, but Hester was an artist, and her concoctions gave infinite zest to small means.

When her bell for meals sounded she knew she could begin to dish the viands. Francis never stopped to gossip, when that hour arrived.

THE SPEEDWELL.

The old, yet ever new, story of the Pilgrim start from Delfthaven in the Speedwell, and her return as unseaworthy, claims much sympathy even at this distant day, as Bradford tells us: "So, after they had tooke out such provision as ye other ship could well stow, and concluded both what number and what persons to send back, they made another sad parting, ye one ship going back to London, and ye other was to proceede on her viage. Those that went bak were for the most parte such as were willing so to doe, either out of some discontente or feare they conceived of ye ill success of ye viage, seeing so crosses befale, and the yeare time so far spente; but others in regarde to their own weakness, and charge of many yonge children were thought least usefull, and most unfite to bear ye brunte of this hard adventure, unto which worke of God, and judgement of their brethren they were contented to submit."

This tells the pathetic tale of the story of life; no place for the weak or young; each one must be "up and doing, with a heart for any fate," but those who could not must bear loneliness and separation. Athletes wanted then, not for record, but serious labor.

THE DEPARTURE.

Those on board the ship, who, with straining eyes, were watching the dear ones, left ashore for reason of infirmity, as time proceeded, realized "if they looked behind them ther was ye mighty ocean, which they had passed, and now was a maine barr, and goulfe to separate them from all ye civill parts of ye world."

Everything points to the belief that all of Francis Cooke's family were to come over in the Speedwell, but misfortune separated them, and left Hester Cooke, in "charge of many yonge children" to follow when the time was auspicious. Only John to go with his father as some compensation for the severed family ties, he, one writer says, was young enough to be led ashore by the Pilgrim's hand.

No wonder his after association with John was so near and dear, through all of the records, the only one spoken of as "his son" from time to time in connection with his father.

FAMILY POSITION.

The founder of the family of Cookes in this country comes to us in his power unawares. He was one of the Pilgrims who immediately occupied a very important place, and while the conviction of his value only dawns upon one as they read continuously, the fact exists, his record accumulates, and proves that he was behind the throne wielding immense influence.

Pursuing the even tenor of his way, his strength grows day by day, until the consciousness comes that he is guiding the "ship of state" with the rare judgment of his strong personality.

Valuable as his record is, it seems so general and wide spreading that everything is taken as a matter of course, hardly requiring recognition.

He and his descendants held firm grip on positions of weight and trust all through their life in Plymouth colony and the surrounding towns.

ARRIVAL OF THE FAMILY.

Hester, wife of Francis Cooke, came out in the famous Anee with her children, and though the time between her arrival and that of the Mayflower was only little over two years, the intervening anxiety had been serious, telling sorely upon the waiting. Still with hope beckoning them, their ship life must have been one of pleasure. All the passengers had the same end in view—one great, eager desire to reach Plymouth and the loved ones, trusting to find them ready and waiting for the deep love they were bringing.

There is the "ring of the true metal" about all of the Cookes. They asked no favors, had no special pleading for preference in any respect, but they always drew the "lucky numbers" in the land divisions.

The rotating wheel in which their lots were cast placed them where they would like to be, and Francis Cooke occupied a house on Leyden street adjoining the residences of Edward Winslow and Isaac Allerton, a distinction of propinquity which places his social position on record. Had he not been acceptable to those magnates there would have been some means devised to prevent or remove his claim. Intercourse during the hours of labor was inevitable, but the familiarity of close residence could be averted, and no questions asked or answered. The present, when written, will tell very much the same history—everything possible if one only knows the right man to approach and secure.

MILITARY CLAIMS.

With the name of Cooke, wherever located the wide world over, comes a strong following of a military character. Infrequent as their intercourse with Europe was, they managed to keep themselves cognizant of affairs abroad, and some of the early emigrants returned to England, enlisted under Cromwell's banner, and died fighting for his cause.

Cromwell's hold upon the Pilgrims and pioneer settlers was of great power, perhaps accentuated by antagonism to the Stuarts, from whose hands they had surely not received many favors, but certainly they responded to Cromwell's beckoning. Love is a great power, but there is a force to hatred that overcomes many obstacles.

The Cooke family had cause for this repetition of military prowess. They carried arms in the Holy wars, and the Courtois Collection gives them as

"Walter Cok went to the Holy Land, 1191. Richard Cok went to the Holy Land, 1191." Add to these Wm. Henry Cooke, Recorder of Oxford, Judge of County Courts, a Magistrate and Deputy Lieutenant of Herefordshire, who wrote three volumes of Collections tow..d the History and Antiquities of County Hereford, in continuance of Duncomb's "History"; also that Sir Anthony Cooke, a learned man, was tutor of King Edward VI. in 1543, and I lead up to the natural inheritance of the special gifts which the Cookes used for the benefit of "Plymouth Colony."

Localities are right, others must search the lines. Our Cookes were prominent people, not great warriors, but scenting the hostilities from afar, ready and willing for the station they were assigned to, with a little token in their hand for presentation to the first Indian who approached.

Doing their part well, was the mark of their birthright, they knew no contrasting life.

There was always another leaf of them to read, no matter how nearly the colonists thought they had closed the book, and sealed it with finis.

Cooke record accumulates with great rapidity in England; in 1612 a Cooke was Chancellor of the Irish Exchequer, Sir Richard Cooke Secretary for Foreign Affairs in the Cabinet of Charles I., 1635; in 1462 a Cooke was Lord Mayor of London, an elective position, all remember, as for 800 years this office was filled by the vote of the various powerful guilds.

Again, Sir Thomas Cook, of Worcestershire, founded Worcester College, at Oxford, and Sir Thomas Cook, of Middlesex, to keep up the connection with the "first comers of our country," was governor of the East India Company.

The history of Essex, England, supplies Cookes ad libitum, the men of position by birth and marriage, the females completing the history, marrying well, and themselves recorded as altogether lovely, strong of intellect, reproducing in their children the best of both parents.

In the army, the navy, the church, in literature and the learned professions, in politics, in the pulpit, in the mother country it would be asking little of them with such a backing to be much to the land of their adoption and birth, whatever the demands it might make.

With the arrival of the Ann, and not only Hester, wife of Francis Cooke, and their family, but so many others of the Pilgrim following, increasing the members in the little family of the colonists, came the call for room, the expansion also demanded by their experience in the yield of the land, Plymouth being notedly barren.

From there to Rocky Nook, on Jones River, a place within the limits of Kingston, was Francis Cooke's next move. Here he made a home in its full meaning, bringing up his children to bear their part in everything connected with the needs and regulations of all parts of the colony.

Studying this man's character all through his life, it is easy to see a certain exclusiveness of association, always being with his own, as represented by his family, and the early inhabitants who brought with them known credentials from the mother country.

HIS AGE.

History places Francis Cooke as about 40 years of age when he reached Plymouth; so he had passed "his green and salad days" before he was made Freeman in 1633, 1634 referee in settlement of various affairs between members of the colony.

And in 1636, as was usual with people of "high degree," received an apprentice, John Harmon, son of Edward Harmon, of London, tailor, for the indenture period of seven years.

These records all through this early life accentuate the history of that period as to the relation of master and servant, as this connection is often erroneously placed according to modern view. Inherited regard for the customs and laws of England must continue with this people, and they had no feeling in regard to the terms that were in general accepted usage in the homes of their ancestors.

CONTINUOUS DUTIES.

Until 1640 this Pilgrim's name appears constantly in some capacity performing important duties for the government, in which year he was associated with Howland, Pratt and Cash in deciding the boundaries of the lands of Mr. Thomas Prence and Clement Biggs, at Eel River, and in the same year received a large grant with his son John, "bounding on the North River."

Belonging to the "sound currency" party, the gold spoon in his mouth, it was, as is traditional for people thus born, further filled from 1642 to '48 by another grant of land at "A. Medden" by Jones River.

His party being right, himself in full sympathy with "the powers that be," he was continually a committee of arbitration, in 1659 appearing in settlement of land boundaries.

In 1662 he, with his son John and others, was allowed to settle upon a tract of land purchased for a new settlement. This comprised the old town of Dartmouth (now New Bedford), which in 1652 belonged to thirty-six persons, and it is "probable the earliest settlers came from the English township of that name." There is no record of his making it his home, he only seems to have held proprietorship, and John reigned in his stead, the Pilgrim father dying in the following year, aged 87 years.

APPRECIATION OF THE PILGRIM FOREFATHERS.

Weary and worn as the little band were with the exactions of the adventurers, they certainly won on their good behavior, and if there could be a reward, in their opinion they had it, in the letters received from them by the "Ann and Little James," where they encourage them by saying, "Let it not be grievous to you that you have been instruments to break the ice for others who come after with less difficulty; the honour shall be yours to the world's end" (New England Memorial, p. 102).

The verdicts of 1600 and 1800 are the same, in the latter century given, perhaps, with no knowledge of the previous record. For all the intervening years, the world's vote is on the same platform.

THE STORY OF THE TIMES.

The history of a man to be correct cannot be written without an understanding of his environment and restrictions. The history of the day is many-sided; one must read between the lines after all possible research to get at the true inwardness of affairs, and understand the springs of action. In writing for my own part I feel that I am breaking ground under the most favorable circumstances, for a continuance of this search by other historians, giving my suggestions, not assertions.

So I read in "Young's Chronicles" the story of the times where he says: "I think it is a wise course for all cold complexions to come to take physic in New England, for a cup of New England air is better than a whole draught of Old England's ale. Here are also abundance of turkeys, often killed in the woods, far greater than our English turkeys, and exceeding fat, sweet and fleshy, for here they have abundance of feeding all the year long, as strawberries (in summer all places are full of them) and all manner of berries and fruits."

Then, later, Cotton Mather takes up the wondrous tale, and observes: "We New Englanders do dwell in so cold and clear an air, that more of the smaller stars may be seen by our considerers than in many other places."

From this point of view, there is no drain upon our sympathies, to be sure, in regard to the turkeys as a sole means of satisfying hunger. One might recall the bet made that a man could not eat a quail for a certain number of days in succession without resentment, but "all manner of berries and fruits" would suffice for variety as appeasing the appetites of even such toilers in this "clear, cold air," as we know the colonists to have been.

The contrasting story, as told by Bradford, returns us to a knowledge of their hardships, and one's sorrow increases with the realization of the cause. The record reads: "The best dish we could present them with is a lobster or a piece of fish, without bread, or anything else but a cup of fair spring water, and the long continuance of this diet, with our labors abroad, has somewhat abated the freshness of our complexion, but God gives us health."

Poor Bradford, in this low physical state, could not divest himself of the natural desire of mankind, which in the old times included womankind, that they should retain the fresh complexions of youth and plenty.

The guns were loaded ready for action, but it was awfully grewsome and creepy at night in bleak New England, the wind sighing and screaming as if a departed spirit had returned to haunt the world and vent the animosities of earth on the culprit; wolves scenting for prey, and the Indians acting as omnipresent sentries.

For them the ammunition must be saved. Hunger told upon their spirits; but they still lived.

FRANCIS COOKE'S DEATH.

The death of this Pilgrim was an irreparable loss—a man of judgment, of decisive, though not arbitrary action, who could see both sides of the question, even when the necessity of action, on conviction, might be against his interests.

A MAN'S WILL.

The difficulty historians often experience in placing a man's children from the fact they are not mentioned in his will, may perhaps be solved by remembering that a man owning tracts of land in various locations, as a son grows to maturity, and under the influence of the bright, haunting smile of the girl he loves, is ready to "set up for himself," gives him a farm and the paternal blessing as his share of the estate. So further notice of him as an inheritor was unnecessary, and in many instances he is for the time, at least, so far from the "old homestead" that younger members of the family, with the many intervening "olive branches" of those days, scarcely know of this brother's existence.

LACK OF INTERCOURSE.

Frequent intercourse was neither expected or possible.

Every neighbor going to the "cattle show" would be the medium for home news, and was sure of a welcome when waited on by the deputation from the various families, eager to elicit knowledge of the well being of the distant dear ones.

No opportunity for privacy, the secrets of all hearts were laid bare, without the slightest compunction or delicacy, and if the non-resident were detained any length of time by business, a meeting would be called, that, by joint wisdom, fitting advice might be returned as to their children's action in affairs deemed wholly their own.

A parent continued to be a parent, if the child was as strong as Samson and big as Goliath. Only self-reliance as to labor was required.

ACTION OF THE COURT.

If repression has the counter effect of forming character, the chance of development was strongly in the hands of the Pilgrims.

"The General Court, always desiring to have a fatherly care over her subjects, concluded that a few sumptuary laws were required for the welfare of our good fathers and mothers, and that there should be no mistake or misunderstanding about the matter, they enacted a law to regulate their costume, and also to regulate their diet, by forbidding the use of cake or buns, except at burials, marriages, or such like occasions; the wearing of all ornaments, gold, silver or silk lace, was forbidden, as well as hatbands, ruffs, also embroidery or needle work, and the wearing of long hair was an abomination in the sight of God."

The observance of Christmas was considered a crime, savoring of popery, and to "eat fish on a Friday" came under the category of restrictions. From this history, and period, must be viewed the well-balanced character of Francis Cooke, a man with a fine reticence, which descended to his children.

He had expended "considerable estate in promoting the colony," and no one's death has called out such peculiar notice.

He died in 1663, aged about 86, and, though many lived to great age, he is spoken of in the death records as "Francis Cooke, the ancestor," and Bradford states it, as if it were a phenomenon, that he lived to see "his children's children have children."

At all events, his Walloon wife survived him for years, continuing in the "straight and narrow path" of her whole life, going from the sorrows and privations of her own race and sect to the equally narrow life of Plymouth colony, but living to see the changes of time and thought, her nationality fitting her to grow and broaden with the epoch.

Historians differ in opinion as to the children of Francis Cooke, the Pilgrim. Granting this, I must, from my own judgment, as I peruse the records, assimilate convictions and search for the truth in all directions; take Josias, not only as a son, but a strong power in the family, inheriting the qualities of the Pilgrim, prosperous, and of good repute. Savage does not allow us Josias, and record-seekers dearly love to pin their faith on him; still, he would be only human to occasionally pass by the possibilities from which facts grow.

The argument now is founded not upon what was said, but what was not. Certainty is self-evident, requires no assertion, so it seems to me it was not necessary to mention Josias as a son. In these days, when they told the "granite truth," it surely would have been noticed if Josias were not the son of Pilgrim Francis. There was no political slate for an office holder, designating his share of the patronage, firmly closed when the end was reached, unless a lively sense of power to come was evident; then the claim was a moveable feast. Thus it is impossible to believe that, unless a son, Josias should have had such constant, intimate, personal and official association with the family. Francis would naturally choose his own son for preferment if Josias were not a son. He was always in good company, surrounded by his kin and their and his nearest connections; each drew on the same following.

NAME ASSOCIATIONS.

Records and assimilations of names and localities bear me out in this at every step, and it rests with Mrs. H. Ruth Cooke to secure by her wonderful name descents proof that all the early Cookes were in some degree of one family.

In view of the natural sequence of events, there is no intimation in Baylie's assertion that Josias was "probably" son of Francis. Freeman's History of Cape Cod, Rich's History of Truro, Davis in Landmarks of History and the "Cook Memorial," as well as many private records sent me, make ours the majority report.

So, while welcome is given Josias, placing him, as all wish, too, in the family of Francis Cooke, of the Mayflower, truth compels the telling that one of the earliest records of him as a man is where, "March 26, 1633, he is fined for breach of peace," one of his frolicking days when he was "painting the town."

However, he soon "got even" with some one else, for "June 5, 1638, Josias Cooke was a witness against William Adey for working Sunday in his garden."

COOKES ALWAYS TOGETHER.

From 1637 to 1647, Francis Cooke, Sr., juryman; 1639 to 1669, Josias Cooke, juryman; 1640 to 1653, John Cooke, juryman; 1655 to 1683, Jacob Cooke, juryman.

Again, "August 1643, under names of all males able to bear arms from 16 years to 60 years, all of Plymouth, Francis Cooke, Jacob Cooke, John Cooke, Sr.; John Cooke, Jr., his boy; Edward Dotey, Josias Cooke." They gave their all—the call for one secured the rest, and proves their community of interests.

ANOTHER SON.

John Cooke married Sarah, daughter of Richard Warren, of the Mayflower, and soon his story began.

He was ten times a Deputy from Plymouth, and held the valued office of deacon for many years. John's record proves him to have been a man of education; it was always easy on every committee to have the making out of reports fall to his share of the proceedings, not only because of his distinguished position, but from his gifts.

Surely a statesman, perhaps too stalwart for a diplomat, but he had by choice of the people no idle time.

The Cookes being silk mercers, they may have been included in the record that "many of the first colonists at Plymouth were weavers from Yorkshire and Nottinghamshire, and brought over their looms with them."

In their substantial way it is certain they had everything, and how they came to let Miles Standish get ahead and secure a cow for himself, when "a cow and two goats were allowed to thirteen persons," passes my comprehension.

OTHER PURSUITS.

John and his father were men of one mind, and whether from special fitness or a touch of old Neptune in the Cooke inheritance, they came prominently to the front during the building of that great leviathan of the deep, a forty-ton vessel, the pride and joy of the people. Not to disparage the seafaring man, or lose my hold on the "historical hatchet," it is only fair to say of the Cookes that the deficiency in horsemanship was wholly from lack of the horse, all knowing that the first account of one was in 1644, in the estate of Stephen Hopkins.

John, having placed himself on record as a naval architect, he was soon ordered by the court to build a ferry between Dartmouth and Rhode Island. By sea or land the offices were his, but one was the last straw, and when appointed by the Plymouth Colony to attend the Quaker meetings "to endeavor to seduce them from the errors of their ways," he turned sympathizer, realized the wrongs endured by them, forgot Gov. Prince was to the front, and, giving full expression to his feelings, was excommunicated, naturally, for his "opposition to the proscriptive laws of the Prince era."

VARIETY IN RELIGION.

His religion was rather changeable as to sect, when in 1676 he joined in resettling Dartmouth, he cast in his religious views with Obadiah Holmes, of the Baptist church at Newport, and, with confidence in his own powers, even preached at Dartmouth.

Effectively, of course, but his traveling for church purposes on Sunday brought him under censure, though this Baptist connection did not prevent the recognition of his usefulness, and frequent election to the Plymouth General Court as deputy.

Indeed, the record proves that "at a town meeting, the 22d of May, in the year 1674, John Cooke was chosen debity, 'arthur hathaway,' grand juryman, etc."

John Cooke's progress in his religious acquirements is worthy of notice, as Backus, in his church history, states that "John Cooke was a Baptist minister in Dartmouth many years, from whence springs the Baptist church in the east borders of Tiverton."

MILITARY POSITION.

John Cooke was also a warrior bold, volunteering in 1637 for the Pequot war, known always in history by the prefix "bloody," a statement about which there can be no doubt; so as Capt. John Cooke we now must place him, with the positive conviction that if there was any fighting to be done John Cooke was not attached to the "commissary department."

Wherever he locates Josias Cooke keeps in the company of his family. No circumstances are strongly enough beyond their control to estrange them from a common interest.

As Francis and John ruled wisely and well, winning golden opinions from those they were surrounded by in Plymouth, so Josias showed his power in Eastham. He was made magistrate, selectman and deputy by the town, and several times proved his uprightness of deed and intent during his appointment under the court "to examine the accounts of the treasurer of the colony, and as agent of the colony to treat with the Indians in the purchase of land."

From 1634 on he was a tax payer, an evidence of citizenship in vogue in those days as well as now. Though not a stranger, they "took him in" to the extent of all the pressure he would bear, without the kick the Cookes were fully equal to when conscious of imposition.

HIS MARRIAGE.

Not willing to have "taxation without representation," the following year Josias Cooke took to himself a wife, in the person of Elizabeth Ring, widow of Stephen Deane, September 16, 1635, and may, with his ten children, be recorded as having a full house at life's close.

Stephen Deane was one of the adventurers who came out in the Fortune and was authorized in "1633 to build, on Town Brook, a beating mill. Until then every family had a hand mortar, though later little steel mills were not unknown." Whatever his outlook of future prosperity, poor Stephen Deane never lived to see it realized, for in 1634 he left his unfinished work, wife and three children.

Then the "plum" of the period fell into his hands, for, "June 7, 1648, Josias Cooke was allowed to sell wine at Nanset, and to be register keeper for Nanset."

The regulations on this subject were very explicit.

"Early provision was made for taverns and ordinaries. They who kept them were required to be licensed, and were not to suffer any to be drunk, "nor to tipple," "after 9 o'clock at night."

A precedent for the Raines liquor law, the only progression being the lengthening of the time.

The women, too, were allowed their share in the patronage.

"In 1646 Mrs. Catherine Clark, having a family of children, is licensed for £10 per annum, if she provides a fitt man that is godly to manage the business."

NANSET.

Josias Cooke went to Nanset with the old stand-bys, which included in the committees sent by the church to survey Nanset (Eastham), and purchase of the natives; Gov. Bradford, Thomas Prince, John Doane, Nicholas Snow, Richard Higgins and Edward Bangs.

They decided it was too barren to accommodate all of the church of Plymouth; but they bought a tract of land called Pochet and two islands lying before Potanumguat, with a beach, besides all the land called Namkeket.

This grant included Eastham, Wellfleet and Orleans. The church of Plymouth, in consideration of the sum they had paid, conveyed their right to Thomas Prince, John Doane, Nicholas Snow, Josias Cooke, Richard Higgins, John Smalley and Edward Bangs, who immediately commenced a settlement at Nanset.

CONVICTION.

This is not supposition, but record, and tells the tale, which becomes a twice-told one, of Josias Cooke's association with the people, who knew and loved his father, for "Josias Cooke was one of the first proprietors of the present town of Abington, having, June 8, 1664, received, in company with Lieut. Joseph Rogers, Giles Hopkins, Henry Sampson and Experience Mitchell, a grant from the court of all that tract of land lying between Bridgewater and the Massachusetts Bay Company."

All of these the "old comers," people with the pioneer tie, who pulled together naturally and had as little wish for intrusion from the outside element as would come as a matter of course from these people, with the "blood bond," accentuated by long association.

ANOTHER SON.

Jacob Cooke, son of Francis, first attracted attention in the Colonial records in June, 1637, as a volunteer in Capt. Prince's company for the Indian war, and after that he held several offices in Plymouth.

These sons went from their home on Leyden street to the various places of their after life, a home to be known through all history, one of the seven houses of which Longfellow writes in his courtship of Miles Standish—

'Till he beheld the lights of the seven houses of Plymouth
Shining like seven stars in the dark and mist of the evening."

They could ask no better of their future life than that it should keep pace with its beginning. Jacob Cooke married first Damaris, daughter of the Stephen Hopkins, whose friendship and congeniality all claim, making a strong family connection, which was repeated again to the increase of this descent.

After her death he married, in 1655, Elizabeth, daughter of Thomas Lettice and widow of William Shurtleff, who was killed by a stroke of lightning at Marshfield "while sitting with a child in his lap and holding his wife's hand to encourage her, but he alone of his family was hurt."

Goodwin tersely tells that "this storm immediately followed a fast on account of drought, and ended with a hurricane—

"Prayer was too efficacious."

Following the course of Josias, Jacob moved to Eastham, and died there July 7, 1676.

Josias, always a prosperous man, went away from Plymouth first, before John went to Dartmouth, and Pilgrim Francis in his will, after providing for his wife and daughters, left all to his son Jacob, "to be his and Jacob's heirs' forever."

The story, to me, seems complete. The elder brothers, well provided for, had no claim to visible remembrance. They had taken their chance at the start, and as I can find no record of discontent, were satisfied with the will, which was "witnessed by John Howland and John Alden. Inventory, May 1, 1663, taken by Eph Tuckham and Mr. Crowe."

THE COOKE PUZZLE.

As I have felt obliged to put things before the public as I see them, and am very anxious that the result of my labor shall be for the benefit of history, I give the children of Elder John Cooke, son of Francis Cooke, of the Mayflower, sometimes known as Rev. John, just as they came to me from the historian, who, of her kindness, desires to place Capt. John Cooke as the son, not the elder himself.

Much may have to be done as supplementary work before the "Signers" are completed, continuous study affording clews to be worked up, which develop as records are received, pointing to various localities where new search may be made.

Elder John Cooke, eldest son of Francis, of the Mayflower and Plymouth.

I.—Sarah Cooke (3), born 1635; died after 1710; married November 20, 1652, Arthur Hathaway, first Hedaway, of Marshfield, Mass., and had eight children.

This enables those of this descent, through the Hathaways, to search for their records through those bearing the name of Sisson, Hatch, Mott, Clark, Taber, Kempton, Cannon, Nye, Hammond, Wing, Pope, Spooner, Hillman, Delano, Willis and Swift.

II.—John Cooke (3), born 1637 (given by Davis; not given in Memorial).

III.—Elizabeth Cooke (3), died December 6, 1715; married November 28, 1661, Daniel Wilcox, son of Edward, of Portsmouth, R. I. They had nine children. (Look for this descent among the names of Briggs, Butts, Cook, Earle, Tripp, Sherman, Lake, Moon and Cory).

IV.—Esther Cooke, born August 16, 1650; married in 1667 Thomas Taber, son of Philip and Lydia (Masters) Taber.

V.—Mercy Cooke (3), born July 25, 1654, in Plymouth, Mass.; married Stephen West, 1682; died November 21, 1733.

VI.—Mary Cooke (3), born January 12, 1652; married 1668, Philip Taber, Jr., son of Philip and Lydia (Masters) Taber. They had seven children.

Elder John Cooke, it will be remembered, married Sarah Warren. An astonishing number of connections with the Mayflower can be made by the study of these two families.

Now the daughters and Francis Cooke felt his right to pride in good wife and children.

Hester married Richard Wright, one of the adventurers waiting and ready to choose a wife from the "maidens fair to see," who came out in the Ann. Youth was a fault remedied by time, and surely they married on a certainty of personal knowledge not afforded in after years. Richard Wright had a mind of his own, even if the Pilgrims had a way of requiring their will should govern the new comers, albeit they were the men who by virtue of their investment felt they had a word to say in the matter.

"When in 1645 Rehoboth was founded, Richard Wright built a mill, and the next year because he would not leave it to serve as deputy he was fined." Sure proof of his freemanship, that being one of the penalties of their refusing to accept office.

"The public good must be consulted before private interests." Strength of opinion with him came after his marriage, which took place November 21, 1644, and as he was born about 1608 his age was sufficient to suppose he held his own in the future.

INHERITANCE.

Richard Wright, son "probably" of William and Priscilla (Carpenter) Wright, inherited by the will of his wife's father, Francis Cooke, of the Mayflower, "the Old Homestead at Jones River, known as Cooke's Hollow," and had Adam born about 1645, died 1724, married first Sarah, daughter of John Soule and his wife Sarah, by whom he had two children, then for second wife took Mehitable Barrowes, and by true Pilgrim progression had eight children.

Next came Esther Wright (3), born 1649, then Mary (3), again John, afterward Isaac Wright (3), born August 26, 1662.

Adam Wright's marriage with Sarah Soule, through their children, enlarges the Cooke descent, making clear lines to the Mayflower through several ascendants, Isaac, marrying in 1717 Mary, daughter of John Cole, and Joseph, Sarah Brewster (Spooner Genealogy).

COOKE OUTLOOK.

The Wrights were not the only ones to spread and flourish among the "old comers," Elizabeth (3), daughter of Jacob (2), son of Francis, the Pilgrim, married John Doty, son of Edward, of the Mayflower, and Faith (Clark) Doty. She died in time to allow John Doty to seek a second mate, but left ten children to grace the family board, and give Sarah, the second wife, enough occupation to keep her out of mischief, from idle hands.

Through the first marriage the branches spread into the families of the Neisons, Shearmans, Morses, Faunces, Cobbs, Curtises, etc. It would take a Philadelphia lawyer to unravel the various kinships thus entailed, but they lead to much of the history of those early times.

MARY COOKE.

Mary Cooke, daughter of the emigrant, Francis, born in 1626, married John Thompson, December 26, 1645, a man of evident consequence in the colony—supposed to be of Scotch origin. There are various spellings of the name. In his will he writes it "Tomson."

"He closed his industrious and useful life June 16, 1699, nearly 80 years old. He was buried in the first burying ground, Middleborough. His grave is marked by a small stone, which is said to be the second one erected."

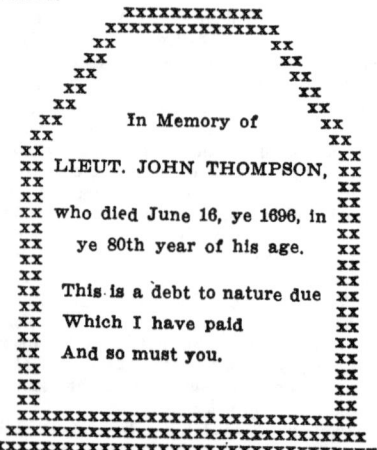

In Memory of
LIEUT. JOHN THOMPSON,
who died June 16, ye 1696, in ye 80th year of his age.
This is a debt to nature due
Which I have paid
And so must you.

Mary, his wife, with inheritance of many days, "died March 21, 1714, in the eighty-eighth year of her age; buried same place with her husband." This marriage leads back to the most prominent of the early families, giving the Mortons, Kemptons, Tabers; making another of the collateral connections with Gov. Levi P. Morton, for Mannasseth, son of Deacon George and Joanna (Kempton) Morton, married Mary Taber, daughter of Capt. Thomas Taber, and Mary Thomson, daughter of Lieut. Thomson, granddaughter of Francis Cooke, of the Mayflower.

PRIDE OF BIRTH.

It is a pleasure to study this lineage; they do their duty in the church, their families and in the government. Deacons, of course, their's the moral force; military men, guards for their country, whether on the "tented field" or sentries to protect the lives of their dear ones and homes; government officials, that the best of themselves may be given to rule wisely and well. The one who has just left us as the highest State officer can record no better than his ancestor, Lieut. Ephraim Morton, youngest son of George and Juliana Carpenter Morton, of the early Plymouth colonies.

JANE.

Jane was in nowise left behind her sisters, and though the courtship began in childhood's sunny hours, her marriage to Experience Mitchell had a very modern method in it, they having crossed the ocean together as fellow-passengers on the Ann.

"Experience Mitchell was one of the founders of Duxbury, and when Bridgewater was set off became a leading man there. Much could naturally be expected of him; he was at Leyden with the Pilgrims and left a brother Thomas, who lived and died there."

It hardly seems possible, as there is a lack of any apparent family connection with the Mayflower people, he was intended for the original start, one of those put back on account of the Speedwell's mishap; his youth would either have secured his coming over or prevented such intention while there were real family ties in Leyden to hold him back.

WOMEN OF THAT DAY.

There has been no new dignity given women in the present day they did not possess in the old colonial times. Men and women worked side by side. The only discussion was the paramount need of the other. Labor was king in those days. No man felt above watching beside the couch of a sick child after a day's toil; the mother needed rest; their interests were in common. Then an approaching storm, with unstored hay or grain, called wife and daughters to its rescue, not as the "beggar's maid" waiting for the king to pass, but the home feeling of the loss all would sustain if worst came to worst. Their family ties regulated everything; the spirit of content was abroad as well as in the home.

They had no long look ahead to the period when machinery, not chivalry, should lessen women's cares, give them time to go forth from home and take, wisely or no, a place in affairs; separate themselves by "women's work," "women's doings" from the place they held so proudly beside husband and father.

Francis Cooke knew with Hester every little ailment of the boys and girls, the spring of their actions, whether requiring curbing or assuring. No need to go outside for advice. Father knew everything and mother was always there to carry out his wishes.

The home life of this family seems written with the records, and though they started sufficient unto themselves, they enlarged and widened until the tangled skein of relationship required the older heads for its unraveling, if it ever truly reached that state.

The Cooke descent is a very large one; the names which claim kinship increase at every turn; the Pilgrims married "early and often," and I find in all who come to me but one opinion.

Without the slightest feeling of pretense, they recognize a certain solidity of start that cannot be improved upon. The early home on Leyden street was one of the seven perpetuated in history, and recognizing that as the lucky number of the early colonists, knowing as all do the claim put forth for those who were of the "seven pillars of the church," there seems to have been an omen of content in the thought that, surrounded by the choice of the neighbors, these Cookes started with the best.

The Cookes must give their own account, but let them read backward before making it indelible.

The Cooke record given in this paper has a very wide scope, both as to location and family.

The references which have been proved entitle those of this lineage to join either Society of Mayflower Descendants or Huguenot Society.

Francis Cooke, of the Mayflower, Plymouth, Mass., 1620, married Hester, the Walloon, in Holland; she came out in the Ann, 1623.

Jane Cooke, of Plymouth, Mass., daughter of Francis and Hester Cooke, came out with her mother in the Ann; married, about 1628, Experience Mitchell, who also was passenger on the Ann, the last of the forefather ships.

Elizabeth Mitchell married John Washburne, Jr., of Plymouth, Duxbury and Bridgewater, Mass., December 6, 1645.

Mary Washburne, of Bridgewater, Mass., married, 1694, Samuel Kinsley, of Easton, Mass.

Benjamin Kinsley, of Swanzey and Easton, Mass., married, 1732, Priscilla Manley.

Martha Kinsley, of Easton, Mass., married May 30, 1762, Seth Lothrop, of Easton and Enfield, Mass.

Thomas Lothrop, of Easton and Leyden, Mass., married, February 20, 1792, Deborah Pope, of Dartmouth and Bridgewater.

Zebediah Lothrop, of Providence, R. I., and Philadelphia, Pa., married, at Providence, February 1, 1825, Elizabeth Terry Earle.

Sarah Eliza Lothrop married, at Philadelphia, Pa., January 31, 1854, Dr. Richard Henry Lee, of Philadelphia.

Edward Clinton Lee.

REFERENCES.

"Lothrop Family Memoir," by Rev. E. B. Huntington, Ridgefield, Conn., 1884.

"Alden Memorial," by Dr. E. Alden, Randolph, Mass., 1867.

"Story of a Pilgrim Family" (Alden), by Rev. John Alden, Boston, 1890.

"History of Plymouth Plantation," by William Bradford, Colls, of Massachusetts

FRANCIS COOKE, OF THE MAYFLOWER.

Mary Cooke	married	John Thompson.
Esther Thompson	married 1675	William Reed, born Oct. 16, 1839.
William Reed, born May 24, 1682; died June 3, 1753.	married 1703	Alice Nash, died Dec. 5, 1757.
Solomon Reed, born Oct. 22, 1719; died 1785.	married 1748	Abigail Stoughton.
John Reed, born Nov. 11, 1751; died Feb. 17, 1831.	married 1780	Hannah Sampson, born 1755; died 1815.
Sampson Reed, born June 10, 1800; died 1880.	married 1832	Catherine Clark, born May 28, 1805.
Thomas Reed, born Feb. 3, 1837; died Feb. 3, 1885.	married 1860	Mary Anne Webb.
Caroline A. Reed	married 1885	Walter Romeyn Benjamin, born Sept. 24, 1854.

Walter Reed Benjamin.

Historical Society, Vol. 3, 4th series, Boston, 1856.

"The Pilgrim Republic," by John A. Goodwin, Boston, 1888.

"History of Easton, Mass," by Rev. Wm. L. Chaffin, Cambridge, 1886.

"Ralph Earle and His Descendants," by Pliny Earle, Worcester, 1888.

"Plymouth Colony Records," Boston, 1855.

"History of Bridgewater, Mass.," by Nahum Mitchell, Boston, 1840.

"History of the Huguenot Emigration to America," by Charles W. Baird, D. D. New York, 1885.

The End.

The Cooke history is only written finished, so far as I am concerned. It rests in abler hands than mine, who already have gathered so much that it seems as if the work were completed.

To Mrs. H. Ruth Cooke and Mr. Rollin H. Cooke much is due, and far more appreciation will be given when all the branches make their proper claims.

To verify the statement that the "Cookes connect everywhere," I give the following chart, which places, for descendants of this line, about ten ancestors on the Mayflower—surely a full hand, and one greatly to be desired. It came to me from Mrs. H. Ruth Cooke, who always rises to everything which places the Cookes where she thinks they are entitled to be.

```
William Mullins
  |
Priscilla Mullins — John Alden      Myles Standish        William White        Francis Cooke
            |                             |               Peregrine White       Mary Cooke
         Sarah Alden — Alexander Standish                  ——— White            Esther Thompson
                   |                                       ——— White            William Reed
              Lydia Standish                               Anna White           John Reed
Isaac Sampson —— |                                              |
              Uriah Sampson                                     |
                      |_____ Hannah Sampson _____|               John Reed
                                           |
                                   Sampson Reed ——————————————————— Catharine Clark
                                           |
                                   Thomas Reed ——— M. A. Webb
                                           |
                                   Caroline A. Webb ——— Walter Romeyn Benjamin
```

THOMAS ROGERS, Eighteenth Signer.

It can hardly be said that the Rogers family have a divided interest, and yet the situation is such in regard to them that, failing one connection, they can fall back upon the other.

However, even looking at it in this light, there is always the strong hope that, having attained to one position, they may lead on to the other.

Thomas, of the Mayflower, is greatly to be desired, but the addition of John, the Martyr, would round off the claim to perfection.

There has always been such an atmosphere of uncertainty about the descendants of Thomas, the Pilgrim, that all except the son, Joseph, who came out with him, have seemed marked "dangerous."

To be sure, Bradford, in 1650, writing of Plymouth Colony, says: "Thomas Rogers died in the first sickness, but his son is still living, and is married and hath six children. The rest of his children came over and are married and have many children."

This surely entitles to Rogers descendants, even if poor Thomas, the Pilgrim, only lived through the voyage, and yielded to the first sickness, consequent upon his privations, lack of space and close personal contact, forced upon the people of the Mayflower by the necessities of the situation.

His only kin companion, Joseph, who came out with him, had to serve for all left behind, fit into his anxieties and bear to the family his sad farewells.

EARLY TIMES.

In these early times each child was welcome. With dire want staring them in the face on every side, a large family was counted a blessing.

Need of their future services became the paramount idea; the increased endurance consequent on the additional mouths to be fed was a matter set aside for the general good, which alone must control them.

Many hands made light work. There were the household "chores" for little feet and hands, duties of greater moment for others of increasing years.

So if records were kept at all, those of the Rogers family must find place somewhere, and another from Bradford says of Thomas Rogers: "He was one of the forty-one persons who signed the constitutions of government on board the Mayflower, and was one of the Pilgrim Fathers. His son Joseph came with him, is married, and has six children. The other children came over afterward, including John, married, and have many children. Thomas died in 1621."

This secures another child to the Pilgrim, placing John on the list without any doubt.

DUXBURY.

For a time Duxbury was really the annex of Plymouth. The colony had spread as to numbers and opinions, so that "Room for the Pilgrims! Room!" was a cry that required attention, though the break was not sudden or immediate. The residents there used this suburb for summer quarters, returning to Plymouth winters, and they also attended church there.

Among those thus inclined were Standish, Brewster and other stalwarts of the "old comers," and for some reason of personal attraction this included both John and Joseph Rogers, for in "August, 1643, they were on the list of men in Duxbury able to bear arms between 16 and 20."

And as evidence they had attained to years of manhood, they were among "those rated March 25, 1633, at nine shillings each." No overestimate of labor and its compensation would be allowed among these experts on the subject of quid pro quo.

LIEUT. JOSEPH ROGERS.

Lieut. Joseph Rogers, as history afterwards reveals him to us, was some time in Duxbury among those sterling, solid Pilgrims who were the backbone of the colony, answering the war cry when it sounded with military alacrity and strong personal patriotism, and joining with equal fervor in the thanksgiving for peace, if such a time ever came to them in those early Indian days.

In 1648 leave was granted this Lieut. Joseph to have meadows purchased from the Potanumsquatt Indians, and February 24, 1652, he was appointed "one of the jurors to lay out the most convenient way from Sandwich to Plymouth."

He had strayed from the original resting place, but was very active in making connection with his early home.

From Duxbury to Sandwich, and then "May 22, 1655, placed on record among the legal voters of Eastham."

Near enough to Plymouth for all practical purposes. A man never forgotten when bravery and judgment were required, step by step he included the offices of worth, and when "in 1658 a council of war was appointed, Josiah Winslow appointed to the supreme command and Joseph Rogers one of his council."

No history accords to any sections surrounding Plymouth great fertility with increase sufficient to maintain those dependent on the crops and supplies, and yet it is given us that "there were plenty of orchards in Duxbury in 1637." This, with the tales of the wild turkey, venison and fish found in abundance, certainly shows our Pilgrims had their choice of market, even against Bradford's convincing statements of dire want.

SANDWICH.

Whatever the improvements in variety and quantity in Sandwich, a sturdy little family surrounded our Lieut. Joseph, claiming and receiving the sustenance necessary to promote the muscle and sinew required in the life of toil and small return awaiting them.

CAPE COD RECORDS.

It will not interfere with the coming surprises to give Joseph Rogers's children, born in Sandwich, Mass., as:

Sarah, August 6, 1633, died in infancy.
Joseph, July 19, 1635, married Susannah Deane at Eastham April 4, 1660.
Thomas, March 29, 1638, married Elizabeth Snow 1665.
Elizabeth, September 29, 1639, married Johnathan Higgins 1660.
John, April 3, 1642, married Elizabeth Twinning.
Mary, September 22, 1644, married John Phinney.
James, October 18, 1648, married Mary Paine 1670.
Hannah, August 8, 1652.

The name connections are satisfactory. Joseph, the young father, desirous of appearing without doubt in his proper relation to his first born son, then the memory of the father so dear to him, required recognition, so Thomas came next in order, and John, the brother named in connection with him, must have place. James we may have to allow to the mother's family, but the name can be looked for, and when found, continued; there is some back ancestor accountable for it.

The poor Pilgrims do not receive much credit for nostalgia; perchance, in their stern, unadorned language, thought of home would be called force of habit, and although Joseph Rogers, son of Thomas, of the Mayflower, had a residence easily availed of, in 1635, from the court records it is learned that "Joseph Rogers was allowed a constant ferry over the Jones River, neer his dwelling howse, and to take a penny for the transportation of each person, he, the said Joseph, maintayning a sufficient ferry at that price"—he was without question much better satisfied that he thus kept up consant communication with Plymouth, its affairs and inhabitants.

COATS-OF-ARMS.

No doubt it was in the spirit of this home-longing, later on, they began to look up, and have prepared for use, the coats-of-arms which, from their variety, are now found to be so perplexing.

The original instinct of obliteration had lessened with time, and the habits of their early life and traditions being strong upon them, they endeavored from memory to produce the coat armour that had been ever present in the homes of their ancestors.

Satisfied with general effect, what cared they whether the arms were heraldicly correct? They conveyed to them their aspirations and the future then was an unknown quantity, in which they had no personal part.

Yeomen in Queen Elizabeth's time were allowed to bear them, the "Guilds" were granted them, and there they were borne with a bravery of display which placed the freemanship thus acquired as a matter of the greatest moment.

These arms were their connecting cable; with them in hall, and book, the new world seemed more their own.

They were silent about their feelings for the home across the deep blue ocean, but the sentiment was the same, and though the tongue told of the abuses from which they had fled, deep down in their hearts they sang with tears in their voices: "There is no place like home, sweet home."

All through this article it will be my endeavor to give as much data as is possible that can be authenticated, and thus place many of the vexed claims. The following were sent me as "miscellaneous records from Harwich":

Zacheus Rogers married Elizabeth King

in Eastham, 1743; children, Eunice, 1745; Mercy, 1747; Elizabeth, 1749; Abigail, 1752.

MARRIAGES.

Elizabeth Rogers and Eli Small, 1786.
David Rogers and Jerusha Eldridge, 1773.
Priscilla Rogers and Thomas Linnell, 1772.
Bessie Rogers and Jonathan Kinnewick, 1783.
Mercy Rogers and Tully Nickerson, 1793.
Eliz Rogers and James Slater, 1775.
Levi Rogers and Mary Andrews, 1777.
Samuel Rogers and Phoebe Crosby, 1791.
Crisp Rogers and Bethia Smith, 1756.
Thomas Rogers, of Harwich, and Elizabeth Smith, of Chatham, November 10, 1748.*
Mercy Rogers and Eli Fuller, 1746.
Tabitha Rogers and Stephen Cole, 1748.
Caleb Rogers and Ruth Rogers, 1767.
Thankful Rogers and Ezekiel Andrews, 1750.
Martha Rogers and Thomas Chase, 1751.
Caleb Rogers and Mercy Ring, 1754.
Sarah Rogers and John Birge, 1756.
Mary Rogers and Judah Mayo, 1758.
Jesse Rogers and Mary Freeman, 1761.
Nathaniel Rogers and Elizabeth Crosby, 1715.
Elizabeth Rogers and Nathan Bassett, 1734.
Henry Rogers (Harwich) and Deborah Nickerson (Eastham), 1761.

The safe child causes no anxiety. Joseph Rogers holds his own all through history, placing himself from the start as with his father on the Mayflower, and known locally in the Plymouth record of 1623.

"The Falles of their grounds which came first in the Mayflower according as their lots were cast. Joseph Rogers 2 akers, lying on the South side of the brooke to the baywards."

Then, to show the good company he kept: "In 1627 in dividing the cattle the 11th lot fell to Gov. Bradford, and those with him, to wit,—his wife Alles Bradford, and William Bradford, and Joseph Rogers."

The intimate relations with Gov. Bradford inclined to a belief of a natural favoritism on his part to the young Joseph. He was fully aware of it, and guarded against any increase of this feeling in the public mind.

"In 1638 Joseph Rogers is granted to have a pcell of land to make him a field or two to plant corn upon, in the place where he desireth, and to be viewed and appoynted him by Mr. Bradford that it may not too much prjudice the comons of the neighborhood there."

Given just what he wanted, our friend could make himself content.

TO LAW WITH EDWARD DOTY.

The steady course of prosperity was not gained by this young Pilgrim without some drawbacks, which required the "strong hand of the law" for their adjustment.

"In 1632 he complayned in Court of Edward Doty for non-performance of covnant between them, wherein six pigges of

*Note.—A correction in regard to this is sent me from Mrs. Osborn Nickerson, of Chatham, Mass. (Cape Cod): "In town records Moses is given, and it is Moses in cemetery records.

"'Mr. Moses Rogers died March 22, 1795, in ye 74 yr of his age. Mrs. Elizabeth, wife of Mr. Moses Rogers, died December 2, 1795, aged 64 years.'"

five weeks old were due unto the plaintiff."

He wanted his "little pigges to go to market," and must have felt it a poor return when all he got out of Edward Doty was, "the case being heard, the defendant was cast in four bushels of corn."

Later on he might have been better able to care for his future bacon, as in 1642 he "is granted the parcel of meddowing, containing four or five akers, lying about Massachusetts Path, about two miles from Mr. Bradford's farm."

Had Stephen Hopkins owned it thoughts of stock raising might have intruded themselves, but if Bradford had such instincts he restrained them, conventional, for fear of "offending his brother," always.

No argument as to his age can be brought from his freemanship, as he was on the first list, "they comprising the General Court found under date of 1633."

THE BROTHERS.

That, however, is a matter of no importance; he was quite young enough to enjoy even in the way of such youthful sports as the epoch and location admitted of, his brothers, who came out to him. Their school of physical culture was a very primitive one, but all the same it was the best they had.

"In 1640 Joseph and brother John are granted 50 akers apeece of upland next where Mr. Vassell's farme is at the North river, with portionable meadow ground." So they were near neighbors, and the fact of Joseph's local authority, for "he was elected constable the same year," may have lessened some of the depredations on their lands, which were the playful Indian habits of the day.

Soon the break came, and Joseph Rogers was called upon to assume the "pomp and circumstance of war," even if it were inglorious fighting against the crafty Indians, and is pposed by the town of Nanset (Eastham) to this Court for lieutenant, to exercise the men in armes, is by this Court appred, and established lieutenant there."

LAST HOME.

About 1655 Lieut. Joseph, wearing his honors calmly, as he felt was due, moved with his family to Eastham, where he spent the remainder of his life, dying early in 1678.

Joseph, Jr., born in 1635, who married Susannah Doane, was killed on Christmas Day, 1660, from a fall while wrestling with his friend Richard Hawes.

"The Governor is authorized by the court to give oath to Susanna, the wife of the late deceased Joseph Rogers, for the truth of the inventory of his estate. March 5, 1660."

To keep his line intact he had one son, Joseph, born January 27, 1661. Then James, who married Mary Paine, left James, born 1673, Mary, 1675, and Abigail, 1678, and Thomas, marrying Elizabeth Snow, had Elizabeth, born 1666; Joseph, 1667; Hannah, 1669; Thomas, 1671, who died in infancy, and, not to lose the name, the next child was also Thomas, born 1672, then Eleazer, 1673; Nathaniel, 1675.

This "Eleazer, grandson of Joseph, was one of a Committee Chose To take Care of the Herrinbrooke and the Herrins," and proving his ability in this direction, had the local and historical importance of being the earliest recorded sexton.

"At a towne meeting held at Plymouth, March 23, 1732, the Town A Greed With Eleazer Rogers to Ring ye bell, sweep the meeting house, Kp the Doores and Windows of sd meeting house shut, and opened for the Congregations use upon all occasions, and Carefully loock after sd house, as above sd, and the sd Rogers is to receive of sd Town three pounds pr year for his sd service, to begin on the 1st of April next Ensuing this date."

Evidently Eleazer fulfilled his duties to the satisfaction of all concerned, for "March, 1733, it was Voted that Eleazer Rogers be Saxton for the ensuing year. There was a vote called, whether they would allow ye Saxton, Twelve pounds for ye ensuing year; it passed in the negative, and Eleazer Rogers being then present, Refused to serve."

If Deacon Wadsworth could secure progressive remuneration for mere church services in early Plymouth, why not one of the Rogers family nearly a century after?

JOHN.

With "John" comes great confusion, and many lines of descent securely placed will need changing. though, in studying them over, I find most are through the John who married Elizabeth, daughter of William and Elizabeth Alden Pabodie, which only necessitates the change in the previous generation, which is a clear title.

The righting of these Johns, giving John, the son of Thomas, his undoubted place, I owe entirely to the deep research of Hon. Josiah H. Drummond, of Portland, Me.

I will not attempt to follow his argument, only give the valuable results of his study, authenticated by records which admit of no dispute.

Mr. J. S. Rogers, of Chicago, Ill., who is compiling the Rogers' history, welcomed the solution thus given to the "confusion worse confounded" he met in his study.

"John Rogers, of Duxbury, son of Thomas, of the Mayflower, was among those proposed March 5, 1638-9, to take up freedom. The latter being the year of his marriage to Ann Churchman, April 16, 1639," goes far toward suggesting that he was a very young child when the Mayflower sailed.

This would be in keeping with Bradford's statement of those left behind who had "yonge children," and future history on this plea may fill gaps which will prove traditions people are wrestling with, knowing they have generations of assertion to build them on. Matters with this John do not stand still. He prepared to establish his claims, and, as Mr. Drummond asserts, made a will which "delights the heart of the genealogist."

THE WILL.

"John Rogers, Sr., of Duxborough," by will, dated August 26, 1691, proved September 20, 1692, gives:

1. To his grandson, John Rogers, all of his houses and lands in the town of Duxborough.

2. To his grandson, John Tisdall, for the use of his mother, Anna Terry, one-half of his land, divided and undivided, in Middleboro, excepting his rights in the Major Purchase, the last to be disposed of according to his mother's mind.

3. To his daughter, Elizabeth Williams (who was the wife of Nathaniel Williams, of Taunton), the other half of the Middleboro land; and his "cattel" were to be equally divided between these three daughters.

4. To his grandson, John Rogers, all of his household stuff and moneys, out of

which he was to pay his sister, Elizabeth Rogers, forty shillings; and twenty shillings each to "his other three sisters," Hannah Bradford, Ruth Rogers and Sarah Rogers.

5. To his daughter Abigail Richmond, "that twenty shillings a year which is my due for four score acres of land which I sold to my two grandsons, Joseph Richmond and Edward Richmond."

6. He appoints his "loving son, John Rogers, sole executor and administrator of this my last will and testament."

This is a strong story. The name of Rogers is one of power always, and, to add to its desirability, John, Jr., married well, secured for a back ancestor Priscilla Molines Alden, who recently, at a woman's society, was put forward as one of the ten great women of history. She certainly claims the love of her descendants, and John Alden is not far behind in the same sentiment.

BRADFORD, ALSO.

This lineage also adds Bradford, and there are those who put him first in their estimate of the Pilgrims.

Rogers, Bradford, Molines, Alden, Southworth demand good citizenship.

The following line which came to me gives the pleasure of showing a descent desired by many who cannot exactly make the connection at various points. I add the wife of the first John only:

1. John Rogers, son of Thomas, of the Mayflower, married Ann Churchman April 16, 1639. Savage says perhaps daughter of Hugh Churchman, of Lynn. 1640.

2. John Rogers, born in 1641, married Elizabeth, daughter of William and Elizabeth Alden Pabodie (or Peabody), November 16, 1666.

3. Sarah Rogers, born March 4, 1677, married Nathaniel, son of Robert and Deborah Searle, born June 9, 1662, Little Compton, R. I., and died February 5, 1750.

4. Deborah Searle, born November 17, 1695, died May 16, 1776, at Little Compton; married, February 20, 1717, George Pearce (son of George), who was born March 2, 1697, died February 22, 1764.

5. Jeptha Pearce, born February 20, 1722, died October 22, 1770; married, February 23, 1749, Elizabeth Rouse, who was born February 23, 1724.

6. Betsy (widow of Benjamin Sayer) Pearce, born October 17, 1756; married April 6, 1800, Capt. Zebedee Grinnell, who was born January 20, 1730, and died December 13, 1811.

7. Brenton Bliss Grinnell, born September 9, 1801, died September 1, 1883; married, January 22, 1825, Nancy Bennett Brownell, born December 8, 1805, died August 15, 1884.

No one can be skeptical in the face of authentic public records, made as events were happening.

So, when a correspondent sent me the following from the Harwich records, with the statement that "she had searched them personally about two years ago," the consummation of the wishes of all concerned was almost startling.

"William, son of first Thomas, settled in Hempstead, Long Island, and died in 1650."

The content of success is upon us all, no discussion left, and for once all are satisfied with a "plain, unvarnished tale."

The work of connection is only pleasure, started with light hearts when the result is sure.

Then to accentuate and increase the certainty there comes from Cape Cod another record which enlarges the claim, giving hope of James and those still signed "possibly."

"Thomas came in the Mayflower with son Joseph, other children, including John and William, coming afterward.

CHANGE OF RESIDENCE.

The local changes of these Pilgrim descendants have a method in them. On the road they made the acquaintance of the "early comers of Cambridge and Dorchester," met their kin and friends from the "mother country." They follow Warham and Hooker and "sit down" in Windsor, Wethersfield and Hartford, gathering recruits for any new movement, whether the end finds them in Sharon, Amenia and "Nine Partners," or stopping on the way at Stamford, they spread sail and trim their canvas for Long Island.

William Rogers, it is claimed, took the natural route to Stamford (though I have no record of him there after leaving Wethersfield), then settled at Hempstead, L. I., removing about 1648-9 to Southampton, and then his household gods, not having root, went to Huntington, L. I., where, together with Thomas Weeks and Jonas Wood, both of whom were fellow associates in Wethersfield, he acquired permanent local rights by purchasing land from the Huntington Indians.

This was, indeed, his last home, for he died soon after this settling, leaving a widow, Anne Rogers, and children, Obadiah, his eldest son, who, however, finding the place to his mind, remained in Southampton; the others, Jonathan, Noah, Samuel, Mary and Hannah, removed with him to Huntington.

NO WILL.

The barrier of "early records lost" meets us here, and there is no evidence of William Rogers having left a will, but all is not darkness, when the will of Anne Rogers is found recorded at Riverhead, Long Island, dated November 22, 1669.

In this testament she mentions her son Obadiah, and his eldest son, also Obadiah, who were residing in Southampton in the very homestead occupied by our William Rogers, before he removed to Huntington.

Between the deaths of the parents, the sons, John and Noah, made home in Branford, Conn., and John died unmarried before 1671. Noah, however, gives us a clear record, marrying April 8, 1673, Elizabeth Taintor, daughter of Michael Taintor.

There is no "probably" written on this will of Widow Anne Rogers, she is herself, no one else, despite any other possible claimants—they are the ones to be avoided, so we write out, Ann Rogers, widow of Henry Rogers, of Setucket, who afterward married George Wood, of Setucket, and survived him, the same to Anne Rogers, wife of John Rogers, of Oyster Bay, for she and her husband were both alive when our Anne, widow of William Rogers, of Huntington, died.

STILL MORE.

If more is wanted to place this family authentically, it can be found in the office of the Town Clerk of North Hempstead, at Roslyn, Queens County, Vol. E, pp. 18, 19, where all can read and digest the quit claim deed of Widow Anne's grandson Obadiah, of Southampton, in which on August 13, 1735, he quit claims to Jeremiah Wood, of the town of Hempstead, "what right I have, or ought to have, to any of the estate in the township of Hempstead, formerly purchased by my grandfather, William Rogers, deceased."

It has been very hard to quietly hold this back, until in the sequence of history it could properly be brought forward. Inclination prompted its being connected with almost any one, but there has been no place for it until it came to its own.

THE MARTYR CLAIM.

The Long Island Rogerses are not the only ones who claim, with Thomas Rogers, of the Mayflower, a line "from way back," which shall give them the increased glory of descent from John the Martyr.

In the "History of Huntington," page 6, there is the statement that Thomas, of the Mayflower, was son of John, of Dedham, who was son of Noah, of Exeter, who was son of John the Martyr, "Prebendary of St. Paul's, Vicar of St. Sepulchre's, and reader of Divinity, who was burnt at Smithfield, February 14, 1555. First Martyr in Queen Mary's reign."

NAME CONNECTIONS.

The name connections are very strong, to most people absolutely convincing. Thomas, the American progenitor name in England, after the fashion of the day, one son John, for his father. Then Noah, the son of William, seems to fit by his naming into the ancestral Noah.

THE MARTYR'S DESCENDANTS.

The history of John Rogers, of Smithfield fame, should certainly be found among the American family of the name, for I have heard of enough Bibles belonging to him, with full records as to identity and lineage, which have mainly perished in the flames, to have kindled his funeral pile, and occupied every moment of his maturer years, to the exclusion even of sleep and sustenance.

Surely he must have descendants, when the nursery tales "of long ago" harrowed the minds of children of that period by pictures of John Rogers at the stake, surrounded by "nine small children, and one at the breast." The works of art were very crude, and though the flames were angry and widespread, our Martyr seemed to bear a charmed life, to endure it all without any physical evidence but that of serene peace and perfect confidence in the truths for the expounding of which he was to suffer the death penalty.

The personal history of this family is very meager, but the lineage, as I have received it, is fine, and cannot fail to establish and call out all there is to be known. The line now given is very comprehensive, follows the Pilgrim beckonings, and must of necessity make authentic the claims of many families.

I. Thomas Rogers, of the Mayflower.

II. Williams Rogers, of Huntington, moved to Southampton, L. I.; a landholder from 1642 to 1645; married Anne, who in 1669 is a widow, and makes a will, leaving her property to her six children.

Obadiah (1), born 1630-5; inherited house and land at Southampton, which since 1650 has been in the family.

John (2), born 1646, of Huntington; Freeman; 1664; married Naomi, daughter of Robert Burdeck; landowner before 1668 in Huntington; removed to Branford about

SIGNERS OF THE MAYFLOWER COMPACT.

1666; landowner in Branford 1668; died in 1676, without issue.

Samuel (3).

Mary (4).

(Jonathan (5). (Town records of Huntington, L. I., published 1889) 1637).

Noah (6), born 1646.

Hannah (7).

III. Noah Rogers (6), born 1646, married Elizabeth, daughter of the first Michael Taintor, of Branford, and Elizabeth Rous (?), April 8, 1673. Noah removed to Branford about 1666. Was a landowner in Huntington before 1668; died 1725; left a large amount of money, besides much land. Issue:

Mary (8), born April 14, 1675; married —— Barnes, of East Hampton, L. I.

John (9), born November 6, 1677; married Lydia, daughter of John Frisbie and Ruth Bowers, June 17, 1713; died about 1750 in Branford (?).

Josiah (10), born January 31, 1679, one of the proprietors of the town of Branford; married Lydia Goodsell. Issue, eleven children.

Thomas, the sixth child, married Rebecca, daughter of Abijah Hobart, of Stonington, Conn., and died about 1750, in Branford, aged 86; had eight children.

Hezekiah (11).

Noah (12), born 1688.

Elizabeth (13), married Abiel Frisbie, of Branford.

Ann (14), married —— Barnes, of East Hampton, L. I.

IV. John Rogers (9), born November 6, 1677; married Lydia, daughter of John Frisbie and Ruth Bowers, June 17, 1713. He died about 1750 in Branford (?), Issue:

Lydia (15), baptized May 12, 1714.

Mary (16), baptized March 30, 1716.

Hannah (17), baptized July 10, 1718.

Elizabeth (18), baptized September 14, 1720.

John (19), baptized October 14, 1722.

Joseph (20), baptized April 29, 1725.

Daniel (21), baptized June 2, 1727.

Samuel (22), baptized October 5, 1729.

Stephen (23).

V. Joseph Rogers (20), baptized April 29, 1725, married, Susannah Pardee August 23, 1748. Issue:

Jason (24), born December 2, 1749 } twins.
Joel (25), born December 2, 1749 }

Abigail (26), born December 27, 1751.

Joseph (27), born in Branford, April 27, 1755, married Lois Hall, December 25, 1779, and died April 19, 1833.

Malachi (28), born November 28, 1763.

VI. Joseph Rogers (27), born April 27, 1755, in Branford, married Lois Hall, of Wallingford, Conn. (born September 25, 1757), December 25, 1779. Died in Claremont, N. H., April 19, 1833. She died May 30, 1829. Issue, all born in Wallingford, Conn.:

Thaddeus (29), born July 20, 1781, married Philina Putnam.

Bennajah (30), born October 3, 1782, married Sally Hartshorn.

Lemuel (31), born July 13, 1784, married Fanny Putnam.

Abigail (32), born February 15, 1787, married George Beeckman September 25, 1810, and second, Henry Hill, May 28, 1827.

Lois Hall (33), born July 31, 1789, married John Alexander January 28, 1810, of Keene, N. H.

Joseph (34), born March 20, 1792, married Alder Petty.

VII. Lois Hall Rogers (33), born July 31, 1789, at Wallingford, Conn., married John Alexander, of Keene, N. H., January 21, 1810, at Claremont, N. H. He was born July 27, 1790, at Winchester, N. H., and died March 18, 1840. She died January 26, 1881, at Cohoes, N. Y. Issue:

Lucius (34), born December 10, 1810, married Sophia Chapin; eight children.

James (35), born October 21, 1812, married Susan Braman; seven children.

Bradley (36), born November 27, 1815, married Frances Hale; six children.

Thankful (37), born March 18, 1818, died September 12, 1819.

Oliver (38), born May 3, 1820, married Lucretia Droune; three children.

Joseph George (39), born May 9, 1822, married Barbara Vickers; seven children.

John (40), born July 12, 1824, married Susan Wood; four children.

Seraph Ashley (41), born November 5, 1827, married 1849, Hon. Joseph Adams Pond, of Boston, Mass., president Massachusetts Senate; five children.

Lois Hall (42), born March 26, 1830, married Thomas W. Bachelle, of Lynn, Mass., March 29, 1853.

Bennajah Franklin (43), born September 7, 1832.

VIII. Seraph Ashley Alexander, born November 5, 1827, married December 4, 1849, Hon. Joseph Adams Pond, born in Boston September 8, 1827, died in Boston October 22, 1867. Issue:

Joseph (41) Adams, Jr.

Alexander Winthrop (42).

Frederic Wilson (43).

Carolyn Ashley (44).

Ellen Josphine Pond (45).

There are surely no limits to the claims of the Rogers family, and the present active interest will unquestionably place matters of ascent and descent right, even if it requires time to put everything in authentic line.

The rare opportunity I am availing myself of leads me to feel that I am only writing the "Pilgrim's Primer," a necessity for after work.

No one is great by themselves, and I can truly feel that, surrounded as I am by hosts of friends and upholders, I should achieve something of true importance.

The following records come from sources that admit of no questioning; the first are the result of the generous offer of Judge Charles N. Daniels, of the Windham County Probate Court, to whom the public will owe far more before the "Signers of the Compact" is complete.

ROGERS.

Copied from Windham Probate Records, Vol. I., Part 1, pages 312, 313.

Will of William Rogers, of Voluntown, dated December 25, 1727, offered for probate July 28, 1729, mentions oldest son John, second son, William, son Mathew Patrick and wife Elizabeth, daughters Anna and Janet and wife Janet. Vol. 2, page 178, date April 6, 1736, find receipt of John to his brother William for his part of his father's estate, witnessed by Mathew Patrick and Elizabeth Patrick.

Vol. 14, page 462, date January 17, 1801—Inventory of estate of Jeduthan Rogers, late of Hampton.

Vol. 15, page 148, date September 18, 1801—Receipt of heirs of Jeduthan Rogers, signed by Jeduthan Rogers, Rufus Rogers, Ambrose Ames and Anna Ames, Amos Green and Lucy Green, Jabez Walcott and Jemima Walcott, Edward Pease and Hannah Pease.

Vol. 14, page 462, date October 5, 1801—Will of Nathaniel Rogers, of Lebanon; wife, Susannah Rogers; sons, Jeremiah, Josiah, Daniel and Harris; daughter, Elizabeth Noyes, wife of John Noyes. Heirs of my daughter Theoda Watrous, deceased wife of Oliver Watrous. Heirs of my daughter, Hannah Stark, deceased wife of Dyar Stark. Daughter Lucinda Avery, daughter Susannah Hyde, wife of Solomon Hyde.

Vol. 15, page 233—Will of Jeremiah Rogers, of Lebanon, date August 10, 1805, probated May 6, 1806. Wife Lucy Rogers; daughters Lydia and Anna, now Lydia Stark; Anna Bartlett; son-in-law Caleb Stark, named as executor.

Vol. 15, page 291—Receipt of the only heirs to the estate of Jeremiah Rogers, late of Lebanon, dated August 23, 1806, signed by Caleb Stark and Julius Bartlett.

Vol. 19, page 339, August 10, 1829—Inventory of estate of Oliver Rogers, of Chaplin, $38.95; afterward declared insolvent, and no mention of heirs to be found.

In Court Book No. 5, Page 181, December 16, 1786—Nathaniel Rogers, of Lebanon, is appointed guardian of his grandson Seth Rose, minor.

One kind act has begotten another, and from Mr. C. H. Dimmick, Town Clerk of the town of Windham, Conn., comes the record of vital statistics of the town of Windham, Conn.

Relating to the Rogers Family.

Hope Rogers to Esther Meacham, marriage November 14, 1715.

CHILDREN.

Joseph, son, born August 5, 1716.

Ishmael, son, born July 7, 1717.

Ichabod, son, born January 19, 1718-19.

Josiah, son, born October 7, 1720.

Jethro, son, born April 14, 1722.

Jeduthan, son, born February 16, 1723-4.

Sarah, daughter, born February 21, 1725-6.

Mary, daughter, born October 6, 1727.

Joel, son, born October 14, 1729.

Ruth, daughter, born August 23, 1732.

DEATHS.

Joseph, son, died August 9, 1716.

Ichabod Rogers to Priscilla Holt, marriage November 10, 1743.

No record of any children born to them.

Jethro Rogers to Hannah Holt, marriage October 8, 1747.

CHILDREN.

Oliver, son, born April 14, 1748.

Bixbee, son, born December 18, 1749.

DEATHS.

Bixbee, son, died December 27, 1749.

Josiah Rogers to Hannah Ford, marriage March 1, 1742-3.

CHILDREN.

Jonah, son, born December 15, 1743.

Josiah, son, born August 2, 1747.

Hannah, daughter, born July 15, 1748.

DEATHS.

Josiah, son, died September 7, 1748.

Jeduthan Rogers to Anna Farnum, marriage October 21, 1747.

CHILDREN.

Jeduthan, son, born May 24, 1748.

Anna, daughter, born December 10, 1749.
Esther, daughter, born March 6, 1750.
Jeduthan, son, born March 4, 1753.
Esther, daughter, born January 7, 1755.
Lucy, daughter, born October 24, 1756.
Jemima, daughter, born July 19, 1758.
Isaiah, son, born February 20, 1760.
Tabitha, daughter, born November 19, 1761.

DEATHS.

Jeduthan, son, died June 24, 1750.
Esther, daughter, died September 6, 1753.
Esther, daughter, died January 21, 1756.
Tabitha, daughter, died April 22, 1763.
Anna, the wife of Jeduthan Rogers, died December 30, 1762.

Jeduthan Rogers to Hannah Knight, marriage October 12, 1763.

CHILDREN.

Hannah, daughter, born August 31, 1764.
Rufus, son, born January 16, 1767.
Asa, son, born March 14, 1769.

DEATHS.

Hannah, the wife of Jeduthan Rogers, died August 13, 1771.

Jeduthan Rogers to Eunice Burges, marriage October 4, 1772.
No record of any children born unto them.

Oliver Rogers to Hannah Coburn, marriage February 11, 1770.

CHILDREN.

Lovewell, son, born January 17, 1772.
Cynthia, daughter, born April 20, 1774.
Daniel, son born November 9, 1776.
Philora, daughter, born September 23, 1778.
Hannah, daughter, born May 26, 1785.
Tryphena, daughter, born December 7, 1788.

From Connecticut to Long Island is only following a Pilgrim impulse; the names show for the translation, and both places should be searched for connections.

The fate of the papers on all sides acts as a warning to those now in possession of valuable records to have copies made and placed in fireproof vaults.

It is hard to know they have been not purified, but extinguished by fire, and the escape of the following records from the Old or First Presbyterian Church, Huntington, L. I., which fell into the hands of the British, seems almost a miracle.

Only the marriages were given by the kind friend, who thoughtfully placed them at my disposal.

Josiah Rogers, married Elizabeth Conklin, March 23, 1724-5.
Hezekiah Rogers, married Ruth Scudder, March 29, 1725.
Philip Platt, married Phebe Rogers, December 15, 1725.
Joseph Rogers, married Mary Conklin, April 14, 1726.
Silas Weeks, married Sarah Rogers, January 23, 1726-7.
Jacob Rogers, married Sarah Smith, May 28, 1732.
Alexander Rogers, married Phebe Wood, August 29, 1732.
Annais Rogers, married Prudence Carle, November 7, 1732.
Cornelius Conklin, married Premella Rogers, November 7, 1732.
John Brush, married Jane Rogers, January 8, 1734.
Jonathan Rogers, married Hannah Whiteman, June 8, 1734; both been married before.
Noah Rogers, married Heziah Whiteman, February 18, 1734-5.
James Rogers, married Mary Smith, March 16, 1736.
John Titus, married Susanna Rogers, October 4, 1741.
Joseph Rogers, married Mary Rogers, widow, July 9, 1746.
Isaac Rogers, married Mary Rogers, November 27, 1747.
Cornelius Conklin, married Elizabeth Rogers, January 7, 1747.
Amos Platt, married Sarah Rogers, April 27, 1745.
Ebenezer Titus, married Jerusha Rogers, July 23, 1750.
Jonas Rogers, married Mary Jarvis, November 21, 1761.
Timothy Rogers, married Jemima Conklin, December 22, 1751.
Joseph Conklin, married Charity Rogers, January 15, 1752.
Thomas Rogers, married Mary Whitson, January 23, 1751-2.
Henry Jarvis, married Sarah Rogers, May 26, 1752.
Silas Sammis, married Ruth Rogers, September 28, 1762.
Zopha Rogers, married Deborah Whitehead, December 7, 1752.
Josiah Rogers, married Ruth Bunce, January 15, 1754.
Jeremiah Rogers, married Abigail Kelsey, March 23, 1757.
Obidiah Rogers, married Mary Rogers, January 23, 1769.
Timothy Rogers, married Mary Thomas, October 2, 1759.
Josiah Rogers, Jr., married Jerusha Rogers, June 10, 1760.
Andrew Leet Coles, Fairfield, Conn., married Elizabeth Rogers, June 11, 1760.
Silas Carle, married Mary Rogers, January 25, 1760.
Philip Rogers, married Phebe Rogers, October 9, 1762.
Zephaniah Rogers, married Mary Jarvis, May 15, 1779.

No matter who James Rogers, of New London, was descended from he had children and made a will, leaving behind him a clear record of his doings, his value in the community and the amount of his estate.

He came to America in the ship Increase in 1635, aged 20 years, always supposed to be a descendant of John the Martyr.

Few people have greater reason for making a claim, or feeling that they substantiated it, than this on the part of James Rogers. It needs no discussion; it comes authentically, so far as anything can, from the librarian of Alfred University, New York State, where the Bible recorded as from John the Martyr, of Smithfield, England, is preserved.

To strengthen and prove its value, I quote verbatim from the copy of the Bible records:

Written on inside of cover is the following:

Cranmer's first edition, to which this accurately corresponds, was first published in 1539. The archbishop was burned by Bloody Mary in 1556. We give this the date of 1549 for fear of antedating. Fifteen hundred and thirty-nine might, with more propriety, have been its date."

The following is written on the first fly leaf:

The
New Testament
of our Lord Christ
Translated from the original Greek by Cranmer,
Lord Archbishop of Canterbury,
in the second year of Edward VI.'s reign
MDXLIX.

The following is written on the second fly leaf:

Hoc Novum Testamentum Republica, eruditissimis viris ostensum est, inter quos alliqui illustres Theologiae Doctores erant, Id cum libris et codicillis amplissimarum bibliothecarum collatum est, et declaratum est Cranmeris Episcopi, primarii Canterbury, editio promulgata anno Domini MDXLIX, et in Brittaniae regis Edvardi VI. secundo anno.
Gulialmus H. Porter,
Waterford, Conn., Oct. 1st, 1839.

The following is a newspaper clipping pasted on a fly leaf taken from the "New London Repository:"

The Bible of John Rogers the Martyr.

Little did we dream, in the days of our boyhood, while, with eager curiosity and childish simplicity we used to pore over the pages of the New England primer, and pause with almost tearful sympathy over the quaint old wood cut representing the burning of the martyr, John Rogers, at the stake, attended by "his wife and nine small children, with one at the breast," that we should ever behold the Bible, the veritable Bible, read, pondered and prayed over by that noble martyr to the Christian faith. But we have the privilege of recording the strange fact that we have seen, handled and perused the identical precious relic of the days of the Smithfield fires and the bloody persecution of the reign of the cruel Mary.

The book itself is a small, thick quarto, containing the New Testament (the translation of Cranmer in 1539), the Psalms and a portion of the liturgy of the Protestant Church at that time. The title page, a few of the first and the last leaves have been lost, the book having been twice rebound. It is printed in the large, full, ancient German text, with ornamental initial letters to a portion of the chapters and a few marginal references.

The chapters are divided, as in King James's version, but they have no division into verses, capital letters in the margin indicating the commencement of paragraphs as they occur in each chapter.

In various parts of the book we find brief notes and memorandums by different persons relative to its carefully cherished and authentic history.

This venerable book, by a careful comparison with a number of ancient copies in the library of Yale College, New Haven, is ascertained by antiquarians to have been printed in 1549, in the days of King Edward VI., under the patronage of Thomas Cranmer, the primate of England, who was burnt at Oxford March 1, 1556, in the third year of Mary's reign, a little more than two years after Rogers was burnt at Smithfield.

The Bible was kept as an heirloom by the family, descendants of the venerated martyr, having been concealed from the minions of the bloody Queen during the remainder of her reign, in a bed, and carefully preserved until it passed into the hands of

James Rogers, a descendant (great-grandson, as by himself stated) of the martyr, by whom, when 20 years of age, it was brought over to this country.

He emigrated to New Haven in 1635, and most sacredly kept the precious relic in all his sojourns in this, then, wilderness, as a protection against the attacks of savage foes, or a talisman against misfortune. It came into the possession of Jonathan, the fifth son of James Rogers, descended to his eldest child, who, by marriage, became connected with the Potter family at Hopkinton, R. I.—Conclusion of Newspaper Clipping.

This Bible has been most religiously cherished in this family about a hundred years, and is now the property of Mrs. Saunders, niece of the late Miss Polly Potter, of Potter Hill, R. I.

It has been confided for a short time, as a precious relic, to Capt. Daniel Rogers, of this city, by whose indefatigable antiquarian genealogical researches its historical connection with every family through which it has passed has been fully established back through the descendants of the former owner, James Rogers, who came to America in 1635, as above stated.

Delays are not always dangerous, and to secure all that can be known requires the giving of sufficient time to leave no stone unturned to gather in the history all are anxious for.

A great searcher is certainly entitled to every consideration. One follows almost blindly their train of thought, and accepts it from the very force of their argument, but even in the face of my own willingness, I cannot see any cause why James Rogers, of Newport, R. I., should claim the place as possible son of Thomas of the Mayflower, as against James Rogers, of New London.

Mr. Drummond has effectually disposed of John, of Milford; left no possible argument in his favor, though even having two sons of the same name in a family is not without historical precedent, as Mr. Ethan Allen Doty found in his searches.

Rhode Island colonial records give that James Rogers was a freeman at Newport, R. I., March 15, 1643; was elected sergeant of the General Assembly March 15, 1643, and continued such until 1664, and was also the Solicitor General in 1657. In 1676 his widow, Mary Rogers (then Mary Peabody), petitions to settle his accounts.

THE MARTYR'S BIBLE.

Experts, whose opinions are all valuable, believe in the Bible now in the Museum of Alfred University as belonging to John, the Smithfield Martyr, inherited by his descendant, James Rogers, of New London, and by him brought to this country.

This coincides with my own convictions, and on this platform I propose to work, acknowledging from the onset that many records which would have been convincing to me a short time since, to-day, from the fact of my long searching among these people of Pilgrim claim, have only led me to make an entire change of belief.

Each historian of this family has given, according to his lights, the opinions formed from the records found.

They have turned all the stones in their line of march, but left many, as a matter of course, to be removed by others.

JOHN THE MARTYR.

John Rogers, the martyr, holds his own always, and all will feel better acquainted with him when they read that he was born about 1500, at Deritend, in the parish of Aston, near Birmingham.

This gives us pause, and tells the Pilgrim story of the Scrooby postroad, of the cities and towns surrounding it, where, from generation to generation the germ of Separatism was being passed on, gathering in strength for the deeds which make the history of our country.

John, of Smithfield, was only in advance of his times, when, from an orthodox Catholic priest, he became a Protestant, and, with the new zeal of his conversion, made the manner of his death such a triumph of faith.

Being the son of John the first, as I reckon him, though many generations behind him are known, and Margery Wyatt, the father a loriner, in our modern view of the calling a saddler, how he must have startled his parents in their simple life by his going out from them to the world he made for himself.

Nature asserted itself in the change of religion, and soon John, of Smithfield fame, took to himself the wife who has been no small part in the history connected with the Martyr.

"Adrianna de Weyden, (the surname meaning meadows, Latin, prata, anglicized into Pratt)," his choice was from Antwerp, and they are found, shortly after their marriage at Wittenberg, where he was in charge of a Protestant congregation, and became a proficient German scholar.

All the names in the biographies, histories, etc., are reproduced in the American descendants, John always to the front, as was fitting, but the roll call, even as known, can be responded to over and over again.

Placing Thomas, of the Mayflower, as a descendant of John, the Martyr, seems to me not only possible, but so conclusive that an argument sent me from Miss Anna B. Williams, of Springfield, Mass., fits so naturally into my own suppositions and needs that I give it entire, hoping the outgrowth may be definite light on the subject.

ANOTHER'S OPINION.

"It seems to me that about the first thing the wife of the Martyr would have done, after the terrible tragedy in England, would have been to flee with all speed, with her young children to her native town and friends, Germany, not far from the very spot whence embarked the passengers of the Mayflower. This stone is conspicuous and has never been turned."

Intercouse with relatives in the sections near Birmingham, and Antwerp, could easily produce the descent, which would send to us Thomas of the Mayflower, and later on the "other children," who bore the names recorded in history.

OTHERS OF THE FAMILY.

Although Thomas, with his young son Joseph, were the pioneers, they were not, as I argue, the only members of their immediate family represented in the early colonies.

It must be remembered that the Cooke and Rogers families intermarried many times in Europe, also that the name of the wife of John, the Martyr, was Pratt.

This serves my purpose, and I call attention to the record of New Plymouth colony. "In the division of cattle on May 22, 1627, the first lot fell to Francis Cooke, and his company joined to him." Among them were Joshua Pratt, Phineas Pratt.

Then to establish them as "old colonies," who were held back to await means of conveyance, they are found on the first list of freeman, 1633, Joshua Pratt coming on one of the "forefather ships," Phineas, supposed of Weston's company.

Kinspeople together, Francis Cooke as always the head of the family. Such things do not come by chance.

JAMES, OF NEW LONDON.

James Rogers, as has been stated, came to America in the Increase, 1635, aged 20 years. The first knowledge of him is at Stratford, New Haven County, Conn., where he married Elizabeth, daughter of Samuel Rowland, their oldest son, Samuel, benefiting by his naming, for he received from his grandfather, Rowland, according to Savage, a large estate.

Next he is heard of at Milford, Conn., where his wife united with Mr. Pruddens Church, (who was the first pastor in Milford), in 1645, and "he himself in 1652." In the same church the children were baptized.

"In ye story of ye Memorial, as told by Nathan G. Pond," in commemoration of the 250th year of Milford's History, there is an account of the stone bridge raised in honor of this event, on one stone of which, as the gift of Hon. Isaac T. Rogers, is inscribed.

```
JAMES ROGERS,
   Obit. 1688.
Elizabeth, His Wife.
```

Whatever his birthright, James Rogers had the spirit of his and every epoch of the world where the man owned the ability, to seek large business interests, and, being of strong stock, he succeeded.

His small dealings with New London "grew and multiplied" until he had to seek a broader field for his workings, and went permanently to New London, the home of Governor Winthrop, of Connecticut, and Jonathan Brewster, between 1656 and 1660.

Before leaving Milford he recorded himself, for in 1655 he was "informed against for bad buskit and flower, and if after that his flower or bread was bad the damage would fall on him."

Being "in transit," he did not hesitate to make further history, and in 1656 "James Rogers was informed against for bringing in liquors and not paying customs duties on them. He was present, and said it was two or three anchors. He was ordered to answer to his neglect."

Safe in New London, he tried his little game again, and in 1657 "James Rogers had three anchors of liquor forfeited."

Honor and prosperity came with his local habitation in the plantation. He soon gained property and influence, found himself sought, and employed in civil and ecclesiastical affairs. Six times chosen representative to the "General Court," and in "Memorial History of Hartford," Vol. I., he is given as one of the men from Saybrook (where he lived for a short time), in the Pequot war.

Wise James, he anticipated the Rogers call for Colonial sons and dames. Gov. Winthrop, mindful of his value, urged his settlement in New London, accommodated him with a portion of his own home lot,

On this Rogers, building for perpetuity, erected a house of stone.

BUSINESS.

"He was a baker on a large scale, often furnishing biscuit for seamen and for colonial troops, and between 1660 and 1670 had a greater interest in the trade of those parts than any other person in the place."

Head of the first "American Biscuit Company". and next to Gov. Winthrop, the richest man in the State.

His landed possessions were very extensive, his outlook was on a broad domain he knew was his own, there were "several hundred acres on 'great neck,' the fine tract of land called "Pachaug farm," several house lots in town, and twenty-four acres east of the river, which he held in partnership with Col. Pynchon, of Springfield, Mass."

The wolf was effectually driven from the Rogers door.

The children, I am happy to give authentically, from Mr. J. S. Rogers, of Chicago, and while I add many personal traits and items, the dates of births, marriages and deaths I place securely from his courtesy.

I. Samuel (James, 1), born 12-12-1640, died 12-1-1713; married (1) 11-17-1662, Mary, daughter of Thomas, and Dorothy (Lord) Stanton, married (2) Joanna, widow of Thomas Williams, of New London.

Their children were:

1. Mary, born 4-17-1667; died, 9-30-1756; married, 10-2-1685, Capt. Samuel Gilbert (son of Jonathan,1), of Hartford, Conn., afterward of Colchester, Conn. He died

2. Samuel, born 12-22-1669; died 2-2-1743; married 1-16-1694, Abigail, daughter of John Plumb. She died 6-7-1732, aged 57.

This is probably the Samuel who married, 1733, Elizabeth Hall, but December 1737, he married Palatiah, widow of John Ames, and daughter of John Stebbins. She died 1-6-1755, aged 78.

3. Daniel, born about 1670, died before 1737; married, 9-24-1702, Grace, daughter of Thomas and Joanna Williams. She was born 1680.

4. Elizabeth, born 5-8-1673; died about 1750; married (1), 1-5-1699, Theophilus Stanton, of Preston, Conn.; married (2), 3-17-1709, Asa Harris. He was born in Boston, Mass, 11-10-1680. Was brother of James Harris, who married her sister Sarah.

5. Anna, born 5-8-1675; died, 7-26-1689.

6. Sarah, born 8-9-1676; died, 11-13-1748; married, 5-10-1696, James Harris, son of James Harris, of Boston, Mass.

When Samuel Rogers and Mary Stanton were married, "the parents of the two contracting parties each pledged £200 as a marriage portion to the couple." Mr. Rogers, in fulfillment of his bond, conveyed to his son his stone house and bakery at Winthrop's Cove, or Mill, where the son commenced his housekeeping and lived for fifteen or twenty years.

II. Joseph (James, 1), born 5-14-1646; died 1697; married Sarah ———; she died 8-17-1728.

Their children were:

1. James, born 1672, died 7-21-1721; married 3-27-1669, Sarah, daughter of James Stevens, of Killingworth, Conn. She born 1680, died 1-4-1752.

2. Samuel, married (1) 3-24-1703, his cousin Elizabeth, daughter of James Rogers; married (2), 4-28-1707, Deborah ———; she died 7-17-1727.

3. Joseph, Jr., died 1, —, 1724; married Deborah ———; she died 7-17-1727.

4. John, born 3-20-1676; died 7-13-1739; married 2-5-1718, Deborah Dayton.

5. Rowland, born about 1680; died 5-16-1712; married Mary ———.

6. Elizabeth, married (1) ——— Chapman; married (2), 4-7-1705, Bartholomew Crossman.

7. Sarah, died 11-21-1729; married 2-18-1712, Thomas, son of Thomas and Susanna Williams. She left her husband after birth of daughter Ruth (born 1713), who married Joseph Huntley, of Lyme. Thomas Williams married again, 1717, Sarah Babcock. Sarah did not remarry.

8. Bathsheba, married, 4-24-1725, Gabriel, son of John Harris; he born about 1686.

9. Jonathan, born about 1683; married Alice Champion, of Lyme. She had her dower set off about 1749. Three minor children.

III. John (James (1), born 12, 1, 1648; died 10, 17, 1721; married (1), 10, 17, 1670, Elizabeth, daughter of Matthew Griswold. She was born 1652 and died 1727. John Rogers, having left the established church and joined the "Seventh Day Baptist" Church, of Newport, R. I., his wife was granted a divorce in 1676. He married 6, 6, 1699, Mary Ransford. This marriage was declared illegal in 1703. He married (3) 7, —, 1714, Widow Sarah Coles, of Oyster Pond, L. I.

At the marriage of John Rogers to Elizabeth Griswold, her father performed the ceremony, accompanied with a written contract, or dowry, the husband prophetically preparing for the separation which occurred.

He was at one time a man of influence in New London, Conn., but eventually becoming a law unto himself, he naturally suffered from the powers he was antagonizing. What he desired, he assumed, taking to himself the ministerial offices of baptizing and preaching, and further to separate himself from the accepted sects organized one of his own, called "Rogerine Baptists," or "Rogerine Quakers." He obeyed the government so far as it did not conflict with his code of conscience or religion. They paid the county rate, but the poor ministers had no rights. They must live on constant "donation parties," and the rate for their maintenance was not only not recognized but abhorred.

Prayer with them must be silent, unless the grace from within was too strong for repression, and burst forth in song or word. To a slight degree they favored in their belief the Christian Scientists. They considered the use of physicians and drugs as sinful, relying on kindness, care and watchfulness for cures in case of sickness.

The Congregational Church was in the ascendant at that time, and vigorous as was the growth of the Rogerines, the other sect, with Thomas Hooker as its expounder, was too deep rooted to have it viewed calmly. Still, with all that can be said on the subject, the granting of a divorce for ecclesiastical reasons, gave evidence of greater bigotry than one should expect, even in those times, though the feeling for Elizabeth Griswold Rogers is much lessened by the knowledge that in less than in two years she married Peter Pratt (August 5, 1679).

The names have come to us again. The Cookes were Baptists, though not of the Rogerine school, and they were Rogers kin, the Tabers through whom so many reach Francis Cooke were Baptists, and to leave nothing unfinished, there was a Pratt, perhaps waiting and willing to marry John Rogers's divorced wife.

The children of John and Elizabeth Griswold Rogers, first wife of John, were:

1. Elizabeth, born 11, 8, 1671; married Stephen Prentiss, son of John Prentiss, of Lyme, Conn., 1689-90.

2. John, born 3, 20, 1674; died 6, 18, 1753; married 1, 20, 1700, his cousin, Bathsheba Smith. She, daughter of Richard and Bathsheba (Rogers) Smith; married (2) 1, 28, 1723, Elizabeth, daughter of Israel Dodge, of New London.

Children by second wife, Mary:

3. Gershom, born 2, 24, 1700; died 1770; married 4, 8, 1725, Sarah, daughter of David Wheeler, of Groton, Conn.

4. Mary, born 3, 6, 1702; died 11, 5, 1781; married 1, 22, 1730, John son of John Hobbs, of Boston.

IV.—Bathsheba (James (1)), born 12, 30, 1650; married 3, 4, 1669-70, Richard Smith, of New London, Conn.; married (2), Samuel Fox.

Their children were:

1. James, who married Elizabeth (daughter of Jonathan Rogers); baptized, 4—12—1674.

2. Elizabeth, married William Camp, of New London.

3. John.

4. Bathsheba, married John Rogers (2), 1, 2, 1700. She died 11, 13, 1721.

5. Richard, died about 1703.

V.—James (James (1)), born 2, 15, 1652, died 2, 7, 1713; married 11, 5, 1674, Mary, daughter of Jefferson Jordan, of Ireland. "Tradition says that Capt. James Rogers commanded a vessel which brought over a number of Redemptionists from Ireland, among them this Jordan family. On his arrival Capt. Rogers became the purchaser of the oldest daughter, Mary, and married her."

In after life he would say "that it was the richest cargo he ever shipped, and the best bargain he ever made."

Their children were:

1. James, born 2, 2, 1674, died 7, 9, 1733; married (1) Elizabeth ———, who died 2, 28, 1713; married (2) Freelove Hurlburt (daughter of Stephen); she was born 1694, and died 1, 26, 1739.

2. Mary, born 5, 1, 1678, died 12, 31, 1720; married 1, 30, 1705, Thomas, son of John Prentiss.

3. Elizabeth, born 8, 27, 1680; married, 3, 24, 1703, Samuel, son of Joseph Rogers; she died 6, 29, 1703.

4. Sarah, born 11, 23, 1682; died, 1776; married (1) Jonathan Haynes; married (2) Elder Stephen Gorton; he was born 1704 (son of Benjamin).

5. Samuel, born 3, 23, 1685; died young.

6. Jonathan, born 4, 13, 1678; lived to at least 1714, but probably unmarried.

7. Richard, born 10, 13, 1689; married, 1710, Mary (or Mercy), daughter of Joshua and Mercy (Sandys) Raymond.

8. William, born 5, 10, 1693; died 1, 21, 1744; married, 8, 27, 1713, Elizabeth Harris; married in Westerly, R. I., but lived first in New London, and said to have removed to New Jersey.

The daughter, Lydia, married John Dodge, October 23, 1748, and from them are descended many prominent families.

VI. Jonathan (James (1)), born 12, 31, 1655; baptized in Newport, R. I., 1674; drowned at Gull Island about 1697; married Naomi, daughter of Elder Robert (of the

Baptist Church) and Ruth (Hubbard) Burdick.

Children of Jonathan and Naomi:
1. Ruth, born 1678; married William, son of Samuel Beebe.
2. Elizabeth, born 1681; married James, son of Richard and Bathsheba (Rogers) Smith.
3. Naomi, born 1686; married, 2, 25, 1708, Benjamin, son of Samuel Fox.
4. Content, born 1688; married 5, 1, 1707, Jonathan Maxson, son of John and Mary (Mosher) Maxson, of Westerly, R. I. He was born 1680 and died 11, 20, 1732.
5. Jonathan, Jr. (only son), born 1690; died 6, —, 1780; married, about 1711, Judith Potter.
6. Rachel, born 1692; married Samuel Fox, Jr.
7. Catherine, born 1694; married 4, 15, 1720, William Brookfield, son of William, of Elizabethtown, N. J.

VII. Elizabeth (James (1)), born 4, 15, 1658; died, 6, 10, 1716; married 2, 9, 1682, Samuel Beebe, of Plum Island.

Their children were:
1. Elizabeth, born 10, 27, 1684; married Nathaniel Newbury, of New London.
2. Mary, born 5, 4, 1686; married John Clark, of Plum Island.
3. Bathsheba, born 3, 16, 1688; married William King, Jr., of Southold, L. I.
4. Rebecca, born 1, 25, 1690; married Samuel Brown, of Southold, L. I.
5. Patience, born 2, 25, 1692; married Elder Thomas Hiscox, of Westerly, R. I., as his second wife.
6. Hopestill, twin of Patience.
7. Hannah, born 4, 5, 1695; married —— Lester, of Plum Island.
8. James, born 10, 10, 1701; married Susanna Babcock.

The naming of the children in the various families has a strong bearing on their consanguinity. James, of New London, with good judgment, gives to his first born the name of Samuel; then came Joseph for the brother who coming out with his father, in view of the Pilgrim's death, took upon himself the duties his age would admit of, and stood in his father's place.

The inevitable John, pursuing the Rogers family always, then James for himself.

The will tells the story of the man—his keen sense of justice, devotion to his wife and her interests, mindful of his children's rights, always under their mother, and an abiding faith in the Heavenly Father, who would pronounce the plaudit "Well done, good and faithful servant" for his efforts to lead the life of His appointing.

THE WILL OF JAMES ROGERS.

The last will and testament of James Rogers, Sr., being in perfect memory and understanding, but under the hand of God by sickness. This I leave to my wife and all my children, sons and daughters, I being old and knowing the time of my departure is at hand. What I have of this world I leave among you, desiring you not to fall out or contend about it, but let the love one to another appear more than to the estate I leave you, which is of this world. And for your comfort I signify to you that I have a perfect assurance of an interest in Jesus Christ and eternal happy estate in the world to come, and do know and see my name written in the Book of Life, and therefore do not mourn as they that are without hope.

1. I commit my spirit into the hands of God Almighty, desiring my body, it may be buried (hoping for the resurrection), and what is expended thereupon let it be paid out of the estate I leave. I desire all my debts may be paid out of the estate I leave. I know of no old debts unpaid nor any great matter of debts I owe. My land at Mystic I bequeath to my three eldest sons, Samuel, Joseph and John, it being first by them divided into three parts, and then let it be divided to them by lot, that each may know what his part is, for as the lot falls, so shall each one's part be, they paying to my daughter Elizabeth £25.

2. To my son James I bequeath Goshen Neck, and he shall have a highway to it over the pond where I now go.

3. To my son Jonathan my houses and lands so far back as Magunk fence, which lies within my field fence, and the bounds between my son James and son Jonathan, which is, so to say, between Goshen and my field shall be the great rock which lies between the pond, and the sea on the north side of the beach, a line being run north and south from the said rock shall be the bounds between them. To my son Jonathan I bequeath the twenty acres in the new pasture joining his house and running on the south side of my field fence, and bounded on the east by the lane running between the head of my son James his home lot and my son Jonathan his own dwelling house.

To my son John and son Jonathan I bequeath all the rest of my land lying in the new pasture, as also all the rest of my land lying in the General Neck, it being divided by them into two parts first, and then, as the lot comes forth shall each one know what his part is, and my will is that my son James pay to my daughter Elizabeth twenty pounds within a year after the death of his mother (my wife), and that my son Jonathan pay to my daughter Elizabeth fifty pounds within three years after the death of my wife, ten of it the first year after her death.

To my son Joseph I bequeath the land I had of Obadiah Bowen, called Bruin's Neck.

To my son John I leave the land I had of Robert Allyn, lying on the east side of the river that goeth to Norwich, he paying to his sister, my daughter Bathsheba the sum of twenty pounds within a year after the death of my wife, and if he sees cause not so to do, my daughter Bathsheba shall have said land.

And all the rest of my estate, as cattle, household goods, debts and personal estate, I leave to my wife to dispose of as she sees good, only to pay to my daughter Elizabeth ten pounds if she sees good, with the advice of my son John.

I also give liberty to my wife to sell or dispose of any part of my land or estate here willed, if she sees cause so to do, without offense to any of my children, and to have the use of my houses to live in or to let out.

Some cattle was left with me by my son John to use as my own, not giving me power to give or will away, but did promise me what I sold or killed for the family's use he never would demand pay, but for only those that should be remaining in my hands. The chamber where my son John now lies I leave to him with the room under it for him to live in during his lifetime if my wife sees cause not to order it otherwise.

If any difference should arise about my land here willed, or any part of my estate, for want of a plain discovery, whether about bounds or otherwise, my will is there shall be no lawing among my children before earthly judges, but that the controversy be ended by lot, and so I refer the judgment of God, and as the lot comes forth so let it be.

And this I declare to be my last will and testament, as witness my hand this eleventh day of the ninth month, one thousand six hundred and eighty-three.

James Rogers.

Samuel Beebe, Mary Beebe, witnesses.

Recorded in the third book of wills for New London County this 22d day of July, 1703.

(James Rogers died when the government of Sir Edmund Andros was paramount in New England. His will was therefore proved in Boston, Mass.)

AGAIN THE OTHER CHILDREN.

In speaking of the Plymouth records a correspondent writes: "In only one book could I find anything about his other children (Thomas's), who came over later—William, who settled in Hempstead, L. I.; and John, who owned land in Plymouth, with his brother Joseph."

The statements in regard to this family, made nearly half a century ago must have weight, lesssening as they do the time between the generations who were the participants in the great drama of life, so fruitful in results, enacted at Cape Cod. I give a "note of a discourse on the 'History of the Congregational Church Society' of North Branford, Conn., January 6, 1850, by Rev. George I. Wood, then pastor of the church, in which he says that the first meeting house there was built about 1724 (!!), gives names of the Building Committee, including name of Josiah Rogers, and in a foot note says: 'This Josiah Rogers, the ancestor of the Rogerses of North Branford, was a lineal descendant of the fifth generation from John Rogers, who was burnt by the Roman Catholics at Smithfield in 1554.'"

No one can realize better than I do that I am presenting "an unvarnished tale" to the public. I have courted kindly criticism step by step—very little has come to me—but I do not rest in consequence in the belief it has not been made. All I ask is that it shall be public—that history may benefit by the discussion.

What remains for me to do is to give a few records that will lead to sectional clews, and not to neglect an ancestry dearly prized, which I think is only part of what has gone before. I copy:

"The records of another branch, taken from books in the Historical Rooms, Newark, N. J."

"Rev. Nathaniel Rogers came to America in 1636. His descendants claimed descent from John the Martyr, through Nathaniel's father, John Rogers, of Dedham, England. The family records in manuscript (Nathaniel being first writer) are now in possession of Lucy M. Harris, of Albany, N. Y.

"Nathaniel was born in Haverhill, England, in 1598, graduated at Cambridge University and became a noted preacher, married Margaret Crane, of Coggeshall, England, settled at Ipswich, Mass., died 1655.

"Children—John, Nathaniel and Samuel.

John was president of Harvard College at his death, in 1684.

"His son John, the second writer in the book, was born at Kittery (now Elliot), Me., in 1692, graduated at Harvard 1711, married Susannah Whipple, was a preacher at Kittery, and died 1773.

He was the father of eight children, the eldest named John. There was a John in every Rogers family, including the Martyr, for fourteen generations. The conclusions of Joseph L. Chester, a descendant of Nathaniel, and who made an exhaustive research in English records, are that there is only the slightest possibility that John Rogers, of Dedham, was a grandson of the Martyr. Chester traces the maternal ancestry of Thomas Rogers, grandfather of the Martyr, from Charlemagne, down through William the Conqueror, Henry I., Henry II., King John, Henry III. and Edward I.

First generation, John Fitz Rogers, who married a daughter of Sir Simon Furnep.

Second generation, Sir John Fitz Rogers, married a daughter of Sir Thomas Etchingham.

Third generation, Sir Henry Fitz Rogers, married a daughter of Lord Stoughton.

Fourth generation, Thomas Rogers, who had two elder brothers, Sir John and James, a doctor of divinity.

Fifth generation, John.

Sixth generation, John.

Seventh generation, John the Martyr (his children were Daniel, John, Ambrose, Samuel, Philip, Bernard, Augustine, Barnaby, Susan, Elizabeth and Hester).

Eighth generation, John, LL. D.

Ninth generation, Rev. John of Chacombe.

Tenth generation, Rev. John of Sherburne. This brings us down to the beginning of the line in this country.

The children of the latter, as copied from Scituate town records, are: John 1682, Alice 1685, Daniel 1688, Elizabeth 1691, Thomas 1695, Hannah 1701, Joshua 1708, Mary 1712, Caleb 1718.

The above John, born 1682, and wife Deborah, had Daniel 1708, Elizabeth 1709, John 1711, and Deborah 1713.

John, 1711, married Plain Wilkinson; their son John, born 1758, in Menden, Mass., married, in 1794, Sally Ballou; their children were Abigail 1795, Nathan 1797, John Adams 1799, George Washington 1801, Eunice and Eliza (twins) 1803, James 1805, Maria 1810, John Wilkinson 1813, and William 1817.

Abigail married Samuel Chaffin, of Holden, Mass., and Eunice Thomas Davis.

The names are all here, Thomas second only to John, the rest male, and female in every branch.

It is the same puzzle, but it is in our hands for persistent effort.

One line takes into the Dutch of Long Island through

1. Thomas, of the Mayflower.
2. William, and Anne, who died 1669.
3. Jonathan, born 1637, married Rebecca, and died 1707.
4. John, and ——, died after 1730, deed was made then.
5. John, married about 1735 Jemima Whitman.
6. John, born 1737, died 1791, married November 26, 1761, Ruth Wood.
7. Mary Rogers, married John Whitman.
8. Anne Whitman, married Zebulon Ketcham.
9. Eliza Ketcham, married Samuel Van Wyck.

Another which leads through Connecticut is valuable. With it the story ends, but fine records will go to the Mayflower Society, too long and numerous for publishing.

1. Thomas Rogers, of the Mayflower.
2. William and Anne, of Long Island.
3. Noah and Elizabeth Tainter Rogers, of Granford, Conn.
4. Josiah, son of Noah, of Branford, who married Lydia Goodsell.
5. Josiah Rogers, Jr., born in 1708, married Martha, daughter of Edward Frisbie, April 24, 1728.
6. Medad Rogers (born August 17, 1750), married Rachel Baldwin July 9, 1787.
7. Amzi Rogers, born December 17, 1793, married Betsy, daughter of Samuel T. Barnum, September 22, 1814.
8. Theodore D. Rogers, born June 10, 1822, resides in Norwalk, Conn.

A choice bit of history is added to the James Rogers, of New London, descent: John Rogers (5), Dr. Uriah (4), James (3), James (2), James (1), born November 3, 1744, and brother of Hannah (Rogers) Kent, mother of Chancellor James Kent, has never been accounted for in any published accounts I can find.

During or before the revolution he moved to Saratoga County, N. Y., then the frontier, married a Scotchwoman, McCrea, had five children, and died there about 1795. There is a record of him as living in Ballston, Saratoga County, N. Y., Dec. 31, 1779, where his assessment was £84 and tax £3 13s., (Hist. Saratoga Co., p. 250).

I can only give positively the descendants of his daughter, Sara Rogers. She married, 1801, William M. Wilkins, whose first born was named John Rogers.

I have often heard my grandfather say his mother was an own cousin to Chancellor Kent, which proves the connection. William M. Wilkins and Sara Rogers had a number of children. My grandfather, John Rogers Wilkins, had thirteen, so you see there are a great many descendants. John Rogers had besides Sara, David Rogers, who married and lived in Corinth, 1820-30, and had a family. Susan Rogers, who married a Shepherd, had two daughters, Jane, who died about 1885, in Ballston, N. Y., unmarried, and Mary, who married a Franchot. Leucretia Rogers married an Anthony, of Little Falls, N. Y. Nancy Rogers married a Taylor; no children.

Another item has come through Mr. L. T. Rogers, of Milton Junction, Wisconsin, who says that when the city of New London was burned by the English during the revolution, the Rogers papers were burned in the house of Peter Rogers.

Whatever information is gained in regard to this family, by the searches now being made in England, will be given to the public in the paper, and added in the third part of the pamphlet.

THOMAS TINKER, Nineteenth Signer.

"Came in the Mayflower, with wife and a son. All died in the first winter."

JOHN RIDGDALE, Twentieth Signer.

"Died before April, 1621. Alice, his wife, died first winter."

EDWARD FULLER, Twenty-first Signer.

The brothers, Dr. Samuel Fuller, the dearly loved physician of the Pilgrim colony, and Edward, came together on the Mayflower, the latter with his wife, Ann, and son, Samuel.

The journey over, the parting was immediate, for the first sickness proved too much for Edward and Ann Fuller, so they answered the summons and went from this world together, to be sure, but the human wrench at leaving behind their son, the "young Samuel," sad as it was, must have been lessened by the fact that another home stood open for him.

Safe in the care of his uncle, the "deacon doctor," the ties soon became but a memory, and as years and strength were accorded him, he took up the duties that came to him with the integrity of his birthright.

Surely his life must have been planned to his dear uncle's satisfaction, for he made him executor of his will, and showed him always the trust begotten of good behavior.

RECOGNITION.

The colony, too, recognized boy's rights, or rather tender claims upon them, for in the division of land three shares were apportioned to him, acceptable, truly, as a sweet, living remembrance that they should thereby perpetuate the memory, and show their respect for the parents, so early taken, and be so far as material life was concerned, in the personal relation of the father to the fatherless.

The home so cordially given him, was the truest and best a child could have or need, and in its wholesome atmosphere, the "young Samuel" grew and thrived apace, until he was made freeman of the colony in 1634.

He did everything well, never with any ostentatious demand, going from Plymouth to Scituate April 8, 1635, carrying with him his credentials of Christian fellowship with the Plymouth Church, which entitled him to membership in Scituate, where he joined the church November 7, 1636, with approval on all sides.

HIS MARRIAGE.

On April 8, 1635, he increased his happiness and position by marrying Jane, daughter of Rev. John Lothrop, and to give a substantial bearing to the whole matter, the ceremony was performed, civil rites being the order of the day, by the stalwart of the colony, Capt. Myles Standish. To increase the rights of his descendants in the present requisites for membership in the various societies the future marriage connections were of the strongest.

Jane Lothrop was born at Edgerly, Kent, England, September 29, 1614. Her father, the Rev. John, being a son of Thomas Lowthropp, of Ellen, Yorkshire. This placing satisfies my plea of local connection with the "old comers," gives acquaintance with George Morton, perhaps Edward Southworth, Brewster, Bradford, Francis Cooke and the like.

People of one intent, only biding the time for change of location.

The Lothrops can carry their line still further back, for Thomas Lowthropp was son of John Lowthropp, of a parish in the East Riding of York, and our Rev. John Lothropp brought with him a strong history. Educated either at Oxford or Christ College, Cambridge, he was the second minister of the First Independent Church in England.

Imprisoned by Archbishop Laud, upon his release in 1634, he sailed to America, remaining nine days in Boston. He next sought Scituate, and then settled in Barnstable, where he was pastor many years.

GOV. WINTHROP'S OPINION.

Rev. John Lothrop's arrival was of importance. Gov. Winthrop made public mention of it, noting and commending the "modesty and reserve of one who had so prominently, so ably, so fearlessly upheld the Puritan faith."

The blood of the Pilgrims and Puritans makes a national claim for these Fullers, and report says that recent researches in Europe have given more of the history of this name than any other.

HIS HOME.

Soon the home nest to which Jane Lothrop Fuller was going was prepared. The sparsely settled neighborhood had no terrors for this Puritan maid. The fact that theirs was but the fifteenth house had no intimidations. She knew the work of making it habitable was before her, and she only had time for such duties.

The records credit Samuel Fuller with a residence in Barnstable as early as 1641, but there seems no certainty until 1644.

No town that had Samuel Fuller for a citizen would neglect to write his name so that it would be known, if he were really there.

Samuel Fuller lived his simple life, as he should from his forbears, retiring in disposition and habit, eminently pious, an honest man, good neighbor and Christian gentleman.

His opinions of such value, such integrity, there was no withdrawal under pressure of circumstances.

Large wealth for the times came of his honest methods. History tells that he was the only one of the Mayflower passengers to settle in Barnstable, where he died October 31, 1683.

The mantle of his uncle had fallen on his shoulders, and the account rendered of him makes the world better for his having existed.

MATTHEW.

Matthew, the son of Edward and Ann Fuller, who came after his parents, was a man of different caliber from his brother.

His talents were as great, but so perverted as almost to be lost sight of. He had a strange political method for the day, was on the fence, giving his opinions with rash freedom, but fell either side when sure of popular approval.

Owning property together, thrown of necessity upon each other for society from the very loneliness they were surrounded by in their home, did not unite them in opinion.

They were in thought and deed the very antipodes of each other.

The world was before Matthew Fuller, but of his own choosing he did not make the best of it.

Considering what he accomplished, because of his strong man's nature, one sorrows to think of the lost outcome if he had only been in earnest.

HIS FAMILY.

Dr. Matthew Fuller came to America about 1640 with wife and three children. His prominence in Plymouth Colony none can doubt. He was "captain in the military, surgeon-general of the Colony troops and served as chairman in the Council of War in 1671." He had two wives—Frances and Hannah—and died in Barnstable, Mass., 1678.

His children were (1), Mary, born in England, who married Ralph Jones, April 17, 1655; (2), Elizabeth, born in England, married Moses Rowley, April 22, 1652; (3), Lieut. Samuel, born in England, married Mary ——; (4), Dr. John, born in Plymouth, Mass., maried Berthia ——; (5), Anna, also born in Plymouth, married her cousin, Samuel Fuller.

SAMUEL, SON OF EDWARD.

Samuel died October 31, 1683, as Savage says, "one of the latest Mayflowers." His children were:

(1), Hannah, born in Scituate; married Nicholas Bonham, January 1, 1659. (2), Samuel, baptized February 11, 1637; married Samuel Fuller. (3), Elizabeth, who married —— Taylor. (4), Sarah, baptized August, 1641; died young. (5), Mary, born June, 1644; married Joseph Williams, November 18, 1674. (6), Thomas, born May 18, 1650; died young. (7), Sarah, born December 14, 1654, and married —— Crow, (8), John, born in Barnstable, 1656; married Mehitable Rowley, and, after the birth of four or five children, moved to East Haddam, Conn.

FULLER TREASURES.

The Fuller cradle is a matter of authentic history, accepted, and, in consequence, placed with the relics at Plymouth, so valuable in the mind of the public that its abiding place is as fixed as the laws of the Medes and Persians. Where it is, it must remain. No beckonings from loan exhibitions will be considered for a moment. Even Chicago could not make a loud enough call to secure it.

Still, there are other treasures claimed to have come over in that immortal ship, which, by inherited right, belong in the Fuller line. One, a carved oaken chest, is now in the possession of Mrs. Maria L. Reid, wife of Rev. Louis H. Reid, of Hartford, Conn.

With the strange perversity of the human mind for following the fashion of the day, some of these beautiful old English oak, carved chests, during the period when "colored chests" were in vogue, the color a dull Roman red, were submitted to the paint brush, and henceforth appeared of more modern conception.

Curiosity led a lady, who, studying the date apportioned to a "coulored chest" of highly prized inheritance, was led to see how it would appear with the color removed, and to her delight, received from the hands of the polisher a rare chest of English carved oak.

Accompanying the chest was a small iron

kettle, which is owned by Henry A. Fuller, of Wilkesbarre, Pa.

This has a delightful homelike sound, leading one to imagine the gathering of the clan at any Fuller home to enjoy, the harvest being over, a sociable cup of tea. In our mind's eye there is a view of the table set with their precious treasures in the way of the delft cups and saucers, teapots and plates. Even Brewster's teapot could be borrowed if the assemblage grew beyond the Fuller possibilities, and—being sure of an invitation, had our lot been cast at that period—at least at this distant day all feel they had some home content.

This thought has been treasured as one "outside the pale," as Popish, and no prayers would avail to save them from perdition if they ventured on such abhorrence.

LOCATION.

The Fullers have gone the right way, stopping all through the Pilgrim sections, and, while they have sought Wilkes Barre, they never forget, or have forgotten, that they made their start when it belonged to Connecticut, and that the Wyoming Valley was peopled by the Yankees from that State.

They are true to their traditions, and when the "Society of Mayflower Descendants" calls to duty there is no postponement of action on their part.

of Massachusetts," and rector of the Church of the Messiah, at Boston, Mass.

This includes Col. Stephen W. Nickerson, a brother of the above, who is president of the "Massachusetts Bimetallic Union."

The next line must of necessity start from the common ancestry, for it leads through such various ways as to rouse the hope of striking unknown descents.

1. Edward Fuller, of the Mayflower.
2. Samuel Fuller, who married Jane Lothrop.
3. Hannah, daughter of Samuel and Jane Lothrop Fuller, born in 1636; married, January 1, 1658, Nicholas Bonham. They lived for a time in Barnstable, then moved to Pis-

John Williams and wife Jane.

Both born in England and who migrated to Newbury in 1633, and thence to Haverhill, Mass., as one of its founders.
Their son, Joseph Williams, married Mary Fuller, daughter of Sam Fuller,
1647-1722   1644-1720
who removed to the neighborhood of Norwich Conn., about 1694.
The son of this couple, "Cap'n" John Williams, lived at Poquetannock, then a part of Norwich—his wife's name, Mary Knowlton, of Roxbury.
1680-1741
"Cap'n" Joseph Williams married Eunice Wheeler, of Stonington. He removed to Brattleboro, Vt., just before the war of the revolution and died there.

1st child. John Williams, 1747-1813, of Weathersfield, Vt.	5th child. Gen. Joseph Williams, 1753-1800, of Norwich, Conn.	6th child. Zipporah Williams, 1756-1820, married in 1776 Timothy Phelps, of Brattleboro, Vt., a prominent attorney of that State.	Benjamin Williams, who died on the "Jersey" prison ship in 1781.	Isaac Williams, who was impressed into the British naval service, and had a leg shot away in an action at sea.
Joseph, Grandson, Hon. Fred. H. Nichols, Weathersfield, Vt.	Edwin Williams, 1797-1854, Author, and at one time Editor of the N. Y. Herald.	John Phelps, 1777, an eminent lawyer in Vermont, who late in life removed to Baltimore.	Charles Phelps, 1781, a lawyer of celebrity of Vermont Bar.	Timothy Phelps, 1792-1822, a lawyer, who died of yellow fever in the South.
	T. D. Williams.		Hon. James H. Phelps, 1847-1893, of Suffield, Conn.	Mrs. Taft, wife of Judge Alphonso Taft, Attorney-Gen. in Grant's Cabinet.
		Gen. John W. Phelps, 1830-1870, of Brattleboro, Vt., distinguished during the civil war; was with Butler at New Orleans.	Gen. Chas. Edward Phelps, of Baltimore, a M. C., served in the civil war and is now Judge of Maryland Bar.	Rev. Charles P. Taft, M. C., Rep. from Cincinnati, Ohio.

read of their privations—there was a certainty of the chafing dish, its very utility secured its possibility, now my ruthless hand must tear away from those who have not searched history this relic of past traditions, even against the evidence of the delft heirlooms.

Tea and coffee were absolutely unknown to our forefathers, and tea was rarely used in England before 1657, and then was sold for from £6 to £10 per pound.

One drawing would have intrenched on their obligations to the merchant adventurers, calling loudly for the blood, as well as pound of flesh of the poor colonists.

Even the aroma of coffee was denied them, though tales of its fragrance may have reached them from England after 1641, when it was first brought to the mother country.

I love to accept the pleasant traditions of the past. They have grown dear to my heart, but searching is unveiling, and one must have some slight foundation in the truth of their statements in view of the figures found.

FOOD OF EARLY DAYS.

The morning and evening meal of the early Pilgrims and Puritans was easily provided, no great variety to arouse capricious appetite to desire for a change. Milk, hominy, broth, or porridge, as they called it, prepared for the epicure by boiling in it a piece of salt pork, must suffice.

Later they learned to know and value pork and beans for Sunday night, and on Saturday those on fashion intent had minced codfish, potatoes, rye and Indian bread.

To eat fish on Friday would have put them

LINES OF DESCENT.

The following lineage comes from Chatham, Mass., the Cape Cod of then and now, and will, I am sure, aid many lines:

1. Edward Fuller, signer of the Mayflower compact.
2. Capt. Matthew Fuller, participated in King Philip's war; died in 1678; married Frances ——?
3. Lieut. Samuel Fuller, married Mary ——? Killed in King Philip's war, 1675.
4. Ann Fuller, born 1670; died July 2, 1722; married April 29, 1689, Joseph Smith, born December 6, 1667; died March 4, 1746.
5. Rev. Thomas Smith, born February 6, 1706; died July 7, 1788; married August 28, 1734, Judith Miller, at Yarmouth, Mass., who was born August 23, 1716; died July 31, 1785.
6. Hon. Josiah Smith, born February 26, 1738; died April 4, 1803; married Mary Barker, June 15, 1760, at Pembroke, Mass., she was born May 2, 1740.
7. Ruth Barker Smith, born April 12, 1773; died September 9, 1855; married at Pembroke, Mass., October 20, 1796, to John Barker, who was born July 24, 1773; died August 17, 1839.
8. Mary Smith Barker, born December 23, 1800; died September 29, 1860; married June 22, 1826, at Foxborough, Mass., Stephen Tillinghast Westcott, born November 22, 1799; died June 13, 1874.
9. Martha Tillinghast Westcott, born August 20, 1829; died August 16, 1868; married January 6, 1848, Thomas White Nickerson, born January 6, 1826.
10. Thomas White Nickerson, Jr., born June 25, 1858; a "member of Colonial Wars

cataway, Middlesex County, N. J. They had eight children.

4. Mary Bonham, their daughter, born October 4, 1661, married July 15, 1681, Rev. Edmund Dunham, who was also Justice of the Peace in Piscataway, N. J., commissioned by Queen Anne, January 23, 1709. He was born in Plymouth Colony, New England, July 25, 1661, and was the third in descent from Deacon John Dunham, of New Plymouth, who came to America in 1630.

5. Rev. Jonathan Dunham, son of the above, born August 16, 1694; died March 10, 1777; married, August 5, 1714, Joan Pyatt.

6. Their daughter Elizabeth Dunham, married, 1738-40, Micajah Dunn, who was born September 12, 1716; died September 11, 1779; served in the revolutionary war. She died December 4, 1771.

7. Joel Dunn, born October 22, 1747; died July 27, 1845; married, October 2, 1771, Rachel Runyon, fourth in descent from Vincent Runyon, the Huguenot. Joel Dunn served in the revolution as private, and in the wagon brigade.

8. Sarah Dunn, born December 19, 1796; died April 2, 1883; married, February 3, 1819, Benjamin T. Field, who was the tenth in descent from John Field, the celebrated English astronomer.

9. Jane Fitz Randolph Field, their daughter, born September 23, 1832; married, April 10, 1853, Thomas Eastburn MacDonald.

10. Their daughter, Mary White MacDonald, married April 30, 1874, James Moses.

To give the present matter its full value, I must quote it as it came to me from Rev. M. E. Dwight, of Plainfield, N. J., who has stood by me in historical research, without regard to a personal family interest.

The following has just been found at East Haddam, Conn.:

"Deed from Ephraim Fuller and Shubael Fuller, both of East Haddam; quit claim.

"To our loving sisters, Lydia Gates, Thankful Brainerd, Zeniah Bill, Hannah Daniels and Rachel Hurd, all our right, etc., etc., to a certain tract of land in Middletown, east side of the Connecticut River, belonging 'to our honored father, Mr. Shubael Fuller, late of East Haddam, deceased.'" Date of deed June 22, 1748.

Middletown deed book 12, page 567.

"Mr. Shubael Fuller" was the son of "little" John Fuller, of Barnstable, Mass., and Mehitabel Rowley, born January 11, 1660, daughter of Moses Rowley, of Barnstable, Mass., and Elizabeth Fuller, daughter of Capt. Matthew Fuller, eldest son of Edward Fuller. John Fuller was the son of Samuel Fuller, brought by his father, Edward Fuller, in the Mayflower.

Since Shubael Fuller married Hannah Crocker, daughter of Jonathan Crocker, of Barnstable, and Hannah Howland, daughter of Lieut. John Howland, eldest son of Hon. John Howland, of the Mayflower, the marriage names of these daughters will prove of the greatest public interest.

JOHN CRACKSTON, Twenty-fifth Signer.

John Crackston died the first part of March, 1621. His son, "John Crackston, Jr., froze his feet, while lost in the woods, and died from a resulting fever."

The Pilgrim left a daughter Ann, at Leyden, who married Thomas Smith, a wool carder, from Bury St. Edmonds.

JOHN TURNER, Twenty-second Signer.

The history of the Turners is bristling with possibilities, each one giving a hope of reaching the goal, or absolute residence in England, where one can date from, with any certainty.

Even the mother country would not be reliable, when their Norman claim is in the ascendant, and others with a strong historical pull, put them with the Tourneurs of early New Amsterdam.

At all events John Turner came out on the Mayflower, with two sons. Before the first winter was over father and sons had succumbed to the first sickness, and, if they were allowed marked graves, even they may have been lost in the general decay, when Marjorie, the daughter he left behind, and who is said to have reached this country, arrived.

Always allowing the "perhaps" of early history, I place her, as of Salem, Mass., and that she married the first Richard Paul in 1638. This, again, I leave to some other historian.

A complicated tradition has also reached me, and being by no manner of means impossible, though marked "dangerous," that too, I give.

"Mrs. Jane G. Austin, in 'Betty Alden's Daughter,' tells of Elder Brewster's daughter Mary, marrying John Turner, and leaving Plymouth. If she was correct, this John must have been the son of the Pilgrim who came in the Mayflower. The theory of John Turner being a son of the Mayflower Pilgrim is not accepted, as he was clearly son of Humphrey Turner, of Scituate, but that Mary was a daughter of Elder Brewster is positively stated by some. The tradition in one family is that the son or grandson of John Turner, Mayflower Pilgrim, was one of the first settlers in New Haven, Conn., his name Nathaniel Turner.

"One of the descendants, a first settler of Hartford, Conn.—from there John Turner also a descendant—went to Norfolk, Conn., and was one of the first settlers there about 1758."

In connection with the above, there is some Pilgrim evidence in the fact that the Windsor, Conn., Browns, who are supposed to descend from Peter Brown, went, as was natural under such circumstances, to Hartford and Norfolk, Conn., as well, with the Turners.

These records cannot be ignored, if one wants to; the wisest, broadest plan is to accept what is natural, until proof is furnished to the contrary, working always to make it historically correct.

The Turner name certainly carries with it the Brewster record, and as the various marriages make as many lines, I give it in the chart as sent to me:

Humphrey Turner, died 1673; was of Scituate, Mass., in 1633. Married Lydia Garner.

Their eldest son, John Turner, born in England November 12, 1645, married Mary Brewster, daughter of Jonathan Brewster and Lucretia, granddaughter of Elder William Brewster.

Benjamin Turner, born March 5, 1650, died April 14, 1692, married Elizabeth Hawkins.

Capt. Hawkins Turner, born August 24, 1704, in Scituate, Mass., married Lucy Starr, of New London, Conn., born July 18, 1707, died March 16, 1809.

Jonathan Starr, of New London, Conn., married daughter of Elizabeth Morgan, of Groton, Conn.

Samuel Starr, son of Comfort Starr, married Hannah Brewster, daughter of Jonathan Brewster and Lucretia, granddaughter of Elder William Brewster.

Many notes come to me from all quarters in regard to the Turner family. All will be useful to future historians. My attention was called to "Historical Collections of Grantham, England," by Edmund Turnour, Grantham, southwestern part of Lincolnshire.

Although the present generation spell the name Turnour, it seems, from the book, to have been formerly Turnor or Turner. As this place was near the vicinity of the other Pilgrims, it seems possible John Turner, of the Mayflower, may have come from here.

In Dr. Eggleston's "Beginners of a Nation," published in 1897, on page 130, is reference to a book of Dr. Bound's on a stricter Sabbath. Page 139: "It is Thomas Rogers, the earliest opponent of the doctrine of Greenham and Bound, etc. Preface to Thirty-nine Articles, paragraph 20."

Can this be Thomas Rogers, of the Mayflower?

Mr. Alfred R. Turner, of Malden, Mass., who has stood bravely by both Turners and Rogerses, as a lineal descendant, sends the line of Humphrey Turner.

Humphrey Turner and wife Lydia came to Plymouth in 1628 and settled in Scituate, near Coleman's Hills. They had John (1), John (2), Thomas (3), Daniel (4), Nathaniel (5), Joseph (6), Lydia (7), Mary (8). John (1) married Mary Brewster, daughter of Jonathan, and granddaughter of Elder William Brewster, November 12, 1645. They had thirteen children. Joseph, who married Bathsheba Hobart, had Bathsheba, Margaret. Ezekiel, who married Susanna Keney, had Ezekiel, Grace, Lucretia, Sarah, Ruth, Mary, Elizabeth, Lydia, Hannah, Susanna. John, who married Abigail Padeshall, had Richard, Abiel, John, Margaret, Lydia, Abigail. Elisha, who married Elizabeth Jacob, had Elisha, Elisha, Mary, Jael, Jane, Elizabeth, Mary. Benjamin, who married Elizabeth Hawkins, had John, Joseph, Benjamin, William, Hawkins, Grace, Elizabeth. Jonathan, who married first Martha Bisbee, second, Mercy Hatch, had Isaac, Ignatius, Jesse, Martha, Deborah, Keziah, Jonathan, Mary, Jemima, Ruth. Amos, who married Mary Hiland, had Amos, Ezekiel, Seth, Jane, Mary, Lydia, Anna. I am not informed in regard to the rest—Joseph, Lydia, Mary, Ruth, Isaac Grace.

MOSES FLETCHER, Twenty-seventh Signer.

"His first wife was Maria Evans. In 1613 he married, at Leyden, Sarah, widow of William Dingley."

Savage says: "He came in the Mayflower, without wife or child, and died within four months."

FRANCIS EATON, Twenty-third Signer.

This passenger on the Mayflower is so mixed as to his marriages and descendants that it would take the infallible Philadelphia lawyer to place them authentically.

His first wife and infant Samuel came out with him, but the wife's brief existence carried so little weight that she passed from the places that had known her with scarce a thought on the part of those she was surrounded by.

But the boy grew and thrived, lived to be an old citizen, and, after a sojourn with his father in Duxbury, when he reached maturity moved to Middleboro, where appearances of success were against him, as he died insolvent. This, however, was not an unknown condition of affairs among the early settlers, so he can hardly be ostracized, unless one admits that he was in good company. Affairs were not apt to be in a prosperous condition when so much depended upon a return from land culture alone.

This Samuel was something of a real estate speculator. He watched his chances, and, finding Love Brewster was willing to dispose of his beautiful property, by the bayside, he bought it with the loving hope that Martha Billington, whom he married, would enjoy the rest and content he had prepared for her. This, however, was not to be; they must again pick up their belongings, and, having sold the property to Josiah Standish, in 1663, make another move.

Sampel himself may have had more to do with this roving, restless spirit, which governed all their proceedings, than appears, for "in the year next before 1652 the General Court admonished Samuel Eaton and Goodwife Hall, of Duxbury, for mixed dancing."

Samuel had at least gone through other motions, as he bound himself (which sounds like a voluntary act) an apprentice to John Cooke in 1636, for seven years.

THE PILGRIM.

Francis Eaton, the Pilgrim, came out as a carpenter, which in those times was an occupation very highly respected. The man who built church and house had a place of his own in public estimation.

He married for second wife "Mrs. Carver's maid," and she, too, had no "length of days" to record, so that, in the land division of 1627 he had, as Bradford states, taken a third wife, and by her had three children, of which, he adds, "one was married and had children; the other two were living, 1650, but one was idiote."

HIS THIRD WIFE.

The last wife, Christian Penn, a passenger in the "Ann," 1623, survived her husband. The second wife left one daughter, Rachael, who married Joseph Ramsden, and he led her, to say the least of it, a very singular life.

They were only married March 2, 1645, and "in 1652 Joseph Ramsden was ordered to live no longer in the woods remote from neighbors, whereby his wife has been exposed to great hardship, and peril of losing her life," but that he bring her with all speed to some neighborhood.

In 1656 the order was repeated, and in case of non-compliance "his house was to be torn down."

ANOTHER SON.

Benjamin Eaton, son of the Pilgrim, in 1636, was bound to Mrs. Fuller; "she to keep him at school two years."

On the 4th of December, 1660, he married Sarah, daughter of William Hoskins, and moved to Duxbury, but in 1655 returned to Plymouth.

Christian Penn Eaton, to give her life its full variety, married for second husband Francis Billington, perhaps a jump into the fire, but she had reached years of maturity and judgment.

JOHN GOODMAN, Twenty-eighth Signer.

"Goodman had a lot assigned him in Leyden street, in 1620." Young, in his "Chronicles," says: "Nothing more is known of him, except that he died before the end of March."

JAMES CHILTON, Twenty-fourth Signer.

To the narrow mindedness of the royal family of Stuarts the world undoubtedly owes much of their ignorance of the times during which they reigned.

"They had an instinctive jealousy of the free press, and so far as possible kept it under strict supervision."

What may come to us from the records too unimportant to meet the eyes of those in power, remains to be seen. The present relations with England, which have led to the returning of the original history, written by Gov. Bradford, may unfold in the same spirit other matters of equal importance.

James Chilton, the Pilgrim, never came ashore. For him "the promised land" was reached through "the pearly gates of the New Jerusalem." Provincetown, Cape Cod, was but a name, and the spirit which returned to Him who gave it December 3, 1620, soon had the companionship of the wife of his youth, who died shortly after landing.

Mary, their daughter, known as the "Pilgrim Orphan," left her "footprints" as history names it, on Plymouth Rock. She married John Winslow, brother of Gov. Edward Winslow, who came over by reason of the going back of the Speedwell, in the Fortune, 1621.

Mrs. Robert Hall Wiles, president of the Illinois Federation of Women's Clubs, who is a lineal descendant, gives the historical proof of their residence in Plymouth, from the fact of their certificate of dismissal from the Plymouth Church to the Boston Church, being in Plymouth Hall, Mass.

SAVAGE.

Savage says, speaking of the Pilgrim Chilton: "His daughter Mary, who accompanied her father and mother, has by vain tradition been made the first to leap on Plymouth Rock, as that honor is also assigned to John Alden, when we know it is not due to either, married John Winslow, and in 1650, Bradford says, she had nine children, of whom one was married, and had a child. She died 1679, but another daughter of Chilton was left by him in England where she married, and came to our country."

REMOVAL.

John Winslow, moved to Boston in 1655, was a shipping merchant and led a prosperous, important life. One daughter married Edward Gray, who was quite prominent in Rhode Island, much being written of him by Austin and other historians; next their daughter, Mary Winslow Gray, married William Abbott, son of George Abbott, who came from Yorkshire, England, about 1640, and settled in Andover, Mass., in 1643, one of the pioneers of that town.

Susanna Winslow became the wife of Roger Latham, of Bridgewater, in 1649. At this time he was living in Plymouth, but his previous home was Marshfield, where in 1643 he held the office of constable, but true to his first home, he returned to Bridgewater before 1667.

BURIAL.

"Mary Chilton and her husband, John Winslow, are buried in King's Chapel Burying Ground, in Boston, their names upon a slab at the gate in Tremont street, with those of other Mayflower Pilgrims buried there."

The honor of this descent is wide-spread, the accident which kept John Winslow from being one of the Mayflower pasengers, is redeemed by his marriage, and the name of Winslow from this line can take its proper place on every honor roll.

No descendants of the daughter who "came after" have come to me. If they are ready for the third pamphlet, history will be satisfied.

DEGORY PRIEST, Twenty-ninth Signer.

Prince says: "The year begins with the death of Degory Priest." "Priest is set down in the Leyden 'Records' as 'from London,' and had been many years a member of the Leyden Company." "It is on record that he married, November, 1611, Sarah (Allerton) Vincent, widow of John Vincent. November, 1615, he was admitted a citizen of Leyden, and in April, 1619, he (calling himself 'a hatter') deposes that he is forty years of age, and knows one Nicholas Claverly. This would make him forty-one to forty-two when he died."—Leyden MS. Records.

"His widow married Cuthbert Cuthbertson, a Dutchman, who also was of the Leyden Company, and Winslow calls him Godbert Godbertson, probably the name he owned in early life; and it met with the changes which seemed to come to the Pilgrims and those in marriage connected with them."

Everything will be done to secure the descendants of his two daughters, who came out in the Ann with their mother.

A claimant has also arisen bearing the name of Priest, but time sufficient has not elapsed since the communication to really know anything about it.

The Mayflower Society have made a search with good results, but want "more." This, too, will come in both paper and pamphlet, third part.

JOHN BILLINGTON, Twenty-sixth Signer.

Gov. Bradford says in his history: "The said Billington was one of the profanest men among us. He came from London, and I know not by what friends shuffled in among us."

A superficial search makes this possible, but the conviction grows as one proceeds that there is more than ordinary cause for the Billington family being on the Mayflower.

Our reason resents the idea that in a vessel so cramped for room that families are divided, husbands and wives separated, young daughters left without the protection of their parents, Robert Cushman, one of the important factors in the equipment of the ship, remaining to wait future means of transportation to the colonies, and there are four stowaways from one family.

It was a simple impossibility. They had been together several days at least, by virtue of the mishap to the Speedwell, which attended their start, and John and Francis Billington were not boys to be suppressed or reduced to the subordination of extinction. The situation was one their hearts craved, and the spirit of April fools' day was not regulated for them by the calenadr.

THEIR POSITION.

The Bylingtons were people of high standing in England, belonging to the Judges in Henry VIII.'s time, and I am inclined to think that John Billington, of the Mayflower, being too much for his family, was shown that his "room was better than his company," and the wherewithal provided in unstinted measure to secure foreign travel for him—his destination not a matter of consideration.

However, this in no way prevented his claiming rank among the Pilgrim Fathers.

A recent work says: "The Pilgrim Fathers were all those members of the Separatist Church at Leyden who voted for the emigration to America, whether they were able to go there or not—together with such others as joined their church from England.

"Membership in the Pilgrim Church was the first qualification; intended or actual emigration to New England was the second one. This general definition includes Christopher Martin and his wife, Richard Warren and John Billington, Sr., and his family, who came from London."

THE BOYS.

The Mayflower company, if not wiser and better for having the Billingtons on board, at least had the monotony of the voyage varied by the exploits of the boys. Their youthful pranks were the terror of the whole community. Nothing held them back when roused to action.

The little piece of pleasantry on the part of John, when he threw the light into the gunpowder, which fortunately was discovered in time to prevent serious consequences, was only in touch with the spirit of his inheritance, a lawless disregard of surroundings and the rights of others. No condign punishment awaited him at his father's hands and he was left to live this life of unconcern.

With them, the choice being between "hot water" and fire, they took the one available. "All was grist that came to their mill." The Billington makeup was not in favor of obedience. John Billington, the Pilgrim, resented it, and, while he knew the power vested in Standish was real, that his mandates would be carried out by the strong arm of the law, he refused to obey him, uttering threats for his own satisfaction even when perfectly cognizant they would be of no avail.

Capt. Standish did not wear his sword for ornament. It was his insignia of the power he held, even paramount to the Governor's.

For his insubordination the punishment "converted" to Billington was that "he was adjudged to lie for a time in a public place with his neck and heels tied together."

An opportunity of thought in which to hatch more mischief.

JOHN.

John, the oldest son, feeling the restraints and monotony of the little settlement, as Bradford tells us, "lost himself in ye woods & wandered up & downe some 5 days, living on berries and what he could find. At length he light on an Indean plantation, 20 miles south of this place, called Manamet, they conveid him furder of te Nawsett, among those peopl that had before set upon ye English when they were costing, whilest ye ship lay at ye Cape as is before noted. But ye Gov'r caused him to be enquired for among ye Indeans, and at length Massassoyt sent word wher he was, and ye Gov'r sent a shallop for him and had him delivered. This act of justice, and protection, was sorely against Gov. Bradford's desires, time so valuable, and the services of those he detailed so needed that the matter of John Billington's appearance, seemed of little moment. The young John hardly timed his expedition to his own advantabe. Later he would have enjoyed the Beech plums, wild gooseberries, and white grapes, which Young in his Chronicles says "were found here in great abundance."

FRANCIS.

There was no Sahara for the Pilgrims to dread, the whole country was rendered attractive and picturesque by the variety of pools, lakes, creeks, etc., they met during their wanderings.

"Plymouth Bay is a most hopeful place, innumerable store of fowl, and excellent good, and cannot but be fish in their seasons; skate, cod, turbot and herring we have tasted of, abundance of muscels, the greatest and best that ever we saw, crabs and lobsters in their time infinite. It is in fashion like a sickle, or fish hook." Plymouth was surrounded by these various forms of water, and Francis Billington had the honor of perpetuating the name by finding a body of water, which has always been called Billington Sea.

This swarmed in the season with a species of herring called alewives, which in the needy condition of the colonies proved a valuable addition to their resources.

Matters of individual taste were left wholly out of the count, and though the Frenchwomen saw with their minds' eye the many delightful possibilities of even this homely article of food, time, utensils and condiments were wanting to their perfection, and in the stern necessities of the situation they forgot even to mention the cravings which came with the home thoughts.

Later these alewives, which in the future prosperity had no attractions were used for farming purposes, and were so valuable that the office of keeper was made for their protection.

HIS CRIME.

John Billington had many faults; perhaps he deserved his sad end. Still I can but feel that his suffering the death penalty was the effect of the times. It is easy to imagine in the light of the present day a more lenient sentence.

John Newcomen had interfered with his hunting, and was warned by Billington to desist. Not appreciating the manner of man he had to deal with, he continued his annoyances until on one occasion, when he hid behind a tree on the approach of his enemy, the irresistible impulse to rid himself of this "cumberer of the ground" was too much for Billington, and he fired the shot which proved fatal.

A record from Bradford's history may place this in a rather different light:

"They assemble by beat of drum, each with his musket or firelock, in front of the captain's door; they have their cloaks on, and place themselves in order, three abreast, and are led by a sergeant, without beat of drum. Behind comes the Governor, in long robe, beside him on the right hand, comes the preacher, with his cloak on, and on the left side the captain, with his side arms, and cloak on, and with a small cane in his hand, and so they march in good order, and each sets his arms down near him."

Habit becomes second nature. The colonists were never without arms. Intuitively they sought them for every obstruction. "Eternal vigilance was the price both of liberty" and life.

No Indian or prowling beast, for whom he was prepared, could have more surely represented the evil beyond endurance than the sight of John Newcomen hidden in his terror behind the tree.

I do not defend the act, but the impulse. Then, too, there was the same wearing of arms on Newcomen's part, and he might have fired the shot as well as John Billington.

The instinct of self-preservation glows more or less in every human heart, only the fact exists that both suffered, one by a single hand, the other under force of the law.

VIEW OF THE COLONISTS.

This offense was a matter of great moment in the colonies. It was a proceeding that must be made an example of.

The question of their rights in the case caused much discussion.

They felt themselves powerless to act, so, to secure not only better judgment, but power for conviction or forgiveness, they consulted "Winthrop and other leaders of the Bay, whose authority under the crown was beyond question," and they, with much sorrow and paryerful regard, decided that Billington "ought to die and the land be purged from blood."

A life for a life.

The death sentence was carried out September, 1630, memorable in American history as the first execution in the colonies.

The punishment consummated, sorrow followed, and the generous minded remembered only what was good in him. He had been with them in all their trials and privations, bearing willingly his share in their labors, through sickness and poverty.

BAD LUCK.

Misfortune, for a time, certainly followed the name. John had died before his father. John Billington's wife, only a unit while he lived, took up his story and furnished much uninteresting litigation to the colony.

Francis, through whom all descent comes, in 1634 married Christian Penn, widow of Francis Eaton.

They proved a thriftless pair. Their growing family of eight children seemed too much for them, and they were forced to bind most of them out to secure means for their existence.

Francis was occasionally sued and fined, and once had the choice of a whipping or paying £20. If the sentence was carried out I greatly fear the family exchequer would require the whipping.

However, years brought a change, and, having reached the time of life when, as a Frenchman aptly says, "our vices leave us," he was on committees, boards of reference and other organizations, which gave evidence of his standing in the community.

Martha, his daughter, married Samuel Eaton January 10, 1660, and so far as she was concerned the name no longer existed.

Helen, or Elen, as she is variously called, widow of the Pilgrim, succeeded to the farm at Plain Dealing, two miles north of Plymouth Rock, and in 1638 gave it to her only living child, Francis Billington, on account of the "natural love she bore him."

Later in the year she married Gregory Armstrong, and it is to be hoped that her declining years had some of the peace and comfort to which she had a claim.

THE BILLINGTON FAMILY.

The feeling of the authenticity of name connections, which always leads me to search other companies of Pilgrim times for history in this family has been well rewarded. I found in Capt. John Smith's company, Virginia, 1620, a Francis Billington.

There can be no chance about this, and he is easily placed as a brother of Pilgrim John Billington's, while the children's names make good claim—John for the father, Francis for the uncle.

A John Billington was at Portsmouth, New Hampshire, in 1645. He settled at Kittery, Maine, opposite.

His descendants took the name of Billing, and later it became Billings. This is the story, and with natural associations, there were Williamses among the early settlers of Kittery, later on one bearing the name of Francis Williams. Then there is a Brewster supposition from this section. All this unraveling seems but the work of time, but why not avail of the present and hasten the welcome day when one need no longer puzzle over supposition.

THOMAS WILLIAMS, Thirtieth Signer.

"Thomas of Plymouth, 1620, passenger in the Mayflower, one of the signers of the memorable compact at Cape Cod in November, had no family, and died soon after the landing, as Bradford tells."—Savage.

There is a very general belief that Thomas Williams either did not die or left a son. One tradition is that he settled in Kittery, Me., where the family intermarried with the Billings (Billingtons); another comes to me from Cape Cod, claiming him as "perhaps" "our Thomas Williams, of Plymouth and Eastham," writing: "I think he is the same bad boy Thomas whom Mistress Warren had reprimanded, because he is saucy and sweared. Might he not have been the thirtieth signer, or a son?"

PETER BROWN, Thirty-third Signer.

Being "two Dromios in the field" claiming the same position as to descent from this Pilgrim, with my earnest desire to draw out all discussion, correction and history, I give them as I have found them, or they have come to me.

Coming to America single in the Mayflower seems to have been no drawback to Peter Brown, for in the next thirteen years he availed himself of his opportunities by marrying twice.

He came out as a carpenter, which gave him when the individual interest was allowed, and a man secured the personal result of his labors, a fine opportunity for wealth from the very necessity of his occupation. His the master hand, and every one who could "drive a nail" more or less his assistant.

Still though he must have added much to the comfort of the colonists, from lack of other ties, which made a claim on his time, his "single blessedness" told against him in the land division of 1623, when by virtue of that fact he had but one acre of land in the assignment.

PETER BROWN A BENEDICT.

Early difficulties in the way of local possession, however, were overcome, and in 1627, in the division of cattle, he was to the fore, claiming for "Mary and Martha" their share and making it good by the records.

The "probably" of the situation, where decided identification of wife and child as to the time of marriage and birth unknown, was merged into certainty, and it is history to state that he married Martha Ford, who came out in the Ann. "Marrying and giving in marriage" went on even during the times when the colonists held their property in common, cultivated the land without regard to ownership, and all was deposited in the general storehouse, to be drawn out by the authorities in proportion to the numbers requiring means of livelihood.

What the arrival of the Fortune must have been to them, my pen fails to describe. News from the home country, the presence of Jonathan Brewster; and yet Bradford in this hour of hope could feel that the "Plantation was glad of this addition to its strength, but could have wished that many of them could have been of better condition and all of them better provisioned, but that could not be helped."

Five hundred miles to the north of them (Nova Scotia) five hundred miles to the south of them (New Amsterdam) for neighbors did not develop social instincts.

CHANGE OF TACTICS.

With the division of land, which meant absolute ownership, ambition and enthusiasm was aroused. The farmer "homeward plods his weary way," to be sure, still the summing up of his day's labor gave him an account on his own side of the ledger. Possesssion brought self-respect, and a spirit of progression was aroused. The homestead was very primitive, but it belonged to the family.

DUXBURY.

From Plymouth to Duxbury was claimed to be a step in the right direction, and Peter Brown took it, so was registered among the early settlers of Duxbury, "most of them men of high repute among the Pilgrims, and often elevated to the highest offices among them." The Pilgrims were not the Puritans of "law and order" 'fame, but no laxness in the way of absence from duty was permitted them. Casting their eyes over the whole colony was a very simple matter, and the authorities, grasping the situation, found that Peter Brown, a freeman, and consequent example, had not answered the roll-call as "present" at the General Court in 1633, so this Pilgrim, upon other duties, perhaps pleasures intent, was fined according to law 30s., from which there was no redress.

DEATH.

The "divine gift of silence" came to Peter Brown in 1633, and his inventory was presented October 4, 1633.

His family position is very peculiarly stated, when his estate was being settled by order of the court, he is mentioned as having "divers children by divers wives." His widow was Mary, his second wife, and as he is said to have left four children, the consideration shown his widow and administratrix seems unusual, for, "aside from £15, sitt on his two daughters," she received the "remainder of his estate for support of her young family." Standish and Brewster took the inventory.

History may some time make more of these records in regard to Peter Brown's wives and children. Two marriages and four children in Pilgrim times would hardly bear out the statement of "divers children by divers wives."

PETER, THE SON.

The early demise of the father left the continuance of the history with the children and for our purpose, so much hinging on his after residence, Peter will answer for "he, with Gov. Bradford and thirty others were among the first purchasers of Dartmouth in 1652," making him, as he was born in 1632, only twenty years of age when admitted to this enterprise of the "solid men."

Some affinity to Connecticut, perhaps a drawing to Jonathan Brewster (James Rogers), and other wanderers from the fold of Plymouth's claims, took him to Windsor, Conn.

He went from Duxbury there, and the benefit of his Dartmouth venture may have told for him as an investment.

PETER, JR.

Dr. Stiles, in his history of ancient Windsor, simply announces Peter Brown, of the Mayflower, giving the usual records, then puts as "Family 2, Peter (son of above), born 1632; removed from Duxbury, Mass.; married, July 15, 1638, Mary (probably daughter of Jonathan or Nathan) Gillet; he admitted to Windsor Church June 22, 1662 (O. C. R.); bo't in Windsor, same year (June 28), house and lot of Robert Hayward, 'near the mill," and doubtless resided there until he bought the Josias Ellsworth place, near William Phelps, Jr., January 31, 1664, which since has been called the Peter Brown place, and became conspicuous about the beginning of the present century, because of the opposition of its then occupant (a Peter Brown) to the opening of a new road, which left his house in the lot, etc.

"This house was demolished some thirty years since. He contributed 9s. 7d. to the Connecticut Colonial relief fund for the poor of other colonies, 1676; his wife owned Half Way Covenant, in Windsor Church, July 17, 1659, O. C. R. Peter Brown died March 9, 1692, aged 60, estate £408 15s. 6d."

This Peter Brown was a miller, and, January. 1658-9, at town meeting, it was voted "that Peter Brown that keeps the mill, should take but single toll, or the sixteenth part of all grain for his grinding, only of Indian corn it was voted by the major part that he should take toll and half, from this time until 25th of March next ensuing, but no longer."

The Indian corn being more difficult to grind, larger rates were required as compensation.

JOHN BROWN.

If this man is Peter Brown, son of Peter Brown of the Mayflower, the lineage of John Brown, of Ossawatomie, and the invasion of Virginia, October, 1859, comes in its direct descent.

The branches which lead to it are widespreading, claiming some of the "great and good of the land." For the benefit of those who have never looked into this matter I give his line: Pilgrim Peter, Peter (2), John (3), John (4), Capt. John (5), then Owen Brown (6), who married first in Simsbury, February 11, 1793, Ruth (daughter of Lieut. Gideon and Ruth Humphrey) Mills, and granddaughter of Hon. Oliver Humphrey, of Simsbury.

In this little town, near Weatogue, Windsor, and so many of the places of great historical interest, where "God's acre" in the very heart of the place, is full to overflowing with the names that live, was born in 1793 this Ruth, from whose marriage with Owen Brown came Capt. John Brown, born May 9, 1800, at Torrington, Conn. where his parents had made a new home, who died in compliance with the law at Charlestown, W. Va., December 2, 1859.

Time and the record "marches on," and it is well to leave this part of the history with the man whose fate must always rouse divers opinions, but to read his enforced farewell to earth will surely call forth a parting tear over his generosity and his purpose, which he claims was a single one, for the good of mankind.

THE OTHER STORY.

To secure exact history I must mainly quote the records so kindly loaned me, and to give perplexing statements a start, state that John Brown, of Plymouth, was an older brother of Peter, and both lived on the Duxbury side.

John was married in England, where some of his children were born, but the year of his coming out is not known.

To make the matter clear, I take the Pilgrim Peter Brown, then his son Peter, born, as this record gives it, in 1628, and died in 1658, six years after the purchase of Dartmouth, with Gov. Bradford and others in 1652.

Now the strange story begins, which will

give, in view of the other long accepted, much opportunity for search.

"Six years later his (Peter 2) two sons, Thomas and Hachaliah, with their friend, Peter Disbrow, removed to Rye, which was in 1664. (See also "History of Rye," by Dr. Baird, and Bolton's "History of Westchester County," Vol. II.

Thomas Brown, the eldest brother (son of Peter 2), never married. Hachaliah had five sons and three daughters. His sons were Peter (3), Hachaliah (2), Thomas, Benjamin and Deliverance. Jonathan Brown, of Rye, a grandson of Hachaliah, had a daughter Sarah, who married a descendant of Rev. Thomas Hooker, also of Capt. Thomas Willet, the first (English) Mayor of New York; and the Snowdens, of Philadelphia, are descended from them.

Peter Brown, son of the first Hachaliah, married Martha, daughter of Peter Disbrow, who, with Thomas and Hachaliah Brown, was one of the most prominent men in the colony.

Hachaliah Brown, second son of the first by that name, was, says Dr. Baird, called

John Trumbull—Mary Swan.
│
Joseph Trumbull—
Benoni Trumbull—Sarah Drake,
Aug. 10, 1684,
obit. July 24, 1770.
│
Benj. Trumbull—Mary Brown,
born May 11, 1712. │ Aug. 28, 1708–Nov. 19, 1763.
│
Ashabel Skinner—Sarah Trumbull,
│ July 11, 1745.
│
Sylvester Skinner—Polly Wilcox,
1765–May, 19, 1848. │ obit. Dec. 1859.
│
Jonathan C. Brown—Julia Skinner,
Oct. 1808; │ June 30, 1810;
ob. Sept. 26, 1872. │ ob. Dec. 6, 1890.
│
Elsie Brown.

Mayflower Mary
Peter Brown—Martha Ford.
│
Peter Brown—Mary Gillett,
Oct. 4, 1632,
Mch. 9, 1691.
│
Peter Brown—Mary Baker,
March 12, 1664.

Major in 1752. He was Justice in 1755-6, and Mr. Bolton states that he commanded the Westchester Levies under Gen. Lord Amhurst. Jonathan Brown, of Rye, a grandson of Hachaliah, had a daughter, Sarah, who married a descendant of Rev. Thomas Hooker, also of Capt. Thomas Willet, the first (English) Mayor of New York, and the Snowdons, of Philadelphia, are descendants from them. A later Sir Anthony Brown Lord Montague was a prominent character in Devonshire, England, in the early part of the last century. His daughter, Content Brown, married Rev. John Rathbone, of Stonington, Conn., January 8, 1751, when about 18 years of age.

Having left Rye so young, very little is known of her, although prior to 1850 most of the older members of the family were familiar with the name, and expressed themselves in regard to her as a near relative.

She died at Ashford, Conn., September 30, 1804, aged 72 years.

HER FAMILY.

Rev. John Rathbone and Content Brown had thirteen children. Prudence, their fourth child, married Samuel Satterlee, of Stonington, and they later removed to Ballston, Saratoga County, N. Y. After the fashion of the day, the hair of this couple has been preserved in a locket, which is now in the possession of one of the Browns of Rye.

A granddaughter married Hon. Samuel B. Ruggles, of New York, and another granddaughter, Content, married Robert Cheesbrough.

Perhaps to the fact that a descendant is now writing Cheesbrough genealogy, I owe some of the data I am so fortunate as to be able to give to the public.

Hachaliah Brown (2) married Ann Kniffen, of Rye, and died about 1794.

BOLTON'S HISTORY.

To make a correction, as sent me, I must quote from "Bolton's History," which says: "Brown—This family was a younger branch of the Browns of Beachworth, in the County of Kent, England, founded by Sir Anthony Brown, who was created Knight of the Bath at the coronation of Richard II. He left issue two sons, Sir Richard, his heir, and Sir Stephen, who was Lord Mayor of London in 1439.

His eldest son, Sir Robert Brown, was father of Sir Thomas Brown, of Beachworth Castle, who was treasurer of the household of King Henry VI., and was Sheriff of Kent in 1444 and 1460.

Thomas Brown, Esq., of Rye, County Sussex, England, emigrated to Concord, Mass., in 1632, from whence he removed to Cambridge, where he lived some time. His sons were Thomas, of Rye, and Hachaliah, of Rye."

MISTAKE.

"Mr. Bolton was misinformed in regard to above statement. The Thomas he refers to was a cousin of Mayflower Peter, and not the ancestor of the Browns of Rye. The father of Peter of the Mayflower was Thomas, who was grandson of the first Sir Anthony." The famous "Battle Abbey" was given by Henry VIII. to Sir Anthony Brown. A later Sir Anthony Browne, Lord Montague, was a prominent character in Devonshire, Eng., the early part of last century. Montague, Mass., is named for him.

This makes the claim of the name connection. Collins's "Peerage" will give the student more of this history. The story of these Pilgrims is the "living present," a mathematical use of the data furnished, which tells the story of one, at the same time all of the colony.

Hutton's statement in his "Original Lists" that "the proceedings which were taken chiefly against the nonconformists, caused many English families to leave their homes, helps the story. Some were sent to distant parts of the country. "Thus a delinquent belonging to Essex would be sent, perhaps, to Wiltshire or Yorkshire, and under pain of severe punishment, forbidden to leave the town in which he was located, where, by the way, under the semblance of being a free man, he was compelled to earn, or at least procure, his own living."

SEPARATION.

The field of separatism assumes greater proportions and influence as the search goes on. Captain Hooker, the historian, recently told me that he had found a line of it running from Wales to Devonshire. This will explain the Cooke connection with Lieut. John Thompson, of Wales, and so many others not distinctly placed.

Some of the early historians of New England give the birthplace of Mayflower Peter Brown as Yorkshire. This is quite possible, as we know many people of distinction were compelled to stay there.

Knowledge of them is lost from their leaving secretly, Hutton claiming that even at that early period vessels left almost daily for America. "Among the thousands who emigrated to New England, it cannot be doubted that a large number left to avoid payment of the hateful subsidy, and that they would not take the oaths of allegiance and supremacy."

Lists of the passengers were not kept, so the doubters should not deter people from the natural assimilations of history until absolute records prove them incorrect.

With one more of the statements that have come to me I will leave this history to public opinion and correcting, trusting no supposed delicacy will lead any one to hesitate about expressing any suggestions that will be of benefit.

"Peter of Plymouth, and Peter of New Haven, were undoubtedly the same person."

This chart I am glad to give. Some of the records are worthy of full search:

Peter Brown, married Mary Hard; died 1633 at Plymouth. Peter Brown, married Elizabeth Knapp (?) 1628-1658, Plymouth. Hachaliah Brown, married, 1671, Ruth Mead. Hachaliah Brown, married Ann Kniffen (?) about 1728; major in 1752; judge in 1755; died July, 1789. Content Brown, January 8, 1751, married Rev. John Rathbone, of Stonington, Conn., 1729-1826. Prudence Rathbone, 1757-1827, married Samuel Satterlee, 1741-1831. George Cary Satterlee.—George Cary Satterlee, married March 19, 1833, Mary Le Roy Livingston, 1811-1886. Francis Le Roy Satterlee, married Laura Suydam, December 9, 1868. Madeleine Le Roy Satterlee.

GEORGE SOULE, Thirty-fifth Signer.

Although not on the records of the Pilgrim start, a man of distinction, even in those days of plain living and plain speaking, George Soule held his own as a citizen where "essential servies" were needed.

He came out as of Edward Winslow's family, leading to the supposition that he was indentured to his chief, in connection with his business interests and Brewster.

The love he bore Winslow continued always, and the next generation, at least, acknowledged the bond with great loyalty.

Everything he held in the way of office was on his own "probity and integrity," a wielding of his personal power, which was felt during the whole of his long life.

ENGLISH HISTORY.

The History of Normandy and England, by Sir Francis Palgrave, third volume, edition of 1864, in its accounts of the "Baronial Castles of the Contentin, Avanches and the Bessin" (page 661), mentions that the "Chateau de Soule," under Henry II. (1154-1189), was held by Guillaume de Soule; a family of Soule subsists in England under the name of Sole.

The association of names in the following record brings us even to the present day, with intervening generations accredited.

Upon the "Catalogue des Grands Seigneurs Normans, Qui pesseunt la mer et combattirent pour Le Duc Guillaume quand .. conqueste l'Angleterre," may be found the name of Le Sire Guillaume de Soulle, associated with such distinguished Norman Barons as Robert, Comte de Mortaine (Morton), Le Sire de Puy (Depew) and Le Sire de Tracy.

Coming down to more modern times, knowing the family were in the counties of Kent, Cambridge and Worcester; also in London, where, upon the records were found the following extracts, bearing evidently upon the family of the young Norman Pilgrim with whom we have to do, there is a feeling that the start is really made:

"George Soule, married Alice Edwards June 26, 1625, at St. Saviour's, Southwark, London."

"William Sole, son of Robert, baptized in St. Butolph's, Bishopgate, London, October 18, 1607.

"Elleyn Sole, marryed John Owenstead, January 29, 1608 at St. Botolph.

"John Soule, of St. Buttoulphe (Butolph) without algat, and Ruth Fox, of this Parish, were married in St. Dionis Backchurch," London, December, 1581.

It is merely a historical sequence to suppose that these were the parents of the Pilgrims. The name argument increases the possibility—the first born taking that of his possible grandfather, John, the unwritten sentiment, deep down in the Pilgrim heart, asserting itself at the sight of the welcome son. Too, there was a Fox following in the early colonies.

IN AMERICA.

Some military connection is imputed to this family, for all through, the generations living at the same time as the Pilgrim did more than good service. George Soule made his record as "one of the volunteers to aid those of Massachusetts Bay, and Connecticut against the Pequod Indians."

His home at Duxbury, where he was appointed in 1642, "to provide forces against them (the Indians) for an offensive, and defensive war," must have been very satisfactory. In 1637 the records tell us that "a garden place is granted George Soule at Duxborrow to lye his grounds at Powder Point."

Housekeeping on the primitive plan of that place, would save many steps, though there is a modern sound about their "one large room a bedroom, and kitchen on the first floor, with two large and two small rooms above," then sometimes that part is dear so a woman's heart "an attic above all."

CURIOS.

How the present relic hunters would enjoy searching for the treasures sure to be in the garrets of those seafaring Soules, where generations of curiosities were stored away almost forgotten by the ocupants. China galore, and such ebony desks, filled, beside the evident beauty, with secret drawers, receptacles for the trusty gold, the modus operandi of reaching it known only to the initiated.

These cottages were fortified, and had gambrel roofs, which though of older English architecture than some of the hastily constructed buildings, were considered very desirable as a means of firing upon the treacherous Indians. This was a time when the claim of ambush was made for themselves. The leanto, for reasons out of my power to give, was also called a salt-box.

THE OLD AND THE NEW.

The idea of Pilgrim and Puritan neatness has been handed down so decidedly that one is fain to accept it without a thought. Yet even this tradition is susceptible of discussion as to its inheritance from "Old England." The stories of the merry-making there are extant, only the reading to freshen the memory and tell us that

"Old King Cole was a merry old soul,
And a merry old soul was he.
He called for his pipe, he called for his bowl,
And he called for his fiddlers three."

This was the finale, the mint and chartreuse for digestion. What had gone before had ceased to be of interest, but the surroundings told the tale of the Boar's head and plum pudding eaten, the refuse thrown to the dogs, the unbidden guests, their Board of Health, and then, when overcome by satiety, they mounted a sleeping guard, the abundant rosemary came into play, filling the air with its sweet perfume.

Barren Plymouth did not furnish the rosemary; there was no imitation, the sincerest flattery possible, so appreciating the necessity, they sawed the trees through the middle, putting the smooth part on top for their flooring. This must be scrubbed, and from it has grown out beautiful New England floors in their primitive neatness.

OTHER CUSTOMS.

From these cold, cheerless houses Puritan usage required that the first Sunday after its birth a child should be taken to church for baptism. Without Dr. Cornwall's explanation of the cause of disease in New England, it is evident there would have been much without any insidious germ of predestination.

As early as "1636 every household in Plymouth Colony was required to keep a ladder which would reach the top of the roof in case of fyer." In the same year, November 15, 1636, a law was passed by the Colony Court ordering "cattle marks," by which alone claim of ownership could be made.

George Soule, it is shown by Plymouth records, must have a "piece cut out like a x of the under side of the right eare downwards," and he and Anthony Thatcher "were shosen a committee to draw up an order concerning disorderly drinking of tobacco." Protection against "cigarette fiends," for "drinking" tobacco was then the common term for smoking."

DUXBURY.

The bay about Duxbury, being well protected, is quite free from rocks, only a few about Powder Point, where the sportive trout secured themselves from observation, are known as Zachary's rocks, probably after the son of the Pilgrim, who, rejoicing in an unusual name, secured easy identification. His father early lived at Powder Point.

The Soules were emphatically men of the sea. Not the wise men of Gotham who made their venture in a bowl, but stalwart seamen, armed and equipped for a whale or smaller game. Only they must have something as a reward for their labors. The Delanos and Soules shared this glory, and the danger gave zest to their enterprise, as around Cape Sable they sought both means of livelihood and pleasure. This trade grew upon them, their hairbreadth escapes not confined strictly to a landsman's style of narrative made them welcome patrons of the Duxbury ordinaries, where they found refreshment for man and beast.

Those abodes of sociability were in good hands; the convival spirit was worked always under the restraint of the law. The ordinaries, which having become Puritan taverns, were not allowed to be kept without a license by an express order of the court, and the choice seems to have been a matter of great moment, only the sober ones and strong were considered equal to the gravity of the case, and were enjoined to keep matters quiet and to take care that none should "drink over much." The regulating of the precise quantity must have required a neighborly knowledge.

THE SEABURYS.

Think of "Mr. Seabury," of Duxbury, who in 1678 was granted a license to sell liquors "unto such sober-minded neighbors as hee shall thinke meet, soe as he sell not lesse than the quantitie of a gallon at a time, to one person, and not in smaller quantities by retaile to the occasioning of drunkenes."

The chance for a royal time was provided, but the means to it must be taken on the sly. And this was a member of the family of Bishop Seabury.

The early settlers of Duxbury are recorded as "men of the highest respectability, of the highest repute among the Pilgrims," occupying military, ecclesiastical and civil positions with much honor to themselves and the community they represented. You can take your choice. George Soule was among them, whether you spell his name Sole, Soal, Soul. The family of Sole are of ancient English origin, with armorial bearings.

It is all in the story to tell that the Soules were traders, always in good company, for they had Alexander Standish for one and Major Judah Alden for another to participate in all that could accrue. Facts are stern things, whether met in the broad daylight or in the privacy of the midnight lamp. Either way Joshua Soule stared the matter in the face and proved beyond doubt that "the most profitable sales of the period were those of intoxicating liquors."

SHIPPING MERCHANTS.

To own two vessels, the Seaflower and the Dolphin, was quite a shipping interest, and the journeys to Virginia, Maryland and the Carolinas aided much to the filling of the "ancestral halls" which grew with their wealth.

The Soules were always to the front in maritime affairs. Every branch fitted into their desires. They could fish, trade and sail their own vessels; then, given the chance, if for the benefit of their country, turn them into "saucy privateers" at a moment's notice. Church interests were not forgotten by the Soules. The Pilgrim was one of the petitioners for a church in Duxbury. He died in 1680, very aged, and his wife in 1677. He was called one of the "old stock," also a member of the original company for the "Pilgrim Suez," which Cape Cod isthmus, with Buzzard's Bay for its Red Sea and Plymouth its Aleppo, was so happily called.

George Soule, with others, "lived several years after a route for a canal had been traced there," and claimed interest of the Massachusetts Bay Colony.

He married Mary Becket, and had John, who lived, as was fitting, to be seventy-five years of age. He owned the right to having his "days long on the land which his God gave him." His father's touching tribute to this claim tells, "and for as much as my eldest son, John Soule, and his family, hath in my extreme old age and weakness, bin tender and careful of mee and very healpfull to mee, and is likely for to be while it shall please God to continue my life heer, therefore I give and bequeath unto my said son, John Soule, all the remainder of my housing and lands whatsoever."

Then George, who inherited half of his father's lands at Dartmouth. Benjamin, killed in the spring of 1675 by the overwhelming force of the Indians at Canoncut. Zachariah, who lived at Powder Point, died in 1663; Nathaniel, who, like his brother, inherited land in Dartmouth; Elizabeth, who married Francis Walker, of Middleboro; Susanna, then Mary, placed to John Winslow, 1652, for seven years, though the joining of these names prevents fear of hard usage, still, fortunately, she had a home of her own, for she was married before 1672 to John Peterson.

A long line of sea captains follow this name. They fly to the east, they fly to the west, and if old ocean sometimes claims them, there is that in the blood which, even with this knowledge, would send other members of the family out, if they knew the same fate would be theirs.

George Soule, one of the Pilgrims who came in the Mayflower, in 1620, landed at Plymouth, and afterward settled at Duxbury, Mass.

He had a grant of "one acre west of the watering place," at Plymouth, which he sold to R. Hicks and Thomas Southworth, and removed to Duxbury in 1645.

FIRST GENERATION.

John Soule, born 1632, at Duxbury; married Esther Delano about 1638, daughter of Phillippe De La Noye (de Lannoy), who came out in the Fortune 1621 from Leidon, a lineal descendant of the Seigneur de Lannoy, who died September 12, 1733, aged 95. He died 1707, aged 75.

SECOND GENERATION.

Joshua Soule, born October 12, 1681, of Duxbury, who married Josanna Studley. He died May 29, 1767. He left, with other children:

THIRD GENERATION.

Joseph Soule, born March 15, 1722, of Duxbury, who married Mary Fullerton, in 1742. He had, with other children, Ruby Soule, who married Eden Wadsworth, and:

FOURTH GENERATION.

Joshua Soule, who married February 14, 1765, Mary Cushman, born December 22, 1744; died in Philips, Province of Maine, March 27, 1819. They had with other children: Joshua Soule, late senior Bishop of the Methodist Episcopal Church, and,

FIFTH GENERATION.

Ruby Soule, born in Bristol, Me., October 1, 1777; died February, 1844. She married Peter Dudley (lineal descendant of Gov. Thomas Dudley, of Massachusetts), who was born in Maine, A. D., 1777; died in Mainville, Waren County, Ohio, in 1819. They had, with other children:

SIXTH GENERATION.

Rhoda Dudley, born in Maine, April 21, 1806; died October 27, 1846; married March 28, 1830, in Mainville, Ohio, Hon. Abram Teetor. Their son:

SEVENTH GENERATION.

Henry Dudley Teetor was born November 16, 1834, at Goshen, Clermont County, Ohio, who married, January 26, 1864, at Glendale, Ohio, Miss Sarah Lee Cilley, daughter of the late Judge Jonathan Cilley, of Cincinnati, Ohio, and great-granddaughter of Major-Gen. Joseph Cilley, of New Hampshire, who distinguished himself in the War of the Revolution as Colonel Commanding the First New Hampshire Regiment, afterward president of the Society of the Cincinnati of New Hampshire.

GILBERT WINSLOW, Thirty-first Signer.

"Baptized October 29, 1600. A brother of Gov. Winslow. Returned to England about 1626. Died 1650."

EDWARD MARGESON, Thirty-second Signer.

Edward Margeson, single man; died early 1621.

RICHARD CLARKE, Thirty-sixth Signer.

Tradition will not allow the early death record of this Pilgrim to stand.

The claim of descent from him is constant, and from many sections. The tales of long ago are deep rooted, and any doubt of the authenticity of their statements would be, from their point of view, too ridiculous to arouse even interest.

It is one short, to them conclusive tale; and as such mainly from Hatfield's "History of Elizabethtown, .N. J.," I state it.

The story, while not giving any of the antecedents of Richard Clarke, the Mayflower Pilgrim, states that "Richard Clarke, a shipwright, was from the east end of Long Island. In a deposition made March 22, 1741, his son Richard, then 'aged about fourscore years,' states that he was born, as he hath heard, at Southampton, on Long Island, and that he was brought to Elizabethtown by his father, named Richard Clarke, when he was between sixteen and seventeen years of age.

"The father's name is not found among the early inhabitants of Southampton. He was living in Southold in 1675."

There is a strange possibility about this record; not more so than some others, however. Long Island has many secrets to unravel. The Pilgrims were no strangers there. It was a place of traffic, its wilds increasing the number of "skins," both the New England States and New Amsterdam found such valuable articles of commerce. A little colony of the best people had already "sat down" there, and, too, there was a drift of those not to water inclined for New Jersey.

The instinctive desire on the part of many to cultivate the soil found better opportunity among the inland towns. Matters of health, too, entered their calculations. Bleak Long Island could be within visiting distance, but the home in more balmy New Jersey.

RICHARD CLARKE, SENIOR.

Richard Clarke, Sr., with his wife Elizabeth, daughter Elizabeth and five sons, Richard, John, Joseph (Joshua), Samuel and Ephraim, came to Elizabethtown about 1678. Two sons, Thomas and Benjamin, were born to him after his arrival.

The first five were all admitted as associates in 1699-1700. The will of Richard Clarke, Sr., is dated New York, April 1, 1697, where he may have been taken ill, and where probably he died a day or two later. His estate was valued at £159.5.1½.

His son Thomas was the grandfather of Abraham Clarke, the signer of the Declaration of Independence.

RECORDS.

The story in Elizabethtown is easily substantiated. Dr. J. Henry Clarke, M. D., of Newark, N. J., to whom I am indebted for this history, has the above from family records left him by his father and grandfather, perhaps by them given to Dr. Hatfield.

They had no doubt of their descent from Richard Clarke, the Mayflower Pilgrim, and were satisfied that the second Richard came, as so many did, to Long Island from the New Haven colony.

One record shows Richard Clarke as "having property in Southold in 1675, bounded by the property of James Emot, and the Westbrook in right of himself and wife.

"Also is recorded as possessing property in Southampton in 1664 of upland bounded by William Oliver, Charles Ludlow and George Rose."

The accompanying chart, part of which was sent to me, I have added to as I recall the history. If incorrect, I alone am to blame.

Exceptions are taken to this record, as was expected, but an effort will be made in the third pamphlet to give the reasons for them.

In the Rahway cemetery, on St. George's avenue, is a monument erected in 1848 to the memory of the signer. Upon the four sides of this are the following inscriptions:

Abraham Clark,
Born at Rahway, 16th Feb., 1726,
Died 15th Sept., 1794.
In private life a Christian.
Exemplary, consistent, zealous.
In public life a statesman and a patriot.
In 1775 a member of the first Provincial Congress.
In 1776 one of the Committee of Public Safety.
A delegate to the Continental Congress and a signer of the Declaration of Independence.
Erected by the citizens of Rahway,
4th July, 1848.

Richard Clark, Signer of the Mayflower Compact.				
Richard Clarke, of New Haven? Southampton, Southold and Elizabethtown.				
	Richard Clarke, of Long Island and Elizabethtown.			
		Thomas Clarke, born in Elizabethtown.		
			Thomas Clarke, son of Thomas, who had one son, Abraham.	
				Abraham Clark, signer of the Declaration of Independence for New Jersey, who married Sarah Hatfield, had three sons and three daughters.
				Children of Abraham Clark, the signer, born about 1720; Abraham Clark, M. D., married Lydia Griffith, daughter of Dr. John Griffith, of Newark, N. J.; died July 28, 1854, at the house of his daughter.	Had one child, Eliza, who married John P. Beekman, of Kinderhook; had two daughters, Catherine, who died two years ago; Anna Rosalie, who is living, single, and the only descendant of the signer.
				One son, single, died young in the "Jersey Prison Ship."	
				One son, single, died at home of "jail fever;" was in "N. J. sugar house."	
				One daughter, Hannah, who married Capt. Mellyn Miller.	No children; both dead.
				One daughter, Henrietta, who married Major Clarkson Edgar, Rahway.	No children; both dead.
				One daughter, Abbey, who married Thos. Salter, of Elizabeth.	Had one daughter, Louise Salter, who died, single, at about 80 years of age.

On the old brown stone which marks the grave the following is engraved:

A. C.
In Memory of
Abraham Clark, Esq.,
Who died Sept. 15, 1794, in the 69th year of his age.

Firm and decided as a patriot, zealous and faithful as a servant of the public. He loved his country and adhered to her cause in the darkest hours of her struggles against oppression.

This grave, with that of Capt. Richard Skinner and Sergt. Abraham Trufberry, were marked by a committee from the Elizabethtown Chapter, No. 1, of the Sons of the American Revolution. Every year these gentlemen go to the different cemeteries and put marks on the old patriots' graves.

EDWARD DOTY, Fortieth Signer.

No one can write of Edward Doty, without recognizing his various attractions, though some of his proceedings run counter to one's general expectations of the staid and serious Pilgrims.

The supposition of his youth when he started for new fields to conquer is eagerly accepted in extenuation of acts which in that light seem only the overflow of the exuberance of early life, without "malice aforethought" in his acts.

Allowing that traditions are truth, until disproven, it is easy to accept the information given by history, and coming to me from various sources. All are backed by genealogical search, for, in 1873, Albert G. Welles, president of the Gen. Society, and M. T. Foreman, the secretary, made a genealogical search, and as a result gave it that "Edward Dotey or Doughty, of the Mayflower, was an English youth, belonging to the same family as Sir Charles Montague Doughty, or Doty, of Therburton Hall, Suffolk County, England, formerly of Lincoln County.

The family has an ancient and honorable record that dates back to the Norman Conquest.

Edward Doty, being a minor, came over in the employ of Stephen Hopkins, and was one of the forty-one "Signers" of the compact signed on the Mayflower, November 11, 1620."

RIGHT OF PLACE.

The locality is certainly in favor of Edward Doty's relation to the Pilgrims before his start, and as Goodwin, in his "Landmarks of Plymouth," places Stephen Hopkins as possibly of Scrooby, from his employes, Doty and Leister, that is corroborative of the statement.

Another of the records written between the lines of history that evolve truths as the result of a general search, unites these people in one body politic, giving one keynote of action.

The statement in my possession that "Edward Dotey ran away from home, in resentment of his oldest brother's inheritance of the home and emoluments," has a foundation in truth, but there is more to it than this fact, though it may have been the last straw, which gave the active impulse to the final act.

ENGLISH LAW.

The article on "Descent" preceding Virginia Genealogies, by Rev. Mr. Hayden, of Wilkesbarre, places Edward Doty on a platform which has no question as to acceptance; it is infallible in its relation to the people of that epoch.

"The law of primogeniture, or right of the oldest son to inherit all of his father's estate, if held by knight's service, introduced into England soon after the Norman conquest, by the influence of Norman lawyers, has determined the descent of land in England for the past 800 years. True, its direct effect has been to enrich the oldest son and beggar the rest of the family.

"Yet it has this advantage, in that while it creates a privileged class of landed gentry, it disperses the younger sons to seek their homes and fortunes elsewhere without in any way affecting their lineal traits and mental and social investments."

This was Doty's situation; a younger son, as the research of experts shows, of an authenticated family, he was obliged, in common with all others, under the laws of England, to serve his apprenticeship of seven years to earn the rights of citizenship.

Stephen Hopkins, a prominent resident of his own section of country, personally attractive, drew him to make his start of indenture with him, and under such tutelage, as well as the necessary trade, taught him as he himself was taught the Separatist doctrines, and during the serious twilight hour imbued his young mind with a longing for adventure, and what would soon be called a broad, liberal education.

Part of his apprenticeship was behind him when his master, a man strong in his convictions, decided to cast in his lot with the outgoing Pilgrims. The prospects as well as necessities suited Edward Doty, and the citizenship to be earned could be accomplished as well with Stephen Hopkins in other lands as with the same person in his own.

AGAIN ENGLISH LAW.

"A freeman, which class alone was entitled to elect civil officers, was one who had served his apprenticeship to one of the sixty odd Livery Companies, or Craft Guilds, and had received his discharge from indenture.

"Into these Livery Companies went, as indentured apprentices to learn the craft, or trade, the best blood of England.

"To the Companies even royalty joined itself."

This name may be found in England and here, spelt in many ways. They are only the accidents of the times, common from the variety of sectional pronunciations, and the indifference of the owner.

Such error has pursued people always, and in the early days the desire being to put their personal identification out of the power of those they were surrounded by, they were willing to drift into any spelling, no matter how far from the truth it rendered the pronunciation.

In an old deed made October 17, 1752, Abner White (whose son Charles married Elizabeth Doty) deed, entered in Charlotte Precincts, recorded in book 2, is signed by William Dougherty, Town Clerk, February 13, 1771.

Abner White in his will places the name as Doty.

SERVANT CONTINUED.

The word servant in the past had not the same significance of menial position as in the present. It was an English form of speech to which no one took exception, and in the large English houses in China, it was usual for any one not of the firm to speak of himself as servant of the house of "Blank."

Fresh from countries where the feeling of caste was wool-dyed, no necessity would have led Gov. Carver, whose conversatism was a matter of fact, to choose this youth as one of the "ten principale men from the volunteers" to go on the third exploring party, an expedition of the greatest importance, requiring judgment, if possible experience, involving the destiny of the whole colony, if he were not educated up to it. It was not a time for experiments, the people ready and waiting, longing and needing, must have the speediest housing and settling for the well-being of their venture.

THE RIGHT VIEW

So Edward Doty was a servant to Mr. Stephen Hopkins, not for personal, menial service, but living naturally with his master, as was the custom of that day, and many which followed it, eating at his table, as people so circumstanced have for time out of date. Then, when his time was up, marrying, if they so desired, a daughter of the house, with the accompaniment of a father's blessing.

History had precedent for such procedure. Modern methods are the same, only the terms are different. Edward Doty and Edward Leister were confidential clerks from the start.

I have no desire, for it in no way detracts from Edward Doty's character, to make him other than he was, a wild, harum-scarum fellow. Not being a clubman, and having no Monte Carlo to seek when he desired a little outing where the numbers who were on the same mission hid the single action, our Edward, who never could dance a "pas seul," rendered his account wholly, freely, regardless of Bradford's willing pen or the Plymouth records which, centuries after, would be searched for his credentials before he could present himself to the august board who would pass sentence on his admission to the "Society of Mayflower Descendants."

Our "young blood," imbued with the spirit of the times when Drake, Hawkins and "Sir Walter Raleigh, the master spirit of England for romantic enterprises, and a passionate desire to discover, explore and settle other countries," had infused the lougings for what must be called piratical adventure into the minds of men, expected more of an expedition than the hum-drum life of narrow ship's quarters, surrounded by women and children.

He hadn't shipped for this. There must be some place for his opinion and action; at least he valued it, and history shows that others took the same view of it.

Edward "Dotte" was not alone in feeling that an ordinary mixed ship's company could be dispensed with; other spirits like unto himself saw with his glasses and felt it incumbent on themselves to enjoy each day as it came.

THE ADVENTURERS.

The bond binding them to the merchant adventurers in the future, men who were "outgrowths of the craft guilds," bore heavily on their future, and they were to avail themselves of all the liberty of unorganized ship life to store up retrospective pleasure. Years of trial, work and the discipline of "a barren country, which is a great whet to the industry of people," never entirely effaced this part of his character.

The boy nature remained with the man of riper years.

At the start all had land, to be sure, but

SIGNERS OF THE MAYFLOWER COMPACT.

it was by yearly tenure, everything on the co-operative plan.

The old saying that everything was provided for the "lame and the lazy" did not take deep root in the Pilgrim mind. Naturally the thrifty resented this procedure, and at the request of the people, in 1623, there was a distribution of ground plots, each man receiving one acre, permission being allowed the father to claim one acre for each member of the family.

Edward Doty had but one allotment, which proves conclusively and satisfactorily that he was a single man at the time. No rights on his part would be left unclaimed.

What his own act had to do with his state of single-blessedness no one will ever know. But he lived it down, although the record can never be effaced that "on the 18th of June (1621) the whole company were convened to adjudge upon the record of offense which had been committed in the colony." This was a duel fought with sword and dagger between Edward Doty and Edward Leister, the servants of Stephen Hopkins, in which both were wounded.

The company sentenced them to have their heads and feet tied together, and so to remain for a day, without meat or drink; but within an hour they were released by the Governor.

LENIENT PILGRIMS.

Soft-hearted Pilgrims, they were still themselves without the austere learning which came with the Puritans, fresh from the cruelties of other countries.

Puritanism partook of the temperament of the person in power, who was often a law unto himself. Pilgrimism, if it can be so called, saw always the lenient side of everything, they sounded the modern war cry of wishing "to be left alone" with their beliefs and desires.

A household religion, strong of purpose, loving and tender in authority.

They made no compromises with their consciences, but held to the form of Christian service which kept their daily life the best they knew, not looking backward for regrets, or forward to the unknown future beyond their control.

The Pilgrim toleration was not in the Puritan "articles of faith," who were tempest-tossed religiously and meted out to those under them punishments with an iron will which was not velvet-gloved.

A WILLING SINNER.

For my part, I would not have trusted Edward Doty had not punishment stared him in the face, not to repeat the same offense at a moment's notice on the slightest provocation. It was the irresistible something in the man's nature that hal to be worked off, regardless of circumstances.

Why have a sword if not for use? They were not collecting relics for home adornment.

GOVERNOR'S POWER.

"The Governor, in some cases previous to the establishment of juries, remitted punishments. He remitted that of the duelists, Doty and Leister, after it had been partially administered."

Having no patent of their own by which to live and guide public affairs, the officials were peculiarly placed as to their actions. They were still wholly under English law and must creep slowly into power. The adventurers migh at any time "vent their spleen" upon them, and so represent affairs to the government abroad that the official hand would fall with undesired weight.

LAND DISTRIBUTION.

The second distribution in 1627 spoke well for the progression of the people, in idea and material; also for a national dependence on each other; so "to make it all easy we take every head of a family, with every young man of age and prudence, both of the first comers and those who have since arrived, into partnership with us. Each single freeman to have a single share. Each father to have leave to purchase a share for each of his family."

Each share is allotted twenty acres of tillable lands, besides the single acres with the gardens and homesteads they had before (in the allotment of 1623).

Each single man was requested to unite with some head of a family, in order that there might be as few families as possible. Still, Edward Doty was unmarried, and could claim but one share.

EDWARD A BACHELOR.

Edward Doty, sowing his wild oats, with all the freedom he could command, did not stop to realize "that a plantation can never flourish till families be planted, and the respects of Wives and Children fix the people on the soyle."

Why should he, when he did not suffer for his single blessedness, and the little cherub who sits aloft had sped no arrows for him? Beside John Howland's hospitable board he found all the comforts the colony could command, and under his peaceful influence there was nothing to arouse his belligerent spirit.

CALM BEFORE MANY STORMS.

After this the record is very quiet, and it is only as one reads from Bradford, when, in 1650, he says: "Edward Doty, by a second wife, hath seven children, and he and they are living," that one realizes how, between 1627 and 1635, joy and sorrow have come to our Pilgrim, and that the wife of his youth was one of the loved and lost. Gone from his earthly to her heavenly home.

"On the 6th of January, 1634-5, Edward Doten and Fayth Clarke were married."

This young bride, daughter of Thurston Clarke, only 16 years of age, knew whom she loved, and that she was sure of happiness with Edward Doten, a "thrifty, active citizen."

A man who, if given a choice of the place, could, or at least would, try to occupy any or all at once.

What matter which, so long as they caused him to present himself at court, whether as plaintiff or defendant was a matter of perfect indifference to him, and when going too far he found himself a prisoner, it was only for a mere trifle, the too free use of tongue or fists!

There is no doubt of his capacity in either respect.

THE INHERITANCE.

By heredity his sons took up the wondrous tale and repeated history so far as their attendance upon court was concerned.

Still, again, like the Pilgrim, they were energetic, useful citizens, although litigation was the very "breath of their nostrils."

The Pilgrims and "old comers" brought with them a deal of human nature, resentment of imposition, and rebelled with a modern spirit at the requirements of the times.

"For the young men that were most able and fitte for labour and service did repine that they should spend their time and strength to work for other men's wives and children without recompense. The strong, or men of parts, had no more devission of victails and cloathes than he that was weake and not able to doe a quarter the other could; this was thought injustice.

"The aged and graver to be ranked and equalized in labours and victails, cloathes, etc., with the meanner, and younger sorte, thought it some indignitie and disrespect unto them, and for men's wives to be commanded to doe service for other men, as dressing their meate, washing their cloathes, etc., they deemed it a kind of slaverie; neither could many husbands well brooke it."—Bradford's Plimouth Plantation, pp. 135, 136.

EDWARD DOTY'S FEELINGS.

Imagine Edward Doty remaining quiet under such regulations for an instant. Every instinct of the man would call out against it, and few, and necessary, as were the "cloathes" he owned, he would surely "turn and rend them" that his wife might have full occupation for every moment at home, or if the necessity which knows no law compelled her to some share in the work required for others, would take care there should only be time for a hasty "running over" of these outside duties. His wife, his time, would have suited his husbandly requirements far better.

Allowing that there are two sides to every question, and that I may naught extenuate or give false value to, each view shall have its place.

The acknowledged authority on Edward Doty, of the Mayflower, is certainly Mr. Ethan Allen Doty, and when preparing this article, I was glad of the personal friendship which enabled me to seek him last spring, and secure the expert opinion which I knew was his.

True to his desire to have only real, authenticated history, I found he felt there was not the slightest foundation of fact in the many statements of the connection with the Doughty family of Suffolk County, England.

Indeed, if I mistake not, the family nationality is rather attributed to Germany. Goodwin pronounces it French, and allows this birthright to plead for many faults of temper.

However this may be, and admitting, as "the historian" claims, that he was an ignorant lad, 20 years of age, who signed the Compact and future papers, including his will, in 1655, with a mark, this, if accepted as evidence of his inability to write, would place many of that epoch as uneducated.

OTHERS SIGN WITH AN X.

Having already called attention in previous papers to Alice Southworth Bradford's will, also that of Peregrine White, signed with an X, I doubt not I could find much similar evidence that would make Edward Doty in good company. My own conviction grows with the search into a belief that there was some method in this mode of procedure, recognized by the period.

The days are not so long ago when lack of practice and inclination made writing a labor, and all who have reached years of maturity can give evidence from precedent of the large number of people who rarely took a pen in their hand.

No one doubts Louis XVI.'s royalty, and

SUCCESS.

Edward Doty's success in life in attributed to his ambition and shrewdness. Certain is it that by 1640 he was a considerable land owner and a man of position and influence.

Arriving in America in 1620, the early part of the time tied to the needs attendant upon the sickness that made such havoc in the colonies; then the contract with the adventurers, which bound a man hand and foot, with no outlook of liberty of action; again the barrenness of Plymouth, which was labor with scarcely a return; and yet with these years against him Edward Doty, young, strong and fearless, made great strides to accomplish such a material advancement more than equal to the average, certainly, at 40 years of age, with all the drawbacks of the situation.

Strive as I may, I can but feel that there was more backing to Edward Doty than would come from an ignorant, untutored lad, as many allow him to have been.

One must recall that the intellectual progression of that day was at a very low ebb; there was no goal before people that placed them in early training. Indeed, truth compels the assertion that this method of educational economy of time hardly reaches two generations, and it is asking too much of the Pilgrims that they should be postgraduates in the "arts and sciences" in those early days.

EDWARD DOTY'S SECOND WIFE.

Faith Clarke Doty was not exempt from the sorrows of life. In 1655 she was called to part with her husband, and in 1661, before time had lessened her grief, her father, Thurston Clarke, was frozen to death while on his way by land from Plymouth to Duxbury. A hard fate to come all the way from Ipswich, England, in the Francis, to meet!

HER HOME.

Faith Doty had a very beautiful house at Plymouth, on the High Cliff, and other residences, and there came to her Edward, John, Desire, Samuel, Thomas, Elizabeth, Isaac, Joseph and Mary, two of them born after Bradford's account in 1650—where he says: "Edward Doty by his second wife had seven children living in 1650, but his will mentions only wife and one son" (Savage's Gen. Diet, vol. II., p. 61, Bradford's Plymouth Plantation, p. 455; Mount's Relations, p. 45).

Can I have better argument for the doubters in favor of many other children left out of their fathers' wills? Only his namesake, Edward, to show out of nine children! Why not the same privilege allowed to Elder William Brewster, to Stephen Hopkins, and others who have not left a title clear for their descendants to prove these "back-fathers" as their own?

That this was usual there can be no doubt; in fact, with the above authority, all must be silenced if not convinced.

HER SECOND MARRIAGE.

Being a second wife, Faith Clarke Doty retaliated by having a second husband, marrying March 14, 1667, John Phillips, of Marshfield, Mass. This unfortunately does not give claim to the Mayflower descent, that only coming through the Dotys.

This ancestry is naturally so much desired that kindness prompts any assertion that prevents false hopes, only admitting every possibility among those "old comers" of reaching that ship by the various intermarriages.

Thinking people must pause before they relegate the present interest in ancestry to a place among the "fads" of their times and realize the powerful, worldwide strength growing day by day as each one enlists under the Mayflower banner, the "Founders and Patriots," the Sons of the Colonial Wars, Colonial Dames, for a future time of need. These societies are making a band with but a single thought for their country. Children are growing up, with the currents of patriotism running through every fiber of their being, to venerate the flag all hold so dear, and with the pull all together hold it aloft, the pride of a whole nation.

"Imitation, the sincerest flattery," will spread its influence over others until time gives them the born right to place themselves in their turn as the example.

PILGRIM HEREDITY.

One thing the Pilgrim Fathers brought with them could well be dispensed with, but "hope comes with the morning," and science, which has a barnacle-like tenacity of purpose in averting disease, has laid hold upon the fell destroyer, determined to place it, so far as human knowledge controls, with the things of the past.

For a long while I have studied during our work in the library under Dr. Edward E. Cornwall, M. D., while he was tracing to its source the cause of the early disease known as the "first sickness," which devastated the colony at the start.

Now that his article is published, I have the opportunity of quoting from it, and accounting for the rapid spread of that sickness. Dr. Cornwall attributes it to quick consumption. The infectious disease which had spread over the country some two years before the arrival of the Pilgrims, making such havoc among the Indians, seems to have had no connection with the after sickness, and is scientifically attributed to smallpox or measles.

All the circumstances attending the arrival and life of the Pilgrims were in favor of the development of the very disease this article goes to prove. Still, there must have been an exciting cause, and search has proved conclusively that "the tubercular bacillus was present on the Mayflower."

Dorothy May Bradford was drowned, Gov. Carver died of apoplexy, and then the sad tale is taken up, all in favor of the presence of the disease that "walketh at noonday."

Consumption, which medical science places as most certain between the ages of twenty and thirty, took from this little band the flower of its company, and to spend still further its venom, fastened itself upon the crew of the Mayflower, after the Pilgrims had left the ship, and they, happy in better quarters, sought the places vacated by the Pilgrims, probably receiving therefrom the germs for future disease.

Mary Brewster's death appealed to us, knowing she was wasting away, even when all her heart desired had gathered around her.

The Lord's will with them was not a matter of rhetoric, or assuagement; the victim must meet it with the undying faith which overcame harsh methods, and weak as poor human nature has always been, bear testimony of the horrors overcome, as sick, nervous and alone they were to accept their fate.

THE CREW OF THE MAYFLOWER.

History enables us to feel a little vindictive toward the captain and crew of the Mayflower, but all, allowing for the lapse of time, pass over the never to be forgotten wrongs when they read that "they that had been boone companions in ye time of their health and welfare began now to deserte one another in this calamity, saing they would not hasard their lives for them, they would be infected by coming to help them in the cabins."

This is a long "looking backward," to search for personal inheritance of disease, and some of the descendants of the "tough ones," who survived all ills, may take much unction to themselves for their exemption, but the present era of enlightenment, which "carries healing in its hand," will still allow all Pilgrim descendants pride in their birthright.

There was nothing of the "dinna ken, or dinna care," about the Dotys; what they had, what they did, was recorded.

Edward Doty, or Doten, and Faith Clark, daughter of Thurston Clark, had nine children, and I owe it to Mr. Ethan Allen Doty that I can account for them all.

One very important and convincing argument for the Dotys is that they married well, the majority of them not "early and often," as the history of the times records for many of the families. Still, frequently enough to show they were not out of the count in the way of attractions.

It is a very convincing lineage, as to the aspirations, desires and success of those of the name.

The Pilgrim's will tells the tale I love to dwell upon, recall, and repeat. Made May 20, 1655, and recorded at Plymouth, at his death, August 23, 1655, with nine children, while it gives his lands to his sons, mentions only Edward the eldest, and provides for his widow.

So, if wills are infallible, history is only sure of the first-born, from this source.

QUAINT INVENTORY.

Thirty-five years of accumulation, and the enumeration of his possessions, assures us that his thrift met with its reward, as he leaves "three score acres of upland, with meadow adjoining," valued at £10, while "a yoake of working oxen," true to the necessities of the times, are placed at £12, and a cow, his children's friend, is appraised at £4.

It is a pleasure to notice that he had some of the comforts himself, among them a large number of household utensils, and, as in those days a "chafing dish for live coals" was included, Faith Doty could join a club and spread such tempting viands as venison and wild turkey before the members that the only excuse offered for absence would be sickness.

Chairs, "chists," hammers, hinges, "kitles" and, above all things, "a bed and covering," estimated at the high value of £5, figured in the inventory. How they disposed of the "nine little" Dotys, with only one bed, is a matter of conjecture.

THE CHILDREN.

Mary, the youngest child, effaced herself completely after she had participated in the settlement of her mother's estate in 1677, and the records announce, for the benefit of

SIGNERS OF THE MAYFLOWER COMPACT.

aspirants to Mayflower ascent, that she was unmarried.

Edward Doty, Jr., married, at Plymouth February 25, 1633, Sarah Faunce, daughter of John Faunce, and Patience, his wife, and no historian neglects to chronicle that she was a sister of the famous Elder Faunce, while those who read accept his worth unhesitatingly.

This Edward, being a man of many virtues, having the Doty "intelligence, integrity and thrift," seemed fitted for a better end than to be drowned with his son John and Elkanah Watson, in Plymouth Harbor February 8, 1690.

There is one comfort. He made his mark on ages to come, for his daughter Sarah married James Warren, justice of the peace, captain, and ancestor of many patriots dear to all.

Mary, another of his daughters, married Joseph Allyn, whose distinguished family honor Connecticut, and soon removed to Wethersfield, that State, there becoming identified with the history of the colony.

Then an Allyn daughter, with inherited ambition, became the wife of James Otis, colonel, and Judge of Barnstable, whose son James was the great orator and patriot of his times.

A BROKEN TIE.

Here history has a sad side. While collecting material for these articles, no one was more interested than Mr. Albert Boyd Otis, of Belfast, Me., in securing for my use and advancement all of record and tradition possible.

To-day my historical work among the Pilgrims is nearing its close, but no word of encouragement or congratulation will come to me from him, unless the angels in Heaven are permitted to minister on earth.

The history of the Dotys could not be written with the Warrens left out, so, true to precedent, Mary, daughter of James, and Mary Allyn Otis, married her cousin, James Warren. This marriage was on a very equal footing; no woman versed in modern ways could be more than Mercy Otis Warren, the historian of the revolution, was, and she found, as was wise, a fitting mate in the never-to-be-forgotten James Warren, president of the Provincial Congress.

The world honors him, without a personal claim—his were deeds, not words.

AGAIN THE CHILDREN.

Two sons of Edward Doty, Jr., and Sarah Faunce, Samuel and Benjamin Doty, settled at Saybrooke, Conn., and place the world in touch with themselves, in the present, through Rev. Dr. William D'Orville Doty, of Rochester, and the late Clara Doty Bates, of Chicago.

John Doty, the second son of the Pilgrim, found his happiness in Plymouth, owning good citizenship, marrying for his betterment, in 1667, Elizabeth Cooke, who was born in Plymouth, January 18, 1649, daughter of Jacob Cooke and Damaris Hopkins, and then adding to all that was best of himself by caring for the brothers and sisters, who naturally needed his protection.

This John Doty, who was a farmer, with the tendency of the times to allow the spelling of their names to be at the mercy of the individual, his family for generations having lived on the New England coast, were and are found as "Doten."

Elizabeth Cooke Doty, mindful of her duties, left behind her nine children, dying November 21, 1692; and John, backed by Biblical and Pilgrim lore, feeling the loneliness not good for man (!) even with all of these "olive branches," secured the hand (a woman's heart in those days was supposed to be in her work) of Sarah, daughter of Giles Rickard, and, to make the round dozen at the family board, had three children.

Thomas Doty, the third son of the Pilgrim, took a different view of life from his stay-at-home brothers; his talents required greater scope for their development, so Cape Cod became his home, took to himself a wife, and made Mary Churchill happy during his stay, dying in 1679. Their only child, also Thomas, to keep the family title clear, had by his wife, Elizabeth Harlow, a son, Col. Thomas Doty, born in 1704, who was a distinguished officer in the war of 1756, and then, having acquired the martial knowledge, which gave him something to talk about, made himself known during the war of the Revolution, as landlord of the famous "Doty Tavern" at Stoughton, Mass., where the patriots were always welcome.

Here they met to crack their jokes, plan campaigns, place their pickets, and then, everything being arranged to their satisfaction, they did not neglect themselves or leave "mine host of the Doty Tavern" in the background.

Col. Thomas Doty made his country his bride, never marrying, giving all of his time, thought and strength for the use of the patriots who "most did congregate" under his trusted roof.

Samuel, the fourth son, to vary the family history, commenced his career as a seaman, lived on Cape Cod, fished for a change, perhaps livelihood, and, though his subsequent career fails to prove him one of the whalers of that location, probably took a hand at any such sport if opportunity offered.

CHANGE OF RESIDENCE.

However, he left this life of supposed peril behind him, removed to Piscataway, N. J., and soon became a warrior bold, lieutenant of Capt. Francis Drake's company. He married Jane Harmon, exchanged anchor and gun for the pruning hook, became a farmer, and, stretching forth for the ground to till, gained wealth, a "local habitation and a name."

Edward Doty, the Pilgrim, would "rise up in his wrath" if Desire, his lovely, attractive and intelligent daughter, had not the place to which she belonged. She married, first, Christmas, 1667, William Sherman, of Marshfield, Mass. (son of William Sherman, who died in Marshfield October 25, 1697, and Prudence Hill), who "fell destracted" under pressure of the trials of King Philip's war, and a grateful nation granted her £20 for her relief. Only this for Hannah, born in 1668, who married William Ring, Elizabeth, William, Patience, Experience and Ebenezer.

The only record well authenticated to the present day I have, is that of Mr. George W. Sherman, of Lynbrook, N. Y., taken from the records at Marshfield Hills.

William Sherman, who married Prudence Hill, their son William Sherman, wife Desire Doty. Ebenezer Sherman, their son, who married Margaret Decro (or, as it is said, Margaret D'Esqurureaux), and had Elisha Sherman, who married Lydia Walker, then their son Ebenezer Sherman, who married Mary Simmons, and had a son, Aaron Sherman, whose wife, Lydia Mitchell, added another Aaron Simmons Sherman, father of George W. Sherman.

OTHER HUSBANDS.

Desire Doty next took to herself Israel Holmes, a fisherman, who, to fill her cup of sorrow to overflowing, was drowned 1685, in Plymouth Harbor.

However, the third time she was successful, and in the love and protection of Alexander Standish, heir apparent, and oldest son of the great Capt. Myles Standish, life assumed new beauty. In this line comes Mrs. Russell Sage and her brother, Col. Slocum, honored members of the "Mayflower descendants."

To her was granted length of days, for she died, as appears by her grave stone in the Cedar Grove Cemetery at Marshfield, December, 1731, aged 86.

Elizabeth, who owned Edward Doty the first as father, has a short tale to tell. She married at Marshfield, Mass., January 13, 1675, John, son of John and Annis Peabody Rouse; they had one son, also John, born 1678, died 1704.

The one who makes the full rounded history of the Dotys, which gives great satisfaction to the historian, is Isaac Doty, the seventh child of Edward and Faith Clark Doty. Not to forget the Pilgrim claims, he lived for a time in Sandwich, Mass., and then the same magnet as to locality drawing him as it did others to Long Island, about 1672, he removed to Oyster Bay, and with the adaptability given to sparsely settled regions, fitted into the work to be done, became vestryman of the Episcopal Church, and, to keep up the connection, was buried in its graveyard.

With wise forethought, perhaps knowledge, he married Elizabeth, daughter of William and Elizabeth England, of Portsmouth, R. I., and of this union there were six children accounted for that in no way prevents others being found who have the same claim.

Nine was the lucky number in the Doty family.

No one need confine themselves to Episcopal records in this search, many of his descendants united with the Society of Friends on Long Island and in Duchess County, so they may look under the broad-rimmed hats and Quaker bonnets for their long-lost cousins and aunts.

Prosperity has followed this branch. They have not doffed their practical common sense, while donning the gray garb which has brought to them peace and exemption from the adventure their ancestors started with. This family are a little mixed with the name of Doughty. I leave to them the unraveling of the start. Perhaps it may fall on Mr. Spencer Cary Doty, of this line, who carried his gray into the civil war, winning for himself an additional society in the "Loyal Legion" of New York.

THE LAST OF THE CHILDREN.

Mary, with the claim of her youth and lack of history, was accounted for first, and now there is no choice left us. Only Joseph, the eighth child and youngest son, can add to the history, in which there is so much to revere. Having surveyed and laid out the town of Rochester, Mass., as it is to-day, it is natural he should have chosen a "garden spot" to his liking, and, farmer as he was, till the ground to his personal advantage, until he became at least one of its largest landowners, which would, in consequence, place him as a prominent citizen.

Joseph Doty's life was relieved from monotony, being three times a wooer (shall I say lover?), marrying first Elizabeth Warren, who was born September 5, 1654, daughter of Nathaniel Warren and Sarah Walker; then for second wife choosing Deborah, born about 1662, daughter of Walter Hatch and Elizabeth Holbrook, and again, to increase the undoubted strength of the family connections he made by his marriages, took Sarah Edwards to his "heart and home."

His descendants have spread and increased with time, following a Pilgrim trail from which I expect much history. They have gone from Rochester and Hardwick, Mass., to Sharon, Conn., and the adjoining towns, to "Nine Partners," and the "Oblong" tracts in New York.

This "Oblong" has so much historical significance, is so constantly in local evidence, that I sought Rev. C. M. Selleck, the historian, of Norwalk, Conn., to place it positively. He says it is between Ridgefield, Conn., and New Canaan, in the same State.

The Dotys have given us Gov. James Duane Doty, Governor of Wisconsin, both as Territory and State, and then, as a gift from the honored Lincoln's hands, Governor of Utah; Commodore George W. Doty, of the navy; Rev. Elisha Doty, the missionary, and, of course, as has been told, the Warren and Otis claim, but there is still a very rugged one to add in Ethan Allen, of revolutionary fame, the "Green Mountain boy," who needs neither title nor description to place him; every schoolboy in the land is waiting and longing to follow his example.

One more line of descent to afford a clew for search and my story is done. The Dotys prove themselves so much in the present that the Mayflower is only an accessory, not a necessity.

1. Edward Doty, of the Mayflower, who married Faith Clark.

2. Edward Doty, Jr., who married Sarah Faunce.

3. Samuel Doty, who married Ann Buckingham, and lived at Saybrook, Conn.

4. Samuel Doty, who married Margeria Parker.

5. Samuel Doty, who married his cousin, Mercy Doty. He also lived at Saybrook, and with all of his sons who were above sixteen joined the revolutionary army, doing good service through the war.

6. Ethan Allen Doty, married Keturah L. Tompkins.

7. Warren S. Doty, married Sarah M. Child.

S. Ethan Allen Doty.

The original record reads "In answer unto the petition of Desire Sherman unto her husband, William Sherman, Jr., who fell destracted in the service of the country, the court allows her the sume of £20 towards the releiffe of them and theire familie, being by reason of great charge and nessesities in great straightes."—Plymouth Colony Records, Vol. V., 1668-1678.

RICHARD BRITTERIDGE, Thirty-fourth Signer.

"Richard Britteridge, Plymouth, came in the Mayflower 1620. Died ten days after landing, being the first of the sad roll."—Savage.

EDWARD LEISTER, Forty-first Signer.

The records of the early historians simply give him as coming over with Stephen Hopkins, as Edward Doty did, and that he went to Virginia.

A correspondent has claimed descent from him, and adds: "Andrew Leister, his brother, was licensed to keep a house of entertainment at Gloucester February 26, 1648; births of four children are recorded at that place.

"Andrew died June 7, 1669; his oldest child was born 1642."

RICHARD GARDINER, Thirty-seventh Signer.

"Richard, of Plymouth, 1620, one of the passengers of the Mayflower, was living late in 1624, but though he partook of the division of lands, early in that year, he had no share in the division of cattle—1627. No more is known of him but what Bradford tells, that he became a mariner and died away, and he had no wife."

JOHN ALLERTON, Thirty-eighth Signer.

"John Allerton, a sailor on the 'Mayflower,' who decided to join the colony; signed the 'Compact,' but died before the vessel set sail to return."

THOMAS ENGLISH, Thirty-ninth Signer.

"Thomas Plymouth, one of the passengers in the Mayflower, 1620, died in the general sickness early next spring, leaving no wife nor child. He had been a sailor, says Bradford, hired by the Pilgrims."—Savage.

"MAYFLOWER LOG."

The hope, which was the result of the wish, has given cause for a wrong impression as to the contents of what is called the "Mayflower Log," a misnomer surely, and for that reason a disappointment to those who expected to have all difficulties solved which had crossed their pathway while searching for the history of the Pilgrim Fathers and early colonists.

Our knowledge remains as of yore. To us has only come the original manuscript of Gov. Bradford's journal, the book from which all subsequent history must have been taken, varied only so far as the writer was a participant in the events narrated.

Bradford made no special plea for its value while writing it. He was plain of speech, as befitted the times, but one needs no telling to know that, in his position, he was the one of all people fitted to the work he undertook and accomplished. He was in the midst of events as they occurred, and, with his conscious gift of description, has done as all so blessed always have and will, put it on paper in his leisure hours.

The Pilgrims were a living history, told by themselves in the passage of time. That their Governor and strong dependence should chronicle their life was more than natural. They had been driven from England, after enduring persecutions beyond human nature to bear, at a time when everything connected with the government was at the lowest ebb of integrity. They were looking for more from life than was given them. They had, as a celebrated clergyman recently said in a sermon before the Fort Greene Chapter of the Daughters of the American Revolution, "found their souls," and, in order to keep them, they must leave the depravity surrounding them and seek new fields, where their purity of purpose should not be strangled by the difficulties they could not control.

LEYDEN.

Leyden, their next home, to them, went so far and no farther; there was a limit of time set upon their freedom to worship the living God as they were finding Him. The twelve years' truce with Spain, nearly over to them, meant possible defeat, only the faithful to live and die by their beliefs, while the future of their children was the cause of their greatest anguish.

Next their pilgrimage to America, and the silver lining to the dark cloud was evident, even through all their vicissitudes and dire want.

Of this situation of affairs, thanks to Gov. Bradford's journal, all have been fully aware, and, though it is claimed by some historians that the original manuscript was stolen from the belfry of the church in Boston, it certainly was carried in some unaccountable way to England, and found a resting place in the library of Fulham Palace.

Nothing is hidden that shall not be revealed, and as the historians of the early colony had borrowed largely in their writings from Bradford's journal, the quoting by Bishop Wilberforce of passages from this hidden journal, made their source easy of identification.

The temptation no one had a desire to resist, led the Massachusetts Historical Society to seek at least to copy what they deemed their own, and in 1856, under the supervision of the late antiquary Charles Deane, an edition of surely five hundred copies were published, and soon were being eagerly read and digested by the historian and searcher in the various libraries.

ANOTHER TREASURE,

Too, there is a fac-simile edition by the photogravure process, with an introduction by John A. Doyle, Fellow of All Souls' College, Oxford. No writer has ever claimed more for Bradford than he does, and his high appreciation shows where he tells "The practical temper of the man, his power of bringing common sense, with a touch of humor, to bear on an administrative difficulty is well illustrated by his account of the second Christmas day spent at Plymouth." The same conviction will come to every one as they read in Bradford's quaint language, after knowing that in the autumn before the colony had received an addition of thirty-five newcomers.

"Most of them were lusty young men, and many of them wild enough, who little considered whither or about what they went.

"When Christmas day came round these new-comers refused to work, as against their consciences. Bradford then told them that if they made it a matter of conscience he would spare them until they were better informed.

"When the rest of the settlers came in at noon from their husbandry, they found the new-comers amusing themselves with games in the street. Bradford therefore took away their implements and told them that it was against his conscience that they should play and others work, and henceforth games were no more seen in the streets of Plymouth."

AUTHENTICITY OF THE HISTORY.

The newly returned "History of Plymouth Colony" carries with it proofs of its authenticity. Samuel Bradford, perhaps with some intuition of the dangerous surroundings of new colonies, on one of the blank leaves has written a short account of the early history of the manuscript.

"This book was rit by goerner William Bradford, and gifen to his son Mager William Bradford, and by him to his son, Mager John Bradford, rit by me Samuel Bradford March 20, 1705."

Many of the early historians had free access to Gov. Bradford's Journal, Morton, surely, and Prince, who tells of Gov. Bradford's "History of Plymouth People and Colony," "all in his own handwriting." Hubbard continues this tale in his history of New England, and Gov. Thomas Hutchinson gives full credit to the Bradford manuscript.

Bradford, without, or with very little, competition, could easily be the great historian of his time. Still much of his value in relation to future needs is a matter of temperament. He enjoyed the petty details that would ahve been irksome to other men; matters of seemingly no importance, now so highly treasured, that came under his official eye, were to him worthy of a place with the events of the day, and in the present much greater detail would be forgiven him. He saw things from all sides, and I gather from my study that he was not a really conventional man, as were many of that period. This strikes one when they recall his state visit to Mrs. John Winthrop, of Massachusetts. He allowed himself time to pay his respects, as was due, but, that function through with, sought Capt. Prince on his vessel for a chat.

THE PRESENT.

This is the time when there will be no neglect in disseminating whatever can be added by the return of this history. Public interest demands and commands that it be made available for all.

Rev. Anson Titus, of Tufts College, to whom I applied for information, writes me: "The Massachusetts Great and General Court has authorized a full account of the return of the original manuscript to be published. The same will be of great interest, in that it will contain information in brief compass."

STUDENTS.

No one from Savage down will say aught against "Bradford's History." It has been an entertainment and benefit all these years. Searched with avidity, an authority without competition, and yet there is surely sorrow that the accidental changing of the long-treasured name to the "Mayflower Log" led to anticipations of new fields open to the student, knotty, puzzling questions set at rest, and all with their welcome, include a regret that they had not the unknown to deal with.

SIGNERS
—— OF THE ——
Mayflower Compact

—— BY ——

ANNIE ARNOUX HAXTUN.

PART III.

REPRINTED FROM
THE MAIL AND EXPRESS,
NEW YORK,
1899.

Fore-Words to PART III.

AFTER much consideration, I have determined to compile this pamphlet, with many faults to be corrected.
"Ye olden time" is making history so fast in the present that it seemed wiser to thus arouse the discussion which would lead to the securing of hitherto untold genealogical history.

To this end a number of blank pages have been left, that when the corrections come, which will be published in The Mail and Express Saturday edition there will be space to add them to the pamphlet.

The historical tangles which to me seem of the greatest importance are the finding of an authentic list of Elder William Brewster's children. My own study of the Pilgrims does not reconcile me to the number accounted for, in view of the sympathy so constantly given Brewster for his large family and inadequate means for their support. Rev. Nathaniel must have his authentic place in his family, and Hanna Brewster's two husbands should be recorded.

Edward Brewster, who joined the expedition with William Brewster and Stephen Hopkins, is not fully received as the Elder's son. He wants his recognition.

Elizabeth Tilley, who long ago I proved by old records not to have been the daughter of John Tilley, the Pilgrim, by his wife, Bridget van der Velde, wants what tradition from all quarters of the country gives her, and from which no arguments will turn the Howland descendants—her historical right to being Gov. Carver's granddaughter. In 1895 I wrote of this from Mr. Cowles's Hartford Bible.

The parents of Richard Warren, of the Mayflower, and his wife Elizabeth, cannot be found. I felt grateful for the start in the right direction when now some years ago I found his wife was not Elizabeth Ivatt, widow of ——— Marsh, but this knowledge was only leading to more search in the endeavor to really record them. Col. Chester, in "London Marriage Licenses and Allegations," page 1,418, gives under the head of Warren, Richard, haberdasher, and Elizabeth Evans, of St. Mildred, Poultney, London, spinster, at St. Leonard, Shoreditch, 2 January, 1592-3, B. ("B." means Bishop of London's office.) This would appear to place Richard Warren's wife, and account for it by the confusing of names, making Evans, in the variable spelling of the day, Ivans, as the name was often spelled in connection with the Widow Marsh. Mr. Inglis Stuart, of New York, and "Nauset," of Boston, disposed of that claim by impossibility of dates.

Two wives are wanted for Francis Cooke, of the Mayflower, and the arranging of all the grandchildren as well as children attributed to him.

These and many other questions are before you; each will help the other, and no one need hesitate from any sensitive feeling in criticising or correcting me. I only want true history, will be very proud of that which I can substantiate myself, and willing to accord all honor to those who accomplish what I fail to do.

My willingness to help goes without saying, and in asking the active good will of those who have records it is hardly personal when the whole world may share in these benefits. With gratitude to the public for the courtesy and consideration always shown me,

ANNIE ARNOUX HAXTUN.

No. 56 St. Felix street, Brooklyn, N. Y., July, 1899.

For copies of the Mayflower Pamphlet address
THE MAIL AND EXPRESS,
No. 203 Broadway, New York City.

PART III.

SEQUEL TO
Signers of the Mayflower Compact.

The Brewster Records and Passengers on the Forefather Ships.

The following records have many sponsors, and I am indebted first of all to Mr. Ripley Hitchcock for the liberal interest which started this paper on its way to the public. An inheritor of the ascent of both Brewster and Bradford, he not only put in my way the tangible evidence now given, but kept alive the desire to enlarge these historical benefits.

Then to Rev. Joshua W. Wellman, of Malden, Mass.; Judge Charles N. Daniels, of the Windham Probate Court; Mr. C. H. Dimmick, Clerk of the Town of Windham, Willimantic, Conn.; Mr. Joseph F. Swords, Mr. Weaver and Mr. George E. Hoadley, of Hartford, Conn.; Dr. Charles Inslee Pardee, of New York; Mrs. Calvin Durand, of Lake Forest, Ill.; Mrs. Wilhelmus Mynderse, and Mrs. Mary Brewster Minton, of Brooklyn, N. Y.

THE RECORDS.

The following genealogy of the Brewster family was printed some years ago in some newspaper or magazine, then cut out, and the slips pasted into a scrapbook. This record thus preserved was kindly forwarded by mail October 11, 1894, by Miss Ellen D. Larned, of Thompson, Conn., to Rev. Joshua W. Wellman, of Malden, Mass., in response to a letter of inquiry from him. She is the authoress of the invaluable history of Windham County, Connecticut, in two large volumes.

In a letter accompanying this record of the Brewster family, she says: "This record was compiled by W. L. Weaver, of Windham, who died before his researches were printed in book form; but though unfinished they have proved very valuable. He had access to many sources, and is very trustworthy." The printed copy of record, which was so kindly forwarded by mail, and which, after being carefully copied, was returned with many thanks to Miss Larned, was most generously cut by her from her own scrapbook.

I.—COPY OF THE BREWSTER GENEALOGY.

William Brewster, the famous ruling elder in the Plymouth Church, was born at Scrooby, Nottinghamshire, England, probably in 1563, and educated at Cambridge. In 1607 or 1608 he went to Holland, was ruling elder in Rev. John Robinson's church in Leyden, and came in the Mayflower as chief of the Pilgrim band, with his wife, Mary, and two younger sons. He died April 16, 1643.

CHILDREN

1. Jonathan (2), born in England, came over in the Fortune in 1621, settled in New London, was prominent there, and had a family.
2. Love, born probably in Holland, came with his father in the Mayflower, removed to Duxbury, married Sarah, daughter of William Collier, May 15, 1634; had Sarah (3), who married Benjamin Bartlett; Nathaniel; William, who was deacon in church in Duxbury; he had William and Benjamin, who was born in 1714, and Wrestling (3).
3. Wrestling, born in Holland, came with his father, and died a young man, probably unmarried.
4. Patience, came in the Ann, 1623, and married Thomas Prince, who was afterward Governor of the Colony.
5. Fear, came with her sister in the Ann, and in 1626 married Isaac Allerton, as his second wife.

Wrestling Brewster (3), of Duxbury, son of Love (2) and grandson of Elder William (1), by his wife Mary had children:
1, Jonathan (4); 2, Wrestling; 3, John 4, Mary; 5, Sarah; 6, Abigail; 7, Hannah.

Jonathan Brewster (4), son of Wrestling (3), of Duxbury, Mass., called of Lebanon, though no account of him is found in Lebanon records, bought land of Amos Dodge, near the meeting-house in Windham, July 26, 1729-30. He purchased sixty acres of land with house of Amos Woodward, east of Merrick brook, January 12, 1729-30. This, we suppose, became the Brewster homestead, now in Scotland, near the old Brunswick meeting-house, a little north of the Williams family, and near the burying ground in that neighborhood. His will was proved September 29, 1754. From the will and town records it appears that Jonathan and Mary (daughter of John Partridge) Brewster, who were married May 6, 1710, and removed to Windham, Conn., had the following children:

1. James (5), born in May, 1714-15, married Faith Ripley March 15, 1739; died October 2, 1775.
2. Peleg, born about 1717, removed to Canterbury, Conn.
3. Jonah, of Windham, married January 25, 1743-4, Joanna, daughter of Edward Waldo, and died June 3, 1750. Will dated May 15, 1750, proved July 10, 1750, names wife, Johannah, and her father, Edward Waldo, children Jonathan, Nathan, Ezekiel, Ann (child unborn).
4. Hannah, married Barker or Baker (probably John).
5. Mary, married 1st Reuben Lillie, 2d Jeremiah Bingham.
6. Jerusha, married Zebulon, or Zeburton, Rudd.
7. Sarah, married Jehephat Holmes.
8. Elijah, born in Windham, March 12, 1731; died about 1755, unmarried. In his will, dated April 24, 1755, he gives his "blue coat and camlett jacket and my best hat to John Baker for reasons best known to myself."
9. Jonathan, born May 1, 1737, married Joanna, daughter of Edward Waldo. He died November 24, 1753.

"The probate records of Windham County, Conn., show that Jonathan Brewster died November 24, 1753; his will was probated January 21, 1754."

Capt. James Brewster, born May 15, 1739, (5), son of Jonathan (4) above, who was son of Wrestling (3), of Duxbury, who was son of Love (2), who was son of Elder William Brewster (1), of Plymouth colony, lived in Scotland parish, and was a tanner and currier. He married Faith Ripley (5) March 15, 1738-9, daughter of David (4) and Lydia (Carey) Ripley.

CHILDREN.

1. Lydia (6), born March 18, 1739-40; married William Ripley January 11, 1757.
2. Faith (6), born May 30, 1742; died September 28, 1745.
3. Olive (6), born June 18, 1744; married —— West, of Renselear, N. Y.
4. Faith (6), born November 18, 1746; married Samuel Pardee, October 12, 1769, at Sharon, Conn., and died in 1815.
5. James (6), born January 8, 1748-9; died February 22, 1777.
6. Mary (6), born June 30, 1751; married David Gould, son of Job Gould, of New

Milford, November 4, 1772; died March 2, 1840. Job Gould was son of William and Abigail Gould.

7. David (6), born December 21, 1753; married Hannah Paine 1776. He died. She married (2) Capt. Caleb Jewett, of Sharon, Conn.

Peleg Brewster (5), the son of Jonathan, the Windham settler, married, and had a family and removed to Canterbury. We have not the record of his family except—

John (6), born in Scotland, June 14, 1739.

Jonah Brewster (5), son of Jonathan (4), married Joanno Waldo, daughter of Edward, January 25, 1743-4. He died June 3, 1750.

CHILDREN.

1. Jonathan (6), born August 25, 1744.
2. Nathan (6), born January 31, 1745-6; married —— Slack, of Killingly, and died in Pennsylvania, aged nearly 90.
3. Ezekiel (6), born July 19, 1747.
4. Ann (6), born February 12, 1748-9.
5. Jonah, born September 1, 1750.

Doctor John Brewster (6), son of Peleg (5), was the first physician settled on Hampton Hill, and was an eminent practitioner, and a prominent man in that society. He studied medicine with Dr. Barker, of Franklin. He married first Mary Durkee, daughter of Captain William Durkee, of Hampton, November 6, 1760; she died June 4, 1783, aged 41; he married second, Ruth Avery, daughter of Rev. Ephrian Avery, of Brooklyn, June 4, 1789. She died May 18, 1823, aged 69. He died August 18, 1823, aged 84.

CHILDREN BY FIRST WIFE.

1. Mary (7), born September 9, 1762.
2. William (7), born June 17, 1764, died June 4, 1789, aged 25.
3. John (7), born May 31, 1766, was deaf and dumb.
4. Augustus (7), born May 30, 1768, died January 3, 1789, aged 22.
5. Royal (7) born July 13, 1770, died March 1835.
6. Abel (7), and
7. Sophia (7), twins, died young.

CHILDREN BY SECOND WIFE.

8. Elisha (7), born June 18, 1790, died aged two days.
9. William Augustus (7), born December 10, 1791, was a physician; married Lucy Chamberlin, of Brooklyn, March 14, 1813, and died at Danielsonville, July 24, 1856, aged 65. They had children: William Henry, born July 3, 1814, died in Mexico, February, 1842; Francis Augustus, born July 18, 1817; Mary Sophia, born January 23, 1819, married —— Segar, and died June 18, 1840; Lucy Maria, born August 17, 1828.
10. Sophia (7), born April 9, 1795, died April 24, 1810.
11. Betsey (7), Averey, born September 11, 1798, married Joseph Prentiss, died October 17, 1838, aged 40.

Jonathan Brewster (6 or 5), probably son of Jonah, though he may have been youngest son of Jonathan the settler, married Eunice Kingsley February 12, 1767 (Mr. Weaver, of Hartford, says he was son of Jonathan, who died 1753), and had:

1. Orson (7), born August 18, 1767.
2. An infant that died soon.
3. Eunice (7), born January 8, 1770.
4. Oher (7), born August 28, 1771.
5. Oramel (7), born October 31, 1773.
6. Joanna (7), born July 29, 1775.
7. Lydia (7), born January 2, 1779.

8. Jonathan (7), born October 17, 1781.

"William Brewster appeared in Windham about 1753, of what branch of the family we have not ascertained. He had:

1. Benjamin, born February 6, 1753; lived in Windham Centre; married Susannah Green September 8, 1786; she died March 24, 1808, aged 47. He died March 23, 1825, aged 72. Margaret, their only child, born November 12, 1794, married the late Dr. C. S. Avery.
2. Hannah, born October 26, 1754.
3. Elizabeth, born January 21, 1759.
4. Cynthia, born July 25, 1762.
5. William, born January 21, 1765.
6. Cyrus, born August 15, 1769; married —— De Witt, and had William, Cyrus, Nancy and Maria, who went, we believe, to Montreal. He died suddenly September 28, 1818.
7. Bowen, born April 19, 1773.

"Asa Brewster, married Ruth Badger, daughter of Samuel, May 28, 1776. He died March 10, 1811, aged 71.

CHILDREN.

1. Edward, born January 12, 1767.
2. Oliver, born March 17, 1769.
3. Erastus, born March 15, 1773; died October 15, 1775.
4. Abigail, born October 28, 1775.
5. David, merchant in Ashford."

Portions of the above Brewster records have long been obtainable by all, but for one part of them there has been of late a laborious and until now fruitless search. The living descendants of Lydia (Brewster) Ripley, of Cornish, N. H., have been asking "Who were her immediate ancestors on her father's side; and can her lineal descent from Elder William Brewster, of Plymouth Colony, be clearly traced?"

It had been known that she was born in Windham, Conn., March 18, 1740, and died in Cornish, N. H., November 2, 1829; that she was married in Windham January 11, 1757, to William Ripley, who was born in Windham February 12, 1734, son of Joshua, Jr., and Mary (Backus) Ripley, and grandson of Joshua, Sr., and Hannah (Bradford) Ripley, who came from Hingham, Mass., and who were among the first settlers of Windham, Conn., and that she, with her husband and children, removed to Cornish, N. H., in June of 1775, but none of her descendants now living, so far as known, had any knowledge of even the given names of her parents or grandparents. But a single letter of inquiry recently addressed to Miss Ellen D. Larned, of Thompson, Conn., brought out of an old scrapbook in her possession the long desired information. The records of the Brewster family thus obtained show conclusively that Lydia (Brewster) (6) Ripley was daughter of Capt. James and Faith (Ripley) (5) Brewster (5); that Capt. James Brewster (5) was son of Jonathan and Mary (Patridge—elsewhere spelled Partridge) Brewster (4), who came from Duxbury, Mass., to Windham, Conn.; that Jonathan Brewster was son of Wrestling and Mary Brewster (3), of Duxbury; that Wrestling Brewster (3) was son of Love and Sarah (Collier) Brewster, of Duxbury; and that Love Brewster (2) was son of Elder William and Mary Brewster, of the Pilgrim Band, who came over in the Mayflower in 1620. Therefore, Lydia (Brewster) Ripley, of Cornish, N. H., was a descendant of Elder Wilham Brewster, the Pilgrim Q. E. D.

Faith Ripley (5) who was married to Capt. James Brewster (5) and became the mother of Lydia (Brewster) (6) Ripley, was the eldest daughter of David Ripley (4), who was the son of Joshua and Hannah (Bradford) (3) and also younger brother of Joshua Ripley (4), Jr., who married Mary Backus and became father of William Ripley (5) Esq., of Cornish. David Ripley (4) was born in Windham May 20, 1698, and died February 16, 1781. He married March 21, 1720, Lydia Carey, who was born in 1705 and died April 9, 1784, in Scotland, Conn. (Originally a part of Windham).

CHILDREN OF DAVID (4) AND LYDIA (CAREY) RIPLEY.

1. Faith (5), born May 6, 1722; married March 15, 1739, Capt. James Brewster (5), who was born in May, 1714; died ——. She married 2d a Mr. Caleb Jewett.
2. Lydia (5) b. February 20, 1724, who married Rev. Samuel Wood. He was a chaplain in the Revolutionary Army, and died in the British prison ship Asia.
3. Ann. b. August 27, 1726, died September 6, 1792; married October 31, 1745, Nathaniel Ripley (5), son of Joshua, Jr., and Mary (Backus) Ripley. She married 2d May 17, 1769, Samuel Bingham, of Scotland, a part of Windham, Conn.
4. Irene, born February 11, 1729; died February 24, 1804; married 1st Dr. Timothy Warner; married 2d Nathan Hebard (spelled elsewhere Hibberd); married 3d Rev. James Cogswell, D. D., pastor of the Congregational Church, in Scotland, Conn.
5. David, Rev., born February 7, 1731, died in September, 1785. He graduated from Yale College in 1749, and was minister of the Congregational Church in Abington, a part of Pomfret, Conn., for twenty-five years (1753-1778).

David Ripley married Betsey Elliot. Their children were: David, born July 11, 1761; died September 9, 1764. Mary, born August 26, 1763; died January 28, 1826; married Dr. J. E. Warren. Utica, N. Y. Augustus, born November 1, 1765; died March 24, 1769. Elizabeth, born September 5, 1768. David William, born July 17, 1770; died August 2, 1771. (1) David Bradford, born February 14, 1777.

(1) David Bradford, Rev., married in 1807 Betsey Payson; born Aug. 15, 1786; died Oct. 20, 1840. He was pastor of the Congregational Church at Marlborough, Conn., about twenty-eight years, went West and died at Endor, Ill. Children: Elizabeth, born February 23, 1810; died March 21, 1838. Homer, N. Y. Caroline, died in infancy at Marlborough, Conn. Caroline, born August 9, 1813; married October, 1841, Rev. L. C. Gilbert, Prairieville, Minn. Cynthia Williston, born June 29, 1816; married (1) David Jay, married (2) Cornelius Williams, of Missouri. David Elliot, born April 16, 1819; married February 5, 1850, Chloe Shaw, of Northfield, Minn. Catherine, born January 6, 1823; married February 4, 1851, Liberty Ruggles, of Northfield, Minn. Mary, born October 10, 1826; married September 18, 1852, Rodney A. Mott, of Fairbault, Minn.

William and Lydia (Brewster) Ripley were members of the First Church in Pomfret for several years previous to their removal to Cornish, N. H. They were kindred of Rev. David Ripley, pastor of another Congregational Church in the same town. William was his cousin and Lydia was his niece.

6. William, born July 12, 1734; died in Scotland, Conn., November 11, 1811. (He married, March 10, 1757, Rebecca Marcy, who died November 6, 1818, aged 83. Their son David was born January 18, 1761; died June 11, 1782.)

7. Gamaliel, born April 19, 1736; died May 20, 1737.

8. Alathea (more properly spelled Alethea), born April 24, 1738; married to Dr. Elisha Lord, who was the first physician in Abington parish in Pomfret, Conn. Dr. Lord married a sister of the young minister, David Ripley.

9. Gamaliel, born October 20, 1740; died April 15, 1799; married Elizabeth Hebard, who died January 10, 1765; married (2), January 23, 1772, Judith Perkins; she died July 6, 1803. They had ten children, one of whom married Joshua Adams, who was principal of Phillips Academy, Andover, Mass., twenty-three years.

10. Hezekiah, Rev. and D. D., born February 14, 1743; died November 29, 1831. He graduated from Yale College in 1763; was ordained February 11, 1767, and was pastor of the Congregational Church at Green's Farms, in Westport, Conn., for fifty-four years (1767-1821); was an intimate friend of Timothy Dwight, D. D., president of Yale College, and was a member of the corporation of that college for twenty-seven years. He is described as "a man of commanding presence, of a tall, athletic, dignified frame. His fine countenance beamed with intelligence and kindness, and yet there was something in his look which gave assurance of unyielding firmness." He was a distinguished man in his day and wielded a powerful personal influence.

Dr. Ripley married, January 9, 1765, Dolly Brintnall, of New Haven, Conn. "Their union continued for more than sixty-six years, and was dissolved by the death of Mme. Ripley in August, 1831." His own death followed only a few months later. They had five children, one of whom, William Brintnall, graduated at Yale in 1786 and became an able minister of the Gospel. (See Sprague's "Annals of the American Pulpit," Vol. I., p. 647. "A Sketch of Rev. Hezekiah Ripley, D. D.")

11. Bradford, born December 26, 1744; lost at sea.

12. Hannah, born February 23, 1750; married a Mr. Waldo—was a widow in 1803.

Faith Ripley (5), the eldest of the above twelve children, afterward Faith (Ripley) Brewster, and mother of Lydia (Brewster) (6) Ripley, of Cornish, and grandmother of all the children of William and Lydia (Brewster). Ripley, of Cornish, belonged herself to a large and distinguished family. Two of her brothers were able ministers of the Gospel, two of her sisters married ministers of the Gospel, and two married physicians, one of them, however, marrying first a physician, Dr. Timothy Warner; second, Nathan Hibbard, and, as her third husband, a minister, Rev. James Cogswell, D. D., a man of high repute.

CHILDREN OF CAPT. JAMES (5) AND FAITH (RIPLEY 5) BREWSTER.

Their names have already been given in the records obtained from Miss Larned, but further information has been obtained respecting some of them.

1. Lydia (6), born March 18, 1739-40, in Scotland Parish, in Windham Conn., died in Cornish, N. H., November 2, 1829. She married January 11, 1757, William Ripley (5), who was born in Windham, February 12, 1734, son of Joshua (4), Jr., and Mary (Backus) Ripley. Children, 1, Faith; 2, Aletheam; 3, Alethea; 4, James; 5, Selinda. James was born in Pomfret, Conn., and probably Selinda was also.

2. Faith, born May 30, 1742; died September 28, 1745.

3. Olive, born June 18, 1744; died about 1838, and must have been about 94 years of age. She married a Dr. West. She resided at one time in Sharon, Conn; as Olive Brewster, in 1768, loaned money to William Brewster, and in the note is spoken of as Olive Brewster, of Sharon. But in 1808 Mrs. Olive West was not living in Sharon. Probably William Ripley and family, in 1798, were residing in Pomfret.

4. Faith, born November 18, 1746, married Samuel Pardee and died in 1815.

Genealogical history of the Pardee family, compiled from the "New England Genealogical Dictionary," Savage, vol. II., and from family Bible of Samuel Pardee:

George Pardee came to New Haven, Conn., in 1644. He was born in 1619 and married Martha, daughter of Richard Miles, in 1650. Issue of above:

Joseph Pardee, born New Haven, Conn., April 27, 1664; married July 31, 1688, Elizabeth, daughter of first Thomas Yale. Therefrom issued John, born in 1689; Thomas, born October 26, 1695.

*John (2), born February 6, 1698; Mary, born 1700; Elizabeth, born 1704; Daniel, born 1706; Rebecca, born 1708; Josiah, born 1711; Ebenezer, born 1714; Samuel, born 1718; Sarah, born 1720.

George Pardee, born February 10, 1676, went to New York.

From old family Bible:
*John Pardee, born February 6, 1698; died July 13, 1766, aged 69 years. His wife, Betsey Horn, died on the 8th day of January, 1762, in the 63d year of her age.

From *Thomas Pardee's Bible, bought February, 1767; price £2.

(This Bible was left by will to *Samuel Pardee.)

* Thomas Pardee was born October 31, 1722. He was married to Weltheon Cook (who was born August 20, 1724) on the 24th of November, 1743. Issue:

Irene, born December 25, 1744, died April 12, 1745.

*Samuel, born March 7, 1746.

Weltheon, born December 25, 1748 (both daughters born on Christmas).

Gamaliel, born November 26, 1750, died December 8, 1750.

Gamaliel 2d, born May 31, 1752; was in the War of the Revolution.

William, born March 3, 1754, died January 1, 1767.

Argulus and Petchena, twins, born April 22, 1756, died May, 1756.

Calvin, born July 26, 1757.

Alena, born February 24, 1759.

Weltheon, wife of Thomas, died November 19, 1804.

* Samuel Pardee, born March 7, 1746. Married Faith Brewster, born November 18, 1746, on the 12th of October, 1769.

Issue of Samuel and Faith Brewster Pardee:

Laimia, born October 3, 1770.
Augustus S., born October 12, 1772.

Thomas, born December 21, died January 21, 1775.

Betsy, born February 21, 1776, died September 2, 1778.

Arceneath, born July 22, died September 1, 1778.

Luther, born October 4, 1779, died June 16, 1846.

* Orrin, born January 27, 1782, died December 6, 1857.

James, born June 14, 1785, died April 29, 1815.

Laura, born May 15, 1787.

Faith Brewster Pardee, died at Sharon, Conn., December 26, 1815, aged 70.

Samuel Pardee, died at Sharon, Conn., April 26, 1827, aged 82.

A bill of mortality kept by Samuel Pardee:

My grandmother, Betsey Pardee, died January 8, 1762, in the 63d year of her age.

My grandfather, John Pardee, died July 13, 1766, aged 69 years.

My brother, Gamaliel Pardee, died April 21, 1777, aged 25 years.

My mother, Weltheon Pardee, died Novem 19, 1804, aged 80 years.

My sister, Alena, died June 7, 1777, aged 19.

My father, Thomas Pardee, died August 1, 1806, aged 84.

My brother, Calvin, died at Steventown, N. Y.

My sister, Weltheon Dumour, died at Great Barrington, Mass., May 26, 1814, and I only am left, the survivor of ten children of my father's family, and may God grant me to consider.

Issue of Orrin, son of Samuel and Faith Brewster Pardee:

Charles Inslee Pardee, born April 13, 1838; married to Frances Gertrude Snow Beecher (a lineal descendant of the Pilgrim Snows), November 28, 1893.

Edward Luther Pardee, born February 25, 1842.

Richard Gay Pardee was married to Rebecca Camp in Sharon, April 12, 1836; died in New York.

Laura Pardee married Charles Inslee November 14, 1837. She died in Waterloo, Seneca County, N. Y., September 6, 1896.

Frederick F. Pardee married Maria Conklin February 8, 1838.

Augustus Pardee married Emily McKnight.

Albert Pardee married Adelia Jones.

Walter Pardee married Almira Bennett.

Myron Pardee married Cynthia Wilcox, 1848.

Helen Pardee married Charles Seymour, 1855.

Frances S. Pardee married James Boughton, 1859.

Orrin Pardee died in East Bloomfield, Ontario County, N. Y., December 6, 1857.

Sophia Gibson Pardee died in Victory, N. Y., about January, 1863.

YALE FAMILY.

"The first Thomas Yale, of New Haven, born in Wales, came in 1637 to Boston, with Theophilus Eaton; went in 1638 to plant in New Haven; married Mary, eldest daughter of Capt. Nathaniel Turner; had John, born 1645; Thomas, born 1646; Elihu, born 1648, governor of the East India Company, and by his legacy became founder of Yale College; Elizabeth, born January 29, 1667, the youngest daughter of the family of ten, married Joseph Pardee, son of George Pardee, in 1688."—Savage, volume iv.

George Pardee, born in 1629, came from England or Wales to Boston, and to New Haven in 1644.

He is supposed to be of Huguenot descent. The above from Dr. Charles Inslee Pardee.

In pursuance of my policy having given one record, I also submit another, which being from Mr. Charles Henry Townshend, will secure attention.

"Thomas Yale, my ancestor, second son of David, born in Wales, came probably in 1637 to Boston, with Theophilus Eaton, who had married for his second wife the widowed mother of David and Thomas Yale.

"David Yale, the eldest son, returned to England, and by wife Ursula, had sons Thomas and Elihu.

"Thomas, the eldest son, in will dated London, September 29, 1697, proved January, 1697, O. S. (no issue), bequeathed to 'My dear mother, Mrs. Ursula Yale, and to my brother Mr. Elihu Yale, estates here and India. The Hereditary Estate in Co. Denbigh to my brother Elihu Yale's male issue if he have any. Failing such then to the heirs Male of my uncle Thomas Yale, in New England, and to his heirs forever.'"

5. James, born January 8, 1748-9. One James Brewster witnessed the signature of a deed given by John Cotton to William Ripley in Pomfret, Conn., March 29, 1766. This seems to indicate that some James Brewster was then residing in Pomfret. This witness may have been James Brewster, Sr., or James Brewster, Jr. The latter at that date was 17 years old.

6. Mary, born June 30, 1751; died March 2, 1840, aged 88 years and 6 months; married David Gould. They lived through life in Sharon, Conn. He died at 77 years of age. They had ten children, "raised up" nine; had seven living in 1829. One was Rev. Vinson Gould, minister in Southampton, Mass., thirty-one years. He was born August 1, 1774, graduated at Williams College in 1797, was tutor there 1800-1801; ordained August 26, 1801. The youngest son, William Ripley Gould, graduated at Yale in 1811 and at Andover in 1814, and then had several pastorates. One daughter of David and Mary (Brewster) Gould, Sarah Gould, married a physician, Dr. Downs, of New York City.

DOWNS FAMILY.

The following history is given me by a descendant, so I copy verbatim, though knowing there may be errors, still hoping from that fact to have the matter corrected and placed properly in the third pamphlet.

Revolutionary War. Intelligence of the battle of Lexington was brought to Sharon on the Sabbath.

The minister at the close of the morning exercises announced it from the pulpit, and his remarks tended to arouse the sprit of the congregation to firmness and resistance.

As soon as the congregation was dismissed the militia and volunteers to the number of one hundred men paraded on the street and prepared to march to the scene of action.

David Downs, Esq., captain.
James Brewster, lieutenant.
David Gould (who married Mary Brewster, November 4, 1772), ensign.
Children of David and Sarah Downs:

Betsy Downs, died 1785.
David Downs, Jr. (married Polly Baird), died 1812, aged 44.
Clarissa Downs, marrier Rev. Julius Gregory.
Erastus Downs, died young.
Sarah Downs, married Lyman Gould.
James Downs, married Sarah Gould.
Abel Downs, married Jerusha Hempstead.
John Downs, married Mary Gregory.
David Downs, Esq., was from New Haven and came to Sharon in 1768. He married a daughter of Thomas Day.

He was a captain of a company in the revolutionary service, and was, with his company, taken prisoner at the Cedars in Canada, 1776.

He was for many years a magistrate of the town and a member of the Legislature for several sessions.

David Downs, died December 15, 1813, aged 77 years 7 months 15 days.

Sarah Day Downs, his wife, died December 14, 1808, aged 66 years.

Buried in Sharon Cemetery are the following:

Jonathan Day, died January 8, 1763, age 32.

Sarah Day, amiable consort of Rev. Jeremiah Day, died August 25, 1767, aged 21.

Mary Day, wife of Thomas Day, died August 15, 1768, age 66.

Thomas Day, died February 28, 1772, age 82.

Job Gould was from New Milford, settled on Sharon Mountain. He had two sons, Job and David.

Job Gould died February 27, 1795, age 95.

Sarah Gould, died March 17, 1788.
David Gould, died April 19, 1824, age 77.
Mary Gould, died March 2, 1840, age 88.
Sarah Gould was married to Dr. James Downs at Sharon, Litchfield County, Conn., February 25, 1803. (They had nine children.) Sarah Gould Downs died at 79 Grand street, New York City, in her 54th year.

Myron Day Downs (sixth son), born January 3, 1815; married February 27, 1839, Lydia Elizabeth Allen, and died July 31, 1891.

Sarah Gould Downs, their daughter, married, January 17, 1867, Calvin Durand, of Chicago, who was son of Calvin and Luis Barnes Durand, of Charlotte, Vt., and grandson of Francis Joseph and —— Weed Durand, of Norwalk, Conn.

The children of Calvin and Sarah (Downs) Durand are Jennie Elizabeth, who married Elisha Herbert Allen, of Orange, N. J., September 19, 1889.

Henry Calvin married Mary Alice Platt, June 20, 1895.

Harriet Allen.
Married Cornelius Trowbridge.
Mabel Edna.
Bertha Josephine.
Ruth.

Another daughter, Betsey Gould, married Rev. Sylvester Woodbridge, D. D., who was born in Southampton, Mass., November 9, 1790.

7. David (6), born December 21, 1753, youngest son of Capt. James (5) and Faith (Ripley) (5) Brewster and the youngest brother of Lydia Brewster (6) Ripley, of Cornish, was living in December, 1829. He married Hannah Paine in 1776. He died about 1836. He had a family of five children. One of his sons was a college graduate and by profession a lawyer; another was a physician. Some of his children were eminent for their piety and Christian devotion. The lawyer resided in Oswego, N. Y., and was a member of Congress.

It thus appears that Lydia (Brewster) (6) Ripley was the eldest of six children, and this record of her brothers and sisters, though fragmentary, gives hints of the high intellectual and Christian character of the family of which by birth she was a member.

It has already been shown from genealogical records presented that Lydia (Brewster) (6) Ripley was a descendant from Elder William Brewster, one of the leaders of the Plymouth Pilgrims, and that she belonged to the sixth generation of Brewsters in this country.

It may now be added that she was also a descendant from Gov. William Bradford, of the same Pilgrim band. Lydia (Brewster) (6) Ripley was daughter of Capt. James and Faith (Ripley) (5) Brewster (5). Faith (Ripley) (5) Brewster was daughter of David and Lydia (Carey) Ripley (4). David Ripley (4) was son of Joshua (3) Sr., and Hannah (Bradford) (3) Ripley.

Hannah Bradford was the daughter of William Bradford (2), Jr., and Deputy Governor of Plymouth, and William Bradford (2), Jr., was son of William (1), Sr., the famous Governor of Plymouth Colony. Therefore Lydia (Brewster) Ripley was a descendant of Gov. William Bradford, Q. E. D.

But William Ripley (5), who married Lydia Brewster (6), was also a descendant from Gov. Bradford. William Ripley (5) was son of Joshua, Jr., and Mary (Backus) Ripley (4), of Windham, Conn.; Joshua Ripley (4), Jr., was son of Joshua (3), Sr., and Hannah (Bradford) (3) Ripley; Hannah Bradford (3) was daughter of William Bradford (2), Jr., a Deputy Governor of Plymouth Colony, and William Bradford, Jr., was son of Gov. William Bradford, who came over in the Mayflower in 1620. Therefore William Ripley (5), of Cornish, was a descendant of Gov. William Bradford, Q. E. D.

Hence it follows that all the descendants of William and Lydia (Brewster) Ripley, of Cornish, N. H., are descendants of Elder William Brewster, of Plymouth Colony, and are also, through two lines of descent, descendants of Gov. William Bradford, the Plymouth Pilgrim.

William (5) and Lydia (6) (Brewster) Ripley.—They were married in Windham, Conn., January 11, 1757; removed to Pomfret in 1761 or early in 1762. Removed from Pomfret to Cornish, N. H., in June, 1775.

CHILDREN.

1. Faith (6), born probably in Windham, Conn., October 13, 1757, died in Richmond, Vt., May 31, 1824. She married, January 14, 1779, in Cornish, N. H., Jabish Spicer, of Cornish. They resided in Cornish until 1810, and removed to Richmond, Vt., where he died January 6, 1823.

2. Alethea, born August 23, 1759; died September 5, 1759.

3. Alethea, born in Windham, Conn., January 11, 1761; died in Cornish, N. H., October 15, 1841. She married, March 30, 1788, James Wellman, Jr., of Cornish, N. H., who was born July 30, 1754, in Sutton, Mass., Second Parish (now Millbury) and died in Cornish, November 28, 1841; was son of Rev. James Wellman, who was

born in Lynn End, (now Lynnfield), Mass., May 10, 1723, and graduated from Harvard College in 1744. He was ordained and installed pastor of the Second Parish in Sutton, Mass., October 7, 1747. Was dismissed July 22, 1760, and was installed first pastor of the First Church, in Cornish, N. H., September 29, 1768. He married November 8, 1750, Sarah Barnard, born in Watertown, Mass., July 22, 1729, daughter of Isaac Barnard, Esq., of Sutton, Mass. They had nine children.

4. James, born in Pomfret, Conn., April 4, 1765; died in Cornish, August 9, 1842. He married first, March 7, 1792, Lucy Eaton, of Hartford, Vt., who was born in Woodstock, Conn., October 15, 1765, and died in Cornish, N. H., December 23, 1807, aged 42. He married second, in Tarringford, Conn., September 2, 1810, Florella Mills, who was born in Tarringford, July 5, 1779, and was daughter of Rev. Samuel John and Esther (Robbing) Mills, and sister of Samuel J. Mills, Jr., so famous for the part he took in the organization of the American Board for Foreign Missions and the American Colonization Society, and who died at sea, June 15, 1818, in the thirty-fifth year of his age.

This Mills family, descendants of Peter Mills, known in Windsor, Conn., as "the Dutchman" (the original name being Van der Meulen), and which the emigrant ancestor had changed by law to Mills, the name translated being "of the Mill."

The full history of this Mills family, which has furnished such wonderful descent, can be found in "Stiles's History of Ancient Windsor."

Florella (Mills) Ripley died in Cornish, September 21, 1858. She was a woman of sweet and gentle spirit and of sincere piety, was in full sympathy with her brother's earnest missionary spirit, and in her quiet way did not a little to awaken a similar spirit in many Christian people in Cornish.

James Ripley was a man of prodigious energy and of great executive ability. He became famous as a military man and attained the rank of colonel. He inherited many of the characteristics, not only of his noble father and accomplished mother, but also of his Pilgrim ancestors, Gov. William Bradford and Elder Brewster. He had no children.

5. Selinda, born Pomfret, Conn., April 4, 1773; died in Cornish, N. H., June 4, 1854; married April 4, 1790, Eliphalet Kimball, of Cornish. This youngest daughter of William and Lydia (Brewster) Ripley received from her mother an ancient "baptismal robe," or "Christening blanket," so called, which, according to tradition, and as her mother affirmed, came down to her as an heirloom from Elder William Brewster and his wife Mary of the Pilgrim band, and has been used in the baptism of infant children in all the intervening Brewster families. This robe was subsequently cut up into small pieces, which were distributed among the kindred. One piece is now preserved in the Congregational Library in the Congregational Home, Boston, Mass.

William Ripley (5), Esq., who married Lydia Brewster (6), served in the War of the Revolution, holding the rank of adjutant in Col. Jonathan Chase's regiment in Gen. Stark's Brigade of New Hampshire Militia.

JABISH AND FAITH (RIPLEY) (6) SPICER.

Jabish (sometimes called Jaber) Spicer was born in Norwich, Conn., September 11, 1753, where he resided until 1771, when with his parents he removed to Cornish, N. H. His father's name was Zepheniah and his mother's name Sarah. The family came to Cornish in 1771 from Norwich, Conn., four years before William Ripley and family came from Pomfret, Conn., and only six years after the arrival of the first settlers. Jabish Spicer died January 6, 1823, aged 70, and his wife died May 30, 1824, both in Richmond, Vt.

CHILDREN (ALL BORN IN CORNISH, N. H.)

1. Erastus, born November 21, 1779. He went to Richmond, Vt., where he married Abigail R. Richards, who died at Richmond, Vt., August 10, 1818. Their daughter Leucretia was born July 14, 1810, the year in which his father removed to Richmond.

2. Lydia, born February 19, 1781, married Erastus Eaton, a brother of Lucy Eaton, first wife of Col. James Ripley, of Cornish, and born about 1779 in Woodstock, Conn.

3. Amy, born December 11, 1782, died April 11, 1785.

4. William Ripley, born July 19, 1784, married Betsey Sherman. Their daughter, Aurillia D. Spicer, appears to have married a Mr. Lothrop, and to have died May 17, 1835.

5. Peter Bradford, born June 4, 1786. Married June 18, 1817, in Cornish, Miriam Wyman, who was born in Pelham, N. H., January 31, 1794; was daughter of Joshua and Miriam (Richardson) Wyman, of Cornish, N. H., and died May 26, 1824, in Richmond, Vt. He died March 22, 1855, at Mercer, Maine, having married for second wife, April 11, 1825, Susan B. Briggs, who was born in Wiscasset, Maine, April 23, 1799.

CHILDREN BY FIRST MARRIAGE.

1. Mary, born in Richmond, Vt., July 10, 1819, and died in Cornish, May 8, 1839, aged 19 years and 9 months.

2. Pamela, born in Richmond, Vt., September 13, 1821, died in Newport, N. H., June 1, 1858. Some years after her mother's death she was received into the family of her mother's sister, Pamela Frost (Wyman) Chapin, of Newport, N. H. She married Stillman Timothy Fletcher, of Newport, N. H.

CHILDREN BY SECOND MARRIAGE.

3. Wyman, born January 24, 1826, at Morristown, Vt., died at Bradford, Me., February 17, 1851, aged 25.

4. Lucy Miriam, born in Morristown, Vt., February 21, 1827, married October 19, 1853, William B. Chapman, son of Jebish and Faith (Ripley) Splea.

6. Jabez, born March 12, 1788, married Mary Hovey, and died in New York 1854-5.

7. Sarah (or Sally) born March 16, 1790; married Phinehas Kimball. They resided in Hartford, Vt., and afterward in Weathersfield, Vt. She died in Texas in 1842 or 1843.

8. Mary (or Polly) born August 4, 1792; died June 6, 1813, at Richmond, Vt.

Elija, born January 31, 1798; died at the home of her niece, Pamela (Spicer) Fletcher, in Newport, N. H., October 3, 1845. She married, December 6, 1816, Abner Warner, M.D., who was born November 30, 1787. They resided in Camillus, Onondaga County, N. Y., where Dr. Warner died October 3, 1822. They had one son, Abner Spicer Warner, born in Camillus, September 7, 1818. After the death of Dr. Warner, his widow, with her boy, removed, first, to Richmond, Vt.; then to Cornish, N. H. The son resided for a time with his great-uncle, Col. James Ripley, and fitted for college at Kimball Union Academy, Meriden, N. H.; graduated from Dartmouth College in 1842, and from the medical department of that college in 1848. He was principal of the Academy in New Ipswich, N. H., 1842-44; of a village school in Newport, N. H., 1844-46, and was a student of medicine at Dartmouth, 1846-48. Since 1848 he has been in successful practice as a physician. He was surgeon of the Sixteenth Infantry Regiment of Connecticut volunteers, 1862-63; physician of the Connecticut State Prison, 1848-1891; member of the Connecticut Legislature in 1878, and during all his professional life has been physician and surgeon at Wethersfield, Hartford County, Conn. He married, first, Caroline C. Kimball, of Cornish, N. H., November 23, 1847. She was the daughter of William Ripley and Eliza (Dorr) Kimball, of Cornish. She and her husband were great-grandchildren of William and Lydia (Brewster) Ripley. She died September 12, 1866. Dr. Warner married, second, Jane M. Spalding, June 7, 1869. She was daughter of James Spalding, M.D., of Montpelier, Vt.

CHILDREN OF F. ABNER AND CAROLINE C. (KIMBALL) SPICER.

1. George Abner, born March 11, 1849; died August 13, 1851.

2. Caroline Eliza, born September 11, 1852; married Ellsworth B. Strong, May 24, 1887.

3. Mary Lucia, born May 20, 1854; married February 1, 1894, James T. Pratt.

4. Elizabeth Williams, born June 18, 1858.

5. Eliza Spicer, born March 7, 1861; died November 9, 1864.

Dr. Abner S. and Jane M. (Spalding) Warner had one child; George Spalding, born December 28, 1871; died, Chicago, Ill., July 29, 1891.

REV. JAMES AND SARAH (BARNARD) WELLMAN (4).

James Wellman (5), Jr. (mentioned before), was born in Sutton, Mass., 2d Parish (now Milbury), July 30, 1754, son of Rev. James and Sarah (Barnard) Wellman (4), and died in Cornish, N. H., November 28, 1841. Rev. James Wellman (4), the first settled minister in Cornish, N. H., was born in Lynn End (now Lynfield), Mass., May 10, 1723, and died in Cornish, N. H., December 18, 1808, aged 85 years.

His wife Sarah Barnard, whom he married in Sutton November 8, 1850, was born in Watertown, Mass., in August, 1729, and was eldest daughter of Isaac and Sarah Stevens Barnard (5), Esq., of Watertown, but he afterward removed to Gratton, Mass., and thence to Sutton Second Parish, Mass.

Israel (5), Isaac (4), James (3), John (2), John (1).

Sarah (Barnard) Hellman died in Cornish, N. H., June 27, 1854, aged 84 years.

Rev. James Wellman (4) was fitted for college by his pastor, Rev. Stephen Chase, minister of the Congregational Church in Lynn End (now Lynnfield), entered Harvard College in 1740 and graduated from the same in 1744. He was a son of Abraham Wellman, Jr. (3), and Elizabeth (Taylor), his wife, who were married in 1717 (published August 23, 1717). Abraham Wellman, Jr. (3), was born in Lynn End, November 25, 1673, a son of Abraham, Sen. (2), and Elizabeth (Cogswell) Wellman, and died in the siege of Louisburg, on Cape Breton, under Gen. Pepperill, in 1745, in the French war. His name is not found on the muster roll of Gen. Pepperill's army, but he may have served as a mechanic in that successful military expedition. That he was in that expedition and died at the siege of Louisburg there can be no doubt, for such was the repeated affirmation of two of his own sons, Jacob and Rev. James Wellman. Abraham Wellman, Sen. (2), was born in Lynn End, probably in 1643, son of Thomas and Elizabeth Wellman (1). Thomas (1) was in Lynn, Mass., as early as 1640, and he died at Lynn End, October 10, 1672. Tradition says he came from Wales. His great grandson, James Wellman (4), was ordained to the Christian ministry and installed pastor of the Second Church and parish in Sutton, Mass., October 7, 1747. He resigned the pastorate and, by the advice of council, was regularly dismissed July 22, 1760. He was installed the first minister of the First Church in Cornish, N. H., September 29, 1768, and moved the family from Sutton to Cornish in 1769. He married Sarah Barnard November 8, 1750. She died in Cornish January 27, 1814, aged 84 years.

CHILDREN OF REV. JAMES AND SARAH (BARNARD) WILLIAMS (4).

1. Sarah, born June 20, 1752; died in Cornish, June 21, 1803; married January 16, 1776, Nathaniel Dustin, of Cornish, N. H.

2. James, born July 30, 1754; died November 28, 1841; married March 30, 1788, Alethea Ripley (noticed above).

3. Isaac, born February 4, 1757; died in Cornish, December 6, 1840; married about 1804 or 1805, Mercy Colton, born in Grantham, N. H. She died April 7, 1845, aged 69. He was a farmer in Cornish.

4. Solomon, born February 8, 1758; died January 21, 1841; married Molly Putnam, of Cornish. He was a farmer; inherited his father's farm, and resided upon it through life.

5. Joshua, born November 16, 1760; died in Sutton November 29, 1760.

6. Martha, born August 11, 1763; died November 5, 1839; married, first, May 27, 1781, Ebenezer Wright, M. D.; married, second, Barnabas Tisdale (widower) December 30, 1802. Dr. Wright resided in the southwest corner of Plainfield, N. H., near the line between that town and Cornish, and practiced in his profession mainly in those two towns. He died October 28, 1798. Barnabas Tisdale graduated at Dartmouth College in 1809; was a lawyer, and died in 1860, aged 72.

7. Joshua, born May 24, 1766; died in Cornish, unmarried, June 20, 1806. He studied medicine, and was a physician in Cornish.

All the above children of Rev. James and Sarah (Barnard) Wellman were born in Sutton, Mass.

8. Lemuel, born in Cornish January 3, 1770; died November 14, 1815; married Esther Steele Russell, of Piermont, N. H. He was a distinguished physician, had great success in curing "the black fever," was taken with fever when away from home and died of it, at Warren, Vt., November 14, 1815.

9. Barnard, born in Cornish, N. H., March 9, 1773, and died April 7, 1773.

JAMES AND ALETHEA (RIPLEY) WELLMAN (5).

James Wellman (5), eldest son of the Rev. James and Sarah (Barnard) Wellman, married March 30, 1788, Alethea Ripley, daughter of William and Lydia (Brewster) Ripley, of Cornish, N. H. Before he was married he went into the wildwoods in the northern part of Cornish, and singlehanded began the enormous labor of clearing off the mighty primeval forest and creating for himself a cultivated and fruitful farm. This land was near that which William Ripley had bought a few years before, and upon which he and his family were now (1788) living. Thus this young subduer of the mighty forest had a good opportunity to become acquainted with Alethea Ripley.

CHILDREN.

1. James Ripley (6), born February 21, 1789; died November 1, 1860; married Phebe Wyman, of Cornish.

2. Alethea, born November 14, 1790; died in New Britain, Conn., at the house of her son, Benjamin Newton Comings, M. D., January 10, 1879. She married November 30, 1815, Benjamin Comings, of Cornish. He was a farmer, and resided on a farm a little south of the center of the town.

3. Lucy, born March 7, 1794; died February 12, 1863, in Cornish; married January 13, 1818, Joshua Wyman, who was born December 26, 1788, in Pelham, N. H., eldest son of Joshua and Miriam (Richardson) Wyman, and who died in Cornish November 5, 1869.

4. Joshua Barnard, born February 10, 1797; died in Cornish, June 9, 1887; married December 18, 1827, Lucy Hough, of Cornish, who was born February 18, 1804, and died in Cornish, February 28, 1897. They resided upon the farm owned by his father, James Wellman (5), Jr.

JAMES RIPLEY AND PHEBE (WYMAN) WELLMAN.

James Ripley Wellman, eldest son of James and Alethea (Ripley) Wellman, a grandson of William and Lydia (Brewster) (6) Ripley (5), was therefore a descendant in the eighth generation of William Brewster, the famous elder of the Pilgrim Church, and also a descendant in the seventh generation, through his grandfather, William Ripley, of William Bradford, who was Governor of Plymouth Colony and who came over in the Mayflower in 1620, and still again a descendant in the eighth generation, through his grandmother, Lydia (Brewster) Ripley, of Gov. William Bradford, as she was a descendant of both the Pilgrim elder and the Pilgrim governor. He married September 22, 1819, in Cornish, Phebe Wyman.

Phebe Wyman (6), born in Cornish October 31, 1796, and died in the same town May 6, 1885. She was the fourth child and second daughter of Joshua and Miriam (Richardson) Wyman, who with their children removed to Cornish from Pelham, N. H., in March, 1794, Mrs. Wyman riding on horseback and carrying her infant child, Miriam, in her arms. Phebe Wyman was a descendant, in the sixth generation, of Francis and Abigail (Reed) Wyman, who were among the first settlers of the town of Woburn, Mass., in 1642. He was in Charlestown as early as 1640. He was son of Francis and Jane Wyman, of Westmill Parish, Hertford County, England. Phebe Wyman's ancestors on her father's side were Joshua (5), William (4), Edward (3), William (2), Francis (1) and Francis in England.

She was also on her mother's side a descendant in the seventh generation of Samuel Richardson, the second of the three notable brothers, who were not only among the founders of the town (now city) of Woburn, but also were among the seven men who "stood forth, one by one, and declared their religious faith and Christian experience" and were organized into "The First Church of Christ," in Woburn. They were afterward called "the seven pillars." Three of the seven were Ezekiel, Samuel and Thomas Richardson. The ancestors of Phebe Wyman were Miriam (6), Joseph (5), Amos (4), Stephen (3), Stephen (2), Samuel (1).

Children of James Ripley and Phebe (Wyman) Wellman. All born in Cornish, N. H.:

Aurilla Phebe, born July 18, 1820; died November 28, 1862; married January 1 1851, Alfred Hitchcock, M. D., of Fitchburg, Mass. He was born in Westminster, Vt., October 17, 1813, and died March 30, 1874, in Fitchburg, Mass.; son of David and Hannah (Owen) Hitchcock. He received the degree of M. D. from Dartmouth College, in 1844; was much respected, a member of the Legislature for several years, a member of the Executive Council under Gov. John A. Andrews, for two or three years during our Civil War, and was a distinguished physician and surgeon. Aurilla P. Wellman, was educated in a public school in Cornish, in a private school taught in her father's house in her childhood by Miss Martha L. Rowell (who afterward married Mr. Edwin Loche, and with him went as a missionary to the Sandwich Islands), in Lebanon Academy, Lebanon, N. H., in 1838, and in Kimball Union Academy at Meridan, N. H. She taught in a public school in Cornish, in a similar school in Meriden, N. H., in the High School in Windsor, Vt., with great acceptance, for a short time in Mrs. David H. Burr's seminary for young ladies in Washington, D. C.; in Francistown Academy, Francistown, N. H., and was teacher of Latin in Mount Holyoke Seminary from 1848 to 1851, and during the first year under the famous Mary Lyon. She was married to Dr. Hitchcock in her father's house in Cornish, January 1, 1851. This was Dr. Hitchcock's second marriage, he having married first December 13, 1837, Fidelia Darens Clark, of Westminster, Vt., who was born in that town April 15, 1812, and died in Ashby, Mass., December 1, 1849. (See genealogy of the Hitchcock family.)

2. Joshua Wyman, born November 28, 1821. He fitted for college in Kimball Union Academy, graduating from the same in 1842, entered Dartmouth College the same year, and graduated from that college in 1846. He entered Andover Theological Seminary in 1847 and graduated from it in 1850. He taught first, at the age of 17, a public school in Hartford, Vt.; next in the winter of 1842-3 a public school in Upton, Mass; then in the autumn of 1843 in an

academy in Bradford, N. H.; in the winters of his junior and senior years in college taught a public school in East Randolph (now Holbrook), Mass.; taught in an academy in Rochester in the summer of 1847, and taught a part of each year, from 1846 to 1850, in Kimball Union Academy. He was ordained to the Christian ministry and installed June 18, 1851, as pastor of the historical First Church in Derry, N. H., where he labored five years, when he resigned to accept a call to the Elect Church, Newton, Mass., where he was installed as pastor June 11, 1856; and after a pastorate of more than seventeen years was dismissed October 23, 1873. He was installed March 25, 1874, pastor of the ancient First Church in Malden, Mass. He remained in this position until May 6, 1883. Olivet College in 1868 and Dartmouth College in 1870 honored him with the degree of D. D. He married, October 24, 1854, Ellen Maria Holbrook, who was born January 31, 1827, in East Randolph (now Holbrook), Mass. She was educated in a public school in East Randolph, in Wheaton Academy in Newton, Mass., and in Bradford Academy, Bradford, Mass.

3. Mary Sophia, born December 20, 1823; died January 10, 1842.

4. Fidelia, born August 13, 1825; died in Kalamazoo, Mich., December 8, 1874. She married, September 16, 1856, Homer Owen Hitchcock, M. D., who was born in Westminster, Vt., January 28, 1827, and died in Kalamazoo, Mich., December, 1888, son of David and Hannah (Owen) Hitchcock, of Westminster, Vt., and younger brother of Dr. Alfred Hitchcock mentioned above. He fitted for college at Kimball Union Academy, entered Dartmouth College in 1846, continued in the same three years, then taught one year in Kimball Union Academy, returning to college at the close of that year, and graduating from the same in 1851. In the autumn of that year he became associate principal of Oxford Academy, at Oxford, N. H., and during the three following terms was principal of that Academy. He graduated from the College of Physicians and Surgeons in New York City, spent one year in Bellevue Hospital in the same city, and began practice in his profession in the autumn of 1856, in Kalamazoo, Mich. He became one of the most eminent physicians and surgeons in that State, was the first president of the Board of Health, and for many years a member of the Board of Trustees of Olivet College, which was a faithful and liberal supporter of the Congregational Church, of which he was a member, and was highly esteemed as a man and a citizen. Fidelia Wellman was educated in a public school in Cornish, in a private school taught in her father's house, in Kimball Union Academy, and in Mrs. Ellis' boarding school for young ladies at Hanover, N. H.

She was principal in 1846 of the female department of the Literary Institute and Gymnasium at Pembroke, N. H.; teacher in a select school in Marlboro, N. H., in 1847-8, and was preceptress in Bradford Academy, Bradford, Vt., from 1849 to 1854.

5. Catherine Hamblet, born May 31, 1827, died in Fitchburg, Mass., January 24, 1893, unmarried. She was an invalid during nearly all her life, and on account of her ill health she was not able to attend any school outside of her native town. Yet she was possessed of brilliant mental powers which she faithfully cultivated by reading and study at home. Her father and mother in disposing of their own hard earned property, carefully and anxiously provided for her support through life. By economy and care, she preserved and even increased what she then received. During almost her entire life she resided on what was her father's and mother's estate, one-half of which after her mother's death she owned. In 1890, upon kind and urgent invitation, she removed to Fitchburg, Mass., and during the last three years of her life resided with her widowed sister-in-law, Mrs. Louise H. (Wood) Wellman. These last years, through the unwearied kindness of her beloved sisters, were made years of great comfort and happiness to the failing invalid. According to her request she was buried in Cornish. She left legacies to her near kindred, to the Congregational Church in Cornish, of which she was a member, and in which she was tenderly interested, and to two missionary societies.

6. James Ripley, Jr., born July 27, 1829; died in Cornish July 25, 1861. He married, May 2, 1861, Louise Holman Wood, of Fitchburg, Mass. She was born July 14, 1834, daughter of Nathaniel and Louise (Holman) Ward. Her mother was born in Bolton, Mass., November 30, 1803, and died in Fitchburg April 24, 1887. Her father was born in Holden, Mass., August 29, 1797. He graduated from Harvard College in 1821, studied law in the Dane Law School, at Cambridge, and in the office of a Boston lawyer, and was admitted to the Bar and began practice in Boston in 1826. In February, 1827, he removed to Fitchburg, successfully followed his profession through the remainder of his life, and died there August 2, 1876. He held many important trusts, was highly esteemed as a man and citizen, was an honorable lawyer and a sincere Christian. His daughter Louise was educated in part at the Oread Institute, Worcester, Mass., and at Lowell Institute, Auburndale, Mass.

James Ripley Wellman, Jr., was educated in part at Kimball Union Academy and at Thetford Academy, Thetford, Vt. He taught in public schools in different towns for several winters, studied medicine at Dartmouth College and graduated from the Medical Department in 1856. He also attended medical lectures and took part in hospital practice in New York City. He began practice as a physician and surgeon in 1855, in partnership with his brother-in-law, Dr. Alfred Hitchcock, in Fitchburg, Mass. After occupying this position for a time he sailed for Europe, and for one year diligently pursued his medical studies in lecture rooms and hospitals in Edinburgh, London and Paris. Returning home in 1857, he opened an office in Fitchburg, and a brilliant career in his profession opened at once before him. His practice was large and he overworked. In a few years he broke down in health. Repairing to his native town for rest, he died there in his childhood home, but his remains were taken to Fitchburg and buried in the cemetery of his brother-in-law.

7. Albert Erasmus, born February 21, 1838, died in Burlington, Vt., July 18, 1892. He married in Cornish, January 6, 1864, Emily Dodge Hall, who was born at Blue Hill, Hancock County, Me., daughter of Lyman and Mary Peters (Dodge) Hall. Her father, Dr. Hall, was a physician for many years in Cornish. Albert E. Wellman was educated in part at Kimball Union Academy, and taught public schools in Lebanon, N. H., and in Kalamazoo, Mich. He resided through life in the old home, and carried on the large farm owned by his father and mother. He was highly respected and beloved in the town. Important trusts were committed to him. He settled several estates, was selectman for several years and for two years represented the town in the State Legislature. The last year of his life he suffered from ill health. At the request of his son he went to the hospital in Burlington, Vt., for the purpose of obtaining better medical aid, and there he died. The funeral services were held in Cornish, and the large audience assembled in the church attested the profound respect and warm affection in which he was held by the people of his native town.

MISCELLANEOUS BREWSTER RECORDS.

The annexed data from the records of the Congregational Church of Middle Haddam, Middlesex County, Conn., are in my possession and care for the purpose of copying, and may be of interest to you, although in a detached and miscellaneous form:

That church was organized in September 25, 1740.

I confine myself to mention of Brewster, Cook, Rogers and Hopkins families.

Yours,   H. M. Selden, Clerk.

Marriages: September 30, 1742, Elisha Brewster and Luca (Prob. Lucy) Yeamans.

Baptism children of Elisha and Lucy (Yeamans) Brewster:

Elisha, ye son, August 21, 1743.
Lucy, ye daughter, June 2, 1745.
Lucretia, ye daughter, November 8, 1747.

Copied from Lebanon (Conn.) Records:

Jonathan Brewster, son of (Elder) William Brewster and Mary Brewster, born in Scrooby, England; married Lucretia. He died in 1661. She died March 5, 1678.

Children:

William, remained in the old Colony in Massachusetts; Benjamin.

Four daughters located in New London, Conn. Jonathan and Lucretia, his wife, were buried in Brewster Cemetery in Preston, Conn.

Benjamin married Annie Dart February, 1659. He died September 10, 1710, aged 77. Children, births recorded in Norwich, Conn.:

Mary, born December, 1660.
Annie, born September, 1662.
Jonathan, born November, 1664.
Daniel, born March, 1666.
William, born March, 1667.
Ruth, born September 16, 1671.
Benjamin, born November 28, 1673.
Elizabeth, born June 28, 1676.

Daniel Brewster, of Benjamin and Annie (Dart) Bewster, born March, 1666, married (1) Hannah Gager, December 28, 1686.

Children recorded in Preston, Conn.:

Daniel, born October 11, 1687.

Hannah, born December 2, 1690.
Mary, born January 2, 1692.
John, born July 18, 1695.
Jerusha, born November 18, 1697; died April 17, 1709.
Ruth, born June 20, 1700.
Bethia, born April 5, 1702.
Ebenezer, born September 19, 1713.

All except Daniel were born in Preston. Daniel was born in Norwich. Hannah Gager, wife of Daniel Brewster, died September 25, 1727. He married (2) Dorothy Witter, December 19, 1727. He died May 7, 1735.

His widow, Dorothy (Witter) Brewster, died March 19, 1759. John Brewster, son of Daniel and Hannah (Gager) Brewster, born July 18, 1695, married Dorothy Treat, daughter of Rev. Salmon and Dorothy (Noyes) Treat, of Preston, Conn., September 20, 1725. Children recorded in Preston, Conn.:

Oliver, born July 20, 1726.
Dorothy, born July 22, 1728.
Hannah, born September 26, 1729; died December 15, 1736.
Daniel, born April 12, 1731.
Sarah, born May 25, 1733.
Sybil, born August 20, 1735.
John, born January 9, 1737.
Eunice, born October 17, 1740.
Levi, born March 17, 1743.
Joseph, born March 7, 1745.

Sarah Brewster, daughter of John and Dorothy (Treat) Brewster, married Moses Parke, of Preston, Conn., November 9, 1752.

Benjamin Brewster and his wife Mary had children, viz.:

Benjamin, born September 4, 1697.
John, born May 25, 1701.
Mary, born April 22, 1704.
Jonathan, born November 4, 1706; died 1717.
Nehemiah, born June 25, 1709; died 1719.
Comfort, born December 2, 1711.
Daniel, born November 21, 1714.

Benjamin, son of Benjamin and Mary Brewster, married Rebecca Blackman. Children:

Jonathan, born September 9, 1723.
Benjamin, born October 12, 1726.

John, son of Benjamin and Mary Brewster, married Mary Terry. Children:

Mary, born January 20, 1726.
Hannah, born May 5, 1734.

Comfort, son of Benjamin and Mary Brewster, married Deborah Smith, December 2, 1736. Children:

Deborah, born December 20, 1737.
Ann, born May 10, 1741.
Betty, born August 20, 1743.
Comfort, born August 20, 1745.
Daniel, born July 20, 1751.

Daniel, son of Benjamin and Mary, married Mary Dimock October 10, 1733. Children:

Nehimiah, born November 21, 1735.
Nehimiah, born April 19, 1738; died 1751.
Ruth, born August 28, 1740.
Eunice, born January 2, 1743.
Mary, born April 13, 1745.
Mehitable, born August 6, 1747; died 1749.

Daniel Brewster died May 7, 1749.

Comfort, son of Comfort and Deborah (Smith) Brewster, married Elizabeth Abel February 15, 1770; he died May 27, 1822; she died March 19, 1825. Children:

Comfort, born April 6, 1771.
Elizabeth, born December 2, 1772.
Lucretia, born February 18, 1776.
Melinda, born October 30, 1778.
Daniel, born August 12, 1781.

Louisa, born March 7, 1787.

William Brewster married Patience. One child, Ebenezer, born February 1, 1703. William died August, 1728.

William married Mehitable Abel December 13, 1716. Children:

Hannah, born March 31, 1718.
Abel, born July 15, 1720.
William, born February 26, 1723; died young.
Elisha, born August 22, 1725; died at Louisburg 1746.
Ann, born August 28, 1727.

Love Brewster (Duxbury).

Will dated October 1, 1650, and exhibited at court March 4, 1651.

To children: Nathaniel, the heir apparent, the estate in Duxbury; William, Wrestling and Sarah and to his three sons, jointly, all such land as is of right due to me by purchase, and first coming into the land, which is in the yeare 1620. His wife executrix.

Witnessed by Myles Standish.

Inventory (including books to the number of thirty volumes) taken Jan. 31, 1651, by William Collier and Capt. Standish. Amount, £97 7s. 1d.

New England Historical Register (Vols. 3-4), page 284.

From Probate Records of District of Windham, Conn.

Furnished by Judge Charles N. Daniels.

Vol. 15, page 324, July 13, 1794.

Will of Joseph Barston (?), of Lebanon; wife, Sybil; sons, Samuel, Job and Micah; daughters, Molly, Lydia, Betty and Mehitabel.

Speaks of daughter, and only heir of my son Joseph, deceased. Says he means to give nothing to his son Charles, he having already had his portion.

Volume 16, page 392, June 13, 1815.

Inventory of estate of Comfort Brewster, Jr., of Lebanon; no names mentioned.

Volume 17, page 90, Oct. 20, 1817.

Inventory of estate of Daniel Brewster, of Lebanon; among list of creditors of this estate find Dr. Dwight Ripley, Justice Brewster and Comfort Brewster.

Caleb and Betsy Brewster were administrators.

Volume 17, page 131. Oct. 31, 1818.

Inventory of estate of Cyrus Brewster, of Windham; no names.

Volume 17, page 364; June 12, 1822.

Will of Comfort Brewster, of Lebanon, wife Elizabeth.

Eldest daughter-in-law, Parthenia Brewster.

Other daughter-in-law, Betsy Brewster. Daughters Melinda and Louisa.

Volume 18, page 385; April 16, 1825.

Distribution of estate of Benjamin Brewster, of Windham.

Wife Betsy, and Margaret Avery, daughter of deceased, are the only ones mentioned.

Volume 19, page 441; March 6, 1830.

Inventory of estate of Silas W. Brewster, of Mansfield; no names.

Volume 22, page 241; January 20, 1855.

Will of Elizabeth Brewster, of Windham. Property left to her nephew, Samuel H. Perkins, of Philadelphia, in trust for her niece, Harietta P. Clark, of Windham.

The Brewster record ends here, so far as records of Windham Probate Court show.

For the following the public is indebted to Mr. C. H. Dimmick, Town Clerk of Windham, Conn.:

"Mr. Weaver, in his examination of the records of vital statistics of this office, was very thorough, the only thing that could be added, possibly, is, some light might be thrown upon the different families mentioned by him as from Windham by the examination of the land records.

"Upon page 6 of said manuscript appears the following:

"'William Brewster appeared in Windham about 1753; of what branch of the family we have not ascertained.'"

William Brewster was the son of Benjamin Brewster, of Preston, and Benjamin of Preston was the son of Deacon William Brewster, and Deacon William Brewster the son of Love Brewster. The first William Brewster mentioned herein was born September 16, 1714; married, March 24, 1737, Damaris Gates, and had Grace, Cyrus, Asa, Damaris and Drusilla. The wife Damaris died, and he married (2d) Esther Sabin, and had Benjamin, Hannah, Esther, Elizabeth, Cynthia, William, Cyrus, Bowen and Benjamin.

The first record we have of him in Windham was by a deed conveying land to him August 3, 1752, in which he is mentioned as of Canterbury.

Damaris married a James Flint. Asa married Ruth Badger, May 28, 1766, and had Edmund, Oliver, Erastus and Abigail, as appears by said manuscript.

Drusilla married William Ely, of Springfield, Mass.

Cyrus married Nancy Dewitt (daughter of Henry Dewitt, who married Hannah Dean, of Norwich, 1772). They had William, Cyrus, Nancy and Maria, as also appears by said manuscript.

This record comes through the kindness of Mrs. Henry Minton. It is given in full, even if there are some repetitions:

Elder William Brewster, born in Scrooby, England, 1560, died 1644; married Mary, who died in 1624, aged 56, or before 1627. Came to Plymouth in 1620.

Children:

Jonathan, born 1593, died 1661; married Lucretia.

Patience came in the Ann, died 1634.

Fear came in the Ann, died 1633.

Love came in 1620.

Wrestling came in 1620.

Capt. Edward.

Jonathan Brewster, eldest son of Elder William, and Mary, his wife, born at Scrooby, England, 1593. Came in the Fortune to Plymouth in 1621; married Lucretia. He removed to Duxbury in 1632; afterward to New London in 1648; died 1661.

Children:

William, born in Holland, died 1645; Narragansett war last known of him.

Mary, born in Holland; married John Turner.

Jonathan, born about 1627-1649; last known of him, probably killed in battle.

Benjamin, born 1633, died September 10, 1710.

Elizabeth.

Ruth.

Grace.

Hannah (she was aged 37 in 1680).

Benjamin Brewster, son of Jonathan and Lucretia; married in February, 1659, Anna Dart, of New London.

Children:

Mary, born December, 1660, at New London.

Ann, born September, 1662, at Norwich.

Jonathan, born November, 1664.

Daniel, born March, 1667.

William, born March, 1669.

Ruth, born September 16, 1671.

Benjamin, born November 28, 1673.

Elizabeth, born June 23, 1676.

Jonathan Brewster, son of Benjamin and Anna Dart Brewster, married Judith Stevens, December 18, 1690, probably daughter of James and Sarah Smith Stevens.

Children:
Lucretia, born November 3, 1691.
Jonathan, born April 2, 1694.
Joseph, born April 13, 1698.
Sarah, born April 1, 1700.
Mary, born May, 1703.

Joseph Brewster, son of Jonathan and Judith Stevens Brewster, of Preston, married Dorothy Witter, born December 11, 1702, daughter of Ebenezer and Dorothy Morgan Witter, married March 17, 1723.

Children:
Elijah, born September 3, 1724.
Joseph, born August 20, 1726.
Nathan, born December 25, 1729.
Elizabeth, born August 8, 1732.
Jonathan, born September 13, 1735.
Ezra, born March 31, 1738.
Jacob, born January 26, 1741.
Stephen, born March 4, 1744.
Jabez, born March 16, 1747.

Recorded April 8, 1763, at request of Joseph, Norwich Town Rec. Vol. 2, page 335. He died 1770; wife died April 30, 1779.

Dorothy Morgan, born February 29, 1676, married May 5, 1693, Ebenezer Witter; was daughter of Lieut. Joseph and Dorothy Park Morgan, married April, 1670; settled in Preston.

Stephen Brewster, of Preston, son of Joseph and Dorothy Witter Brewster, married Mrs. Hepsibah Rudd, of Norwich, February 25, 1763. He was of Franklin, Conn., later.

Frederick, born 1763.
Edna, born 1765.
Asneth, married; died before settlement of estate.
Stephen, Jr., married; died before settlement of estate.
Clarissa.
Cinthia.
Jacob.
Darius.

Estate settled June 28, 1823. Probate Court, Norwich, Conn.

Norwich Town Records, Volume 2, page 250.

Stephen Brewster, Jr., son of Stephen and Hepsibah Rudd Brewster, born in Franklin, Conn.; died before 1816; married Mary Robinson; born Cheshire, Mass., September 25, 1778; died October 30, 1854, in Tyrone, Steuben County, N. Y. They were of Cooperstown or Otsego, Otsego County, N. Y., in 1804.

Children:
George Robinson, born December 20, 1804.
Stephen.
Darius.

Mary Robinson Brewster married (2), in 1816, Abel Kendall; one son, Elmer Kendall, born 1817; died October, 1841.

George Robinson Brewster, son of Stephen, Jr., and Mary Robinson Brewster, married May 19, 1831, Achsah, daughter of Daniel and Ruth Steele Morgan; born May 8, 1811, in Tolland, Tolland County, Conn.

Children:
Mary, Helen, Julia, Samuel, George, Charles Morgan.

Mary Brewster, daughter of George Robinson and Achsah Morgan Brewster married April 8, 1857, Henry Minton, M. D.; born March 4, 1831; died June 1, 1895.

The great and increasing interest in the Brewster family, and the various ramifications of relationship connected with them, makes me pause before even thinking of an ending.

Still, that time must come, and though much has been revealed, there are still connections to be made, and the spirit of the times demands authorities for everything.

Traditions have become romances until they are verified, so it should be a point of honor with all, to bear their part in developing this history.

The sponsors of the start have increased and multiplied with an activity worthy of the cause.

For my own part there was always a puzzle I could not solve. Taking the Pilgrim and early view of matters, when families were simply mentioned as numbering fifteen, eighteen or twenty, only a record without comment, Brewster's family was considered, and constantly reverted to as so large, yet the numbers did not at all equal the record of the times. Capt. Edward was found; also the young child who died in Leyden, still they do not suffice for the history as given.

I cannot but feel that there are other children to be accounted for, and with the growing desire to search to the bottom all records trust this history will be made.

A DOUBTFUL SUBJECT.

In ye olden times, connection by travel, or letter, was almost impossible, and a man lost sight of, could be placed as dead without further thought, having secured his patrimony he went where his fancy led him, made himself a home, and formed ties that bore no relation to the past.

This maintains in regard to Wrestling Brewster, and "some writers think the Governor mistaken (as to his death, unmarried), as there is a deed of land in Portsmouth, N. H., commencing in these words: "Portsmouth, sixth day of December, 1629. Joseph and Hannah Pendleton (convey to) Wrestling Brewster 80 acres of land for £8, adjoining land belonging to said Wrestling. These lands have descended by inheritance to the Brewster family at Portsmouth, who claim to be descendants of this Wrestling Brewster, until within the memory of the present generation."

MORE RECORD.

Again, in the family records of Portsmouth, N. H., Wrestling Brewster was married to Elma Story, in 1630, and had a son, John, born January 20, 1631, and a daughter, Love Lucretia, born May 3, 1636.

Statements are not proofs, but there is a familiar sound which increases the willingness to make continuous search.

The Brewster records cannot be written without the Ripleys, and in the face of the added Bradford connection they are doubly valuable, so I give, as so kindly sent me by Judge Daniels, the following:

From Probate Records, District of Windham, Conn., volume 15, page 77, July 1, 1803:

Will of Judith Ripley, of Windham, son Harvey Ripley.

Betsey Adams, wife of John Adams, Bradford Ripley, Sephaniah and William.

In heirs' receipt Bradford signs his name David B. Ripley.

Volume 15, page 229, March 20, 1806:

Nath Manning, guardian of Samuel Ripley, a minor, makes return of sale of land.

Volume 15, page 548, April 14, 1810:

Will of Eleazer Ripley, of Windham, wife Miriam.

Sons Josiah, Jeremiah, Eleazer and Nehemiah.

Volume 16, page 65, August 10, 1811.

Inventory of estate of Ebenezer Ripley, of Windham, no names.

Hezekiah Ripley was judge of the court at this time.

Volume 16, page 107, May 7, 1805.

Will of William Ripley, of Windham, wife of Rebecka.

Nephew Hezekiah Augustus Ripley, and his wife Hannah, niece of my wife mentioned.

A Mrs. Eunice Ripley witnesses this will, as does also Asa Brewster.

In a codicil mentions David Ripley, son of Hezekiah and Hannah.

Vol. 17, page 238, November 4, 1820.

Report of commissioners on estate of Ralph H. Ripley, of Windham. Eliphalet Ripley was administrator.

Vol. 17, page 378, August 8, 1822.

Will of Rev. William Ripley, of Lebanon; wife, Lucy; sons, William, Hezekiah W., Willis C., Edwin David, Henry E. and Samuel W.

Vol. 19, page 42, December 5, 1822.

Will of Ralph Ripley, of Windham; wife, Eunice; sons, Christopher, James, Eliphalet. Gives his son Bradford, now resident of the Island of Trinidad, Barbados, $300 provided at the death of his wife Eunice. Bradford is a resident of the United States.

Two grandchildren mentioned, Lydia S. Young and James R. Young; speaks of three daughters, but not by name.

Vol. 19, page 233, December 24, 1828.

Estate of Widow Eunice Ripley, is mentioned with no names.

Vol. 21, page 290, April 11, 1843.

Assignment of Luther Ripley, of Chaplin, is recorded.

Vol. 21, page 334, April 9, 1844.

Estate of Nehimiah Ripley, of Windham, set out of widow's dower to Lucy, widow of Nehimiah.

Same volume, page 353.

Commissioners' report on insolvent estate of above. Among list of creditors find Selina, or Salina Ripley, and Abby Ripley.

Vol. 22, page 312, May 11, 1857.

Will of Anna Ripley, of Windham; sons, William and Justus; daughters, Elizabeth, Ann and Harriet Ripley.

Vol. 22, page 661, June 6, 1864.

Will of Charles H. Ripley, of Windham; mother, Olive H. Ripley; brother, Frank A. Ripley.

The desire to have this history as perfect as possible, brings records, and, when needed, I am happy to say, corrections from every direction. The one I shall now give, I am sorry to say, will not prove acceptable to some. It has been widely circulated, and in some cases authorities have been given.

Mr. Sewall A. Faunce, of Boston, Mass., who is a Pilgrim so far as descent is concerned many times, furnishes the argument, and I know I am safe in saying that no one will be better pleased than himself if there are proofs of two Elizabeths or anything in the records at variance with absolute truth to have them now settled.

The statement made is that Rev. Samuel Fuller, the first minister to Middleboro (son of Dr. Samuel, of the Mayflower, their "Luke, the beloved physician"), born in 1624 and died August, 1695, married Elizabeth, daughter of Jonathan Brewster, son of the elder. Did he?

Elizabeth Brewster, the daughter of Jonathan, was a flower of Connecticut soil, and though not left to "blush unseen" long at that time, was apparently unknown to the "Old Colony."

Neither Goodwin nor Winsor discovered the existence of such a person. But according to New London records she was born in 1638; married first Peter Bradley, who died in 1662, and afterward Christopher Christophers.

Christophers's first wife died in 1676; Christophers died in 1687, and his widow, "relict of Peter Bradley," died in 1708.

All of these dates are important in consideration of the above statement.

Turning now to Rev. Samuel Fuller, it appears by Plymouth probate records that he died in 1695, leaving a widow, Elizabeth, and seven children, and Plympton town records show that Samuel's said widow Elizabeth died in Plympton in November, 1713. It is true also that in the same year that Peter Bradley's "relict" became the widow of Christopher Christophers (1687), Rev. Samuel Fuller's grandson, Nathaniel, was born.

It is evident, therefore, that the Elizabeth who, as wife of Samuel Fuller, then living, became the grandmother of Nathaniel Fuller in 1687, was not Elizabeth, daughter of Jonathan Brewster, who became the widow of Christopher Christophers the same year.

BRADLEY.

Bradley's "relict" was 24 years of age when she first became a widow (1662); there is indisputable evidence that she was still his widow in 1673.

She married Christopher Christophers after 1676, became his widow in 1687, and died in 1708, five years before Fuller's widow died in Plympton.

Therefore if arithmetic is a better witness than theory the statement must be answered in the negative.

ALDEN.

The history of this family of Brewsters reaches everywhere, and thanks to Mr. W. J. Ripley, of Chicago, who is compiling the Ripley genealogy, I am able to furnish this Alden record, which will be invaluable to many:

"In your 'Brewster Records' published July 24, you mention William Ripley (5), Joshua (4-3), John (2), William (1), who married Lydia Brewster, etc.

"It may be of interest to know that Elizabeth Ripley (5), (sister of William), born November 4, 1724, married October 9, 1744, John Alden (4), Andrew (3), Capt. Jonathan (2), John (1), of the Mayflower, (1620), of Lebanon, Conn.; for reference see Alden genealogy.

"John (4) was born July 23, 1716; died March 26, 1789.

"Their (the following) children are descended as well from Gov. Bradford through Joshua Ripley, and his wife, Hannah Bradford."

Children:

1. Parthenia (5) Alden, married Woodbridge Little, Esq. (It would be well to look up this Woodbridge. Some branches of that family lead to Gov. Dudley.)

II. Violetta (5) Alden, married Isaac Fitch.

III. John (5) Alden, resided at Lebanon, Conn.; served in the revolution; ensign Twentieth Continental Infantry, Col. John Durkee, January 1 to December 31, 1776. (Conn. Men in the Revolution, page 106, and Heitman's Hist. Reg.)

IV. Judah (5) Alden, resided at Lebanon, Conn.; served in the Revolution, captain in Col. Samuel B. Webb's addition Continental regiment; commissioned January 1, 1777. Killed in a skirmish in Westchester County or Staten Island, August 22, 1777. (Conn. Men in Rev., page 246, and Heitman's Hist. Reg., page 591.)

V. Roger (5) Alden, born 1748, graduated at Yale College. Served in the revolution; adjutant of Fifth Continental Line, January 1, 1777; lieutenant June 15, 1778; captain September 1, 1779, of Second Regiment; brigade-major Huntington's brigade, at Peekskill, July 13, 1777; wintered at Valley Forge 1777-78; at battle of Monmouth June 28, 1778; appointed aide de camp, with rank of major, to Gen. Huntington, in division orders, Springfield, N. J., April 1, 1780; resigned February 10, 1781. (Connecticut Men in Revolution, various pages, and Heitman's Hist., Reg.) Settled after the revolution in Meadville, Pa. A member of the Connecticut Cincinnati. Appointed ordnance storekeeper at West Point January 20, 1825, and continued to hold the office until the time of his death, November 5, 1836.

He had a daughter, who married Capt. Henry Swartwout, U. S. A., and a son, Bradford Ripley Alden, who was captain United States Army, and died September 10, 1870.

VI. Elizabeth (5) Alden.

VII. Son who died in infancy.

VIII. Son who died in infancy.

Can there be a more beautiful record, and there are many who make the three descents—Brewster, Bradford, Alden!

The true spirit has ben roused in the Brewster family, which means in the present day many other names, so that as one location furnishes record, another, in its pride of its local data, sends still more for the public benefit. Quite a little, hardly complaint, but attention has been called to the lack of record in regard to Love Brewster's family. All in due time, now I will give for a start an item from History of Bridgewater, page 366, where it says that Sarah, daughter of William Collier (widow of Love Brewster), married for second husband a Parks. This is a new field for me, and while not a Brewster descent, it gives the Parks family, if there are any descendants, a collateral relation with the Brewsters.

NEW MATERIAL.

A correspondent sends the following, but dreading the possible letters which may ensue, prefers his name should not appear:

"I have been much interested in the Brewster genealogies being published, and can add an item from the record at Plymouth, Mass., in regard to James Brewster, of Windham.

"Probate records, book 2, page 131. John Partridge's will, dated December 31, 1730, names his daughter, 'Mary,' wife of Jona Brewster, to her son, James Brewster, devises 'my smallest gun which his father, Jona. Brewster, hath sometimes used.'"

Mary Partridge, born in Duxbury May 2, 1693, daughter of John Partridge (1), and Hannah, daughter of Dr. Samuel Seabury (1), married Jonathan Brewster, born March, 1709-10. They removed to Windham, Conn., after 1728.

John Partridge (1), of Duxbury, born November 29, 1657, was eldest son of George Partridge (1), and Sarah, eldest daughter of Stephen Tracy (1), and Tryphosa Le——, who came over on the Ann 1623.

John Partridge married (2) Mary, the widow of Wrestling, the son of Love Brewster.

Lydia Partridge, sister of John (1), married William Brewster, son of Love. Through Dr. Samuel Seabury the Brewsters and Partridges are also related to Rev. Ralph Partridge, first pastor of Duxbury Church (who was probably uncle or cousin of George Partridge, 1st), as follows: Elizabeth, youngest daughter of Rev. Ralph, married Rev. Thomas Thatcher, May 11, 1643. They had a daughter, Patience, who married Mr. William Kemp at Weymouth, Mass., and they had a daughter, Patience Kemp, who married Dr. Samuel Seabury, and who had a daughter, Hannah, born July 7, 1668, who married John Partridge, 1st.

PARTRIDGE.

This adds another family, with many offshoots to the Brewster claim. They intermarried often in Plymouth or Duxbury, and after settling in Windham and Lebanon, Conn., continued to increase the relation through the younger branches.

All of this is the Pilgrim trail and should bring out much history and place some of the "probablies" on a solid basis.

ANOTHER LINE.

This line, which has been authenticated, takes the records into some families not before touched upon.

Elder William Brewster.

Jonathan Brewster.

Mary Brewster, married in 1645 John Turner.

Amos Turner, married in 1695 Mary Hiland.

Jane Turner, married Solomon Otis.

Amos Otis, born in 1737, married in 1798 Nancy Farnsworth.

Amos Otis, born in 1801, the historian and genealogist.

STILL ANOTHER.

Although from an entirely different source this weaves in with the Partridge record:

"I find among my Tilden records James Thomas, born 1683 (grandson of original John Thomas, one of the founders of Plymouth Colony, and who afterward settled at Marshfield, Mass.), married Mary Tilden and settled at Duxbury. They had Mary, born 1693; James, born 1696, and Hannah, born 1698, the wife of Deacon Wrestling Brewster, of Kingston."

E. A. S.

BREWSTER RECORDS CONTINUED.

NEWSPAPER RECORDS.

The following sent me by Mr. George E. Hoadley, of Hartford, Conn., are both quaint and valuable:

Horrid murder, Windham, April 29, 1802. Died at Canterbury on Wednesday of last week, widow Jerusha Brewster, aged 62. Poisoned with arsenic.—New London Gazette, May 5, 1802.

Died at Preston, Conn., on the 29th of April in the 81st year of his age, Mr. Simeon Brewster.—Gazette, May 13, 1801.

At Canterbury, Peleg Brewster, aged 84. —Gazette, May 27, 1801.

At Preston on the 5th inst., Miss Polly, daughter of widow Elizabeth Brewster, aged 15 years.—Gazette, October 24, 1798.

New London, January 3, 1772. About a month ago Mr. Comfort Brewster died in Lebanon in a sudden manner.—Gazette, January 3, 1772.

Died July 23, a child of Benjamin Brewster, 2½ years old, near Preston, Conn.— Gazette, October 1, 1773.

At Hanover, N. H., on the 14th of September, Mrs. Hannah Brewster, aged 35. consort of Gen. Ebenezer Brewster and daughter of the late John Avery, of Preston.—Gazette, April 8, 1805.

At Lebanon, Mrs. Lydia Brewster, aged 98, relict of Ichabod Brewster. Her descendants are 8 children, 74 grandchildren, 220 great-grandchildren and 23 of the fourth generation.—Courant, February 14, 1815.

At St. John's Island, S. C., September 11, Dr. Ichabod Brewster, aged 29, formerly of Lebanon.—Mirror, October 11, 1813.

At Chapel Hill, N. Y., Charles A. Brewster, aged 28, of New York, formerly of Hartford.—Courant, March 29, 1815.

At New York, Benjamin A. Brewster, aged 15, formerly of Norwich.—Courant, November 21, 1815.

At Preston, Peletiah Brewster, aged 58. —Gazette, April 8, 1812.

At Demarara, Joseph Brewster, of Norwich, aged 40.—Gazette, November 20, 1805.

At Franklin, Hepzibah, wife of Stephen Brewster, aged 86.—Gazette, November 8, 1820.

In Griswold, Margery, wife of Elias Brewster, aged 56.—Gazette, January 29, 1823.

At Hampton, Dr. John Brewster, aged 84.—Gazette, September 23, 1823.

At Griswold, Mehitable, wife of Simeon Brewster, aged 72.—Gazette, November 30, 1825.

In this city, Abel Brewster, aged 56.— Hartford Courant, March 27, 1832.

"THE BREWSTER BOOK."

The manuscript sent herewith was recently copied by me from a quarto manuscript of some thirty or more pages, which I found in the Boston Public Library.

This manuscript was written by some one who signs the initials "F. P. B.," and who had evidently seen the original "Brewster Book," mentioned in Vol. III. of the "Vermont Historical Gazeteer," under "Hyde Park."

F. P. B. describes the book as follows:

It is a small quarto volume, with leaves 7½ by 6 inches.

There are now 121 leaves, besides two torn off and lying in the book, making 123.

A considerable more leaves are gone, a few from each end, and some from different places here and there.

It has the original stamped calf covers, now separated from the book. It was capitally bound, and the book is as firm as ever.

It was a blank record book, and the matters in it indicate the following history of the volume:

1st Owner—A scholar and business man, and he owned the book at time of the first emigration to N. England, who copied into the book various public documents relating to the settlement of N. England.

Lists of goods, notes of direction about emigrating, etc.

This person may have been Elder Brewster.

2d Owner—A person less learned than the first, but of recording propensities; very inferior writing. They entered births and deaths and some notes historical and theological.

3d Owner—Less cultivated people, who noted genealogy and a few business accounts.

4th. Lastly, it has been scrawled over and abused by children.

It is badly stained and eaten for from one to three inches back from front margin. The paper has been wet, and become hard and brittle. This has damaged the oldest entries.

The later records have mostly been written within the limits of the margins on uninjured paper.

There are a great many different handwritings and variations in spelling, worse and worse to the end.

Various series of notes of births and deaths, covering long periods are noted by the same hand, as if transcribed from a record, and in one or two cases, a different hand in ink, notes last the death of some person thus registered. Chief matters registered are:

1st. Copy of the charter or grant of New Scotland to John Mason and Anthony Alexander in 1621.

2d. License to Thomas Weston to transport ammunition and ordnance to New England, date February 17, 1621. No. 3—xx— No. 4. Ex. xx No. 5.

The New England patent of thirteen or more pages.

No. 6. Seventeen pages of household farming and trading goods and directions.

No. 7. Commission granted by the Council for New England (name left blank; a license for a voyage).

No. 8. Penmanship too poor to make out.

No. 9. An estimate for the outfit of "a shippe of 200 tonnesses." Three pages items carried out that foot up £526 12s 8d.

No. 10. Poor writing, not easy to decipher, with various scrawls, followed by six pages clearer, written the other way of the book, being notes on a theological discourse.

12. Two pages Fitch "Genealogical Notes."

13. The Fitch epitaph.

14. About fifty leaves (many blank) having scattered genealogical items. Brewster and other items.

15 and 16. Some Latin extracts of historical acccounts concerning Spain and other countries.

No. 3. Genealogies.

"Johnnathan Brewster was borne at Scrooby, in Nottinghamshire, the 12th of August, 1593. (Note Elders oldest son.)

Mary—The wyfe of Wm. Brewster dyed at Plymouth in New England, the 17th April, 1627.

William Brewster dyed at Plimouth, in New England, ye 10th of April, 1644.

William Brewster, the son of Jonathan Brewster, borne at Plimouth, in New England, the 9th of March, 1625.

Mary Brewster, the daughter of Johnathan, borne at Plimouth, 16th April, 1627.

Johnnathan, the soun of Johnathan Brewster, born at Plimouth, 17 July, 1629.

Ruth, the daughter of Johnnathan, borne at Jones River, the 3 of October, 1631."

[Two blank pages, leaves gone; then, in a different handwriting:]

"Benjamin Brewster, the soun of Johnnathan Brewster, borne at Duxborow, the 17th November, 1633.

"Elizabeth, the daughter of Johnnathan Brewster, borne at Duxborrow, the first of May, 1637.

"Grace, the daughter of Jonathan Brewster, borne at Duxborrow, the first of November, 1639.

"Hanna, the daur. of Jonathan, borne at Duxborow, the 3d of Novr., 1641.

(In a later hand at foot of page.)

"The above named Benjamin Brewster died in Norwich ye 14th of September, 1710, and was buried in Brewster Plain.

[Next page, in the old handwriting, same as before.]

Johnnathan Brewster, marryed Lucretia Oldham (?), of Darby, the 10th of April, 1629 (?), who had children—William; Mary, Johnnathan, Ruth, Benjamin, Elizabeth, Grace and Hanna. Note by J. P. B. The marriage date here is evidently incorrect— if William was born 9th of March, 1625. His parents were probably married before that, or the ceremony came after marriage.

Mary Brewster (aged 18) marryed John [Warner?], of Situate, the elder, the 10th of November, 1645. [Note by J. P. B. should be John Turner.]

Ruth Brewster maryed John Pickett the 14th of March, 1651.

William Brewster maryed Mary (Greame?) of London the 15th of October, 1651.

[Two blank pages, leaves gone, then in a different handwriting.]

Daniel Witherell maryied to Grase Brewster August the 4th 1.6.5.9. Elizabeth Brewster, maried to Peeter Brawley the 7th September, 1653.

(?Bradley) Elizabeth Brawley, born March 16th 1654 (?was later); Hannah Brawley, born 17th September, in New London 1656; Peeter Brawley, born 7th September in New London 1658.

In another handwriting:

Lucretia, the Dafter of Peter Bradle, borne at New London, August the 16, 1661.

Peter Bradle the husband of Elizabeth dyed Aprell 3, 1662.

Johnnathan Brewster deyed in the year of our Lord 1659, in August, the 7th day.

"Beniaman Brewster mareed Ann Parte (?) the last day of febeare, 1669' (this date is carefully rewritten).

(Note by J. P. B., no doubt Anna Dart.)

Marie, the dafter of Beniman Brewster, borne 10th day of December 1660.

Ann, the dafter of Beniman Brewster, borne at Mohegin 29 September 1662.

Jonathan—sonn of Beniman, borne at Mohegan November the last, 1664.

Daniell—sonn—born Mohegan 1st March 1667.

(Scrawled up and down in inner margin of the page in another hand:)

Ann Brewster, the wife of Beniaman Brewster, departed this life May the 9th, 1709.

(Some pages further on in another hand:)

Ruth Pickett, widow—ye d. of J. B., m. to Charles Hill of Barley in Darbyshire the 2d July, 1688. (This date is evidently wrong, should be 1668.—J. P. B.)

Jane, their d., born 9th December, 1669. Charles, son, b. New London, 16th October, 1671, New London.

Ruth, ye wife of Charles Hill, deyed the 1st of May, 1677.

Note.—The following genealogy comprehends all the important particulars I found in the "Brewster Record," which was, no doubt, owned by Jonathan Brewster, Elder William Brewster's oldest son.

Joseph P. Beach, Cheshire, Conn.

1. Elder William Brewster, died April 10, 1644; married Mary ——; dyed Plymouth, April 17, 1627.

Children:

2. Johnnathan, born at Scrowby, August 12, 1593; dyed August 7, 1659; married Lucretia Oldham, April 10, 1629. (? Date missing.) She dyed March 4, 1678-79.

Children:

3. William, born March 9, 1625; married Mary Graeme, October 15, 1651.

4. Mary, born April 16, 1627; married John Warner, November 10, 1645.

5. Jonathan, born July 17, 1629.

6. Ruth, born October 3, 1631; married John Pickett, March 14, 1651.

7. Benjamin, born November 17, 1633; married Anne Parte (should be Dart), February 28, 1669.

8. Elizabeth, born May 1, 1637; married Peter Bradley, September 7, 1653.

9. Grace, born November 1, 1639; married Daniel Wetherell, August 4, 1659.

10. Hanna, born November 3, 1641.

No. 3. William.

Born March 9, 1625.

Married Mary Gaeme, October 15, 1651.

No. 4. Mary, born 1627.

Married John Warner, 1645.

No. 5. Jonathan, born July 17, 1629.

No. 6. Ruth, born October 3, 1631; died May 1, 1677.

Married (1st) John Pickett, March 14, 1651.

Married (2d) Charles Hill, July 2, 1688 (1668, J. P. B.)

Children by second marriage born at New London:

Daughter Jane, born December 9, 1669.

Son Charles, born October 16, 1671, 4 o'clock a. m.

Adam Pickett, son of John and Ruth, born November 15, 1658, was married to Hannah Wetherill.

No. 7. Benjamin Brewster, born November 17, 1633; died September 14, 1710; married Anne Parte, February 28, 1669; died May 9, 1709.

This is no doubt intended for Anne Dart, and date should be 1659.—J. P. B.

Children:

11. Marre, born December 10, 1660; married November 28, 1678, Samuel Fitch, son of James Fitch.

12. Ann, born September 29, 1662.

13. Johnnathan, born November 31, 1664; married Judith Steven; died November 20, 1704.

14. Dannell, born March 1, 1667; married December 23, 1686, Hannah Guyer (?).

15. William, born March 22, 1669.

16. Ruth, born September 16, 1671; married Thomas Adgate, June 15, 1692.

17. Benjamin, born November 2, 1673; married Mary Smith, December 17, 1696.

18. Elizabeth, born June 23, 167—(torn off)—probably 1675; married to Daniel Meeks, July 4, 1706.

No. 8. Elizabeth, born May 1, 1637; married Peter Bradley, September 7, 1653; died April 3, 1662.

Bradley children:

Elizabeth, born March 16, 1654.

Hannah, born September 17, 1656.

Peeter, born September 7, 1658; married, May 9, 1678, Mary Christopher, daughter of Christopher Christophers; died August 26, 1687.

Lucretia, born August 16, 1661.

No. 9. Grace, born November 1, 1639; married, August 4, 1659, Daniel Witherell, born at Kent, November 29, 1630.

Wetherill children:

Hannah, born March 21, 1659, married Adam Pickett, May 26, 1680, Wednesday, and had a son, Adam, born September 7, 1681.

Mary, born October 7, 1668.

Daniell, born January 26, 1670.

Marye, borne 1672. Lived 2 mos. and dyed.

Four sons successively "borne and dyed" nameless immediately after their births.

The above Wetherell entries are all in one handwriting, as if copied from some record.

Then in different hand:

Grace Wetherell deyed Aprel the 22d, 1684.

No. 10. Hanna Brewster, born November 3, 1641.

No. 11. Marre (Mary) Brewster.

Born December 10, 1660, married November 28, 1678, Samuel Fitch, son of James Fitch.

Fitch children born at Mohegan:

Mare (Mary), dafter, born March 10, 1679-80.

Samuel, 1681; Hezekiah, 1682; Elizabeth, 1684; Abigel, 1686; Samuel, 1688; Beniaman, 1691; John, 1693; Jabus (Jabez), 1695, died March 28, 1779, age 84; his wife Anna died August 25, 1770, aged 81; Peltiel (Pelatiah), 1698.

No. 12.

No. 13. Jonathan Brewster, born November 31, 1664; married Judith Steven, December 18, 1690, she being then 20 years of age, wanting seven days.

Children:

18 a. Lucretia (dafter), born at Mohegan, November 3, 1691.

18 b. Jonathan, born at Mohegan, April 2, 1694.

No. 14. Daniel Brewster, born March 1, 1667; died May 7, 1735; married December 23, 1686, Hannah Guyer (? Gager); died September 25, 1727.

Children:

19. Dannell, born Norwich, October 11, 1687; married, August 8, 1710, Elizabeth Freeman.

20. Hanna, born at Preston, December 2, 1690; married, December 2, 1708, Joseph Freeman.

21. Mare, born at Preston, January 2, 1692, probably wife of Christopher Huntington.

22. John, born at Preston, July 18, 1695; married, September 20, 1725, Dorothy Treat (died April 17, 1704 (?); another entry says March 7, 1711).

23. Jeruca (Jerusha), born at Preston, November 18, 1697.

24. Ruth, born at Preston, June 20, 1701.

25. Bethujah (Bethia), born at Preston, April 1702; married William Parrish, May 23, 1738.

26. Jonathan, born at Preston, June 6, 1705.

27. Ebenezer, born at Preston, September 19, 1713; married Hannah or Susannah Smith; died October 7, 1739.

Benjamin, born November 25, 1673.

Married Mary Smith December 17, 1696.

Children:

28. Benjamin, born at Mohegan September 24, 1697.

29. John, born at Lebanon May 25, 1701.

30. Mary, born at Lebanon April 24, 17— leaves gone and torn.

No. 22. John Brewster.

Born July 18, 1695.

Married, September 20, 1725, Dorothy Treat.

Children:

31. Olivour, born at Preston July 20, 1726.

32. Dorothy, born at Preston January 22, 1727.

33. Hannah, born at Preston September 26, 1729.

34. Daniel, born at Preston April 12, 1731.

No. 27. Ebenezer Brewster, born September 19, 1713.

Married Hannah or Susannah Smith.

35. Benjamin, born at Preston April 15, 1736.

36. Ebenezer, born at Preston April 25, 1740.

Then follows several pages of marriages and births of the Wedg, Fitch, Niles, Deming, Rudd, Freeman, Fobes, and copy of inscription on tombstone in Lebanon, Conn. Mr. James Fitch, born 1622, minister at Saybrook, and after at Norwich, Conn.

(Graveyard memoranda from "Brewster Book.")

Preston, June ye 14 Day, 1756; then Daniel Brewster (sic), Departed this Life in the 69th year of his age.

(Written on a loose slip). November, A. D. 1790, Anna Lord Rudd, died, aged 12 years.

January 20, 1781, Mrs. Lurene Rudd, died age 49, September 22, 1795.

Mr. Samuel Rudd died, age 73.

Another entry reads: John Christopher (son of Christopher Christophers), was borne at New London, September 3, 1668. Christopher Christophers deyed July 23, 1687.

Mary, wife of Christopher Huntington, departed December 24, 1749.

Matthew Coy married Ann.

Entries of Freeman children, born at Preston:

Daniel Brewster, married Dorothy Witter, December 19, 17—(torn).

Mr. Joseph P. Beach, of Cheshire, Conn., to whom I am indebted for the records from the "Brewster Book," of course, claims no responsibility for the above, knowing that in it there are doubtful dates, which he, however, thinks will be explained and settled by other evidence. Mr. C. Ernest Bowman, I have been told, had the same record of Jonathan Brewster's marriage to Lucretia Oldham. Whether gained from the same source I do not know.

Mr. Beach's present contribution, though

I am promised more records by him, closes with "Ye Brewster Book."

It is described in the second volume (not third, as printed) of the Vermont Historical Gazetteer on page 628, under an account of "Hyde Park," 1781, as follows:

"The Brewster Book, a curious old manuscript volume, is in the possession of the family of Jabez Fitch, born in Norwich February 15, 1737, married June 3, 1760, Hannah Perkins. He died at Hyde Park, Vermont, February 29, 1812."

The writer of the article continues:

"The Brewster Book was evidently commenced in the sixteenth century. Having three times crossed the Atlantic and been exposed to the action of salt water for some time on one of the voyages, the edges of the leaves have been partially destroyed. They appear exactly as if charred by the action of fire, and from one and one-half to two inches of the writing is gone or illegible."

"The family records having been subsequently made are entire."

The writer in the "Historical Gazetteer" after describing some of the contents of the book, suggests that the Vermont Historical Society should preserve the contents of the Brewster Book

The above article is followed by "Fitch's Diary," a very interesting document covering several pages.

Very naturally this "new find" has revived search into the old records, and as the conviction has been constantly forced upon me that the whole of the Brewster history of the early days has never been reached, I quote from Henry Martyn Dexter in his notes to "Monet's Relation," page 140, where he says: "Jonathan Brewster was the eldest son of the Elder. Mr. Savage says he was born in Scrooby, England, but I have in my possession a copy of an affidavit from the Leyden records, which states that he was about sixteen years old, June 25, July 5, 1609, which would back his birth to 1585, eleven years anterior to Mr. Hunter's record of the preference of his father at Scrooby. This would make him 37 at landing.

Much supposition can come from this. Being a Pilgrim, with their surroundings of their history, it is not in the nature of affairs that Jonathan Brewster had not been married before 37 years of age.

At Pomfret, Conn., Dr. William A. Brewster, of Hampton, to Miss Lucy Chamberlain.—Mirror, March 29, 1813.

At Bolton, on the 25th inst., Anson Brewster to Miss Aurelia, daughter of Capt. Samuel Alvord.—Courant, January 2, 1805.

At Windham, David Brewster to Miss Sally Donance.—Gazette, March 9, 1803.

At Stonington, Mr. Azel Pierce to Miss Eliza Brewster.—Gazette, October 8, 1800.

At Norwich, Abel Brewster to Miss Sally Leach.—Courant, February 20, 1816.

At Poquetanock, Capt. John Brown to Miss Eunice Brewster.—Gazette, September 13, 1797.

At Preston, Elisha Brewster to Mrs. Jane Harkers.—Gazette, January 25, 1804.

At New Haven, James Brewster to Miss Mary Hequembourg.—Connecticut Mirror, September 24, 1810.

At Franklin, William S. Gere, of Groton, to Miss Louisa, daughter of Frederic Brewster.—Courant, March 5, 1816.

At Preston, Jeremiah S. Halsey to Miss Sarah, daughter of the late Capt. Jabez Brewster.—Gazette, September 23, 1818.

In New Haven, Simeon Lester, of Norwich, to Miss Hannah Maria Brewster.—Gazette, December 29, 1819.

At Brooklyn, N. Y., Benijah A. Brewster to Miss Lucy Potter, both of New London.—Gazette, June 20, 1821.

At Preston, by Jonathan Brewster, Esq., William P. Nash to Miss Clarissa Brewster.—Gazette, October 20, 1824.

Many lines can be traced from the following record: Capt. Elisha Brewster (son of William, son of Deacon William, son of Love, son of Elder William) was born October 29, 1715; married September 30, 1742, by Rev. Benjamin Bowers, first pastor of the Congregational Church, of Middle Haddam, Middlesex County, Conn. (the church was organized September 25, 1740), to Lucy, daughter of Jonathan, and Sibbel (Harris) Yeomans. She was born April 7, 1715; died August 15, 1775. He died March 26, 1789. The second pastor was Rev. Benjamin Boardman.

Children:

Elisha, born August 19, 1743; died June 12, 1745; baptized August 21, 1743.

Lucy, born May 30, 1745; baptized June 2, 1745.

Lucretia, born October 31, 1747; baptized November 8, 1747; married Dr. Elihu Tudor.

Lott, born September 18, 1749; died about June, 1795.

Elisha, born July 8, 1751; married Margaret Curtis.

William, born February 21, 1753.

Sarah, born November 20, 1754; married Dr. Oliver Wetmore.

John, born November 10, 1756; died December 17, 1758.

Hopestill, born April 15, 1759.

Lydia, born September 12, 1762; married Peter Van Deusen.

John, born June 22, 1764; died August, 1764.

Ruby, born November 22, 1765; married William Kippen.

From New London records:

"John Picket ye sonne of John Picket and Ruth his wife born ye 25 July 1656.

Elizabeth Bradley, ye daughter of Peter and Elizabeth his wife born ye March 16, 1654.

Peter Bradley, ye son of Peter Bradley and Elizabeth his wife born ye 7 September 1658.

Adam Pickett, son of John and Ruth Pickett born November 15 1658.

Daniel Wetherell, ye son of William Wetherell—clericus of Scituate, in New England—married unto Grace, the daughter of Jonathan and Grace Brewster of New London the 4th of August 1658.

Mistake of Recorder. Lucretia was wife of Jonathan Brewster.

Hannah Wetherell, daughter of Daniel and Grace Wetherell born March 21 1659.

Mary Pickett, daughter of John and Ruth Pickett born January 16 1659-60.

Samuel Starr, was married to Hannah, daughter of Jonathan Brewster 23 December 1664.

Samuel Starr, son of Samuel and Hanah Starr, born 11 December 1665.

Charles Hill, sonn of George Hill of Barley in Dartshire old England was married unto Ruth Pickett the widow of John Pickett 16 July 1668.

Thomas Starr, son of Samuel and Hannah Starr born 27th of September 1668.

Mary Wetherell, daughter of Daniel and Grace Wetherell born 7th October 1668.

Jane Hill, ye daughter Charles and Ruth Hill was born 3 in ye morning 9 of Sept. 1669.

Daniel, son Daniel and Grace Wetherell, born 26 Jan 1670.

Thomas Dymond of Hartford was married to Elisabeth daughter of Peter and Elizabeth Bradley September 22, 1670.

Benjamin Shapley, ye sonn of Nicholas Shapley of Charlestown was marryed unto Mary, ye daughter of John Pickett, of New London, ye 10 of April 1672.

Ruth Shapley, daughter Benjamin and Mary Shapley born 21 December 1672.

Elizabeth, daughter of Thomas and Elizabeth Dymond born Aug 14, 1672.

Jonathan Hill son of Charles and Ruth Hill was born ye December 1673-4.

Benjamin, sonn Benjamin and Mary Shapley, born ye 20 March 1675.

Thomas, sonn Thomas and Elizabeth Dymond, born July 22, 1675.

Ruth Hill, wife Charles Hill died 30 April, 1677.

Mary, daughter Benjamin and Mary Shapley, born ye 26 March 1677.

NEW LONDON RECORDS CONTINUED.

Moses Dymond, son of Thomas and Elizabeth Dymond, born May 14, 1677.

Ezekill Turner, ye son of John of Scituate, marryed Susannah the daughter of John Keeney of New London 26 December 1678.

Peeter Bradley, the sonn of Peeter, was marryed unto Mary the daughter of Christopher Christophers May 9 1678.

Christopher, son of Peter and Mary Bradley, ye 11 July, 1679.

Adam Pickett, of New London, marryed unto Hanna daughter of Daniel Wetherell, 26 May 1680.

Ruth, daughter Thomas and Elizabeth Dymond, born September 12 1680.

Benjamin Starr and Lydia Latham, marryed on Wednesday the 20th of May 1702.

Benjamin, son of Benjamin and Lydia Starr, born Tuesday 4 December 1702.

Mary, daughter Benjamin and Lydia Starr, born December 26 1703.

Lydia, daughter Benjamin and Lydia Starr, born October 25 1705.

Elizabeth, daughter Benjamin and Lydia Starr, born October 4 1707.

Jasper, son Benjamin and Lydia Starr, born March 21 1709-10.

Elizabeth Starr departed this life March 30 1710.

Adam Pickett, son Adam and Hanna Pickett, born ye 7th September 1680.

Richard Christophers, son of Christopher Christophers marryed unto Lucretia the daughter of Peter Bradley of New London January ye 26 1681.

Joseph Shapley, son of Benjamin and Mary Shapley, born 15 July 1681.

Samuel Ffosdick, sonn of John ffosdick, of Charlestown in New England, marryed Mercy Pickett, the daughter of John and Ruth Pickett the 1st day of November 1682.

Christopher, son of Richard and Lucretia Christophers born ye 2nd December 1682.

Samuel ffosdick the sonn of Samuel and Mercy ffosdick born August 16, and departed this life 28 November 1683.

Sarah, the daughter Ezekiel Turner, and Susannah his wife, born Oct. 28, 1683.

Samuel the son of Samuel and Mercy ffosdick born 18 of September 1684.

John Pickett, son of Adam, and Hanna Pickett, born July 28, 1685.

Richard, son of Richard, and Lucretia Christophers, born August 18, 1685.

Susannah, daughter Ezekiel and Susannah Turner born Jan. 2, 1685.

Anna Shapley, daughter of Benjamin and Mary Shapley born Aug. 2, 1685.

Mercy, daughter Samuel and Mercy Ffosdick born 30 November, 1685.

By looking back to The Mail and Express of September 11, 1897, searchers, through the courtesy of Mr. Cyrus Brewster, of Derby, Conn., will be able to finish a line from Cyrus Brewster, who married Nancy, daughter of Henry De Witt.

Their son, Cyrus, (7) married for first wife Ann Tappan, who had two children, Annie T. and Jacob D. He married for his second wife Sarah E. Mills, of Huntington, Conn.

This gives five collateral branches, as Sarah E. Mills was one of the noted Mills family, before told of, descended from Peter Van Der Menlen, of Windsor, Conn., who had his name changed to Peter Mills, and who was a student at Leyden University, Holland.

They had seven children, Sarah M., Cyrus, Mary A., Alice M., Samuel M., William J. and Jessie.

Ann T. Brewster, daughter of Cyrus (7) and Ann Tappan Brewster, married Joseph Tomlinson, of Huntington. They had five children, Nettie, Rosalie, Joseph, Annie and Cyrus Brewster.

Jacob Brewster married Louisa Keefer, of Thorold, Ont. They had seven children, Frank H., Katherine G., John T., Maggie L., Robert K., Henry G. and Charles B. Jacob D. was captain and afterwards brevet lieutenant-colonel, and was on the staff of Major-Gen. Herron in the Civil War. He died October, 1896, in Derby, Conn.

Cyrus Brewster (8), son of Cyrus (7) and Sarah E. Mills, married Laura R. Lyman, of Batavia, N. Y. They are now living in Derby, and have two children, Charlotte Lyman and Cyrus (9), both born there.

The only other married child of Cyrus (7) and Sarah E. Mills is May A., who married E. W. Hend, of Boston.

Rosa Tomlinson, granddaughter of Cyrus (7) and Ann (Brewster) Tomlinson, married Rev. Charles W. Shelton, of Derby, Conn. They had two children, Winona and William. Winona died. The family are now living in Derby, Conn.

Cyrus (7) went from his birthplace at Windham, Conn., to Montreal, when he was 18 years old. His two older brothers, Benjamin and William, having gone there before.

Cyrus (6) died in Windham, Conn., in 1818. Cyrus (7) died in Huntington, Conn., June 6, 1888.

The two papers make this line perfect to the Pilgrim Elder, William Brewster, of the Mayflower.

THE FOREFATHER SHIPS FORTUNE, ANN AND LITTLE JAMES.

Just one year after the Mayflower sighted the hills of Cape Cod, the Fortune, "a vessel of forty or fifty tons, or threeabouts," sailed into port, having started from London July, 1621, bringing very unexpectedly to the colonists thirty-five passengers.

Eager as all were for the possible companionship and news from home, the caution of their lives in their new situation made them not only anxious in spirit, but preparation. Their cup of experience was too full to accept the unknown.

Capt. Standish, true to his instincts of anticipating a foe while he longed for a friend, surveyed the means at his command and called all to their posts.

"The stranger drew into the harbor, and when sufficiently near them sent out from her 'ancient staff' the red cross of England."

It was a supreme moment, conflicting emotions would soon be satisfied, and perhaps tangible aid come to them in their great need.

Fate was against them, there was a welcome for some, and others were not acceptable; indeed, so different a type, that even Elder Brewster and Gov. Bradford resented the contingent thrust upon them by the Adventurers. True, Robert Cushman was one of their agents, sent to spy out the land and guard their interests, yet giving the Pilgrims little companionship, as he was to return in the vessel.

THE FORTUNE.

This hastily equipped vessel brought the mouths to fill, at the time when the people, "weary and worn," were in an exhausted condition for want of food, the colony reduced to a minimum as to supplies.

Exasperated by the sight of game they could not secure, every particle of ammunition hoarded as necessary to protection against the Indians and wild beasts, which prowled about night and day seeking whom they might devour; starving in reach, if not of plenty, at least of food which would render life more endurable, they could not compass what this increase of numbers might mean.

More endurance was an impossiblity; they had reached the limits of everything; the "spirit of mortal had ceased to be proud."

All that was left them was the brute instinct of self-protection.

WINSLOW.

Winslow tells us in his "Good News from England" "that the passengers on the Fortune came so unprovided, not landing so much as a barrel of bread or meal for their whole company, but, contrariwise, received from us for their ship's store homeward. Neither were the settersforth thereof altogether to be blamed therein, but rather certain amongst ourselves, who were too prodigal in their writing and reporting (by the Mayflower) of that plenty we enjoyed."

The fearful first sickness and consequent depletion of their stores, that the dear ones might have all available comforts, had not then to be accounted for. This knowledge might have lessened the numbers. But they came, and the list, so far as possible to authenticate it, was:

John Adams, Edward Bompasse, William Bassite, William Beale, Jonathan Brewster, Clement Brigg, John Cannon, William Conor, Robert Cushman, Thomas Cushman, Stephen Dean, Philip De La Noye, Thomas Flavell and son, Widow Foord (4), Robert Hicks, William Hilton, Bennet Morgan, Thomas Morton, Austin Nicolas, William Palmer, William Pitt, Thomas Prince, Moses Simonson, Hugh Statie, James Steward, William Tench, John Winslow, William Wright.

The Adventurers may have been greedy for returns on their investment, but, if as a punishment, they had a severe one, the "Fortune being taken by a French man-of-war off the English coast and carried to the Isle of Use." Like many, in all ages, the captain was lavish with the property of others, and "presented the vessel and company thereof, being thirteen persons, as prisoners to Monsieur the Marquis de Cera, Governor of the Isle."

The papers were searched; nothing piratical could be found; the commission correct, and yet the Marquis de Cera "kept Capt. Barton close prisoner in his castle, commanded his soldiers to pillage them and left them without so much as a kettle to boil their meat in nor can to drink in."

And all this while Cushman looked on powerless to avert the confiscating of the beaver skins and other commodities sent out in payment of the debt to the Adventurers, knowing full well the trouble it would be for the poor colonists to make reparation.

Then, perhaps saddest of all, the Marquis with the refinement of cruelty, "sent for all their letters, opened and kept what he pleased, especially, though he was much intreated to the contrary, a letter written by (William Bradford) the Governor of our colony in New England, containing a general relation of all matters there."

Being the winners, Americans can laugh now, but there have been weary years of mourning over the loss of this manuscript, and in the present, to many, disappointment that, as it is now our own, it should only contain the pages so often perused.

THE ANN AND LITTLE JAMES.

The welcome for the Ann and Little James was ready and waiting. They had given the navy toast to "Sweethearts and Wives" more than the customary Saturday nights, and they were longing for tangible results.

"In August, 1623, the Ann, of 150 tons, and the little James, of forty-four, arrived, bringing about eighty more passengers."

To Gov. Bradford and Miss Standish came expectedly their future wives, to Elder Brewster and Richard Warren the dear ones left behind, and so on through the list, of those who were to make the one great family, gathered on New England's bleak shores.

The rest of the story is told over and over again in the intermarriages that resulted from propinquity, the participants never knowing how different their lives might have been had the field been larger and they given more choice.

"No passenger list has been preserved, but unless some died before the division of lands, in 1624, the following names, referred to in that division, must approximate to accuracy."

Anthony Annable, Jane Annable, Sarah Annable, Hannah Annable, Edward Bangs, Robert Bartlett, Mary Buckett, Faith Brewster, Fear Brewster, Edward Burcher and wife, Thomas Clark, Christopher Conant, Hester Cooke, Cuthbert Cuthbertson, wife and four children; Anthony Dix, John Faunce, Mannasch Faunce (Kempton), Goodwife Flavel, Edmund Flood, Bridget Fuller, Timothy Hatherly, William Heard, Margaret Hickes and three children, William Hilton, Mrs. Hilton, William Hilton, Jr.; —— Hilton, John Jenney, wife and children; Robert Long, Experience Mitchell, George Morton and family, Thomas Morton Jr., Ellen Newton, John Oldham and a company of nine, Francis Palmer, Christian Penn, two servants of Mr. Pierce, Joshua Pratt, James Rand, Robert Rattliffe, Nicholas Snow, Alice Southworth, Francis Sprague, Mrs. Sprague and child, Barbara Standish, Thomas Tilden, Stephen Tracey, Tuphosa Tracey, his wife, Sarah Tracey, Ralph Wallen, Joyce Wallen, his wife; Elizabeth Warren, Mary Warren, Ann Warren, Sarah Warren, Elizabeth Warren and Abigail Warren.

References: Davis's "History of Plymouth," p. 27; "History of the Town of Plymouth," W. T. Davis, pp. 30, 31; "Good News from England," by E. Winslow; "The Story of the Pilgrim Fathers," by E. Arber, pp. 506, 507.

JOHN ADAMS.

Only thirteen years of life granted John Adams in his new home in Plymouth, New England, after sustaining the hardships of the voyage on the Fortune, arriving November 9, 1621.

He was a carpenter and by this pursuit was able to leave his widow and children a "decent estate for that day." And yet the necessity for absolute "bread winning" being wanting, his widow, though he died in 1633, his estate recorded October 24 of that year, married the following June Kenelon Winslow, perhaps a business associate and boon companion of poor John Adams, for both were carpenters.

The placing of the wife of John Adams turns, as history so naturally points, on her maiden name, which, as Ellen, or Elinor Newton, makes her the one who came out in the Ann, 1623.

Savage accords this sagacity of interpretation to Judge Davis.

John and Elinor Newton Adams had three children, James, John and Susanna. This James, though of Plymouth, had a natural leaning to Marshfield, the home of his stepfather, Kenelon Winslow, but he soon tired of being under the family eye and moved to Scituate, where he married Frances, daughter of William Vassall, July 16, 1646.

This marriage was certainly no drawback as to position, for William Vassall, who was a son of John Vassall, Alderman of London, brought much to this country in the way of solid claims to consideration. His father was a man of fine organization, placing himself on record for his successful plans for resisting the Spanish Armada in 1588. People of this desire and intention were apt in those times to find their way to the Low Countries, and as a result imbibe some of the Pilgrim ideas and tenets.

William Vassall's own position was a high one, starting out as assistant of the Governor and Company of the Massachusetts Bay, named in King Charles's charter. For some reason he went back to England, but what he had seen produced the desire to return, and in 1635 he appeared on the Blessing, with wife and children.

His first stop was at Roxbury, but for the future benefit of John Adams his next "sitting down" was in Scituate, though he died in the Barbados.

The other son, John, was of Marshfield, and married, Dec. 27, 1654, Jane James.

John Adams came over in the Fortune November 9, 1621, died 1633. Married Eleanor Newton.

Their son, James Adams, married Frances Vassals.

Their son, Richard Adams, married Rebecca.

Their son, Richard Adams, married Mary Cady.

Their son, Peter Adams, married Priscella Warren.

Their son, Philemon Adams, married Sarah Day.

Their daughter, Sally Adams, married Curnel O. Tarbox.

Their son, Hiram Tarbox, maried his cousin, Eunice Tarbox.

Their son, George W. Tarbox, married Caroline E. Lewis.

Their children—Ida Caroline Tarbox, Kate Lewis Tarbox, George W. Tarbox.

Philemon Adams enlisted January 17, 1778, in Capt. Branches Company of Col. Johnson Regiment.

Windham County History, volume 2, page 188: "Mrs. Philemon Adams, of Brooklyn, Conn., left by her husband ere her home was finished, laid the floor herself and made the house ready for occupation of her family."

WILLIAM BASSETT.

William Bassett would have added much to the interest of his history if he had only recorded a little more of his life in Leyden and in England before seeking the Low Countries.

His story might have unraveled other knotty questions. The tale as it comes from Leyden records that "His Bans were published first with Mary Butler, on the 19th of March, 1611, but she died before the third publication."

Fate was surely against him, but his was not a faint heart, so he soon found another bride, and as "William Bassett, Englishman, widower of Cecil Lecht, he appears July 29 and August 13, 1611, accompanied by Roger Wilson and Edward Goddard, with Margaret Oldham, maid from England, accompanied by Wyham Pautes (? Pantes) and Elizabeth Neal."

History naturally points to this Margaret Oldham as being a sister of John, and if Jonathan Brewster's wife is established as Lucretia Oldham, opens a possibility of another sister to this family.

The Bassetts are in the right line for almost anything; it is a field worthy of fine searching, and surely will reward the time spent upon it.

This is not all, however, for William Bassett's family relations, as "In the division of the lands by the General Court of the colony, on the 22d of May, 1627, the name of the wife of William Bassett is given as Elizabeth Bassett, as there are two of that name mentioned in the family." In the History of Duxbury she is given as Elizabeth Tilden (?).

This has an historical ring, as Thomas Tilden, who arrived in the Ann, probably brought out wife and children, as evidenced by his three shares in the cattle division of 1623; and there being none of his name in the allotment of 1627 it seems as if they were daughters, who had merged their rights in other families by their marriages.

OCCUPATION.

William Bassett's share in the equipment of the colony was as a blacksmith, a laughable misnomer of occupation as it is known in the present day, when it is recalled that the first horse on record (1644) was owned by Stephen Hopkins, the Pilgrim. There is no precedent in the Bassett family, as I place it in England, to suppose our William spent the years from 1623 to 1644, as one of the "lame and lazy" of the "old comers." A pride in the outfit they felt necessary may have made them desire to place on their list artisans of every conceivable guild or trade. They were part of the English requirements. Why not continue the blessings and escape the wrongs? The names given sound strangely, in view of the warehouses and counting houses of modern times. Everything possible was gathered under one roof, as was evidence of the working capacity of one man. Probably William Bassett was a general repairer, using wood more frequently than welding iron, a ship builder forsooth, when the article desired was for heavy travel, at what they conceived to be long distances. Without horses, there were perforce no wagons, and the oxen, though capable, were utilized on the farms. The agricultural implements during Bassett's life few and crude, so I give him a broader field, and feel I am only doing him justice.

One of my notes says he was a "journey mason from Sandwich, Eng.," and though the authority was not taken, the combination would cover the ground.

The first home of the Bassett family in this country was Plymouth, in 1627, but, joining those who desired the church to have an offshoot in Duxbury, the change came with this consummation, and until 1637 they are found there. After that in Bridgewater, where William Bassett died 1667, having been one of the pioneers of the place.

THE CHILDREN.

Goodwin, in Plymouth Republic, gives

the names of the children as William, Nathaniel, Joseph, Sarah, Elizabeth, Jane and Ruth. Savage announces Nathaniel as a son, William, of New Haven, "probably," while of Joseph he merely says he was of Hingham and married, October, 1677, Martha Hobart.

William married, in 1648, the widow of William Ives. Nathaniel, of Yarmouth, in 1672, married a daughter of John Joyce.

Sarah married Peregrine White, and every history of early times is bristling with the demands of her husband by accident of his bring the first native born Englishman. It added much to their possessions that his claims were allowed, for she, living until 1711, had a long period in which to enjoy them.

Elizabeth married Thomas Burgess, a neighbor, November 8, 1648, and after thirteen years' hardly to be recorded as wedded bliss they were divorced June 10, 1661. The History of Bridgewater says she married William Hatch. If so, it must have been a second marriage, and certainly previous experience did not prevent another trial on the part of Thomas Burgess.

Jane cast in her lot with Thomas Gilbert 1639.

Elizabeth married John Sprague, son of Francis, in 1655, who joined "Michael Prince's company at Philip's war, and was killed at Pawtucket March 26, 1676," and his widow married for second husband ———— (?) Thomas.

The Adams and Bassett marriage relations bring them together into the families of William Vassal, William White and the Winslows. Taking the "Hundred of Basset Lawe," which filled the northeast corner of Nottinghamshire, striking Yorkshire and Lincolnshire, as bearing on the Bassett family, who were as the records show in Leyden the natural supposition being that they came to the Pilgrim or Separatist Church, the history multiplies and strengthens.

About midway of this Great Northern Post Road it is my earnest endeavor to prove as the vital power of this Pilgrim movement, "where this court posting service was originated by Edward IV. to obtain war news from Scotland," lies this section from which we bring the Mortons, Southworths, Cooks, Bradfords, Canns, etc., and within easy distance the names prominent in the history of the time.

"It is supposed the hundreds of subdivisions of the Shire were so-called for the numbers of families in each at the time the counties were originally divided by Alfred."

One may well look back upon these roads with pride when they read of the results of the excavations of the present era, showing that our modern improvements are but a repetition of the past, handled by machinery instead of soldiers. All around Coventry are the Roman roads, proved by coins found there to at least reach Nero's reign. The solid work which has so resisted time shows the method to have been layers of broken stone and mortar, the surface covered with shell. There being no "Department of Public Works" it has remained intact until the explorer's spirit unearthed it as a matter of history.

THE TIMES.

There is a great division of opinion among searchers of the present time in regard to the "early comers," the "builders of our nation." It is hard to put them in any position and keep them there, in the public estimation. Those belonging to these families claim too much for them; it is not necessary, they could be placed with royalty on their habits and cultivation without any attempt at supposition, the "plain, unvarnished tale would suffice."

Not even the arrivals, repudiated by Brewster and Bradford would be described in more forcible terms to their disadvantage than Froude has handed down in regard to Queen Elizabeth.

"She was free of access to her presence, quick-witted and familiar of speech with men of all degrees. She rode, shot, jested and drank beer; spat, and swore upon occasions—swore not like a 'comfit-maker's wife,' but round mouth-filling oaths which would have satisfied Hotspur, etc."

And this was one of England's greatest sovereigns. When discussing their forefathers, don't try to place them above the throne, expect of them what the times gave.

Take William Bassett, to Lincolnshire, Nottinghamshire, Yorkshire or any surrounding county, reached by the various roads to the Great Northern, let him renew his acquaintance with George Morton, and Edward Southworth, the merchants, and history may prove him as well born and bred, quite enough so to have his descendants feel a natural pride in the citizenship which dates back to the arrival of the Fortune in 1621.

ROBERT HICKES.

Robert Hickes started his life in the New World in a manner entirely unfair to his antecedents, his unfriendly conduct to the government, in conveying news of their actions to the Adventurers, laying him open to severe criticism.

To his credit, however, it can be said, on Goodwin's authority, that he ultimately became a good citizen, and left to his descendants a fine record.

His history in London opens large historical possibilities, giving such strong circumstantial evidence that, but for the necessary certainty in these days, when traditions are a thing of the past, would be accepted without a thought to the contrary.

"Robert Hickes, a merchant (leather dresser), of Bumenlesdy street, Southwark, London, England, son of John Hicks, came to Plymouth Colony in the ship Fortune, 1621."

From similarity of occupation there is every possibility of his intimate relations with Stephen Hopkins, which would take him back to the expedition of Somers and Gates, to Elder Brewster and his son, "Capt. Edward."

After the manner of the day, he made over his business in London to his son Thomas, a child by his first wife, and, having married well a second time, left England to purchase a home of sufficient comfort for his wife, Margaret Winslow Hickes, and her six young children.

Again this wife's maiden name attracts attention. His venture on the Fortune is made with John Winslow as a fellow passenger, suggesting, as a natural sequence, that they were blood relations sufficiently near for her to feel a drawing to the country where she had such a contingent of kin, occupying places of trust as each one presented himself to the notice of the powers in office.

DESCENT.

The "Barton Genealogy" is authority for the following, which will be found on pages 189-90:

1. John Hicks, of Tortunth, County Gloucester, England, a lineal descendant of Sir Ellis Hicks, who was knighted by Edward, the Black Prince, on the field of Poitiers, dying in 1492, left two sons, Thomas and Robert. The latter was father of Sir Michael Hicks, and of Baptist Hicks, Viscount Camperden. The elder son,

2. Thomas Hicks, of Tortunth, who died in 1565. By wife, Margaret Atwood, he had John, and

3. Baptist Hicks, of Tortunth, born about 1526, who married Mary, daughter of James Everard, Esq., by whom he had Baptist, who died unmarried, and

4. James Hicks, who married Phoebe, daughter, perhaps, of Rev. Ephraim Allyn, of Hertz. He had besides three daughters, John, Ephraim, who died young; Robert, Samuel, whose two sons, Timothy and Richard, emigrated to New England; Thomas, a linen draper of London, who followed his brother Robert to New England, and James, a clerk in the warehouse in London of his cousin, Sir Baptist Hicks.

5. Robert, born 1580, married (1) Elizabeth, daughter of John Morgan, by whom he had sons, Thomas and John, married (2) in 1610 Margaret Winslow, whose parentage has not been found, by whom he had six children.

CHILDREN BY FIRST WIFE.

Thomas, the son by first wife, Elizabeth Morgan, is already placed, as succeeding to his father's business, leaving John, the son who was destined for the profession of law, and entered college, but some call strong enough drew him to his father and the New England of so many hopes and fears.

He was known as being in Rhode Island in 1641, and from there, with the custom of intercourse between the two places, he removed to Newtown, L. I., but finally, with prescience of the honors that awaited him, he settled at Hempstead, and as early as 1664, his legal mind serving him in good stead, he was a justice under commission from Connecticut, the same year being also a deputy from Hempstead, and married (1) Hewdias Long. His second wife was Rachel (a very unusual name in early history), daughter of Josiah (or Thomas) Starr, of Scituate. He died June, 1672. The honors descended, for Thomas Hicks, his son, was a judge of Queens County, L. I.; married to increase the solid history of the day Mary, daughter of Richard Butler, of Stratford, Conn., and widow of John Washburn, whose family hold power of descent with any of the early settlers. There a Long Island name, for his second wife was Mary Doughty. Change of location altered the blood interest, and their son, Thomas Hicks, of Flushing, L. I., by marrying a daughter of Daniel Whitehead, took of the best as he was surrounded.

Jacob, brother of Thomas, so son of Thomas and Mary (Butler) Hicks, born about 1669, married Hannah Carpenter, and their son John, who married (1) Martha Smith, (2) Phoebe Powell, brings us where the story opens a large field, as he was father of Elias Hicks, the Quaker preacher, who was certainly "known and read of all men" in this section of the country.

ELIAS HICKS.

If modern times did not give precedent for youthful precocity, lacking not experience but years, the story of Elias Hicks would assume, to mature ears, something almost ludicrous.

Born March 19, 1748, at Hempstead, Queens County, L. I., son of John and Martha Hicks, a man described as of commanding person, powerful build and indomitable will, it is hard to realize that he began life when the youth of the present are little more than nursery darlings.

When only 13 years old (!) he was placed with one of his married brothers, and "being without parental restraint, and mixing with his gay associates, he lost much of his youthful innocence and was led from the path of true religion, learning to sing vain songs and to take delight in running horses."

The location may have brought the taste, Hempstead Plains as early as 1750 drawing large concourses of people to the horse races, and he, poor boy, following his own inclination, which later would have led him to the circus, vented his youthful enthusiasm on what he had, and others were enjoying.

In his twenty-second year he married Jemima Seaman, daughter of Jonathan of Jericho, and never having studied modern physical culture, he tells with pride that his wife was not of a very strong constitution; but she lived to be the mother of eleven children, four sons and seven daughters.

This strongly developed paternal instinct had a drawback in the fact that several of his children died in early youth, owing to this inherited maternal weakness, but bearing in mind his own early temptations, to which he succumbed, with much philosophy he states, "The weakness and bodily infirmity of our sons tended to keep them out of much in the way of the troubles and temptations of the world."

Too, Elias Hicks was spared the personal experience of much of the care of this large family and the sorrow attending the sickness preceding their passing from the home circle. The record of the amount of traveling he accomplished in pursuit of his ministerial duties seems incredible, and his power is told by results.

THE SECOND WIFE.

The children of Margaret Winslow Hicks, according to Davis in "Landmarks of Plymouth" (p. 133), were Elizabeth, Ephraim, Samuel, Lydia, Daniel and Phoebe.

1. Elizabeth, married John Dickarson, of Plymouth, and died before July 10, 1651.
2. Ephraim married September 13, 1649, Elizabeth, daughter of Pilgrim John Howland, and died three months after the marriage. His young widow married July 10, 1651, John Dickarson.
3. Samuel Hicks, married Lydia, daughter of Deacon John Doane, of Plymouth, and of Eastham (History of Scituate gives the year as 1645), and had, according to Davis, Samuel, born 1651, and Margaret, born 1654. (Gen. Notes of Barnstable Families, Vol. II., p. 272, gives a second daughter Dorcas, born February 14, 1652.) History of Scituate, says this Samuel (son of Robert), was a deputy from Nanset, (Eastham), 1647-8. He lived at Barnstable, Mass., until 1670, then removed to Yarmouth, and finally to Dartmouth, Mass.
4. Lydia Hicks, married after 1627, Edward Bangs, of Plymouth, her fellow passenger on the Ann, 1623, and had a large family.
5. Daniel Hicks, of Scituate, Mass., married Elizabeth Hanmore, September 19, 1657, so says the Colonial Records, and Davis also, but Savage gives as record that he married September, 1659, Rebecca, daughter of John Hanmur.
6. Phoebe Hicks, married 1635, George Watson, of Plymouth, born about 1602, son of Robert Watson, of Plymouth.

ROBERT HICKS.

The first list of Freemen in the records of Massachusetts is under date of 1633. Here is found Robert Hicks, and by virtue of this position he became one of the General Court, who chose the officers of the government and made the laws. Mindful of the needs of the colony, he left a "cow calf to the town of Plymouth." Whether he ever saw Scituate, or not, he surely owned land there, the colony record giving that "in 1662, Margaret, his widow, confirms a sale of 50 acres on the North river, sold by her husband in his life-time to Elnathan, youngest of the sons of President Chauncey."

Robert Hicks, properly of the Pilgrim party, coming out on the Fortune, died March 24, 1647, leaving a descent which covers many States, and embraces the peculiarities of religious belief, as exemplified by the Hicksite Quakers.

Authorities: "Dean's History of Scituate," Davis's "Landmarks of Plymouth," Savage, "Barton Genealogy," "History of Barnstable," "Long Island Genealogies," by Bunker; "Samuel Bonas's Journal," "Life of Elias Hicks."

ROBERT HICKS OF THE FORTUNE.

The corrections and interrogatories for this article have come to me from different sources, so I will merely state them as received, hoping thereby to draw out other history, or at least to set matters right.

Mrs. Charles N. Alden writes: "I want to correct one statement. Lydia Hicks, who married Edward Bangs, only had one child, John Bangs. She died before 1651. Her son married, but left no children.

"Edward Bangs married, second, Rebecca —— (?), who was the mother of his other children. What proof is there that Thomas was son of Robert?

"In 1639 Mr. Hicks, of Plymouth, styled 'planter,' sold to his 'eldest son,' Samuel Hicks, etc. There was a Zachariah Hicks, of Cambridge, before 1652, and it has been claimed that Robert came first and later Zachariah and Thomas followed (brothers or relatives). Zachariah stayed in Cambridge. Thomas found his way to Long Island. The Hicks family, of Rhode Island, Tiverton, came from Thomas (3), Samuel (2), Robert (1). References, Bangs's Genealogy, History of Cambridge, N .Y.; Paige and Austin's Gen. Dict. of R. I."

Another correspondent writes: "I have a record giving date of marriage of Lydia Hicks to Edward Bangs, 1636. Their daughter, Lydia Bangs, born in 1642, married Benjamin Higgins December 24, 1661. I have also a record of the births and marriages through the Higgins line from Lydia Hicks and Lydia Bangs to the present generation."

Again, a very complete statement comes from a descendant, who says: "You make Daniel Hicks, who married Rebecca Hanmer, a son of Robert Hicks by his second wife. In the inclosed pedigree of Mr. Austin, of Providence, he gives Daniel, son of Thomas and Margaret (West) Hicks. I sent this pedigree to Mr. Hicks, of Long Island, who made the researches in England, and he confirmed it in every particular."

I copy as carefully as possible this line of descent:

Thomas Hicks (1), died 1653, Scituate, Mass. He was brother of Robert Hicks, who had lived in Southwark (London), Eng., but who came to Plymouth in 1624. Thomas in his will, January 10, 1653, mentions wife Margaret, and sons Zachariah, Daniel and Samuel. Married Margaret; died 1666.

I. Children—Zachariah Hicks (2), born 1628; died August 5, 1702; married October 28, 1652, Elizabeth Gills, born 1636; died April 28, 1654; daughter of John Gills, Cambridge, Mass.

Children—Elizabeth 3, born April 28, 1654; Zachariah 3, born September 28, 1657; John 3, born April, 1660; Joseph 3, born 1662; Thomas 3, born July 3, 1664; Hannah 3, born March 4, 1666; John 3.

II. Daniel Hicks (2), died 1694; Swanzey, Mass. Married September, 1659, Rebecca Hanmer.

I. Children—Daniel Hicks (3), born 1660; died March 21, 1746; Swanzey, Mass. Married February 11, 1695, Sarah Edmonds, born February 17, 1678.

Children—Sarah 4, born May 30, 1700; Joseph 4, born October 8, 1702; Hannah 4, born April 11, 1705; Isaac 4, born May 11, 1708; Benjamin 4, December 1, 1711.

II. Thomas Hicks (3), Swanzey, Mass. Married Abigail ——.

Children—Martha 4, born January 26, 1707; Mary 4, born July 15, 1709; Michael 4, born June 29, 1713; John 4, born April 6, 1716; Thomas 4, born February 19, 1719.

III. Ephraim Hicks (3), Rehoboth, Mass. Married 1st ——; married 2d, September 20, 1712, Hannah Mills. In 1717 he deeded fifty acres to son Ephraim, and to son John fifty acres more.

Children—Ephraim (4), married February 18, 1708, Sarah Kingsley, who died October, 1727. Perhaps he had a second wife, Eunice, who died February 25, 1749;

1, John (5), born March 12, 1712; 2, Ephraim (5), born March 28, 1714; 3, Barnard (5), born April 11, 1719; 4, Alitha (5), born February 18, 1724.

II.—John Hicks (4), Rehoboth, Mass., married September 16, 1714, Priscilla Wheaten. 1, Mary (5), born October 11, 1716; 2, William (5), born October 11, 1716; 3, Elizabeth (5), born November 5, 1718.

III.—Samuel Hicks* (4), born 1730, Rehoboth, Mass., married September 13, 1713, Mary Rainzey. Nathaniel, 5; Lydia, 5; Jane, 5; Mary, 5; Experience, 5.

IV.—James Hicks* (4), born 1730, Rehoboth, Mass., married October 22, 1713, Mary Wells. Hezekiah, 5; James, 5; Mary, 5; Freelove, 5; Lois, 5.

III.—Samuel Hicks (2), married September 27, 1665, Dorchester, Mass., Hannah Evans.

*These two were probably also sons of Ephraim.

From above memoranda (culled from Rehoboth and Swanzey town records, probate records, Bristol Co., etc.,) it will be seen that Thomas Hicks (1) had a son Daniel (2) who went to Swanzey, and that Daniel (2) had a son Daniel (3), Thos. (3) and Ephraim (3). The first two of said sons settling at Swanzey, while Ephraim (3) went to Rehoboth, an adjoining town. The said Ephraim (3) had a son Ephraim (4), who had a son John (5), born March 12, 1712. This John is the right generation for your John.

Thanks to Hon. Daniel Cleveland, of San Diego, president of the Sons of the American Revolution of Southern California, the record in regard to the English home of the Hicks family is added:

1. There is a parish of Tortworth, County Gloucester, Eng., which is thus described in "Magna Britannica," Vol. II., page 784, as follows: "Tortworth, which stands on the south side of it (the Avon), a parish of eight miles in compass, consisting of pasture, arable, wood grounds and large commons."

2. In the "Paine Records," by Dr. Henry D. Paine, Vol. II., pp. 156, 172, and in the "New England History and Gen. Reg.," Vol. XXII., pp. 60-4, the English residence of early generations of the Hicks family is given as Tortworth, County Gloucester.

It may be stated that there is no mention of the Hicks family in connection with Tortworth in the "Magna Britannica."

Sir Baptist Hicks, of the third generation before Robert Hicks, is mentioned as having been created a baronet by James I., and afterward Viscount Camden, and as being the owner of Camden Manor in Gloucester (Vol. II., p. 803).

GEORGE MORTON OF THE ANN.

The Mortons can look backward, place them where you may, not anxious to assert as to their emigrant ancestor, laudable though their pride in him is, but willing to count for themselves, having taken the honor of their ancestry into their own hands, acting well in the living present.

They belong to "the forefathers, who," as President Dwight says, "were inferior to no body of men whose names are recorded in history during the last 1,700 years."

There may be other Mortons in the field, but with them there is absolutely nothing to do, only as passengers in the forefather ships, which reached America by 1623, has the name any place with us.

FRANCIS COOKE AND GEORGE MORTON.

Between Francis Cooke, the Pilgrim from Bawtry, and George Morton, passenger on the Ann, the first of the name to found a family in America, who was born, as is claimed, in Yorkshire, England, about 1585, and is believed without doubt to be of the ancient family of Morton, there is great similarity of history.

Both were of Roman Catholic families, won over to the Separatist movement by the strong pressure of religious conviction which spread along the line of the Great Northern road leading from London to Scotland. In the hands of men of great power and persuasion it is not at all wonderful that they renounced the religion of their inheritance and "fell into the ranks of the Protestant Puritans," or, rather, to better define the start, the Pilgrims who, guided by Brewster and Bradford, led them to the Low Countries, and thence to the Mecca of these people, where they could pour out their hearts in praise, prayer and song, according as it proved, in the Plymouth Colony, to their individual convictions and needs.

This faith was strong and dear to them, continuing through all their wanderings, privations and sorrows until they turned their faces toward the New Jerusalem and joined the "choir invisible."

SUGGESTIONS.

It is poor history to rely wholly upon "suggestions," but they often prove great powers as clues, and one takes naturally to this thought as furnished by Hunter in his "Founders of New Plymouth," that the George Morton hitherto accounted for in the family of Anthony Morton, of Bawtry, one of the historical families of England, was one George Morton, the Pilgrim on the Ann.

Great possibilities follow this location. The surroundings fit exactly into the historical mosaic, which, if absolutely proven, must include many other families. The story is old, indeed, as it is known that at "Harworth, near Bawtry, Yorkshire, on the edge of Nottinghamshire, Robert Morton, Esq., founded before 1361 a hospital for an ecclesiastical master and certain poor, which is still in existence and in the gift of the Archbishop of York."

EVIDENCE.

Of one item in the way of data all are sure, as the Leyden records announce with the positive assertion of the history that can be known and read of all men, that "George Morton, of York, England, accompanied by Thomas Morton, his brother (though I have been told he was proved not to be a brother), and Roger Wilson, his acquaintance; with Juliana Carpenter, maid, from Bath, England, accompanied by Alexander Carpenter, her father, and Alice Carpenter, her sister, and Anna Robinson, her acquaintance."

"The banns published 6-16 July, 1612.
"The marriage took place 23-2 July, 1612."

INCREASED HISTORY.

All of this makes large family history, the interweavings of kin explaining the actions of each, giving the text for a start in searching locations for other names. The claim made by historians that blood relation dies out in two hundred years had no power in Pilgrim days, its constant renewal perpetuating the strain.

This accounts for inherited characteristics, the reproduction of the traits of the old Pilgrims, in some instances the strong physical resemblance seeming almost to be a freak of nature.

MORTON POWER.

Everything points to George Morton's efficiency as well in England as Leyden, a master spirit, needed in both places, who, though "he much desired to embark with the colonists," remained behind the better to arrange matters for their benefit.

As it is claimed for Robinson that his stay in Leyden was to promote emigration, the same reason may have maintained with Morton. At all events, he was agent for sect in London, and it is historical that he "acted as financial agent in London for Plymouth Colony."

Goodwin, in his "Plymouth Republic," states, "Among the merchants and traders, are not unlikely to have been John Carver, Edward Southworth and George Morton."

MOUNT'S RELATION.

"Mount's Relation," so long the treasure trove of early history, is the subject of long argument to prove its place as to the person designated as its author or compiler by the intitials under which the book was published.

Whichever side one leans to, it all resolves itself when rendering a verdict into the belief that William Bradford, Governor of New Plymouth, sent the manuscript to his friend, George Morton. The vessel which carried out this precious history was freighted with merchandise in payment of the colony's debt to the Adventurers.

The pirates roaming the broad seas, seeking for prey, had no hesitation in seizing the little all of the poor Pilgrims, earned by the "sweat of their brow" and self-sacrifice of a heroic nature. The manuscript, from lack of value to themselves, perhaps a little awakened humanity, was forwarded to its destination, which was George Morton.

Young in his "Chronicles of the Pilgrims" (page 175) calls attention to Edward Winslow's ending of his preface, where he says "some faults have escaped because I could not attend on the Press," then speaking of Mount's Relation, he writes: "It was sent over to George Morton, who, not being in London, put it into the hands of one of the Merchant Adventurers, who got it printed."

Something must be given the public as an earnest of the success of this venture, historical correctness not being a requisite.

It is not surprising that with the penmanship of that day mistakes should be made by inexperienced printers in deciphering the manuscript, and dear to our hearts as Bradford's History is, with the added sentiment of our recent possession of the original papers, can it not be possible that some errors may have crept in there with the printing.

It would emphatically be repeating history to tell that George Morton came over in the Ann in 1623, accompanied by his wife and five children, the last, the infant Ephraim, born on shipboard.

From this "man without a country" descends a large proportion of those bearing the name.

This ship, the poetry of the expedition, leaving home with the knowledge that all if not as glowing as their fancy painted it before the first terrible sickness, still enough was attractive to make the coming out desirable.

Two of their number at least joined the expedition as the result of that very sickness, profiting, as so many did at that time, by the will of Providence, which, in His dispensations, had given them a place for their new life in the colonies.

THEIR RIGID LIFE.

The personal griefs of the Pilgrims were cast aside by the grim necessity of the occasion, the glamour spread around their lives by poets and authors, their own descendants, with the enlarged sentiment which follows tradition, must be read with the remembrance there was only a slight foundation in fact in it all.

It takes away from the desire to trace one's ancestry, as many deem possible, back to the great "gardener Adam," to read in Mr. Benjamin Kidd's "Social Evolution" (277), as given by Byington, in his "Puritan in England and New England," that "only five out of five hundred of the oldest aristocratic families in England, at the present time, can trace direct descent through the male line to the fifteenth century." When making such an attempt, one would do well to be of Dutch nationality, the mixing of the spelling and suffixes would allow of belief to even those not wholly ignorant.

In those Pilgrim days family ties were required, women in the minority; they married, of course; it was their only pastime; the father need fear no opposition, because, after the maner of European nations, he received the almost unknown suitor, and, without thought of any will on the maiden's part, gave or withheld consent.

Surely little Ephraim was the gainer by his place of birth, scoring health as against the requirments of those early customs, when a child must be brought from its comfortless home to the unnamed church for baptism before it was three days old!

MORTON PRIDE.

The Mortons have guarded well their pride, by making their collateral relations worthy of the name, deepening the feeling with which they go back, yet how sad to think of George Morton cut off in the strength of his early manhood, "June anno, 1624," with so much achieved for the time allowed him, yet never to know that Nathaniel, the son, only 12 years old when they reached the new world, was to make himself from his personal participation in events a name among the highest, the potentates of the land.

Secretary to the colony from 1645 to 1685, and author of the memorial, which has so far as history is concerned the value of reaching years beyond Bradford.

His six children were daughters, so none bearing the name is lineal descent from him.

Biblically, he had reached the time allotted man "by reason of strength," but his seventy-two years were so well spent, all of manhood with his early start in the service of his country, that the loss was too personal to connect time with him as for other men.

THE CHILDREN.

This Nathaniel Morton, the oldest son of George Morton, the ancestor, was born at Leyden, 1613, though Savage says England; died at Plymouth, Mass., June 29, 1685; married the year he became freeman (1635) Lydia Cooper. She lived long enough to be the mother of his children, and leave him a widower September 23, 1673, though not for long, eight short months after he marrying Ann, widow of Richard Templar, of Charleston, Mass., who, as he died June 29, 1685, and she survived him until December 26, 1690, gave her a few years to be widow of, as Savage calls him, the "dignitary."

Then Patience, born at Leyden, 1615 (?), died at Plymouth, 1691, and, to guard the family position, married, in 1633, John Faunce, of whim it will, as is just, be a pleasure to write.

John Morton, the second son, was born at Leyden, 1616-17; died at Middleboro, Mass., 1673, having married about 1648-9 Lettice or Letys.

Sarah Morton, born at Leyden, 1617-18, married George Bonum, and died at Plymouth, 1694.

Last, Ephraim, born on the Ann, 1623, who died at Plymouth, 1693, having had two wives—Ann Cooper, whom he married in 1644, and in 1692 took a second wife in the person of Mrs. Mary Harlowe, widow of William Harlowe and daughter of Robert Shelly, of Scituate, Mass.

Lieut. Ephraim Morton has a story of his own to tell, and, as I have a point in history I wish to make, will give a line of descent from him in hope the connection may be authenticated by absolute records. His freemanship came on June 7, 1648, and the better to emphasize the colony's need of his services, the same day he was chosen by the General Court constable of Plymouth.

Every office came to Lieut. Ephraim Morton. In 1654 he was one of the Grand Inquest; in 1657 was elected a representative to the General Court of Plymouth, of which he was a member twenty-eight years, and when, by King William's charter in 1691-92, Plymouth colony was merged into that of Massachusetts, Lieut. Morton was chosen one of the first representatives to the Massachusetts General Court.

FURTHER HONORS.

For nearly a quarter of a century he was the head of the Board of Selectmen of Plymouth Military Company, and in 1671 was chosen a member of the Council of War, in which he was of "much service" many years, including King Philip's war, and in March, 1677, owing to the great distress consequent upon the war, was appointed one of a committee of those to distribute to the people of Scituate "the money contribpted by divers Christians in Ireland, and for the relief of those who suffered during the war."

Those old Pilgrims may have been behind in rotation in office, but they verified the saying of the exception proving the rule,

where Ephraim Morton was concerned. His descendants receive from him the record which makes them welcome to most of the present organizations who are placing their roots deep in the history of the past.

Still this was not all; strong as Ephraim Morton was in civil and military affairs, he moral nature had no narrowing or starving from disuse, the six days of labor giving him the seventh, when he could be an example as deacon of the Church of Plymouth, his own son, George, following in his footsteps, and becoming his successor in office.

This same George Morton, born in 1645, married, December 22, 1664, Joanna, daughter of Ephraim Kempton, and died October 7, 1693.

Then, to increase the military claim, Mannaseth, their son, married Mary Taber daughter of Capt. Thomas Taber, and Mary Thomson, daughter of Lieut. Thomson, and granddaughter of Francis Cooke, the Pilgrim on the Mayflower.

Here records place the people without a doubt. Capt. Thomas Taber, with a long look ahead, names his daughter as Mary Morton in his will, and Mannaseth Morton to accentuate, leaves property to his wife, Mary, and sons Taber, etc.

This very Taber Morton, born March 3, 1709, was married in Nantucket, 1732-3, by John Coffin, justice of the peace, to Lucy Burgess (who is she?), and their son Reuben, born November 1, 1747, married Mary, daughter of Capt. John Worth, and, sad to say, followed the fate of many of that and previous dates, by being drowned while crossing a river (Hudson) on the ice, December 27, 1813.

THE CLAIM.

Here comes the point I desire to make—an historical connection of the grandson of this Reuben Morton, through his daughter Sarah, named Washington Morton (his surname of no consequence, but he was of the same family of Mortons as Gen. Jacob Morton, who was son of the patriot John Morton, one of the "Committee of Safety" pledged to defend their country at all hazards.)

A copy of John Morton's will is before me, wholly a family matter, providing with loving care for his wife and children, but giving no possible history of himself antecedent to this last testament, which was admitted to probate June 11, 1784.

One sentence places his sons and trusted friends:

"Item—I hereby nominate, constitute and appoint my said wife, Mary Sophia, during her widowhood, and my sons Jacob, John and James Washington and my friends, Henry Remsen and Elias Boudinot, Esquires, to be the executors of this my last will and testament, etc."

"Witnessed by John Reed, Robert Morris and Robert Boggs."

The other son, George Clark, and daughters Margaret and Elizabeth Susannah, are carefully provided for as to their education and future maintenance.

RELATION.

The kinship between these two branches which was known and acted upon, I had from the widow of this Washington Morton, whose lineage I have given, but, having no interest at the time, made no effort to place it in its relation to the George Morton who came in the Ann.

Knowing the circumstances, I am sure of the blood relation, and have brought the subject forward with the hope that from the proving other history, that seems exactly in line, should be developed.

Secretary Nathaniel Morton had, without discussion, his place. Lieut. Ephraim made his own right to honor. The Faunces and Thomsons can never be ignored. Perez Morton, Attorney-General of Massachusetts (1810-32), and another of the seventh generation; Marcus Morton, an eminent jurist in 1840 and 1843, Governor of Massachusetts, and his son Marcus, Chief Justice of the Supreme Court, on whose bench his father did such long and honorable service, come to us through Ephraim.

Then from John, son of George, our living ex-Governor, Levi P. Morton, and now it remains to be seen whether added strength of family claim can be authenticated and give us President Henry Morton, of Stevens Institute.

NATIONALITY.

The family of John Morton, of the "Committee of Safety," announce themselves as of Irish descent. This nationality, I am told, the Rev. Mr. Griffis claims for George Morton, of the Ann. I leave it with him to explain where this comes in, but if so, can readily understand the possibility of some of the Yorkshire Mortons going to Ireland in government capacity, and from choice remaining there. This was true of Gen. Edward Whalley on duty in Dublin under military orders.

GEORGE MORTON'S WIDOW.

Juliana Carpenter Morton, thus early left a widow, made strong step relations for the family by marrying Manasseh Kempton, Esq., a member of the first, and other assemblies of the colony, one of the "old comers." Her home in this country continued with kin and the friends she loved for many years, and she died at Plymouth, February 18, 1665, in the 81st year of her age.

THOMAS MORTON.

Thomas Morton identified himself with the family by witnessing his brothers's marriage at Leyden, but there were many times, no doubt, when George Morton would willingly have dispensed with this proclamation of relationship.

What Thomas Morton omitted doing was simply for want of thought, no intention of neglect.

There is no escaping Thomas Morton, of Merry Mount; he meant to show himself, and did, antagonizing everybody, and yet considering the land he came from, he was only continuing the sports in part to which he had been accustomed, only he was not with people of his own inclination. They had left England to forget it. The soreness of the parting from their native land gave prejudice to everything, though no one can justly admit that his career was a safe one for the colonies.

People who have no regard for the opinion of others are always a failure. Their utter selfishness is only forgiven when they are in power, or with the wisdom of mature years they see the error of their ways and make atonement. There was no room for people of his tendencies, where every talent was used to the injury of the struggling people, working always for the common good.

The arms necessary for protection, too precious for hunting, by him put in the hands of the Indians, became weapons of destruction, the red man, made desperate by liberal potations of the fire water he kept ready for his own purposes.

HIS VIEW OF THE CASE.

Accredited authority to him was a joke, but he was overcome by numbers, the majority report was against him, his room was indeed better than his company from every point of view, so, under marching orders, he returned to England, there to pose as a martyr, and having the required "pull," his report was accepted.

The return to America was owing to Isaac Allerton, but the natural man, with his inheritance from Adam, asserted itself, and his evil ways coming to the front, be on his own sweet will intent went too far, was brought to trial, and sentenced "to be set in the bilboes, and afterward sent prisoner to England."

It seems ironical to recall that his goods were sold to pay expenses, but justice to burn his house in the presence of the Indians he had wronged by his example.

Thomas Morton lived out of date. His wrong career was not over, and though he unjustly occupied places of trust, he worked against the interests of the colonies to an alarming extent, while outwardly seeming to have retired to the peaceful employment of writing for the press, his "New England Canaan," which was published at Amsterdam in 1637.

Though banished, there was no annihilation for Thomas Morton, and in 1643 he returned to the colonies in the new capacity of agent to Sir Alexander Rigby, "ostensibly to superintend his affairs in America."

Soon, however, it was evident the same old Adam remained, and in the clutches of the law "he was imprisoned a year for the defamation of the colony in his 'New Canaan,' but after sundry findings he was allowed to settle at Agamentius, Me., where he died in 1646."

If Thomas Morton felt unjustly dealt with, that as a free American citizen he could work out his salvation his own way, he certainly kissed the hand that smote him, returning to the country where the rod for him was always ready, and when the period for the calming of man's turbulent passions came, closed his days under the protecting arms of this government.

Authorities: "Goodwin's Plymouth Republic," "Bradford's History," "Morton Memoranda," "Mount's Relation," "Davis's Additional History of Plymouth," Capt. Charles Morton's (U. S. A.) manuscript, family papers, "Young's Chronicles."

WILLS OF
JOHN HOPKINS, PILGRIM FRANCIS COOKE AND JOHN COOKE.

It is a great pleasure to give three very desirable wills, those of John Hopkins, of Hartford; Francis Cooke, of the Mayflower, and his son John.

The first, through the courtesy of Mr. Goodwin Brown, of Albany, N. Y.:

That of Francis Cooke, being sent to me, I feel that I have the right to give it to the public. The one of John Cooke came directly from Mrs. Henry C. (H. Ruth) Cooke, and, while I cannot claim for her its composition, surely the unearthing of it belongs to her for her persistency in the search.

State of Connecticut, office of Secretary of State, Particular Court, Vol. II., Probate Records.

I John Hopkins off Hartford being through the beseting hand of God upon my sick bed and not knowing how soon the Lord may put an end to this my fraille life Being now in perfect memory for the preventing of all differences and the setting of things in a peasable mind after my decease do make this my last will and testament & doe dispose of my estate as in manner following

Imprimis I make and ordaine my loving wife Jane Hopkins my soul execuxeris of my whole estate movable and immovable out of which my will is that my Saide wife shall pay all the debts which I truly owe to any person at the time of my deasense also my will is that my said wife shall pay unto Daughter Bethiah Hopkins the sum of thirty pounds when she shall atain the adg off eighteen years if she shall live thereunto, and my will allso is that the onne half of all my lands and housings should bee my sonnes Stephen Hopkins to be injoyed by him and his heirs for ever when hee hath attained the adg of twenty and two years my meaning is that my Said Sonne shall not require my said wife to make good all such valuables as may befal my Said houses by fire or other wise before he hath attained the adg of twenty and two years But that my Said Sonn shall enjoy the one halfe of all my lands and housings as they shall be when he attains the adg of aforesaid and my will is further, that if my said wife Should marry again then the onne half of the estate that shee shall then possess the former portions being paid or discounted shall be paid in equall proportion to my said sonn and daughter or their heirers after the deasease of my aforesaid wife my will allso is that my said sonne and daughter remaine with and under the government of my said wife until they have attained their severall adges aforesaid, if then living and of my loving ffriends mr. John Cullick and James Ensing whome I desire to be overseers of this my last will and testament, my will allso is that if any of my said children shall depart their life before they have issue or have attained their aforesaid adges that too thirds of their portion now by me bequeathed shall fall to and be enjoyed by that child which survives and the other third part shall fall too and be enjoyed by said wife if then living, my will allso is that in case any difference should hapen between my said wife and children or any of them or between my sonne and daughter about the understanding of my true meaning in any part of this my will the issuing thereof shall be my foresaid overseers being best acquainted therewith.

Witness my hand to this my last will and testament this first day of January, 1648.
John Hopkins.

This was declared to be the last will and testament of John Hopkins aforesaid in the presence of
    Will Andrewss,
    John Cullick
    James Ensing.

This may certify that we under written have received full satisfaction of or beloved brother, Steven Hopkins, too good content for whatsoever is due unto us by the last will and testament of our honored father, John Hopkins, and we doe for us our heirs, executor and administrator, remit, release and quint our clayme to whatsoever is by the sayd will given and bequeathed too us too beloved brother, Steven Hopkins, aforesaid; the same from the day of the date hereof to be to him his heire and assigne forever as witness or hand 1679. Samuel Stocken.

Test, John Allyh, Sec., November 11, 1679.
(Signed)   Bethia Stocken.
State of Connecticut, ss.
Office of the Secretary.

I hereby certify that the foregoing is a true copy of record in this office.

In testimony whereof I have hereunto set my hand and affixed the seal of said State, at Hartford, this 4th day of September, A. D. 1897.
L. S.) Charles Phelps, Secretary.

WILL OF FRANCIS COOKE, PILGRIM ON THE MAYFLOWER.

"The last wil and testament of ffrancis Cooke, of Plymouth, late deceased, exhibited before the court held at Plymouth aforesaid, the first day of June, 1633, on the oath of Mr. John Aldin and Mr. John Howland."

"The last will and testament of ffrancis Cooke made this seventh of the tenth month, 1659.

"I being att ye present weake and Infeirm in body, yett in p'fect memory thro' mercy doe com't my Soul unto God that gave it, and my body to the earth which my will is should be intered in a decent and comely maner

"As for such goods and lands as I stand possessed of I doe will and bequeath as followeth:

"1. My will is that hester my dear and loveing wife shall have all my moveable goods and all my Cattle of all kinds, viz.: neat cattle, horse kind sheep and swine to be at her dispose.

"2. My will is that hester my wife shall have and occupy my lands, both upland and meddow lands which at present I possess during her life.

"3. I doe ordain and appoint my dear wife and my son John Cooke joynt executors of this my said will.
    "ffrancis Cooke.
"Witness—John Aldin, John Howland."

Copy of will of John Cooke, of Dartmouth, from Register of Probate of Bristol County, Massachusetts:

"The last wil and testament of John Cooke, of the Town of Dartmouth, in the county of Bristoll. I being weake of body, but sound and perfect memory, have disposed of my estate which God hath been pleased to bestow upon me in manner following; that is to say:

"In the first place, I give to my son-in-law, Arthur Hathaway, and his wife Sarah, my daughter, all my land in the point at or near the burying place in Dartmouth, the which I bought of John Russell, to them, their heiress and assignes forever, and also I give with my son-in-law, Stephen West, and his wife Mercey, my daughter, one full third part of a whole share of lands in the Township of Dartmouth, with all my housings and orchards thereunto belonging, with all the privileges and appur'es belonging to the same to them, their heiress and assignes forever, they to possess the same after the decease of my wife Sarah.

"Allso I give unto Jonathan Delano one-third part of a share of meadow called Freemen's Meadow, lying within the Township of Rochester, to him, his heiress and assignes forever.

"Allso I give to my grandson, Thomas Taber, my little island caled and known by the name of Ram Island, lying in Cushnat River, in Dartmouth, with one-third part of my share of meadow called the Freemen's Meadow, lyeing in the Township of Rochester, to him, his heiress and assignes forever, and I give to my said grandson my gun and sword; allso I give to my granddaughter, Hester Perry, one feather bed and bolster.

"All the rest, residue of estate, goods and chattels of what sort or kind so ever I give and bequeath to my loveing wife Sarah to use and dispose of the same as she shall see good, and I make my said wife sole executrix of this my last will and testament.

"In witness whereof, I, the said John Cook, have hereunto sett my hand and seal this ninth day of November, 1694. In the presence of
    "John Cooke. (Seal.)
"Aaron Savory, O, his mark.
"Thomas Taber."

"Memorandum, that on the 16th of April, 1696, then appeared Aaron Savory and Thomas Taber, both of Dartmouth, before John Saffin, Esq., Judge of Probate and Wills, etc., and made oath that they were present and did see John Cooke, late of Dartmouth, dec'd, signe, seall and publish this instrument to be his last will and testament, and yet he was of a disposeing mind when he did so to the best of their apprehensions. John Saffin."
John Cary, Register.

This entered, engrossed May the 8th. 1696, by Jno. Cary, December the 7th. 1696. A true inventory of the estate, goods, chattles of John Cooke, late of Dartmouth. deceased.

```
                                       L. S. D.
Impr.—All his housing and land at.200.00 00
His cattle of all sorts.............020.00 00
In silver money.....................025.00 00
His wearing apparel at..............007.10 00
Two beds and bedding at.............019.10 00
For pueter and tin vessels..........001.05 00
One warming pann....................000.12 00
Two Bibles and six other books......002.00 00
Two iron pots, one iron kettle and
    two old skillets................002.00 00
Five bushels of corn................000.15 00
For linnen, yarn and flax teere.....001.06 00
```

	L.	S.	D.
Half a dozen of spoons	000.	02	00
Two chains and plow irons with several other old iron tools at	001.	10	00
Due in debts	008.	00	00
One gun, a sword and powder and bullets	001.	10	00
One pare of andirons	001.	10	00
Two chests, one table and a settle	002.	00	00
For lumber of all sorts at	003.	00	00
	299.	19	00

Taken by us the day and year first above written.   Arthur Hathaway,
Thomas Taber.

April 10th, 1696, the widdow Sarah Cooke made oath to ye above written inventory. Before me,   Seth Pope,
Justice of Peace.

The above named Sarah Cooke being a very antient woman and unable to travile far, it was necessary that her deposition should be taken as above said to the truth of this inventory, the which I do alow and approve and doe hereby order it be recorded in the Register's Office, this 16th day of Aprill, 1696.

Jno. Saffin, Probae.

Jno. Cary, Registe.

Thus entered and engrossed May the 19th, 1696, by Jno. Cary, Registe.

Mrs. Cooke makes very strong arguments in regard to the will of John Cooke, and but for want of space, it would be well to give them in full. Still my own belief very generally is that when children whether sons or daughters are left out of wills, it is because they have for reasons considered good by the parents had the share of property and belongings they felt to be their due.

Finding the will of Hester Cooke would be a treasure indeed, for under the conditions of Francis Cooke's will she had in proportion to his estate much to leave.

At this very time an effort is being made at Fairhaven, Mass., to raise a monument to John Cooke, and to more clearly understand the matter, I will give the tale as told to me by the wife of Mr. Edward Anthony Jr., chairman of the committee to raise funds for the purpose—a matter they hope will appeal to his descendants:

"John Cooke came from Plymouth to this town (Fairhaven) in 1660, at the age of 55, and settled on a broad plot of land including all of Oxford and a mile or more to north of it. He was prominent in church matters and State, having been a deacon and preacher in one, and a representative in the General Court in the other, and was appointed by the colony as Chief Magistrate and General Agent in this part of the State, and at one time was appointed to treat with King Philip.

"He died in 1695, and was the first white man to settle in Fairhaven, and the last male survivor of the passengers on the Mayflower, and lies buried in Oxford village, the upper village of the town, with no monument to mark his grave."

AGAIN JOHN HOPKINS.

For this and many reasons I hail with delight an article recently sent me from the Rochester "Democrat and Chronicle" of March 15, 1898, read by Dr. A. Hopkins Strong, before the Rochester Historical Society, entitled the "Autobiography of Samuel Mills Hopkins," written by the author for his children.

The manuscript which was prepared just sixty-six years ago, has been in the possession of the family for fifty years, and has never been made public. Dr. Strong thought that it had not, till that evening, been read outside of the family.

The conjunction of the name of Strong with Hopkins has led me to hope that the pencil writing of Strong after Jane Hopkins's name, which I saw in the L. I. Historical Library, may prove as true as it seems natural, considering that John Hopkins was a shipmate of Elder Strong on his journey to America, with the Rev. Thomas Hooker, in 1633.

It is a delight to quote from Dr. A. Hopkins Strong's rendering of the autobiography, where he states "that Samuel Miles Hopkins, of Salem, Conn., born in 1772, and died in 1837, was inclined to trace his descent from Stephen Hopkins, who came over in the Mayflower. One link is somewhat hypothetical, and we know certainly only this, that the line can be made authentic as far back as John Hopkins, known as of Hartford.

"That this John Hopkins was the son of Stephen Hopkins, of the Mayflower, has been plausibly maintained, but it cannot be considered as absolutely proved."

The outgrowth of the meeting, the limited time only giving chance for little more than a synopsis of this valuable history, was the forming of a committee composed of Dr. Strong, Charles E. Fitch and George P. Humphrey, to confer with the family in regard to the publication of the manuscript.

No one of Hopkins blood could surely deny so natural a desire, and all descendants will watch eagerly for the publication of the history of their ancestors.

COOKE CORRECTION FROM MRS. CHAS. N. ALDEN.

In reading over your Mayflower book, I wish to call attention to John Cooke's family. It is claimed that John Cooke had more daughters than you give, and most of them, if not all, are proved by deeds of gift before his death.

To the two Tabers, Thomas and Philip, through Esther and Mary, Stephen West and Mercy, Arthur Hathaway and Sarah, ——— and Daniel Wilcox ——— and William Wood ——— and William Palmer. This information came out in the "Transcript," and was sharply criticised (I am inclined to think this material was contributed by Mrs. H. Ruth Cooke), especially by E. C. Leonard, of Dartmouth, Mass.

He was very accurate, and judged of John Cooke's family by his will, which only speaks of Mercy West, Esther Taber, the wife of Daniel Wilcox, and of Arthur Hathaway. (This will was published in The Mail and Express of March 26, 1898.)

Mr. Leonard went to Plymouth shortly after, and, finding these deeds, made acknowledgment of his mistake.

I feel reasonably sure of William Wood and his wife, but am inclined to think that William Palmer married, first, a ——— Paddock, and second, Susanna Hathaway, and that Susanna is granddaughter of John Cooke.

ADDITIONS AND CORRECTIONS.

THE MATE OF THE MAYFLOWER.

A correspondent sends me the following as received in response to an inquiry concerning Thomas Clark, the Pilgrim.

"In regard to Thomas Clarke, the Pilgrim, you are in error in supposing that he was mate of the Mayflower.

"The mate's name was John Clarke. He settled in Virginia and died there. Thomas first came to Plymouth in 1623, in the Anne, when he was but 18 years old, and it is absurd to imagine that he would have been mate of a vessel at the age of 15. He was born in 1605, not in 1599, as has been so often published. I have never believed that he was mate of the Mayflower, and recent investigations have proved the correctness of that belief beyond the shadow of a doubt.

"The statement in Deans's 'Scituate' that Thomas Clarke, of Scituate, was son or a grandson of Thomas, of Plymouth, has no foundation in fact. He is not mentioned in the will of the Pilgrim, nor in any document emanating from him. The names of the children of Thomas, of Scituate, do not, with one exception, correspond with the names of the children of the Pilgrim. See Johnson's 'Clarke Genealogy,' page 14.

"It is a matter of record that in 1664 Thomas Clarke made oath that he was about 59 years old, consequently he was born about 1605, and was 92, not 98, when he died. Hon. William T. Davis, author of 'Ancient Landmarks of Plymouth,' writes under date of June 14, 1897: 'The mate of the Mayflower was not Thomas Clarke, but was undoubtedly John Clarke.'

"Rev. W. W. Johnson, author of the 'Clarke Genealogy,' wrote to me under date of June 25, 1897: 'And now, my friend, I think that numerous Clarke descendants will have to abandon the idea that Thomas Clarke was the mate of the Mayflower.'"

JONATHAN BREWSTER, PASSENGER ON THE FORTUNE

To start this history well, I ask attention to the records and at the same time request all criticism, viewing it as a strong factor in history, also all records, wills, even traditions which will lead to searches, and oftentimes facts well authenticated.

Accepting Bradford as a reliable authority, I quote from him. In the list of passengers on the Mayflower he gives:

"Mr. William Brewster, Mary, his wife, with 2 sons, whose names were Love and Wrasling, and a boy was put to him called Richard More; and another of his brothers, The rest of his children were left behind and came over afterward." Bradford's History, page 447.

From the same history, page 450. At the close of the list of passengers there is a note: "These being about a hundred sowls, came over in the first ship; and began this work, which God of His goodness hath hitherto blessed; let His holy name have ye praise.

"And seeing it hath pleased him to give me to see 30 years completed since these beginnings; and that the great works of His providence are to be observed, I have thought it not unworthy my paines to take a view of the decreasing and increasing of these persons, and such changes as hath pased over them and theirs in these thirty years. It may be of some use to such as come after; but, however, I shall rest in my owne benefite.

"I will, therefore, take them in order as they lye," etc. (page 451). "Mr. Brewster lived to a very old age; about 80 years, he was when he dyed, having lived some 23 or 24 years here in ye countrie; and though his wife dyed long ago, yet she dyed aged. His son Wrastle died a young man married; his son Love lived till this year 1650, and dyed and left 4 children still living. His daughters which came over after him are dead, but have left sundry children alive; his eldst son is still living, and hath 9 or 10 children, one married who hath a child or 2."

Savage records "William Brewster as the earliest of distinguished Puritan laymen in England; came in the Mayflower, 1620, with his wife, two younger sons, the wife of the eldest, and her son William." The same author gives "Jonathan, Plymouth, eldest son of Elder Wm. Brewster, born at Scrooby, in County Notts, on the road to Doncaster, in Yorkshire, from which it is only twelve or thirteen miles distant, in a manor belonging to the Archbishop of York, under which his grandfather was tenant on long lease; had been instructed only by his glorious father either in his native land or the dozen years residence in Holland, where he was left by the Elder to take care of his two sisters, with his own family.

"Without his sisters he came in the Fortune, 1621; in June, 1636, was in command of the Plymouth trading house on Connecticut River, and gave notice to John Winthrop, Governor of the fort at Saybrook, in a letter in my possession of June 18, of the evil designs of the Pequots; removed to Duxbury, of which he was a representative, 1639, the earliest assembly of deputies in that colony; thence to New London before 1649; there was Selectman; died before September, 1659, having in September, 1656, projected to return to England with his family.

"By wife Lucretia he had William and Mary, both probably, but the first certainly, born in Holland; Benjamin, also Grace, Ruth, Hannah and perhaps Elizabeth, some of these born probably at New London."

FURTHER RECORDS.

Vol. I., New England Historical and Gen. Register, page 50, in an article on "The Passengers of the Mayflower, 1620," by Nathaniel Bradstreet Shurtleff, D. D., gives in the list of passengers:

William Brewster x, which means he brought his wife.

Mrs. Brewster (his wife), in italics, denoting she died before the division of cattle in 1627.

Love Brewster, son of William.

Wrestling Brewster, son of William.

Mrs. Lucretia Brewster, wife of Jonathan, the oldest son of Elder Brewster—William Brewster, son of Jonathan.

The division of land on May 22, 1627, gives Jonathan Brewster, Lucretia Brewster, William Brewster, Mary Brewster as having one share each.—Davis Landmarks page 40.

"Jonathan Brewster, one of those to whom land was granted as passenger on the Fortune."—Davis Landmarks.

This article is left as it is, seeming a debt of honor to the willing helpers, that every opportunity should be given the country at large to contribute record or interest people in solving the many vexed questions which have arisen in regard to this family. As I have said before, in the "Signers of the Mayflower Compact," I believe Elder William Brewster had children not yet accounted for, and the present opportunity, by calling attention to this, may result in bringing to light the whereabouts of their descendants.

Bradford, in his "History," says Jonathan Brewster had nine or ten children. Where are the records of them?

No one passes a Brewster ancestry lightly by, and, until proved, it is natural to believe there are many more aspirants for this honor than have yet been heard from.

In striving for so much that seems possible, it is hard to restrain conjecture which has assumed great proportions, and confine oneself to bare statistics.

But records carry positive weight, and I copy from an article on "The true date of the birth and death of Elder William Brewster," by Rev. Henry Morton Dexter, of Boston:

"Archives of Leyden,
"Registry of Affidavits.

"Record of declaration made before Magistrates of Leyden, June 25, 1609, in which William Brewster, Englishman, age 42 years, and Mary Brewster, his wife, age 40 years, and their son, Jonathan Brewster, age 16 years, declare that they have received some cloths which Bernard Rosse, Englishman, living in Amsterdam, had sent them. They resided at Leyden, in the Street St. Ursule.

"Elder William Brewster was near 'four score,' born 1566, died 1644, age 77 or 78."

So Jonathan Brewster, when he arrived in the Fortune in 1621, was 28 years old. This seems to verify Savage's statement that "he was left by the Elder in Holland to take care of his sisters, with his own family."

HIS MARRIAGE.

It is against all Pilgrim precedent that he should have attained his proven age without marrying. All the statements are to the effect that his wife, Lucretia, came with the Elder in the Mayflower, bringing William with her (for he had by wife Lucretia, William and Mary, both probably, but the first certainly, born in Holland; perhaps Mary).

Through all the histories of early times there is more or less omission and assertion concerning "William and Mary."

By some they are placed as children of the Elder. The idea is growing upon me that Jonathan Brewster married twice, and the wife known to the colonists being Lucretia, there was a confusion of names, and the first was made to bear the same as the second.

BREWSTER BOOK.

I have already written of the "Brewster Book" from the accounts furnished me by Mr. Joseph P. Beach, who enjoyed the perusal of a copy in the Boston Public Library which was made from the original by F. B. Perkins, in November, 1874. Fortune continues to follow my historical efforts, and I now have the added testimony of Mrs. Lucy Hall Greenlaw, of Cambridgeport, Mass., who writes me that she had the pleasure of making a copy from the original book itself.

Feeling a certain obligation to the General Society of Mayflower Descendants, she only sent me a synopsis of the manuscript, but says there is not a shadow of a doubt of its authenticity. (I ask close attention to the arguments in favor of this book, for I cannot see any one of them to be stronger than if used for the Old Hartford Bible owned by Mr. Cowles.)

"The internal evidence of the book shows clearly that the elder son, Jonathan, came into possession of it soon after his father's death; that at his death it passed on to his son Benjamin; from him, through his son Daniel to Daniel, Jr., who, dying childless, left it to his nephew, Nathan Freeman."

Mrs. Greenlaw is confirmed in her belief from having examined the original records in Connecticut of the localities where Jonathan Brewster's descendants lived, without finding any contradiction.

She acknowledges the inaccuracy of the Perkins copy in the Public Library, as he makes a mistake of five years in the marriage of Jonathan Brewster and Lucretia Oldham ("of Derby," as Mrs. Eva J. Hamilton, of Chicago, gives it to me).

OLDHAM'S BROTHER.

Long ago I found in "Goodwin's Plymouth Republic" (page 274) that Jonathan Brewster termed Oldham "brother," which naturally prepared me to accept the new find in the "Brewster Book."

The "Old Hartford Bible" has many claims to authenticity. This, too, comes into the Brewster family. Perhaps a comparison of the two would evolve some unexpected truths, which have needed the present enlightenment to make them evident.

Returning to Mrs. Greenlaw: "The extract from Campenella's 'De Monarchia Hispanica Discoveries,' which the first owner copied in a scholarly hand into the book, suggests to me that William Brewster may have had access to the original manuscript of that work in Holland, and that he copied the most interesting part to print in his own press. This suggestion is strengthened by the fact that the copy in the 'Brewster Book' differs from the first known edition published in Amsterdam in 1640, the year after its author's death. Brewster's inventory does not show a copy of Campenella's work among his books.

"Besides the autographs of Jonathan Brewster, Daniel Wetherell, Benjamin Brewster, Nathan Freeman and Cordilla Fitch, there is another striking proof of the authenticity of this old relic, and that is the record of four sales of books by its second owner to persons living near Jonathan Brewster, of which sales every title is found in William Brewster the Pilgrim's Inventory."

PURPOSE OF THIS ARTICLE.

To secure all possible records this article must work slowly, until public interest spreads and increases. The point of Jonathan's first marriage should be established, then William and Mary, as children of the first wife, would represent the family Jonathan was "left behind to take care of," and prepare the way for his marriage with Lucretia Oldham, one of "John Oldham's company of nine who came out in the Ann" (History of the town of Plymouth, by W. T. Davis), in 1623.

After the marriage the nine or ten children recorded by Bradford as Jonathan's in 1650, should be placed authentically.

Then, too, I have a lingering hope it can be proved that Elder Brewster had another daughter Elizabeth, not yet accounted for, which arises from the number of children so constantly attributed to the Elder, which were the cause of his "low estate," and the need for the help he received from his friends in England for his establishment as a printer, which with his professorship in the Leyden University gave him "better days." I was quite astonished one day while pondering over "these other children," to receive a letter from Mrs. Noel, of Tacoma, advancing this very idea, which has grown to a possibility with me.

Other families had children, "who came after." What was there to prevent Elizabeth remaining with her brother Edward in London and joining some party bound to the colonies?

The wish may be father to the thought, but it would settle a puzzle which I have not the temerity to endeavor the unraveling of. I trust I will be understood as making no assertion, simply advancing an idea that if proved would allow this Elizabeth to marry Rev. Samuel Fuller in 1654 or 1656, as his third child Samuel was born in 1659. An argument is advanced that this would be appropriate to Elizabeth, daughter of Jonathan, who Savage states was married in 1654. The other idea would enable Peter Bradley to continue as Jonathan's son-in-law.

LETTERS.

The Brewster descent being much sought after, naturally a great deal of material has come to me, the following letters kindly furnished by Mr. L. E. Fuller, at least, assist in the controversy:

"A letter I received from T. B. Drew, librarian of the Pilgrim Society, Plymouth, Mass., under date of April 26, 1897, states in regard to Rev. Dr. Samuel Fuller: 'One or two authorities have stated that he married Elizabeth, daughter of Jonathan Brewster.'

"The church records of Middleboro have it that his wife was a Brewster, and I know of no other Brewster she could have been but the daughter of Jonathan, yet I have never seen a record of it.

"Rev. George Stearns, pastor of First Congregational Church, of Middleboro, writes me under date of May 18, 1897, that the records of the church state that Rev. Samuel Fuller married Elizabeth Brewster and that she died at Plymton, November 4, 1713."

So much has been done for me by the "cheerful givers" Judge Charles N. Daniels, of the Windham County Probate Court, Willimantic, Conn., and Mr. C. H. Dimmick, the Town Clerk, that I feel they are my Brewster "find," and copy hopefully a very peculiar paper, which tells its own story as Mr. Dimmick has written it to me.

The following is a copy of a manuscript record, found in a volume of a genealogical character, compiled by Jonathan Clark, which I found filed among the records of this office. How it came to be placed here or by whom I have been unable to learn. I send it to you simply for what it may be worth, and not assuming any responsibility as to its accuracy.

It is as near as possible a verbatim copy.

"April 26, 27 and 28, 1852, I was in Hartford and got Dea. Allyn S. Stillman to bind this book, paid him twenty-five cents before it was in sheets and marked W for Windham, H for Hampton, records Nos. 1, 2, 3, etc. Sheets on one letter blank paper was added when bound, and filled in since by Jonathan Clark, of Hampton, aged the 28th, 78 years 7 months and 11 days. I was born on Friday, most noon, September 17, 1773.

"Hampton, February 8, Wednesday, 1854."

Having for five or six years past taken much pains and spent much time and considerable money in obtaining my genealogy, and believing I can obtain very little if any more, I begin this day to make the following records of them.

JONATHAN CLARK.

After giving the Clark genealogical line, he says, on page 519 of the volume above mentioned:

Brewster pedigree and families.

Elder William Brewster was born in N. part of England, 1560, educated at Cambridge, England, removed to Leyden, in Holland, in 1610 (on account of the persecution), where resided eleven years in pastoral charge of Rev. John Robinson; he and family left Delft Haven, in Holland, 22 July, 1620; two ships, the Speedwell and Mayflower, left Northampton, the Speedwell sprung a leak after sailing and the Speedwell leaked and they returned, sailed again, and Speedwell leaked and returned again on 6 September, 1620. The Mayflower set sail with 100 on board, anchored Cape Cod Harbor, 11 November or 21 December, new style, 1620.

Elder William Brewster's children were Freelove, Wrestling, Jonathan, Lavinia, Lucretia, Patience, Fear, William, Mary and Nathaniel.

Freelove B. married Sarah Collins May 15, 1634; their children were Nathaniel, William, Wrestling and Sarah.

Wrestling B.; children were Jonathan, John, Joseph and Nathaniel.

Jonathan Brewster, son of Elder William Brewster, had sons, James, Peleg, Jonah, Elijah and Jonathan. Peleg was born February, 1717, and his son, Dr. John, June 14, 1739, and when 21-4-22, was married to Mary Durkee, daughter of Captain and Abigail, November 6, 1760; she was born November 29, 1741, and was 18-9-7 when married. Dr. Brewster bought his acre lot (S. Capt. Harvey Fuller) March 2, 1761, of Nathaniel Hovey, Jr. Children:

Mary, born September 9, 1762.

William, born June 17, 1764; died January, 1789, aged 25 years 6 months and 17 days.

John, born May 31, 1766; deaf and dumb.

Augustus, born May 30, 1768; died January 30, 1789, aged 20 years and 8 months.

Royal, born July 17, 1770; died March, 1835, aged 64 years and 8 months.

Abel and Sophia, twins, born 1772; soon died.

Mary, wife of Dr. John, died June 4, 1785, aged 41 years 6 months and 5 days, and he married Ruth Avery, of Brooklyn, June 4, 1789; she was born January 13, 1754, and was 35 years 4 months and 21 days old when married; their children:

Elisha, born June 18, 1790; died June 20, 1790, two days old.

Wm. A., born December 10, 1791; died July 24, 1856, aged 65 years 7 months and 14 days, in Danielson.

Sophia, born April 9, 1795; died July 24, 1800, in Hampton, aged 5 years and 15 days.

Betsey Avery, born September 11, 1798; died October 17, 1838, aged 40 years 1 month and 6 days; married Joseph Prentiss.

Dr. John Brewster died August 18, 1823, aged 84 years 2 months and 4 days.

His wife Ruth died May, 1823, aged 69 years 5 months and 5 days.

Dr. Brewster studied with Dr. Barker, of Franklyn, Conn. He was born in Scotland, where his father Peleg lived X Jonathan b Jonathan was son of elder William, who came in Mayflower X. S. E. of Brunswick M. H. Peleg Brewster and his father Jonathan lived in what was called Brewster House, not far from the old Brunswick M. H. Peleg removed to Canterbury, a little north of Williams family, and near the old burying ground for that neighborhood. Dr. John Brewster was the first doctor that settled on Hampton Hill; there was a Dr. Walton who lived on the road; from Hezekiah Hammond's to where old Mr. John Fuller lived it was 20 or more rods south of Lester Holt's little barn.

Pedigree of Sir John Brewster's last wife, Ruth Avery:

Ephraim Avery, first settled minister in Brooklyn; was ordained 24 Sept., 1735; he married Deborah Lothrop 21 Sept., 1738; she was born 9 Jan'y, 1719. Their children:

John, b. 14 July, 1739; Ephraim and Samuel, twins, b. 10 April, 1741 (Samuel died 21 Dec., 1741); Samuel b. 7 Nov., 1742; Elisha, b. 3 Dec., 1744; Elizabeth, b. 5 Dec., 1746, (m. Rev. Aaron Putnam, Pomfret); Deborah, b. 6 July, 1751 (died 13 Feb., 1777, m. Dr. Baker, of Brooklyn). Septimus, b. 21 July, 1749 (died 10 Oct., 1754).

Ruth, b. January 13, 1754; married Dr. John Brewster.

Rev. Ephraim Avery, died 1754, aged 42; his widow then maried Lord Gardiner, so-called; owned east end Gardiner's Island, New London. After his death she married Gen. Putnam, and died during Revolutionary War at Rye, N. Y.

No one can doubt some of the impossibilities of this record; but there are familiar names that seem to argue for some ancestor all are anxious to place properly in this family.

OLD LETTERS.

Going through an accumulation of letters recently I came across one long forgotten, and quote it from its bearing upon a previous paper. Dr. D. E. Crocker, of Boston, who is compiling a genealogy of the Fuller family, writes me: "Tradition handed down from Ebenezer Fuller, the grandson of Rev. Samuel and Eliz. Brewster, a genealogist all through his long life of 94 years, gives Eliz. as daughter of Elder William. This statement was given me by a descendant who kept all the sayings of this revered ancestor in his heart." Further on he says that she died in Plymton, at the house of her eldest son, on land originally granted to Elder William Brewster.

This is very gratifying, and covers a long span of years, as Ebenezer Fuller naturally remembered his grandfather, and treasured his legends and traditions through his whole life.

RELICS

The union of Brewster and Fuller recalls the speech of Rev. W. L. Gage at the celebration of Forefathers' Day by the Congregational Club, reported by the Boston "Journal" January 4, 1888.

The Brewsters claim possession of a teapot brought over by Elder Brewster, which has been duplicated many times for descendants; the same of the Fullers, who have given or loaned theirs to the Plymouth collection. I, in common I suppose with others, in my ignorance, repudiated these heirlooms, basing the opinion on the fact of tea being unknown in England at that time.

It rests with Rev. Mr. Gage to set us right in this matter, and I give the account in his own words:

"THE OLD TEAPOTS.

"It must be remembered that the Pilgrims did not come here direct from England, but from Holland, where they had resided over twelve years. To give the old teapots a chance to assert their claim to authenticity, it is relevant to show that tea, and therefore, teapots, were in general use by the Hollanders at the time of the sojourn of the Pilgrims in that country."

"The World's Progress, by Geo. P. Putnam, 15th edition, article Tea." "First known in Europe, being brought from India by the Dutch in 1610. Brought into England by Lord Ossory and Lord Arlington from Holland, and being admired by persons of rank, it was imported from thence (Holland) till our East India Company took up the trade. (Anderson)."

According to this author the Puritans must have had nine or ten years experience in tea-drinking, before their departure in the Mayflower. The teapots exhibited in the collections may not be the veritable ones brought over, but there is no reason why these painstaking Pilgrims may not have given their careful habits to their Yankee descendants, and a few of the receptacles for the cup which cheers be left to gratify relic-lovers."

The indebtedness to friends continues, and that as much Brewster history may be made public as possible, I return to Elder William Brewster, that the Mayflower chest—I have had the pleasure of seeing in the Wadsworth Atheneum, the headquarters of the Connecticut Historical Society—may have the place it deserves as part of the Pilgrim's journey.

"It is a solid wooden box, five feet long, two feet wide and about three feet in depth. The original heavy lock and key and iron braces at the corners, fastened with rude hand and wrought nails, are intact.

"A paper pasted upon the lid records that it descended to the Elder's son, grandson, great-granddaughter, and finally, in 1842, to a Mr. Day. It was purchased by the Historical Society in 1850."—New York Herald, May 30, 1891.

STORY OF THE CHEST.

Mr. Joseph P. Beach, while in no possible way claiming that he can prove this chest to be a veritable possession of Elder Brewster, certainly opens a large field to search on.

He tells me that the "Brewster chest" is the one, or very like it, that he once sat upon as a boy when visiting his grandmother in the Day homestead, at West Springfield, Mass.

His mother frequently took him there, and his grandmother often spoke of his sister as being the only one entitled to the possession of that chest, because she bore the full name of its "Brewster" owner—his grandmother Day's name, "Drusilla Brewster," in whose family it had been for several generations.

About 1840 the late Benjamin H. Day (the original founder of the New York "Sun"), youngest child, and only son, of his mother, Mary (Ely) Day, induced her to remove from West Springfield, Mass., to New York City, where she was to reside with him.

It was soon after that that her West Springfield belongings were sold. Mr. Beach remembers the lamentations over the scattering of the relics and the loss of the Brewster chest, and while able to furnish every link as complete so far as Mrs. Mary (Ely) Day, of West Springfield, is concerned—as town records, probate records, church records, tombstones, family Bibles and traditions can make them—he does not feel that all that proves the chest as belonging to Elder Brewster.

THE LINE OF DESCENT FROM LOVE BREWSTER.

For once a line comes directly from Love Brewster, who married, May 15, 1634, Sarah Collier, and settled as an original proprietor in Brodgewater, Mass., in 1645.

Of his son, William Brewster, the Duxbury, Mass., record says: "He removed to Preston, Conn." And the Preston record says: "Benjn Bruster and Elizabeth Witter was maryed ye 18th October, 1713-14."

Their son, William Brewster, born in Preston, Conn., September 18, 1714; married, March 24, 1737, Damaris Gates, and after the birth of their first child in Preston he removed to Canterbury, Conn., where five other children were born, among them, according to the record:

"Drusilla, daughter of William and Damaris Brewster, was born November 3, 1745." Soon after this there is an entry on the Canterbury, Conn., records that "Damaris, ye wife of William Brewster, deceased September ye 7, 1751."

William Brewster, soon after the death of his first wife, moved to Windham, now Willimantic, Conn., where he married Esther Sabens, and had by her eight other children.

He was at one time in West Springfield, Mass., and from there went to Weybridge, Vt., where he probably died.

Drusilla Brewster married, October 12, 1766, William Ely, of West Springfield, Mass., and belonging to her marriage outfit was the "Brewster chest, or one like it."

Why should not her "bravery," much of it woven by her own hands, be carried to her new home in the chest of her forefathers? And though there were many such chests in Plymouth Colony and the surrounding regions, what reason could there be that only Elder Brewster's descendants should be denied this natural article of convenience and necessity?

TO CONTINUE THE LINE.

"Mary, daughter of William Ely and Drusilla Brewster, married, May 25, 1794, Henry Day, and in her possession was a 'Brewster chest,' so-called, which was, no doubt, sold by her son, the late Benjamin H. Day."

Whatever the value of the foregoing record, it surely establishes the ownership of a Brewster chest by Mrs. Mary (Ely) Day, a lineal descendant of Elder William Brewster, which became later on the property of her daughter, Drusilla Brewster.

It was handed down, and for one hundred and fifty years the family knew and spoke of it as the Brewster chest.

This may not authenticate it as the veritable chest upon which it is said the Compact was signed, but it goes a long way toward making all the kin desire it and revere the simple article as having passed from the hand of the great Elder to its present resting place.

All of this comes in the course of events. During the lifetime of the Elder, and for a generation or two after his death, the chest was of no importance, one of the household possessions taken as a matter of course. It was only after the passing away of loved ones, giving fond associations, the changes incident to marriage and new homes in other, perhaps faraway localities, that these homely articles of everyday life assumed any value, and even then were hardly relics, only a time-honored connection with by-gone days of the person's childhood and youth.

The desire of history would be fully satisfied if this chest could be proved to be the veritable chest that had such close personal connection with Elder Brewster and his home across the sea.

Jonathan Brewster, passenger on the Fortune, followed so closely upon the arrival of the Mayflower that the beginning of his history is that of many of the "old comers."

His individuality really asserts itself as he leaves them behind and journeys into what for the times were almost far countries, joining issue with other "Pilgrim" descendants, using that word as including many of Winthrop's fleet, who came after hearing the prospects from kin who had made the first start.

Jonathan Brewster received from the division of land May 22, 1627, the one share allotted by the records to himself, to Lucretia, his wife, and William and Mary (Davis, p. 40). Then he was one of those to whom land was granted as passenger on the Fortune.

Also recorded in the "old colony records from Duxbury as Anno, 1632, April 2, among the names of those who promised to remove their families to live in the towne in the winter time that they may better repair to the worship of God." (Davis, p. 121.)

Plymouth, the homestead of the colonies, could not brook to see those once gathered under its command seeking independent fortune, even in an adjacent town. Short flittings could be tolerated, but entire severance in residence and action could not be grasped, though the stalwarts of the colony were the seceders.

OTHER PLANS.

Whatever the drawing to other places, Jonathan Brewster remained long enough in Duxbury to be several times representative from that place.

Watching the history of these early people closely, it is easy to account for the many sectional probabilities of kinship the names of various locations suggest. Jonathan is seen as engaged in the coasting trade the head and front of the affair, master of the vessel, probably its owner, turning aside at will for trade with hitherto untraveled places on his route from Plymouth to Virginia.

Having social intercourse with the Dutch at New Netherlands, and the English representation in Virginia, who, however, were his acquaintances in the Old World.

In all this he was storing up knowledge for future use, becoming acquainted with the Pequot Harbor, as he entered the river to trade with the natives. Winning from them alike affection and good will, which for the benefit of both continued always, giving Jonathan Brewster the right of way, when others presumably as honest dealers failed of intercourse.

TRIALS.

Everything being opened to him, he lived too fast, attempted to guide in the civil government and still continue his own large enterprises, extending over various tracts or hard-to-travel land and water, until, sad to relate, in the spring of 1649, fate overtook him and he was overwhelmed with pecuniary disaster.

Mr. Williams, of Providence, gives this notice of his misfortune to Mr. Winthrop (who was afterward John, the Governor of Connecticut): "Sir (though Mr. Brewster write me not a word of it) yet, in private, I am bold to tell you that I hear it hath pleased God greatly to afflict him in the thorns of his life.

"He was intended for Virginia, his creditors in the Bay came to Portsmouth, and unhung his rudder, carried him to the Bay, where he was forced to make over house, land, cattle and part with all his chest. Oh, how sweet is a dry morsel, and an handful, with quietness from earth and Heaven."

(Mass. Hist. Coll., 2d series, Vol. IX., page 281.)

OPPORTUNITIES.

There were many reasons why Jonathan Brewster, but for his immersion in public affairs should have been prosperous, the laws of the times rendered protective by the needs of the people guarded the most minute interests.

In 1640, mindful of the future, it was "enacted that every family should sow at least one spoonful of English hempseed," and cultivate it in "husbandly manner," for a supply of seed the next year. Tobacco held a high estimate in the opinion of the rulers, its cultivation rendered easy from the rich bottom lands of the Connecticut, was encouraged by every means in their power.

A decree was issued "that whoever after September, 1641, 'drink' (smoke) any other tobacco but such as is, or shall be planted without these liberties, should suffer the heavy penalty of a fine of five shillings for every pound." (Bryant's Hist., Vol. II., page 27.)

THE INDIANS.

The Indians made their own position in connection with the laws by their atrocities, without doubt, yet it was hard to realize they were to be availed of to the utmost in time of need by the white man, taught for their benefit the use of firearms, as against the wild beasts, or other unfriendly tribes, and when a cause no longer existed come under stringent laws.

"It was a penal act after the Pequot War for any one to sell arms to the Indians, or even mend those in their possession."

ELDER BREWSTER.

Whatever the greed of need—and those were times when every little possession told in the household—the fears entertained by many that as Elder Brewster left no will there might be some trouble about the settling of the estate were groundless. Jonathan, the first born, with perhaps the feeling of the times for the heir apparent, offered no claim, "only desiring an equal division."

The "settlement was made harmoniously," everything guided by the good friends of the Elder, watchful that neither harm should come to the living, or disrespect to the dead.

Jonathan, by right of being the "first born," was given his father's arms and a two-year-old heifer; the only exception for Love being an allowance for the board of his nephew, Isaac Allerton, Jr., whom the Elder had left for him "to table." In all other respects they had share and share alike. (Goodwin, pp. 431-432.)

Reading along in the life of Jonathan Brewster, with his large family reverses, credulity and hopefulness, one could almost wish him, a boy when he arrived, to make his mark among the young people, singing the hymns taught them by Ainsworth, playing the pranks not even Pilgrim and Puritan watchfulness could repress or prevent. It is easy to imagine him dearly loved by all. Even the "four grave men for ruling elders, the three able and godly men for deacons, and one ancient widow for deaconess—who did them service many years, though she was sixty years of age when chosen"—would pass by his misdemeanors as too trivial for notice.

The "old deaconess," history tells us, was "honored in her place." Having secured a position of prominence in the congregation, she made a baton of her "lichen rod," waving it to and fro to the alarm of the children, who, in the awful silence of a Pilgrim service, give play to their imagination, conceived of many horrors as a punishment for the slightest deviation from the rules laid down for them by their elders.

Viewing this as a necessity to constitute being "an ornament," she certainly achieved her purpose, through devious paths, each one a terror to their youthful minds as she showed them the error of any way natural to their childish instincts.

But, as time passed on, and their young forms succumbed to disease, there was a compensating side to her character, as she approached the bed of pain, carrying comfort and delicate healing. The hands that sported the rod could bathe their fevered brows racked with pain, deftly easing all ills. Calling the maidens blessed with such gifts to her aid and with them guiding both young and old to health.

HONORS.

According to the interpretation of early days, calling Jonathan Brewster Mister was an honor—fully deserved by him, it is true, by inheritance, and his own personal claims. The restrictions laid upon the trade with the Indians did not include Jonathan Brewster, who, when others required a license to go up the river to buy corn, had such a monopoly that no other efforts met with success.

Being among those who "wrought at the Mill Dam" in 1651, may not have been an evidence of favoritism, but its usefulness entitled him to be recorded.

To this talent he surely owed that "when the grants were copied and registered with more precise bounds in a book by themselves it was referred to as 'the old book under Mr. Brewster.'"

Even as Town Clerk this duty if not the best of him, would have passed on to one more competent, perhaps have had his supervision, but the records were too important to be left to those not gifted with the pen.

The spice of variety was not wanting in Jonathan Brewster's life, often recorded as a member of the Grand Inquest, and one year after attaining his freemanship (1633), he was "appointed for laying out of highways Duxborrow side." Strong in his engineer instinct, "he was constantly employed by the court in the surveying and laying out of lands for the settlers."

Real estate acquisitions were constant, though they were undignifiedly granted for "meddowing."

THE FERRY.

Perhaps the crowning glory of position was his when, September 12, 1638, he entered into an agreement with Peter Meacock to keep a ferry on the North River, "for the transportation of men and cattle." "Brewster to provide a boat or skiff for the transportation of passengers, and another boat for horses and cattle, and Meacock to keep the ferry for three years and have half the profits, and to have from Brewster a deed of 10 acres of land near the ferry, and a servant provided to assist him in his labors, and any damage resulting from inefficient service at the ferry to be on Brewster's responsibility."

This one-sided agreement did not hold long, providing everything, including a bonus, was hardly the road to wealth, and Jonathan Brewster was "presented" for neglecting the ferry at North River, and, probably because this view of the case was evident to every one, was released. This experience, however, did not prevent his being again complained of and "fyned xxs to the colony and xs a piece to Mr. Groomes and Edward Weston if they will take yt."

No wonder impecuniosity came upon Jonathan Brewster. Still he had comfort in the living friendship of the younger Winthrop, the founder of New London, and in all probability this was the inducement for settling in the town called Pequot, now New London.

REV. NATHANIEL BREWSTER OF BROOKHAVEN, LONG ISLAND.

One of the many vexed questions in the history of the Brewsters is Nathaniel, the first graduate of Harvard College.

Although speculative history is very weak, I may be excused if I follow what has been my policy from the start, making the suggestions of certain possibilities, that other students may bear them in mind during their searches, and see if they can be absolutely authenticated.

Rev. Nathaniel Brewster's death took place December 18, 1690, at the age of 70. This would make the date of his birth 1620.

As a matter of history all recall that Bradford shows Jonathan Brewster as being left behind to look after his sisters and his own family.

One part of his charge he did not fulfill, as instead of remaining for the Ann to protect his young sisters, he came out suddenly in the Fortune. Very grave doubts are expressed by many as to the wife of Jonathan Brewster being on the Mayflower, even those most desirous of adding to their ancestry by her presence there, write her uncertain.

His son William, born in Holland, and "probably" Mary, seem to cause no discussion.

Here comes the possibility that Jonathan Brewster's first wife died at or near the time of the birth of Nathaniel, who was left behind, of course, to the care of others, mayhap Edward living in London, and was the deciding cause of Jonathan's coming to America in the Fortune.

LONG ISLAND HISTORY.

In looking carefully over Thompson's "History of Long Island," there is much to found an argument on in regard to Rev. Nathaniel Brewster. The first edition, published in 1839 (page 267), calls him the Elder's nephew, but between that time and the second edition, published in 1843, something must have called his attention to Nathaniel and made him waver in his opinion, as there he admits the probability of his being Jonathan's son, consequently the Elder's grandson.

It was very easy to misplace Nathaniel Brewster, in view of the varying circumstances surrounding his locating for any permanent residence. History records fully his return to Europe, and the fact of his receiving the degree of bachelor of divinity from the University of Dublin. His return to America could hardly be called a voluntary act, arising, as it did, from the "general ejection of the Protestant clergy in 1662."

His first "sitting down" was not on Long Island (Brookhaven) where his sons John, Timothy and Daniel had settled some years before. For three years he preached in various parts of New England, arriving on Long Island in 1665.

INHERITANCE.

To be a descendant of Jonathan Brewster in olden time carried much weight, and, though Rev. Nathaniel could not be the son of Lucretia Oldham (Brewster), who came over in the Ann, in 1623, he might be very fond and proud of her from the records she worthily secured.

The women of the past worked steadily, willingly in their appointed places, but the simple home duties did not deter them from preparation for every emergency that could arise.

Circumstances required them to be general experts, and I can recall no one more fully equipped for such needs than Lucretia Brewster, wife of Jonathan.

RELATIONS TO NATHANIEL.

No actions among these early people but had their meaning, were freely discussed without fear or favor, particularly in regard to religion. Mrs. Caulkins, in the "History of New London," gives, under date of July 10-65 1665):

"In towne meeting

"If it be your myndes yt Mr. James Rogers shall goe in the behalfe of the towne to Mr. Brewster to give him a call, and to know whether he will come to us to be our minister, and yt shall intercead to Mr. Pell first to be helpful to us herein, manifest it by lifting up your hands. Voted."

The person to whom this application was made was supposed to have been Rev. Nathaniel Brewster, of Brookhaven, L. I. No further allusion is made to him.

Many things point to this as a fact, and I will be pleased if, in reading future papers on this family, those interested will look at the various bearings on this subject.

While having a natural drawing to Jonathan Brewster, if his father, the Rev. Nathaniel had probably been trained independently of this parent, and, though glad to be with him on all occasions, still did not feel the same necessity as other children brought up more immediately under his eye.

Long Island was his home, the people his people; other ties had already been formed there, to which I will allude as time goes on, and the constant intercourse between the two places sufficed for the claims of kinship.

It would be very unwise to close writing of Rev. Nathaniel Brewster until opportunity has been given for either discussion or further information. His will has been published, and while it does not tell all one could wish, it is the best there is.

In the meanwhile I copy from the letter of a correspondent the following: "It seems that he (Gov. Bradford) made the statement in his history that Wrestling Brewster (son of the Elder), was supposed to have died young. In the appendix to his history, page 451, you will find: 'Some writers think the Governor mistaken, as there is a deed of land in Portsmouth, N. H., commencing in these words:

" ' "Portsmouth, 6th day of December, 1629, Joseph and Hannah Pendleton (convey to) Wrestling Brewster 80 acres of land, for £8, adjoining land belonging to said Wrestling." ' "

These lands have descended by inheritance in the Brewster family at Portsmouth, who claim to be descendants of this Wrestling Brewster, until within the memory of the present generation.

Love's early death placed him outside of many possibilities. He had led a good life, and dying a memory tinctured by the sorrow that he might not have been allowed a longer span in which to prove himself. His will in the N. E. Historical Reg., Vol. 34, page 284, is as follows:

Love Brewster (Duxbury).

Will dated October 1, 1650, and exhibited at Court March 4, 1651. To children Nathaniel, the heir apparent, the estate in Duxbury; William and Wrestling and Sarah, and to his three sons jointly, all such land as is of right due to me by purchase, and first coming into the lands which is in the yeare 1620.

His wife executrix. Witnessed by Myles Standish.

Inventory (including books to the number of 30 volumes), taken January 31, 1651, by William Collier and Capt. Standish. Amount £97.7.1.

Nathaniel Brewster constantly confronts one with "probably" and "if," and it hardly seems possible that so much mention of him in relation to Elder Brewster can be without foundation in fact. The coming out of a brother of Elder Brewster's would not have passed by unnoticed or have been a matter of conjecture particularly, as some suggest, that the Brewster the Rev. Nathaniel was descended from went down in the "Phantom Ship" from the New Haven Colony.

The assertions or surmises of this descent are not nearly as frequent as in regard to the Chief of the Pilgrims.

Mrs. Eva J. Hopkins Hamilton, of Chicago, called my attention to the following, which I immediately verified:

Ecclesiastical History of New England, Vol. I., page 497.

PLYMOUTH, 1642.

"This year Jonathan (2), son of William (1) Brewster, a chief founder of the Colony, takes the degree at Harvard. He soon goes to the land of his ancestors. He is ordained over a Parish at Norfolk, and gained an estimable reputation.

"He had the degree of Bachelor of Divinity from Dublin. Another person of his surname landed at Boston, under date of October, 1663."

Hull, the minister, writes in his diary:

"About this time here arrived Mr. Nathaniel Brewster, a very able and pious minister, in Mr. Prout's ship from London. Mrs. Norton entertained him and his family in her house. After a while when our church had tasted his gifts they desire a frequent labor amongst us, who together with Mr. James Allin that came hither about August, 1662, carry on the public ministry of our church."

Thus recalled to dispense the words of eternal life he died 1690, leaving many children, John, Timothy and Daniel, thought to be but not proven as grandsons of Elder William Brewster.

AUTHORITIES.

Wood, in his "History of Long Island," page 33, gives "Nathaniel Brewster, as educated at Harvard, graduated in 1642, settled 1665, died 1690."

The very confusion with Jonathan in the quotation I have given is circumstantial evidence of their relation. The parent paying the bills is strong association, which in those days of irregular records placed upon the father the education of the son.

"Sibley's Harvard Graduates," page 68, gives an account of Rev. Nathaniel, and states that he was born about 1620, died December 18, 1690, aged 70.

"Age and infirmity having for some time disabled him from performing constant ministerial duty."

Sibley has the "if" before the speculation as to his lineage, but the very fact of the subject being discussed in the early part of this century goes far to prove the general belief.

I may be allowed to say that I have sought in every trodden and unknown path to place the Rev. Nathaniel Brewster authentically. Every one has been willing to aid, and so long as this article is continued persistent effort will be made. If no further success attends me, I have at least given the public and future writers the benefit of my search.

Copy of ye last Will & Testamt of ye Revd Mr. Nathaniel Brewster, ye first Minister of Brookhaven, in ye County of Suffolk, Province of New York.

COPY.

In ye name of God Amen March ye 16, 1684-5 I Nathaniel Brewster in County Suffolk on Long Island being weak in body but of sound & good memory calling to mind my frailty & ye uncertain estate of this uncertain life do make & ordain this my last Will & Testamt, by these presents revoking & annulling any former Will made by me either by word or writing & yt this only is to be approved my last Will & Testamt & none other.

Imprimis—I commit my soul unto God my Creator in sure & certain hopes of ye Resurrection to life & immortality by ye merits of Jesus Christ & my body to be decentay interred at ye usual burying place of ye 2d town of Brookhaven as my Executor hereafter shall appoint & my worldly goods & give & bestow in manner & form following—

Item—To Timothy my son I give & bequeath ye dwelling house I now live in the house not belonging to it & ye buildings fences & other improvements thereon containing about nine or ten acres more or less & a six acre lot in ye old field joining to Capt. Tookers lot on ye one side & to Benjamin Smiths on ye other side & a five acre lot in ye little neck and five acres at Newtown & twenty acres in Georges Necke & half an acre of Meadow at ye old mans & half ye meadow at ye west meadow & half ye fifty acre lot in Mount Misery & half ye meadow & upland at ye south which meadow & upland at ye south is to be equally divided between Timothy & Daniel Brewster—

Item—To Daniel my son I give & bequeath the home lot & other improvements purchased of John Roe & two 3 acre lots in ye old field five acres in ye little necke and five acres at ye old mans near Andrew Millers the seventeen acres to be laid out the half of ye fifty acre lot in Mount Misery half ye meadow at ye West Meadow & half ye meadow & upland at ye South.

Item—To John Brewster, my eldest son, I give and bequeath fifty acres of land laid out in ye plains as in ye records may appear and in case the second John be deceased or shall not otherwise dispose of it within seven years, it shall return to and be equally divided between my sons Timothy and Daniel, before named.

Item—To my two grandchildren Daniel and Abigail Burr I give and bequeath ten shillings apiece.

Item—To Sarah my wife I give and bequeath all my household goods and chattels whatsoever together with my books and ye husbandry gneares and tools with full and free ordering and disposal of all ye stock I now possess as horses cattle sheep swine &c.—with ye assistance of my two sons Timothy and Daniel I constitute and ordain to be the executrix of this my last will and testam't to perform all things pertaining to ye office of an Executrix, to pay ye aforesaid legacys and to give and provide portions for all my daughters at her discretion out of ye improvements of ye stock aforenamed and with the assistance of my 2d two sons always provided that there be referred to my 2d Executrix a good and competent maintenance out of ye improvements of the lands willed and bequeathed to my sons Timothy and Daniel above named as also ye full and free use of ye house home lot orchards gardens and other improvements thereon which are bequeathed to my son Timothy. In confirmation whereof I do hereinto set my hand and seal the day and year above named.

Nathaniel Brewster.

Signed sealed and delivered in presence of Theo Helme,
Jack Hawkins. (Seal)

By ye tenor of these presents know ye that on ye 3d day of May, 1695, at Brookhaven, in ye County of Suffolk, in ye Province of New York, before Col. Willm Smith, judge of ye Prerogative was proved & approved the last will and testamt of Nathaniel Brewster, decd, at Brookhaven aforesd, on ye —— day of ——, Anno Dom 168— who by his said last Will & Testamt did nominate and appoint Sarah his wife to be his Executrix as by ye 2d will may appear for ye well and faithful administration of all & singular ye goods chattels credits of ye said deceased to whose care and trust was committed ye same being duly sworn to execute & preform her duty herein according to ye tenor of ye said Will & ye laws of this Province.

MISCELLANEOUS RECORDS.

Trusting the suggestion in regard to Rev. Nathaniel Brewster, of Brookhaven, L. I., in his Harvard days, may be looked up by those in the immediate vicinity of the college, the present article will be devoted to records, with the hope that there may be some results, and an active searching on the part of descendants.

The following was sent to me by Mr. H. J. Yerg, of Goshen, N. Y.:

Deed dated May 21, 1784. Record in Orange County Records of Deeds; Book "D," page 97.

To All People to Whom These Presents Shall Come or May Concern:

Nathaniel Brewster, of Suffolk County, in the State of New York, yeoman, sendeth greeting. Know ye that the said Nathaniel Brewster, for and in consideration of the sum of one hundred pounds currant money of New York, to him in hand paid at or before the ensealing and delivery of these presents, the receipts whereof and satisfaction of the same is hereby acknowledged, etc., etc., forever quit-claim unto Nathan Brewster, formerly of the Precinct of Cornwall, County of Orange and State of New York, but now of the County of Albany, yeoman.

Two lots of land in the town of Blooming Grove, etc., which Jeffrey Brewster, of Brookhaven, Suffolk County, aforesaid brother of the said Nathaniel Brewster, conveyed to the said Nathan, etc. (Signed by Nathaniel and Experience Brewster.)

Deed dated September 27, in the 10th year of the reign of our Sovereign Lord George the Second, A. D. 1736. Between Nathaniel Brewster, eldest son and heir of Nathaniel Brewster, of Brookhaven. To William Smith, of New York City, attorney-at-law.

Land in Siscoper or Cheesecocks (now Monroe). Recorded in Book "E," page 370.

Deed dated April 28, 1814. Nathaniel Brewster and Keziah, his wife, of the town of Newburgh, to James Sidmay. Land in the town of Goshen, N. Y. Recorded in Book "2," page 410.

Nathaniel Brewster to Samuel Tallman. Mortgage dated May 1, 1833. Land in the village of Newburgh, N. Y. Recorded in Book 32, page 235. Orange County Records of Mortgages in County Clerk's office, in Goshen, N. Y.

Church records of the Presbyterian Church of Goshen, N. Y., I find the following:

January 19, 1799. Married, John Brewster and Mary Harrison. Deaths, November 23, 1816, Mary, wife of John Brewster, age 48; cause of death, insanity. April 30, 1817, John Brewster. Aged 62. Inflammation of the Lungs.

In Eager's "History of Orange County," page 73, an account is given of the finding of part of the remains of a mastodon. I quote: "In 1845, found about seven miles east of Montgomery, on the farm of Nathaniel Brewster, Esq."

Nathaniel Brewster, Ensign, commissioned as ensign April 4, 1776. In a company of Brookhaven, Smithtown and Manor of St. George and Mericties, Long Is. Commanded by Capt. Selah Strong in Col. Josiah Smith's, of Minute Men. Of Suffolk County.

Archives N. Y. in the Revolution, p. 289.

In The Mail and Express of February 16, 1895, is a record which will gain new interest in the present, and certainly amounts to very much in its relation to the Chandlers, who have already proved themselves as descendants of the Mayflower Pilgrims in another line.

"The following record is taken from Cradock's 'Harmony of Four Gospels,' 1668, verbatim, and bears the name 'Samuel Molyen's Book,' 1703, and later Jonathan Dickinson's book, Ex Dono D. Tilley:"

"In 1762 it was 'Sarah Chandler. Her Book.' The same, doubtless, who in 1768 married John Brewster. Being the next thing to a Bible, it seems to have served them for a family record. My uncle gave my father the book, and he, I believe, got it at an auction. I judge these Brewsters lived in Orange County, for 'Blooming Grove' is mentioned in one place among the scribblings.

"John Brewster, born June 173—(the last figure illegible); Sarah Brewster, April the 15th day ye 1741.

"John Brewster and Sarah Chandler married the 29th day of March, in the year 1768, and had a child—born the 2d day of June (1769 or 1770?) following.

"Nathaniel B., born July the 15, 1770—and had another son Born, April the 3 day 1772, and Died the 12 day of April 1772.

"Benjamin Brewster born May 1st 1774—Joseph Brewster, born June the 14th 1776—Phebe Brewster born Sept the 10th 1778."

On another page is the following:

"Edward Brewster, dyed March the 13th 1775, Abigail Strong dyed August the 17th 1775.

"Samuel Strong and Experience Brewster, married the 13th day of Jany 1777.

"Phebe Chandler, died February the 7th, 1777 Temperance Strong dyed August 11. 1778.

"John Brewster dyed August ye 23d 1778, aged seventy-two years, nine months and eighteen days.

"Nathaniel Strong Esqur, murdered in

his own hous, October the 6th, 1778, between one and two o'clock at night (a later handwriting in pencil says 'By Claudius Smith).'"

"Charity Brewster, dyed November the 19th 1786 aged seventy-five years.

"Isaac Brewster, dyed Sept 5th 1784."

"Nathaniel Chandler dyed Sept ye 6th 1784."

"Sarah Brewster dyed July the twenty-seventh day 1794." H. M. D.

From Mr. John Bissell, Pittsburg, Pa.:

Brewster baptisms in First Church, Lebanon, Conn. No fathers named on record till 1774.

1724, June 28—Charles, probably son of Joseph and Sibil.
1724, July 6—Sarah.
1725, January 3—Jonathan, probably son of John.
1726, January 30—Mary, probably daughter of John.
1726, August 21—Abel, probably son of William and Ann Abel.
1726, August 21—Hannah, probably daughter of William and Ann Abel.
1726, January 21—William, probably son of William and Ann Abel.
1726, August 21—Elisha, probably son of William and Ann Abel.
1727, April 30—Katherine.
1727, September 3—Ann, probably daughter of William and Ann Abel.
1729, March 23—Samuel, probably son of Samuel.
1729, March 23—Mary.
1729, April 6—Elizabeth.
1729, May 4—Deborah.
1731, June 6—Martha.
1732, November 12—Tabitha, probably daughter of Samuel.
1734, May 12—Hannah.
1735, November 23—Nehemiah, probably son of Daniel.
1738, January 8—Deborah, probably daughter of Comfort, first.
1738, April 23—Nehemiah, probably son of Daniel.
1740, August 31—Ruth, probably daughter of Daniel.
1741, May 10—Ann, probably daughter of Comfort, first.
1743, January 2—Eunice, probably daughter of Daniel.
1743, August 21—Betty, probably daughter of Comfort, first.
1745, April 14—Mary, probably daughter of Daniel.
1745, August 25—Comfort, son of Comfort, first.
1747, August 9—Mehitable, probably daughter of Daniel.
1751, July 21—Daniel, probably son of Daniel.
1771, November 17—Comfort, son of Comfort, second.
1773, January 3—Elizabeth.
1775, January 22—John, probably son of Comfort, second.
1779, May 2—Melinda, daughter of Comfort, second.
1781, April 28—Daniel, son of Comfort, second.

Brewster baptisms from Goshen Church, Lebanon:

1733, January 7—Ruby.
1737, April 7—Wadsworth.
1744, June 3—Huldah.
1746, September 21—Betty.
1749, July 9—Prince.
1753, May 6—Ichabod of Ichabod.
1757, October 2—Lishe of Jonathan.
1760, July 20—Hopestill of Ichabod.
1763, January 9—Morgan of William.
1764, December 16—Ruth of William.
1770, April 15—Seth of William.
1772, October 4—Oliver of William.

Brewster marriages, from records First Church, Lebanon:

1744, May 15—Charles, m. Keziah Owen.
1748, May 18—Mary, m. John Johnson.
1752, May 15—Elizabeth, m. Benj. Wesson.
1760, May 12—Samuel, m. Experience Scott.
1759, Feb. 7—Hannah, m. Maverick Johnson.
1724, Feb. 6—John, m. Mary Terry.
1726, Oct. 26—Mary, m. Benj. Paine.
Nov. 30—Samuel m. Tabitha Baldwin.
1730, Feb. 18—Peter, m. Mary Lee.
1740—Elizabeth, m. Caleb Owen.
1744, April—Patience, m. Matthew Wolfe (De.).
1743, May 18—Hannah, m. Constance Crandel.
1744, Nov. 13—Ebenezer, m. Elizabeth De Wolfe.
Nov. 11—Elizabeth, m. Joseph Tilden.

Goshen Church, Lebanon, and other records:

1754, Oct. 16—Hannah, m. Simeon Metcalf.
1760, June 24—Huldah, m. Ozias Coleman, of Colchester.
1768, Oct. 30—Betty, m. Amos Thomas, Jr.
1772—Ichabod, m. Lucy Clark.
1773, April 1—Ruth Partridge, m. Simon Abel.
1716, Dec. 13—William, m. Mehitable Abel.
1728, May 24—Hannah, m. John Barker.
1732—Oliver, m. Martha Wadsworth.
1736, Dec. 2—Comfort, m. Deborah Smith, of Bolton.
1747, Nov. 5—Katherine, m. Eben Richardson, Jr.
1758—Lydia, m. Asahel Clark.
1755—Bathsheba, m. Josh Chappel, Jr.
1759, May 24—Wadsworth, m. Jerusha Newcome.
1753, May 31—Daniel, m. Phebe Williams, at Stonington.
1762, Oct.—Mary, daughter of Samuel, m. Jonathan Strong.
1774, June 2—Daniel, m. Rosamond Richardson.
1775, Feb. 2—David, m. Lucretia Smith.

From Rev. Zebulon Ely records, Lebanon:

1793, Feb. 13—Comfort, Jr., m. Gay.
1797, Oct. 15—John, m. Deborah Terry.
Dec. 17—Lucretia, m. Samuel Porter.
1722—Benjamin, m. Rebecca Blackman.

MORE BREWSTER RECORDS.

Although these lines are given as full as possible to show the general public various localities and names that descended from Elder William Brewster, much detail could be added, only it would simply be a repetition of what has already been published in the "Signers of the Mayflower Compact" and subsequent Brewster records.

The present one of Volney William Foster, of Evanston, Ill., has been thoroughly carried out, and those who can make the same lineage will only have to watch the passengers on the Forefather ships to secure more than usual history with regard to their own ancestry.

William Brewster, as originator of his family in this country, needs no mention; early writers have made his name a household word, and present search only confirms their high estimate of him.

Then comes Patience (2), daughter of Elder William, born in Scrooby, England, who came to Plymouth, Mass., on the Ann, in 1623, "perhaps," and "probably" (as her brother Jonathan, left to guard her, came unexpectedly in the Fortune, in 1621) under the care of Mrs. Edward Southworth, so soon to be the first lady in the land from her marriage to Gov. Bradford. Patience Brewster needed no assistance to her birthright to give her social position in her new home. Marrying Thomas Prence, son of Thomas Prence, of Lechlede, in County Gloucester, August 5, 1624, was to his credit, though the honor was his but a short time, as she died, to the regret of all and deep sorrow of her father, the Elder, in 1634.

The five children of this marriage had equal right necessarily to the Brewster claim, the Prence widened by the second marriage. As Gov. Prence is entitled to his own history as passenger with Jonathan Brewster in the Fortune, he should be thus known rather than by his marriage.

THIRD GENERATION.

Mercy Prence (3) (Patience Brewster 2, William Brewster 1) was the fourth child and third daughter of Gov. Thomas Prence, and was born in that home of the early heroes, Plymouth, Mass., in 1631; married February 13 or 14, 1650, John Freeman, who was son of Edmund Freeman. As the emigrant had the grace to come out in the Abigail in 1635 and settle in Lynn, Mass., there is no claim for reserving his history for a future paper.

Every act of the early settlers being under the strict supervision of both friend and foe, to rise as Edmund Freeman did to distinction was on his absolute merits. Both town and colony gave him important trusts. Grand Juror in 1636 and Assistant Governor from 1640 to 1646.

So John, his second son and fourth child, born in England in 1620, who came to New England with his father, was at least in a worldly sense a fitting mate for the elder's granddaughter.

The record of his youth he preserved to the end, early removed to Eastham, was captain in 1675, and actively engaged in King Philip's war. In June, 1685, was chosen Major of the County of Barnstable, was deacon of the church, one of the condensed honors of that day, and for ten years selectman.

Then he was sheriff of the county under Andross's Administration and the first-named judge of the Court of Common Pleas, after the union of Plymouth and Massachusetts colonies.

Defined as his story is, from the honors

heaped upon him, it is one of the records that Major Freeman bore a reputation equaled by few in the colony at that early date.

Descendants can ask no more than to be able to authenticate that in all his acts while a public servant he was upright and impartial, and as a source of such action correct in his religious walk and conversation.

His gravestone at Eastham bears the inscription:

"Here lies ye body of Major John Freeman. Died October ye 28th, 1717, in ye 98th year of his age."

His wife, Mercy, died September 28, 1711, at 80.

The Pilgrim welcome extended to an indefinite number of children, mainly perhaps from the needs of population to make their numbers in excess of intruders, whether the white man or the Indian, had an active spirit in this family of eleven. The crust, though small, was always capable of subdivision.

FOURTH IN DESCENT.

John Freeman 4 (Mercy Prence 3, Patience Brewster 2, William Brewster 1), the second child and second son, born December, 1651, in Eastham, Mass., married first, Sarah, daughter of William Merrick, December 18, 1672. She was the mother of all children, dying April 21, 1696, when life seemed brightest, the children having arrived at maturity naturally ready to aid their parents and smooth their pathway. History repeated itself, the children numbering eleven.

FIFTH IN DESCENT.

Mercy Freeman 5 (John Freeman 4, Mercy Prence 3, Patience Brewster 2, William Brewster 1), the third daughter and seventh child, was born August 3, 1687, in Eastham, Mass., and married Deacon Chillingsworth Foster, who was born in Marshfield, Mass., June 11, 1680.

Here again the mother raises her family sufficiently to be a comfort to her, which in Pilgrim parlance means helpful, and wearried with doing, dies July 7, 1720, aged 33.

Chillingsworth Foster, bearing testimony to the great merits of Mercy Freeman, marries again, and this time took to himself Susanna, widow of Nathaniel Sears and daughter of John Gray.

Their happiness was not of long duration, she entering the spirit land December 7, 1730, and he availed himself of the opportunity thus given him by marrying Ruth, widow of Samuel Sears, and daughter of William Merrick, December 7, 1731, the anniversary of his second wife's death. Although no relative to the Brewster connection, it is part of early history to state that he settled in that section of Harwich which is now Brewster, was a blacksmith by trade, the iron merchant of the times and deacon in the church from July 4, 1731, till he died.

Chillingsworth Foster's name provides easy means of search, and the records give him as son of John Foster, of Weymouth, Mass., who married, about 1663, Mary, daughter of Thomas Chillingsworth, a settler as early as 1637, of Lynn, Mass.

SIXTH GENERATION.

James Foster 6 (Mercy Freeman 5, John Freeman 4, Mercy Prence 3, Patience Brewster 2, Elder Brewster 1), born January 6, 1706, in Harwich, Mass., was eldest child of Chillingsworth and Mercy (Freeman) Foster, married July 10, 1729, Lydia Winslow, born September 8, 1709, in Harwich, daughter of Major Edward Winslow, of Rochester, Mass., married Sarah (last name unknown) about 1702 or 1703. Among their children were Edward, born November 6, 1703, married December 14, 1728, Hannah, daughter of his uncle, Kenelon; she died September 23, 1745; Lydia, born September 8, 1709, married July 10, 1729, Deacon James Foster; Mercy, born September 11, 1712, married October, 1723, Chillingsworth Foster.

The record is an open sesame to many societies dear to all patriots. The "Mayflower Descendants" is fully established through the Brewsters, Sons of Colonial Wars, by Major Edward Winslow, which now requires a military line, and when founded, as it must be from the nature of history in the present time, "Descendants of the Forefather Ships," there is a large place for this descent.

These pioneer men seem to have been muscular Christians; to be a blacksmith almost insured a deaconship, and James Foster followed precedent.

SEVENTH GENERATION.

Edward Foster 7 (James Foster, 6; Mercy Freeman, 5; John Freeman, 4; Mercy Prence, 3; Patience Brewster, 2; Elder William, 1), fourth son and seventh child of James, was born July 3, 1738, in Rochester, Mass.; married, January 13, 1762, Deborah Bangs, born February 5, 1744, in Harwich, Mass. This Deborah is easily accounted for, as she was the only daughter and eighth child of Seth and Deborah (Nickerson) Bangs, her father being born in Eastham, Mass., July 29, 1705, and married Deborah, daughter of William Nickerson, of Eastham, December 23, 1726.

This Edward Foster, with all the love so freely given to the Eastern States by its sons and daughters, still had the grace with favoring fortune to move to New York State and die at Broome, Schoharie County, January, 1828, at the advanced age of 90.

EIGHTH GENERATION.

Hopestill Foster 8 (Edward Foster, 7; James Foster, 6; Mercy Freeman, 5; John Freeman, 4; Mercy Prence, 3; Patience Brewster, 2; Elder William Brewster, 1), was the fourth son and eighth child of Edward; was born July 27, 1780, in that part of Pelham, Mass., now called Prescott, and married Laura Osborn, February, 1808.

NINTH GENERATION.

Volney Foster, 9 (unnecessary to repeat the line); born October 16, 1816, in Antwerp, Jefferson County, N. Y.; married, November 1, 1846, in the "Yellow Tavern," at Jefferson, Wis., Marianna Torrey (who was born in Aneron, N. Y., August 21, 1820, and died at Evanston, Ill.), daughter of William and Phebe Vander Veer Van Sicklen.

This Torrey line is a very complete one, thoug it only being the intention to lead to important ancestry, people can do their own connecting, as there is too little space to give the history entire of any family.

TENTH GENERATION.

Volney William Foster. 10 (same line), born February 27, 1848, at Aztalan, Wis., married, at Brockport, N. Y., Eva Adelle Hill, born January 30, 1852, and died at Evanston, Ill., October 18, 1887, daughter of Ezra Northrup Hill.

This line, if taken in all its branches, makes many fine connections, principal among them the great Rev. Thomas Hooker.

If nothing comes from the pursuit of Hannah Brewster, in every known and unknown locality, it is only a matter of sorrow, not fault. The interest has been active, the methods painstaking and persistent.

Many steps in the right direction are to our credit, and I am in hopes there will result an outgrowth of real historical value.

Long ago I published in the paper a growing conviction on my part that Hannah Brewster, daughter of the first Jonathan, married twice. It met with no response, and, though sorry is did not provoke discussion, it in no way dampened the ardor of my pursuit for something tangible in regard to it, nor did I change the opinion, which gathered strength with time.

HISTORY.

Miss Caulkins, in her "History of New London," states that "Hannah (daughter of Jonathan) married, December 25, 1664, Samuel Starr. She was aged 37 in 1680."

Kind fate, which in its workings seems like Providence, brought Miss Elizabeth Miner Avery, of Groton, Conn., to my department, and as part of the toll the whole world of my knowledge has been obliged to pay I immediately proposed to her the questions in regard to Hannah Brewster, so near to my heart.

She wrote me the last of 1897, giving me the following: "I copy from the Starr Genealogy, prepared by Burgess Starr Pratt, Hartford, 1879. The first mention of Samuel Starr in New London is his marriage, December 25, 1664, with Hannah, daughter of Jonathan Brewster. She was born 1643. November 25, 1691, was in full communion with the First Church in New London, where her children were baptized. No record of her death. The children of Samuel and Hannah Starr were Samuel, born December 11, 1665; Thomas, born September 27, 1668; Comfort, born August 7, 1671; Jonathan, born February 23, 1673-4."

This is the same as Miss Caulkins's History.

ABSOLUTE PROOF.

Not satisfied that these statements should lose their power for want of absolute proof. Miss Avery verified the genealogies by the New London town records (Vol. 1, Page 4), adding, "She was left a widow because a tract of land was deeded by her as such February 22, 1687-8."

This was not all; light seemed to dawn upon her as she searched and wrote me: "Perhaps she then married a Thompson, for she was only in middle life."

PERSISTENCY.

Next it was the turn of Mr. S. Cleveland, the Town Clerk of Prestouside, Norwich, Conn., to be interviewed, and immediately matters seemed to materialize.

While he had no authority there was one item with a bearing on the case at least strong enough to have found place in his notebook. Soon the name of the one furnishing it was forthcoming, and from Mrs. A. G. B. Hatch I have with the names of Jonathan Brewster's children, Hannah, born 1643, married John Thmopson, of Shetucket, Thames, Conn.; December 25, 1664, married Samuel Starr.

This would have made "Hanna" about twenty-one when she made her second marriage. Not at all an unusual age to marry at sixteen among the Pilgrims, easily verified as custom by reference to Desire Doty's marriage, and Elizabeth Tilley, wife of John Howland. Of course, many, many more.

Mr. Cleveland says Shetucket, which was set off from Norwich, Conn., was a wilderness in "Hannah's" time.

Mrs. Jane G. Austen would have seen the possible vein of romance in the youthful pair avoiding the parental vigilance (for Lucretia Oldham Brewster was not one to be left out of the count when her children's interests were at stake) and seek their Gretna Green far from the stern eyes that might be searching for them.

The Pilgrims believed in marriage, oft repeated if convenient, but discipline must be maintained. A parent was always a parent.

DIFFERENCE OF OPINION.

Miss Avery thought she might have married John Thompson after Samuel Starr's death. That would seem a point of history too easily authenticated, and, reading between the lines, as told by the history of that period, there is every argument in favor of her early marriage and its making little mark from its short duration, all claims to her then being merged in the Starr marriage, well recorded by Church and State.

Again, the persistency worthy of the cause sent me to Rev. William H. Littell, of "The Manse," Setauket, L. I., ninth pastor of the church of which Rev. Nathaniel Brewster was the first.

I quote without alteration from his letter: "According to some authorities, among them Thompson, he (Rev. Nathaniel) appears to have gone to Norfolk, England, with his wife, Sarah Ludlow, of Roxbury—after three sons were born.

"They were left with his sister Hannah and his father Jonathan, who came with them to Setauket. As to the marriage of Hannah to John Thompson, that occurred probably in Connecticut, and they came here."

These close arguments are very dangerous when so many historical threads are being unraveled by one person. But this material furnished by Rev. Mr. Littell just fits into the claims made by the previous statements.

The Rev. Nathaniel Brewster returned to Setauket in 1665, having spent two or three years in other places, as I have already written. At the close of 1664 Hannah Brewster married Samuel Starr, and was ready and willing to give up the charge of her nephews to their legitimate guardians.

Her life in regard to John Thompson was a thing of the past; new duties awaited her, and from that time her movements were recorded. Thus I have told all I know. In gaining this information I have become an historical beggar, seeking of every one the smallest morsel of knowledge in their possession.

This position I shall retain to the close of these articles. It would be very gracious on the part of any one who would lessen my severe labors by voluntary contributions for public benefit.

My reciprocating is not only a matter of duty, but pleasure.

THE CHILDREN.

The Brewsters seem wanderers on the face of the earth in those early generations. The Elder began the wail of a large family and inadequate means. Jonathan continued with his large number of children, and the Rev. Nathaniel had the family trait noted by the public, of more mouths to fill than there was supply for.

With the definite placing of Hannah, in regard to John Thompson, or rather the first I could give to the public for discussion, came a list of Jonathan Brewster's children, which I give without comment, merely as the new suggestions show themselves.

William, in the Narragansett war, 1645, came on the Mayflower. Mary married in 1645 John Turner, of Scituate, Mass. Jonathan, born 1627, married Grace. Hannah (record already given).

John, born January 20, 1631, married July 6, 1665, Mary Knight, died 1692; Benjamin, born 1633, married Annie Dart, of New London, Conn., 1659, died 1710; Grace married Daniel Wetherell August 4, 1659.

Love Lucretia, born May 3, 1630, married Samuel Sherburn December 15, 1668, died 1674.

Ruth, married first, John Pickett, second, Charles Hill.

Elizabeth, born 1638, married first, Peter Bradley, second, Christopher Christopher.

Love Lucretia is a peculiar combination, and must locate somewhere. She is spoken of in connection with Wrestling Brewster, in the records from New Hampshire, where many think he went, taking his portion of goods with him, and ceasing to be locally of the Elder's family.

Love, the young Pilgrim in the Mayflower, in history and records bears that name, but some of the descendants unite in presuming the name was the diminutive of Truelove.

While everything is possible, I still, from the association of Elder Brewster at the time he was secretary to Minister Davison, must cling to the feeling that Mary Brewster, his wife, was a daughter of Edward Love, of whom, as I have already written (the result of Miss Kouse's connections while studying the history of the Dudley family) in the "Signers of the Mayflower Compact," there is no need of repetition.

The local and name weavings of history are realities; to call one son Edward, another Love, when Mary Brewster was the possible daughter of Edward Love, does not seem an accident.

This Love Brewster, unfortunately for his continued mark on the colony, died young, but so far as his life went it spoke well for him.

The marriage of Love Brewster to Sarah (I have seen a record of her with the prefix Miss), daughter of William Collier, was very pleasing to his father, and he being a favorite son the Elder covenanted and pledged the bridal pair that his house and furniture and one-half of his estate and lands should be theirs when he died.

The will of Love Brewster surely indicates from this clause, "And for those books I have that my wife would distribute them to herself and children at her discretion," that he had his share of the Elder's books, and also the perfect confidence he felt in his wife's dignity and good judgment.

There is a very strong list of descendants, among them Right Rev. Chauncey Brewster, D. D., coadjutor Bishop of Connecticut; his brothers, Rev. William J. Brewster, Rev. Benjamin Brewster and Prof. James H. Brewster, sons of the late Rev. Joseph Brewster, Episcopal clergyman, and all Yale graduates.

Dr. Charles Jeremy Hoadley, LL.D., State Librarian of Connecticut, and his brothers, James H., George and Lewis; Benjamin Brewster, who died at his villa, Scrooby, in Cazenovia, N. Y.; Simon L. Brewster, Benjamin Brewster, William Cullen Brewster, Dr. James B. Brewster, Dr. James C. Jackson, Wadsworth J. Brewster. Prof. George T. Ladd, Dr. Walter B. Platt, Edward C. Hagar, Charles H. Buckingham, Dr. George E. Hunt, Henry C. Yergason, Cyrus A. Dodge, Dr. Charles Inslee Pardee, Dr. Henry Brewster Minton, Mr. Walter Brewster, Horace Rogers, who is doubly descended from Jonathan; William F. Brewster, who is descended paternally both from Jonathan and Love, maternally from Jonathan, and Lodwick H. Jones, who had five distinct lines from the elder, two through Jonathan and three through Love.

Of course, this is but a small portion, only enough to convey our indebtedness to Love Brewster for giving to the present men needed, and ready to spend the best of life in his memory.

The spirit of history, even wearied with searching, is not willing to give up any little item relating to Rev. Nathaniel Brewster or Hannah, daughter of the first Jonathan, his sister, as it is written by many, and believed by most. As a last hope, I went over many records to see whether in the possible assimilation of dates, I might not find a clew which would start fresh search.

A little strength was gained by "Nathaniel S. Prime's History of Long Island," where on ecclesiastical matters wholly intent (page 223) he writes of Rev. Nathaniel Brewster, as a "grandson of Elder William Brewster, who filled so distinguished a place in the Plymouth Colony—the Pilgrim of the Mayflower."

Mr. Prime, not seeking entrance on this descent to any society, told this story naturally in 1849 (I believe) with no fear or anticipation of a dissenting voice.

Two points for evidence come from the "History of the Descendants of Elder John Strong" (page 606).

Speaking of Jonathan Brewster, it says his daughter Hannah married in 1656 John Thompson and died at Setauket, L. I., October 4, 1687. Here the "about" so frequently met with in the old books would serve us well for the date of Hannah's birth. The fact of the exceedingly early marriages is not all that is wanted, even for those early Pilgrim times. How invaluable the little "rewards of merit" of the past century would prove, as establishing her in the infant class, or perhaps in her later wisdom, even as a youthful matron under the Sabbath instructions of the Rev. Nathaniel, her brother.

It is impossible, for want of space, to give many lines, as originally intended, but that is no reason why the material should not be collected for some future use. The following line is very broad, as regards names and localities, and surely will aid in suggesting names for unexpected search.

John Prince, born about 1610 (son of Rev. John, who had been bred at Oxford, and was minister at East Strafford County, Berkshire, England), came to New England, 1633, and was in Hingham, 1635, where he received a grant of land.

Freeman, March 4. 1638, removed to Hull about 1638. He married his first wife, Alice Honor, at Watertown, 1637. She died about 1668.

John died at Hull, August 16, 1676, aged 66 years. His will, which names eight children, was made the 9th of May preceding. He received a liberal education at Oxford University, England, and after locating at Hull was a ruling elder there for many years. His children, all by his first wife, Alice Honor, and baptized by Rev. Peter Hobart, of Hingham, Mass., were:

1. John, born May 16, 1638. 2. Elizabeth, born August 9, 1640; married, 1662, Josiah Loring. 3. Joseph, born February 12, 1642; died at Quebec, 1695. 4. Martha, born August 10, 1645; married, 1674, Christopher Wheaton. 5. Job, born August 22, 1647; shipmaster, lost at sea. 6. Samuel, born August 19, 1649. 7. Benjamin, born April 25, 1652; died at Jamaica, West Indies, before his father. 8. Isaac, born July 9, 1654; married Mary, daughter of John Turner, of Scituate. 9. Thomas, born August 8, 1658; shipmaster, settled at Scituate, and married Ruth, daughter of John and Mary (Brewster) Turner.

Mary Brewster was daughter of Jonathan and Lucretia Oldham Brewster, and granddaughter of Elder William.

Benjamin (3), his son, born 1693 or '94, married Aliel, daughter of John and Patience (Morton) Nelson, of Duxbury, April 17, 1717. Benjamin Prince lived for a while at Duxbury, and later removed, 1727, to North Yarmouth, Me., where his wife died September 15, 1744, and he also December 5, 1737.

Paul (4), his son, born May 14, 1720, at Duxbury, married about 1742, Hannah, daughter of David and Rachel (Lewis) Cushing, of Hingham, Mass. She was of the famous Cushing family of Massachusetts, and a descendant of the Cushings of Norfolk County, England. He died November 25, 1809. She died February 6, 1814.

David (5), his son, born May 6, 1753, married November 20, 1777. Elizabeth, daughter of Nathan and Amy (Wyman) Oakes. She died February 19, 1828; he died February 3, 1849.

Lucretia (6), his daughter, born January 26, 1784, married Dr. Elias Banks, January 17, 1805. He died February 9, 1841; she died March 15, 1872.

Elias (7) Banks (son of Dr. Elias and Lucretia (Prince) Banks), born July 14, 1809, married Dorcas Hopkins, of Portland, Me.

Their daughter Elizabeth Hopkins married, first, George W. Whittier; one child, Margaret Deane Whittier, who married Richard Storrs Colton; their child Deane Whittier Colton. Elizabeth Hopkins married, second, Edward H. Tobey; one child, Donald Banks Tobey.

Too many contributions to this history are coming in to admit of its being closed while there is such a chance of search, or holding one's peace on the desires which are growing in strength day by day.

Thanks to Mr. W. J. Ripley, of Chicago, who is compiling the Ripley Genealogy, the Brewsters have the additional line to John Alden added to the Bradford, already secured.

In your Brewster records you mention William Ripley (5) (Joshua 4, Joshua 3, John 2, William 1), who married Lydia Brewster, etc. It may be of interest to know that Eliz. Ripley (5) (sister of William) born November 4, 1724; married October 9, 1744, John Alden (4) (Andrew 3, Capt. Jonathan 2, Pilgrim John of the Mayflower, 1620, 1), of Lebanon, Conn. (See Alden Genealogy.) John (4) was born July 23, 1716; died March 26, 1789. Their children (the following) are descended as well from Gov. Bradford, through Joshua Ripley (3) and his wife, Hannah Bradford.

I. Parthenia Alden (5) married Woodbridge Little, Esq.

II. Violetta Alden (5) married Isaac Fitch.

III. John Alden (5) resided in Lebanon, Conn.; served in the Revolution; ensign of the Twentieth Continental Infantry, Col. John Durkee, January 1 to December 31, 1776. ("Connecticut Men in the Revolution," page 106, and Heitman's "Historical Register.")

IV. Judah Alden (5), resided in Lebanon, Conn.; served in the Revolution; captain in Col. Samuel B. Webb's additional Continental Regiment; commissioned January 1, 1777; killed in a skirmish in Westchester County August 22, 1777. (Conn. "Men in Revolution," page 246, and Heitman's "Historical Register," page 59.)

V. Roger Alden (5), born 1748; graduated at Yale College, 1773; served in the Revolution; Adjutant of the Fifth Connecticut Line, Jan. 1, 1777; Lieutenant June 15, 1778; Captain Sept. 1, 1778, of Second Regiment; Brigade Major of Huntington's Brigade, at Peekskill, July 13, 1779; wintered at Valley Forge, 1777-78; at the battle of Monmouth, June 28, 1778; appointed aide-de-camp, with rank of Major, to Gen. Huntington in Division Orders, Springfield, N. J., April 1, 1780; resigned Feb. 10, 1781 (Conn. "Men in the Revolution," various pages, and Heitman's "Historical Register"); settled after the Revolution in Meadville, Pa.; a member of the Conn. Cincinnati; appointed ordnance storekeeper at West Point, Jan. 20, 1825, and continued to hold the office until the time of his death, Nov. 5, 1836. He had a daughter, who married Capt. Henry Swartwout, U. S. A., and a son, Bradford Ripley Alden, who was Captain in United States Army, who died Sept. 10, 1870.

VI. Elizabeth Alden (5).

VII., VIII. Two sons who died in infancy.

Can any one doubt that clannishness is an instinct of the heart, rising superior to custom, when the claim of a common inheritance gives a person the strength and sinew of the Pilgrim colony?

The "Brewster apple tree" could bring no discord, planted by Elder William Brewster (Hist. of Duxbury, p. 284), said to be the first in New England, and though it was gone during the Revolution, another sprang from it, and continued as the Brewster tree.

MORE OF EDWARD.

What claim Edward's descendants may make for entrance into the Mayflower Society is unknown; from them may yet come, from their local habitation and name, the history so ardently sought for. All I can do is to add, to what has been given in the "Signers of the Mayflower Compact," an item recently sent me.

"In 1637 Edward Brewster had a shop, bookseller with sign of Bible, at Fleet St. Bridge London, subsequently was treasurer of stationers company." — America Neill, p. 95.

LAND RECORDS OF WINDHAM, CT.

From Mr. C. H. Dimmick, Town Clerk and Treasurer of the Town of Windham, Conn.: "The first mention made on the land records of this town relating to the Brewsters is September 22, 1725, when William Brewster, of Preston, bought 158 acres of land.

"In 1749 Benjamin, still of Preston, sold the above land to 'Cyrus Brewster, a minor under 21 years.' A very comprehensive line is in my possession from Mr. Cyrus Brewster, of Derby, Conn., and though lack of space prevents giving it all, two or three generations will be invaluable through the relation to Huntington, Conn. (where the Mills family, of Windsor, Simsbury, etc., were located), also Strathford, Conn. Cyrus Brewster, sixth in descent from Elder William Brewster, married Nancy, daughter of Henry De Witt, he marrying Hannah Dean, of Norwich, Conn., 1772.

"Their children were Benjamin, William, Cyrus, Maria and Nancy.

"Cyrus (7) married for first wife Anna Tappan, who had two children, Annie T. and Jacob D. He married for his second wife Sarah E. Mills, of Huntington, Conn. They had seven children, Sarah M., Cyrus, Mary A., Alice M., Samuel M., William J. and Jessie.

"Ann T. Brewster, daughter of Cyrus (7) and Ann Tappan, married Joseph Tomlinson, of Huntington, Conn. They had five children, Nellie, Rosalie, Joseph, Annie and Cyrus Brewster."

A DUTCH NAME IN DESCENT.

Rev. Mitchell Bronk, of New York, whose line of descent is through our Jonathan, passenger on the Fortune, writes me: "Through my grandfather, Stephen Brewster, born in 1782, I obtained actual word of mouth information about his grandfather, and the first Jonathan's great-grandson, Joseph, born in 1726."

I have in my possession a commission issued to this Joseph as ensign of the Fifth Company of Train Band, in the town of Norwich, Conn., dated 1764, and signed by Thomas Fitch, Captain-General of Connecticut under George III. I also have a sword which belonged to this Joseph and which, family tradition says, was owned and brought from Europe by Jonathan, son of the elder.

To doubters, as all become during their study of history, finding it hard to reconcile apparently truthful statements they cannot substantiate, nothing is so absolutely appalling as the possessions said to have come over in the Mayflower.

And what gives zest to the story, past and present, is that so many, perhaps from greater forethought, belonged to the Brewsters.

The grave soberness and dignity of bearing among the Pilgrims contrasts strangely with the knowledge that the most pious of the "7 pillars of the church" had distilleries in their houses, and discoursed of another and a better world while waiting for the pot concocted with experience of years to reach the temperature consistent with human endurance.

BREWSTER CONSTITUTION.

Too, they were not devoid of variety, the opportunity being given them of mulled cider and spiced drinks, Elder Brewster, as tradition tells, securing the means for such possibilities by bringing the "original and only" mortar on the Mayflower. Adding to continuous enjoyment by planting, as has been told, the first apple tree.

It is now in the possession of a descendant, who received it from the widow of Dr. William A. Brewster, of West Killingly, Conn., who was the son of John Brewster (6), son of Pelig Brewster (5), son of Jonathan Brewster (4), son of Wrestling (3), son of Love Brewster (2), son of the Chief of the Pilgrims.

William Collier comes with this line, giving additional dignity to the ancestry, a man who came as merchant in 1633, and was assistant from 1636 to 1668, inclusive.

It is a beautiful tribute to tell of him that "he was the only one of the Company of London Merchants who came to this country who furnished means to fit out the Mayflower, and he had something more than a mercenary interest in the sending out of the little ship. His conscience went with it, and he followed." (Stiles's "Windsor.")

How little he knew that he was following a man's best instinct, as the future showed, and working for his own, the Collier blood, flowing through many veins, whose descent was from those of the little ship so honored in the present.

The "Massachusetts Historical Collections," third series, volume 3, Joselyn's "Chronology of America," published in London, 1674, says: "1633, arrived in New England, Mr. Thomas Hooker, Mr. Haines and Mr. Cotton, ministers, and Mr. Stone and Mr. William Collier, a liberal benefactor to the Colony of New Plymouth, all in one ship."

The mortar was for general use, but whatever the baser needs of the day, night sent forth the odors of Araby the Blest, as round the council fires were gathered these potent, grave and reverend defenders of the faith, who were like unto other men. What they lacked was the ability to make their surroundings equal to former habit, and not having what they wished, they must be content with what they had.

OTHER POSSESSIONS.

Miss Ada A. Brewster, the artist, whose home in Kingston, Mass., has been in the possession of the name and family for over two hundred years, tells me of the orchard and woods at the rear of the house, the original planting done by Brewster hands, and continued from generation to generation.

One room has not been changed, but kept as a sort of museum. In it is an old-fashioned mirror, said to have come over in the Mayflower, and also the first rocking chair in the colonies, made for the invalid wife of Wrestling Brewster (4) by a sympathetic farmhand by fastening sounding boards on the legs of a low, easy chair.

The best prized of all, however, is the book of sermons used by the Elder, with marginal notes in his own handwriting.

There is more than a grain of possibility in regard to this book. The location is right and continuous, generations having the one garret, and there being no changes requiring the lessening of what to many might appear unnecessary occupation of space in the transportation.

Keeping records seems to have been a Brewster gift; theirs is the name which occupies everything that comes to light, at least in part, and to this trait history may yet owe the clearing up of many doubts to the records possibly quietly stored with Edward's descendants, too content in their English home to care for the messages sent from barren, bleak New England.

STILL MORE.

To Mr. William Fayal, of St. Louis, I owe knowledge of the following addition to Brewster foresight, or perhaps only an evidence of early mode of life which made such things both a necessity and a matter of course to them:

He sent me, as my final resting place, to a daughter of Dr. Oliver Brewster, of Theresa, Jefferson County, New York, who was a son of Elias Brewster.

These older Brewsters, proud of their blood, did sometimes try to preserve family history by visiting aged relatives, and taking word of mouth testimony as to their forbears.

As a result of this spirit Dr. Oliver Brewster sought Elder Timothy Brewster, of Ellesburg, Jefferson County, and after listening to the marvels of the past, received from lips of previous generations, came away the richer for "an iron trammel, something prior to a crane."

This, too, belonged to the Elder of the little Pilgrim band, and did good service unquestionably before the "common house" was in running order. The description proves its ability:

"A large hook at one end goes over a pole in open-air cooking; the pole held up on crooked sticks. At the other end is a small hook for the kettle, which can be raised or lowered by means of a second notched slab of iron, three inches wide, eighteen long. I think this slab is mended in the middle by riveting, which shows that the repairing took place before our blacksmiths could weld, a rather modern method."

THE BIBLE.

Elder Timothy remembered the Brewster Bible; said it had a wooden cover, with Elder William Brewster's name in silver letters let in the cover. "The old man, Timothy, said the boys took the silver out for knee buckles, and the book was all torn to tatteration," but "I saw in the New York 'Sun' some years ago that the Bible was still in existence."

Mrs. Eva J. Hamilton, of Chicago, herself a Brewster descendant, sends me the following from the Town Clerk of Stonington, Conn.:

"It appears from the journal of Lieut. Thomas Minor (wife Grace Palmer, daughter of Walter and first wife) that Mrs. Lucretia Brewster was buried March 5, 1679, and Christopher Avery, the emigrant, March 12, 1679 (of Groton), and from memoranda of Charles Hill, the second husband of Ruth Brewster Pickett."

RECORDS.

Again lack of space requires the curtailing of personal records. Those now given, however, have too strong a bearing on the usual acceptance of Rev. Nathaniel to be left out.

This is the line of Mrs. Clara Mitchell Howell Lyons, who now lives in the house belonging once to her great-grandfather, John Howell, and Elizabeth Brewster, his wife.

Clara M. H. Lyons, daughter of Charles Howell, son of Major John Mitchell Howell, who was son of John Howell and Elizabeth Brewster, daughter of Daniel Brewster, son of Rev. Nathaniel Brewster, of Brookhaven (Setauket), son of Jonathan Brewster, son of Elder William Brewster, of Plymouth Colony.

ANOTHER BRANCH.

In Eager's "History of Orange County" (1846) p. 545, there is mention of the Brewster family of Orange County (Blooming Grove).

It speaks of "Anna Brewster, who was one of the many descendants in Blooming Grove of Elder William Brewster, and she had two (p. 546) brothers, Daniel and John."

Amy Brewster (who married Major Nathaniel Strong, of Blooming Grove), was a great-granddaughter of Rev. Nathaniel Brewster, and was born and married in Blooming Grove, and in the family archives registered as a descendant of Elder William Brewster.

This came from Lydia Strong Howell, whose name, as every student of history will recognize, covers the Brewster trail to Long Island.

A little item of the greatest interest is proper here:

"The History of the Descendants of Elder John Strong" (p. 15) says the Strong family of England were originally located in the County of Shropshire, England.

This tells a story so strongly circumstantial that I would like to call attention to it, and while inviting correspondence ask every one who has friends abroad to interest themselves in the search for the possible history. Edward Hopkins came from near Shropshire, a neighboring town to Coventry, the home of John Hopkins, John Davenport, etc., and I have already told in "The Signers of the Mayflower Compact" of finding a pencil note giving John Hopkins's wife as a Strong, though to my great sorrow all my search fails of getting it again. At the time I saw it I had no desire for authorities, so passed it by.

This is fine material to work on.

To write of surmises and arguments is very hard indeed, and will not be satisfactory to those who want definite authority for every move. Others, too, may be annoyed at having the waters again stirred in regard to Rev. Nathaniel Brewster, of Long Island, but the hope always presents itself that out of the records of one family may grow those of another, which dovetailing with it, may start the ball with anticipation of definite results.

As yet I have never found a single attempt to prove Rev. Nathaniel Brewster as born in this country, and that on the foundation I make, confirms the idea of Jonathan Brewster's having married before he took to wife the Lucretia Oldham of history.

The majority report is in favor of Nathaniel Brewster as a grandson of the Elder's, much of the history with this tendency having been written before the issue was considered of any more importance than the natural desire to own descent from a man both distinguished and beloved, whose achievements were written in the history of the Old World; whose virtues were a tale told in the home of his adoption.

THE OTHER STORY.

To be the son of Francis Brewster, of New Haven, involved no personal hardship; it simply was not a fact as regards Rev. Nathaniel Brewster, taking the tradition of multitudes from every section as a foundation for the statement.

It is only by continuous searching that

one realizes how widespread these family claims are, the counterpart as to traditions coming from every section of the country.

It would be as impossible to eradicate the belief on the part of a descendant of Rev. Nathaniel that two generations behind him the claim was vested in the beloved Elder as to shake the convictions of those of Howland lineage of the Gov. Carver blood flowing through their veins.

To do this subject justice, I must copy from a letter written me in July, 1898, by Miss Harriet Haines Brewster, of Summit, N. J.:

"The only authoritative statement that I have would tend indirectly to confirm your theory that Nathaniel was a son of Jonathan, born in England.

"This is a statement made by my great-great-great-grandfather, Samuel Brewster, to John Adams in the year 1777. Adams in his diary ('Adams Works,' II., 441), November 17, 1777, writes as follows:

"'Dined at Brewster's, in Orange County, State of New York. Brewster's grandfather, as he tells me, was a clergyman, and one of the first adventurers to Plymouth. He died at 95 years of age, a minister on Long Island; left a son, who lived to be above 80 and died leaving my landlord, a son, who is now, I believe, between 60 and 70.

"'The manners of this family are exactly like those of the New England people, a decent grace before and after meat—fine pork and cabbage and turnips.'

"Although there may be a mistake here as to the age of Nathaniel, there seems no doubt that so definite a statement made by such an intelligent a man as was Samuel Brewster is in the main correct.

"Samuel Brewster had three brothers (I quote from the family record still preserved in the handwriting of Samuel's son Timothy, my great-great-grandfather).

"The oldest inherited the property, and remained in Long Island. The names of the other two were Henry and Timothy. Henry settled in the town of Blooming Grove, Orange County, New York. Timothy lived in New York.

"This will account for the large number of Brewster names found in Orange County, before and about 1800.

"Argument in regard to Samuel:

"I believe Samuel to have been a son of Timothy, second son of the Rev. Nathaniel, for the following reasons:

"1. From Nathaniel's will, dated March 16, 1684-5, it would seem that John, the oldest son, might have been for some time an invalid.

"2. This supposition is further confirmed by the fact that in the town records of Brookhaven, John's name is seldom mentioned, while those of Timothy and Daniel frequently occur.

"3. The name of Samuel is not among the children and grandchildren mentioned in Daniel's will.

"In the record of Brookhaven up to 1800, compiled by the town clerk, I have found the name of Timothy Brewster, or that of Daniel Brewster, affixed as town clerk to records and memoranda during the period of time extending from 1688 to 1738."

ANOTHER SEARCHER.

Mr. George Lamb, of Cambridgeport, Mass., has a theory of two Nathaniels which naturally should be left to him to place, but all will aid in the cause if they will send him every minute detail, record, deed, name or address.

This will make three earnest workers in this field, and the willingness on the part of some of the descendants to contribute toward paying for an extended search is surely no drawback.

The "English Quarterly Magazine of Genealogy" should certainly be one means of finding the descendants of Edward Brewster.

Everything being in the hands of guilds in those early times, some reference in the search should be had to them.

Those who have not enjoyed the privilege of reading the weekly records furnished in the paper, would be surprised by reference to a file, and study of the lineage published, to know how insensibly great history has been making. The limits of life and paper space do not admit of all this being carried out, but it is there, to be known and read of all men.

ANOTHER BREWSTER.

Now living on a farm about three miles from Norwich, in the town of Leedyard, the home of his fathers, is Capt. John Brewster, a man who from his own varied positions of honor has had the opportunity of keeping to the front and renewing his memories of the old Brewsters, who have lived and are buried near his home.

Within sight is the farm where, it is said, Jonathan Brewster lived during the time of his trading with the Indians, also the cemetery where Jonathan and Lucretia Brewster found their last resting place.

ANOTHER LINE.

That of Mrs. Emily Brewster Lisk, of Romulus, N. Y., can only be given in the present, but it involves names that have not yet been reached, and takes in some of the new questions aroused by recent history.

Anson Brewster married Louise Mudge. Their children were Caroline, Erastus, Anson H., William Robinson, Emily and Jefferson (twins) and Edward M.

William Robinson Brewster (named for the Pilgrim), born October 26, 1814, died September 1, 1893, married Eliza C. Mitchell, born December 25, 1813, died January 7, 1882. Their children were:

Jane T., born July 1, 1840. She married Mort Wakely.

Edward E., born February 14, 1842, married Sophie Myers. He died December 9, 1891.

Margaret, born February 19, 1844, married Lucien J. Failing, October 25, 1863.

Jefferson, born May 8, 1846, married, April 23, 1871, Ida Philips.

Emily M., born January 7, 1848, married G. I. Lish, June 25, 1872.

MANY LINES.

1. Elder William Brewster.
2. Jonathan Brewster.
3. Benjamin Brewster.
4. Mary Brewster, married Samuel Fitch, son of Rev. James Fitch, who came from England in 1638, and later founded the town of Norwich, Conn.

Another son, Major James Fitch, married Alice, granddaughter of Gov. William Bradford.

5. Jabez Fitch, born, lived and died in Norwich, Conn. Wife 2 had four sons, Elisha, Asa, Peletiah, Jabez, Jr.

6. Peletiah Fitch (son of Jabez), born 1721 in Norwich, Conn., married Elizabeth, daughter of Samuel Burrows, of Groton, Conn. Six sons, Joseph, Chester, Peletiah, Elisha, Benjamin and Asa. Two daughters, Lydia and Elizabeth.

7. Asa Fitch, son of Peletiah, married Abigail Martin; three sons and four daughters.

8. Barbara, daughter of Asa Fitch, married Peter Cortenius Dunlap, and had two sons and three daughters.

9. Mary, daughter of Peter Cortenius Dunlap, married M. Simpson Culbertson (missionary to China), of Chambersburg, Pa., 1844. Surviving children, Helen, Cornelia, Josephine M.

10. Helen, daughter of Rev. M. Simpson Culbertson, married Rev. Leonard Kip, of New York City (now in China), 1865, and has one daughter, Alice.

11. Alice married Rev. Alexander S. Van Dyck, of Brooklyn, N. Y., and had four children, Marjorie, Leonahrd, Katrina, Louis Bovier.

JOHN WINSLOW OF THE FORTUNE.

Through no intention of his own, simply as the result of circumstances beyond his control, John Winslow came to America on the Fortune. The unworthiness of the Speedwell for an ocean trip was not personal to him. The bon voyage was said by many, as the Mayflower, facing the unknown, started for any port where religious liberty would be accorded them and they might find refuge from the ills they knew of.

The first important step was the start, progression and landing of the Mayflower; but second only to it, and a sequence which gave reality to the colony, was the arrival of the Fortune, bringing not only passengers, some of them much to be desired, but "a patent of their land, drawn up in the name of John Pierce and associates, of the date of June 1, 1621." This patent was properly deposited in Pilgrim Hall, Plymouth, Mass.

GLOWING STORIES.

Where the tales of plenty and prospective gain came from it is hard to place definitely, but the "Adventurers" were not minded to see their investment in the New World continue without tangible dividends, and the Fortune was the bird of ill-omen, carrying the means of prodding the poor Pilprims, just rallying from the early sickness, few in number left them, and most of these in a weak and debilitated state, to the necessity of making superhuman efforts to send back by the Fortune merchantable material as evidence of the gains to be found in America.

The fate of this cargo has already been told; the colonists, the losers in everything but the honored few among the passengers; strong in the welcome was John Winslow.

There is no reading between the lines about this family. All is told, all is historical; they are born, christened and leave their home under the proper authorities, a clean bill of health and position accompanying them.

HIS MARRIAGE.

The variety of traditions hardly seems to warrant the suppositions as to the age of Mary Chilton, one of the passengers on the Mayflower, who afterwards became the wife of John Winslow.

If a "bright girl of twenty," as one record gives no wonder the heart of this passenger on the Fortune was torn asunder in the fear of her fellow-passengers and he not there to guard his possible interests. Still, there is a saving clause, when Savage gives the marriage as about 1627, and one recalls that in those Pilgrim days, with James Chilton and his wife in their graves, there would be no possibility of delaying this marriage to such a date, had this been her age.

A well-studied account of this branch of the Winslows places the marriage as on October 12, 1624.

True to local instincts and interests, they remained for years in Plymouth, living in the northern part of the town, their place being called "Plain Dealing," and rendered dear to them as the birthplace of most of their children. No narrow life for the Winslows, and John made Plymouth his trial trip, occupying local positions of prominence, being representative to the General Court in 1654—as Davis tells us, being on the list of freemen in 1633.

SHIPOWNER.

To modern ears, John Winslow as a shipping merchant has a very crude sound, and when it is known that he was considered an extensive one, having large connections with the British merchants, one looks back and recognizes that he was surely a power in his day, importing and exporting all there was for the benefit of commerce.

In 1656, realizing his need of a broader field, they moved to Boston, the goal of his ambition, and there in a house on Jayliffe's lane, corner of Spring lane and Devonshire street, he started the home of his maturer years, easily located as near the present Postoffice.

The deed for this property, which was made out in 1671, is in the possession of the Trott family, of Niagara Falls, and I judge from the description that it is so historically quaint as to render it a valuable addition to the records of this family.

MARY CHILTON.

Romantically speaking, Mary Chilton should have married either John Alden or Peregrine White. As the wife of either of them the story told of her would have no proportions; with Alden she could have shared the glory, if such it were, of being the first to put foot on Plymouth Rock. Then there would be no need of splitting straws as to their different claims in this respect; however decided the honor would be in one family.

Peregrine White's wife would never have any chance of getting ahead of him. He was, and none disputed it, the first born Englishman in the Pilgrim colony, and what accrued to him from this position he never hid.

John Winslow's larger methods made this of little moment. What he cared for in connection with his family was that as he and his wife had been received as members of the Old South Church on July 16, 1671, pew No. 28, should be occupied by an orderly band of little Winslows, who would need no waving rod in the hands of the appointed deaconess to keep them conscious of the requirements of the Pilgrim ritual and their proper behavior in the Old South Church.

John Winslow was making money; the times for him were prosperous. Mary had the wherewithal to give the nine little Winslows the best of everything, either in attire or for their physical wants. So happy within and without, they trudged to church before their parents, mindful that the duties of the Sabbath could be increased if they gave vent to any unseasonable hilarity or sought the repose brought on by their internal content, while the parson was telling them of future punishment or the preordination, which rendered any good behavior of no account.

LAWS OF THE TIMES.

Perhaps these children knew, as is now read in Quincey's "History of Boston," that in "1672, under the authority of colonial laws, the Selectmen ordered parents to put their children out to service or to indent them out, and if they did not, the authority had power to take them from their parents for that purpose."

Home had many privileges, and though punishments might meet the mark the parent meant, they were served to the multitude, and misery loves company.

This colonial law must explain some of the peculiar placing out of children one meets, causing wonder that there should be such necessity in families of wealth and position.

Boston, now famous for its markets, "for more that a century after the settlement of the town was destitute of a public market. Provisions were brought in carts to the doors of the inhabitants, and an opinion generally prevailed that the tendency of a local market was to encourage forestalling and raise the price of provisions."

This method obtained in New Amsterdam, though in part they had a collection of vehicles filled with commissary stores, perishable and unperishable, which was located near Jacob Leisler's house, and was quite an approach to the Faneuil Market, the pride of the Hub.

A very funny record, which shows that after all there was a method in these restrictions, is in regard to Josias Winslow, "Sept. 28th, 1630. Mr. Josias is fined for stealing from the Indians, and condemned to forfeit his title and henceforth to be called Josias." (Quincy's "Boston," page 40).

So after all Steven Hopkins had a claim he never forfeited; the Mr. remained with him to the end of his days.

BOSTON.

Boston has its own place in the hearts of New England people; early in our history it had the same value. John Winslow, growing to his privileges and prosperity, made his home there, brought up his children as nearly to his own idea as the usual parent, and then, the race being run, without any personal volition, sought by Divine decree his last resting place in Kings Chapel Burial Ground.

There, as "Rambles in Old Boston," records:

"1630
Here were buried
Jacob Sheape 1658   John Winslow 1674
Mary Chilton 1679
a passenger in the Mayflower
and wife of John Winslow."

The coat of arms on the tomb was brought from England in 1683.

THE CHILDREN.

As I find and as it is sent me there is a difference of one in the number of children allowed John and Mary Chilton Winslow. Either will do for history, and as his will is in evidence, nine children accounted for will be sufficient to secure to the marriage a plentiful descent.

At all events, Susanna, their daughter, married in 1649 Robert Latham, and here for the benefit of new students I will quote from Savage:

"Robert (Latham) Cambridge, perhaps brother of Cary, lived two years or more with Rev. Thomas Shepard, removed to Marshfield, where he was constable in 1643, thence to Plymouth, where his marriage took place, some of his children were born, and others, at his last residence in Bridgewater.

"Mitchell thinks him son of William.

"William Plymouth came in the Mayflower, 1620, servant to Gov. Carver, only a youth, and in 1627 had a share in the division of cattle, being in the lot with Gov. Bradford, yet was never named as one of the Mayflower Company in 1620, when he was a boy under Carver's charge, and for the division of lands in 1624, with another servant of Carver's, may have helped John Howland to count four heads. By the discovery of Bradford's history his right to passage in the first ship is proved.

"He was of Duxbury, 1637-9, and Marshfield, 1643-8, and in Bradford we see that after so long residence here, he went home to England, thence to Bahamas and died of starvation."

Mitchell's History of Bridgewater, which gives a full Latham descent, speaks of Cary Latham as an uncle of Robert.

ANOTHER DAUGHTER.

Mary Winslow, born 1630, married Edward Gray, January 16, 1651, a merchant and prominent man.

The oldest gravestone in Old Burial Hill, Plymouth, Mass., is that of Edward Gray, and bears date of 1681.

Sarah, the much-married daughter of the House of Winslow, united her fate, first with Miles Standish, the second son of the great warrior Pilgrim, August 15, 1660; next, in 1665, Tobias Payne, who came from Jamaica and died September 12, 1669. Savage says "with so short notice that his will was nuncup."

Destiny now brought to her Hon. Richard Middlecot, who came from Warminster, County Wilts, England, with one son Edward, and, all things being equal, made her his second wife.

THE SONS.

Mitchell, in the history of Bridgewater, where he has quite a little Winslow history, only gives John four sons, John, Isaac, 1644, Benjamin, August 12, 1653, and Joseph, but Savage adds Samuel, 1641.

JOHN WINSLOW'S WILL, 1673.

"In the name of God Amen the twelfth day of March in the year of our Lord according to the computation of the Church of England one thousand six hundred and seventy-three—Anno Requi—Regis Car secundi, Angli xxxvi. I John Winslow sen of Boston in the County of Suffolk in New England Merchant, being weak of Body, but of sound and perfect memory praised be almighty God for the same. Knowing the uncertainty of this present life and being desirous to settle that outward Estate that the Lord hath lent me, I do make this my last will and Testament in manner and form following (that is to say) First and principally I commend my Soul to almighty God my Creator hoping to receive full pardon and remission of all my sins, and salvation through the merits of Jesus Christ my Redeemer and my body to the Earth to be decently buried with such charges as to the Overseers of this my last Will and Testament, hereafter named shall be thought meet and convenient.

And as touching such worldly Estate as the Lord hath lent me my will and meaning is the same shall be employed and bestowed as hereafter in and by this my will is exprest.

Imprimis—I do revoke renounce and make void all wills by me formerly made and declare and appoint this my last Will and Testament.

Item—I will that all the Debts that I justly owe at the time of my decease to any person, or persons whatsover shall be well and truly contented and paid in convenient time after my decease by my Executor or Overseers hereafter named.

Item—I give and bequeath unto my dear and well beloved wife Mary Winslow the use of my now dwelling house with the Gardens and Yards thereunto belonging for and during the term of her natural life.

Item—I give and bequeath unto my said wife the use of all of my household goods for her to dispose of as she shall think meet.

Item—I give unto my said wife the sum of four hundred pounds in lawfull money of New England to be paid unto her by my Executor or Overseers hereafter named—in convenient time after my decease.

Item—After the death of my said wife I give and bequeath my s'd dwelling house, with all the land belonging to the same unto my son John Winslow, and to his heirs forever he or they paying when they come to possess and enjoy the same the sum of fifty pounds of lawfull money of New England unto William Payne, the son of my Daughter Sarah Middlecott, and also to Parnell Winslow Daughter to my Son Isaac the full sum of fifty pounds of like lawfull money and my Will is that both of the said sums be paid into the hands of my Overseers to be improved for them untill they come to age or day of Marriage with the full profit, that they make of the same, and in case either of the said Children die before they came of age or to marriage as aforesaid my will is that the Survivor of them shall then enjoy both the said Sums, but in case both of them should die before they come to age my will is that then the said sums shall be equally divided amongst the Daughters of my Daughter Latham to be paid unto them as they come to age or marriage as aforesaid.

Item—My Will is that my Ketch Speedwell (whereof I am the sole owner) and the produce of the Cargo that I sent out in her be (at her return to Boston) disposed of by my Overseers hereafter named and the nett produce thereof be equally divided amongst my children my son John Winslow only excepted and to have no part thereof.

Item—I give and bequeath unto my Son Benjamin the full Sum of One hundred pounds to be paid him by my Executor or Overseers hereafter named when he shall attain the age of Twenty one years.

Item—My Will is that if my Son Edward Winslow shall see cause to relinquish his said part and interest in the S'd Ketch Speedwell and her proceeds then my will is he shall have one quarter part of my Ketch Johns Adventure unto his own proper use and then the said Ketch and Cargo, to be equally divided among my other Children my Son John excepted as aforesaid to gether with my Son Edward from having any part in the aforesaid Ketch and Cargo.

Item—I give and bequeath unto my Grandchild Susanna Latham the Sum of thirty pounds in money to be paid her at the day of her marriage and to the rest of my Daughter Latham's Children I give and bequeath unto each of them five pounds apiece to be paid unto them as they shall come to age or the day of marriage.

Item—I give and bequeath unto my Son Edward Grey his Children that he had by my Daughter Mary Grey the Sum of twenty pounds apiece to be paid unto them when they come to age or the day of their respective marriages.

Item—I give unto my Son Joseph Winslow's two children five pounds apiece to be paid unto them as aforesaid.

Item—I give unto my grandchild Mercy Harris, her two children, five pounds a piece, to be paid unto them as aforesaid.

Item—I give and bequeath unto my kinsman, Josiah Winslow, now Governor of New Plymouth, the sum of twenty pounds, to be paid unto him by my Overseers in Goods.

Item—I give unto my brother Josiah Winslow, the sum of twenty pounds, to be paid unto him by my Overseers in Goods, both in convenient time after my decease.

Item—I give unto my kinswoman, Eleanor Baker, the daughter of my brother Kenelm Winslow, five pounds, to be paid her in Goods by my Overseers in convenient time after my decease.

Item—My will is that what my estate shall amount unto more than will pay funeral charges, my debts and legacies in this, my will, given and bequeathed, it shall be divided (after the decease of my said wife) among my seven children in equal proportions, except any one of my said children shall have an extraordinary Providence befall them by way of any eminent loss, then that part of my estate that shall remain as aforesaid shall be divided and distributed according to the prudence and discretion of my Overseers hereafter named, or any two of them.

Item—My will is that in case any of my now children shal die before my said wife that then his or their proportion of the said remaining estate shall be disposed to his or their children, if they have any; if not, then that part or parts shall be equally divided amongst the survivors of my said children.

Item—I give to Mr. Paddy's widow five pounds as a token of my love.

Item—My will is that my negro girl Jane (after she has served twenty years from the date hereof) shall be free, and that she shall serve my wife during her life, and after my wife's decease she shall be disposed of according to the discretion of my Overseers, hereafter named, or any tw of them.

Item—I do nominate and appoint my son John Winslow the sole executor of this my last will and testament.

Item—I do hereby nominate and appoint my loving friends, Mr. Thomas Brattle, Mr. William Tailer and Mr. John Winsley, my overseers to see this my will performed so far as they can, and I do hereby give unto my said overseers five pounds apiece in money as a token of my love.

Item—My will is that my said overseers, or any two of them, shall and hereby have power to make sale of any part of my vessel or vessels that I have not hereby disposed of, and also any other goods, wares and merchandise for the best advantage of my aforesaid children and better payment of other legacy's hereby given and bequeathed.

Item—My will is that during the absence of my said executor my overseers above named, or any two of them, have full power to act in all matters and things respecting this my will as if he was personally present.

And, further, my will is that my said executor shall not act in any matter or thing respecting this, my will, without the advice and consent of my said overseers, or two of them, and that my executor shall not under any pretence whatsoever claim any more of my estate than I have hereby bequeathed him.

In witness whereof I, the said John Winslow, Sr., have herewith set my hand and seal the day and year first above written. John Winslow and seal.

Signed, sealed and published by John Winslow, Senr, as his last will and testament, in the presence of John Jayliffe and John Hayward, Sr.

The skeptical present, with all its thoroughness of intent, large business interests and aspirations for wealth, has recognized the value of the past, and now, as if with one thought, is trudging over time and continuing the pursuits so far as personal history is concerned, of past ancestors.

A time was when word of mouth communication with the participants in the events related gave them a real value, handed down to posterity secure in their truth.

The world moved then, as now, according to the spirit of progression; the descendants of the Pilgrims took up the tales that were told and desired to verify them. They had lived beyond the period of martyrdom, wanted to be heirs in the strife, wear the honors claimed for their ancestors, and when the age of retrospection came to them, to tell to their descendants the same tales which delighted their youthful ears, with the modest addition of whatever honors might have come to themselves.

Only doing in the present what those all-revered and looked-up-to did in the past.

For the records which follow I am indebted to Major Francis Lowell Hills, or Delaware, who sent me as his addition to my department a photographic copy of the "Memorials of my Progenitors, taken by Winslow Taylor, as related by my grandmother, Madam Ann Winslow, September, 1769."

Mary Chilton was the first European female that landed on the North American shore. She came over with her father and mother and other adventurers to this new settlement. One thing worthy of notice is that her curiosity of being first on the American strand prompted her, like a young heroine, to leap out of the boat and wade ashore.

John Winslow, another early adventurer, married the said Mary Chilton, from whom have descended a numerous and respectable posterity. My grandmother, now living, and who affords me these memoirs, is their last surviving grandchild, in the 92d year of her age. Edward Winslow remained in England. His sons who came over were Edward, John, Kenelm, Gilbert and Josiah. Edward Winslow, the son of Edward in old England, was my grandmother Ann's father. The maiden name of my grandmother's grandmother was Katherine Hanly, from Old England and died in New England.

My grandfather's grandfather, Edward Hutchinson, was killed by the Indians at Albany. My great-grandmother Winslow, the wife of Edward, whose maiden name was Eliza Hutchinson, died aged 89. Edward Winslow's first wife was Mary Hilton, by whom was John, Sarah and Mary.

Edward Winslow's second wife was Elizabeth Hutchinson, by whom was Edward, Katherine, Elizabeth, Susannah and Ann, all of whom survived their mother.

Thomas Taylor was born in the middle of Wales and Mrs. Ann Taylor was a minister there. Richard Taylor, his son, came over to New England and died here. He left no other child than John Taylor, my grandfather.

Mr. Richard Taylor having sustained a good character in life was lamented in death.

He bequeathed two handsome legacies to the Old Brick and Old South Church, in Boston. John Taylor, my grandfather, the son of Richard, died at Jamaica. My grandfather, John Taylor, married my grandmother, Ann Winslow, the youngest daughter of Edward, by whom was John Taylor afterwards minister at Milton; he died aged 45.

His death is lamented as a gentleman, scholar and Christian. Elizabeth, William (my father), Rebecca and Nancy, children of John and Ann Taylor, were born in Jamaica. My great-grandmother, Elizabeth Winslow, was just 30 years of age the day after the birth of her first child, Edward, my great-uncle.

Kenelm Winslow, one of the first adventurers, was the father of Nathaniel, and Nathaniel was father of Kenelm (my grandfather). He married Abigail Waterman, by whom was Sarah, Abigail, Nathaniel, Faith, Kenelm and Joseph. My grandmother Taylor, whose maiden name was Ann Winslow (after her return from Jamaica) married Kenelm Winslow, the son of Nathaniel.

William Taylor (my father), the son of John and Ann, married Faith (my mother), the daughter of Kenelm and Abigail, by whom were William, John, Abigail, Elizabeth, Winslow, Joseph and Joshua.

The foregoing is taken from a paper said to be written by Winslow Taylor, son to William Taylor, of Milton, who was uncle to my mother. N. G.
(Col. Nathaniel Gilman, of Exeter, N. H., 1759-1847.)
July 25th, 1790.

OTHER LINES.

The Winslow name does not figure so largely in the present as many others belonging to the Pilgrims, but the descent is in almost every family of the early settlers.

Through Josiah Winslow, brother of the Governor, it takes up by his marriage to Margaret Bourne, that line of ascent, which brings them into collateral relation with the Littles and Warrens.

Then, Mary Winslow, daughter of Josiah and Margaret (Bourne) Winslow, married 1662 (?) John Tracy, of Saybrook, Conn., which gives a large and well-known history.

Again, they are relations of the Tildens, and to show how wide these early connections are, I quote a note sent me by (E. A. S.) a correspondent: "Isaac Tilden married for his second wife Rebecca Man, granddaughter of Richard Man, who is said by Davis's 'History of Scituate,' to have come a youth in Elder Brewster's family in the Mayflower, 1620.

"Richard's name was More, afterward called Man. He died in Scituate, 1656. His brother and sister Ellen died the first winter."

HEIRLOOMS.

John Winslow had every right to expect progression from his descendants. By the industry which meant much personal labor he had earned the position of merchant prince, held by birthright a claim to social precedence, and left an estate valued at $10,000.

Among the Dutch of that period there seems to have been a more actively defined craving for education. The Dutch dominies took in teaching as part of their employment, and among the wealthy it was considered important enough to send the young people to Europe that they might have every advantage.

The mercantile spirit of New England shows in the will of John, the eldest son of John and Mary Chilton Winslow, who left a request in his will that its overseers should see that his son, John Winslow, a lad then about 14 years of age, "should be well instructed in arithmetic and merchants' accounts." The arithmetic he studied, from which so much was expected, "Mr. Wyngate's Arithmetic," is still in the possession of the Trott family, of Niagara Falls, to whom I am indebted for copies of John Winslow's and Mary Chilton Winslow's wills.

ANOTHER TREASURE.

To Mr. Marston Watson, in whose home the chest now is, I owe its description. He received it from his uncle, the late Benjamin Marston Watson, of Boston, Mass., and copied for me the inscription on the brass plate fastened to the chest:

This chest was brought to Plymouth in the ship Mayflower Dec. 22, 1620, by Edward Winslow, afterwards Governor of Plymouth Colony, and from him, through his great-granddaughter, Elizabeth Winslow, daughter of the Hon. Isaac Winslow, of Marshfield, and wife of Benjamin Marston, Esqr., of Salem, Essex Co., and afterwards of Manchester, Mass., descended to her great-grandson, Benjamin Marston Watson, of the City of Boston, its present possessor, who has affixed this plate and inscription this 20 day of June, in the year of our Lord 1830.

COPY OF MARY CLINTON WINSLOW'S WILL.

In the name of God Amen the thirty first day of July in the yeare of our Lord one thousand six hundred seventy and six I Mary Winslow of Boston in New England Widdow being weake of Body but sound and perfect memory praysed be Almighty God for the same knowing the uncertainty of this present life and being diserous to settle that outward estate the Lord hath Lent me I doe make this my last Will and Testament in manner and forme following (that is to say) First and principally I comend my Soule into the hands of Almighty God my Creator, hoping to receive full pardon and remission of all my sins, and Salvation through the alone merrits of Jesus Christ my redeemer: And my Body to the Earth to, be buried in such Decent manner as to my Executor hereafter named shall be thought meet and convenient and as touching Such Worldly Estate as the Lord hath Lent me my Will and meaneing is the same shall be inployed and bestowed as hereafter in and by this my Will is exprest. Impr. I doe hereby revoake renounce and make void all wills by me formerly made and declaire and apoint this my last Will and Testament.

Item—I will that all the Debts that I justly owe to any manner of person or persons whatsoever shall be well and truely paid or ordained to be paid in convenient time after my decease by my executor hereafter named.

Item—I give and bequeath unto my Sone John Winslow my great square table.

Item—I give and bequeath unto my Daughter Sarah Middlecott my Best

Gowne and Petticoat and My Silver Beare Bowle, and to each of her children a Silver Cup with an handle:

Also I give unto my Grandchild William Paine My Great Silver Tankard.

Item—I give unto my Daughter Susanne Latham my Long Table, Six Fayned Stooles and my Great Cupboard; a Bedstead Bedd and furniture thereunto belonging that is in the chamber over the roome where I now Lye my small Silver Tankard; Six Silver Spoones, a case of Bottles with all my wearing apparel: (except onely what I have hereby bequeathed unto my Daughter Middlecott and my Grandchild Susanna Latham.

Item—I give and bequeath unto my Grandchild Ann Gray that trunke of Lining that I have already delivered to her and is in her possession, and also one Bedstead Bedd Boulster and Pillows that are in the Chamber over the Hall; also the sume of ten pounds in money unto her within Six months after my desease:

Also my will is that my executor shall pay four pounds in mony per ann foure three years unto Mrs. Tappan out of the interest of my money now in Goodman Cleare's hands for and towards the maintenance of the said Ann Gray according to my agreement with Mrs. Tappan.

Item—I give and bequeath unto Mary Winslow, daughter of my son Edward Winslow my largest silver cupp with two handles and unto Sarah daughter of the said Edward, my lesser silver cup with two handles; also I give unto my said son Edward's children six silver spoons to be divided between them.

Item—I give and bequeath unto my grandchild Parnell Winslow the sum of five pounds, in mony to be improved by my executor until he comes of age; and then paid unto him with the improvement.

Item—I give and bequeath unto my grandchild Chilton Latham the sum of five pounds in money to be improved for him until he comes of age and then paid to him with the improvement.

Item—My will is that the rest of my spoons be divided among my grandchildren according to the discretion of my daughter Middlecott.

Item—I give unto my grandchild Mercy Harris my white rugg.

Item—I give unto my grandchild Mary Pollard forty shillings in money.

Item—I give unto my grandchild Susanna Latham my Petty Coate with silke Lace.

Item—I give unto Mary Winslow, daughter of my sone Joseph Winslow, the sume of twenty pounds in mony to be paid out of the sume my said Sone Joseph now owes to be improved by my executors for the said Mary and paid unto her when she shall attaine the age of eighteen years or day of marriage which of them shall first happen.

Item—I give and bequeath the full remainder of my estate whatever it is or wherever it may be found unto my children. Name John Winslow, Edward Winslow, Joseph Winslow, Samuel Winslow, Susanne Latham and Sarah Middlecott, to be equally divided between them.

Item—I doe hereby nominate, constitute, authorize and appoint my trusty friend Mr. William Tailer of Boston afforesaid merchant the sole executor of this my last Will and Testament:

In Witness Whereof I the said Mary Winslow have hereunto set my hand and seale the day and yeare first above written.

Memorandum—I doe hereby also give and bequeath unto Mr. Thomas Theher pastor of the third Church in Boston the sume of five pounds in money to be pd in convenient time after my decease by my executor.

her
Mary X Winslow, (Seal.)
marke

Signed Sealed and Published by the above named Mary Winslow as her last will and testament in the presence of us after the adding of four lines as part of her will:

John Hand
Francis Harker
John Hayward ser

Mr Wm Tailler nominated Exr appeared in Court pro May 1670 and renounced his Executorship to this will attests.

Ira Addington Cler

Jno Hayward and John Hands made oath before the Honorable Simon Bradstreet Esq. Govr and Edwd Tyng Esq Assist 11th July 1679 that they did see Mrs Mary Winslow signe and seale and heard her publish this Instrument to be her last will and that then shee was of disposing mind to their best understanding. Attests Ira Addington Cler

By the Honorable Governor and Magistrate then met in Boston power of Adminr of all and singular the goods Estate and Credits of Mrs Mary Winslow late of Boston Widdow deced intestate is granted unto John Winslow and Richard Middlecott merchts two of his sons in behalf of themselves and others concerned they giving security to Administer the 2d estate according to law and the declared minde of the deced annexed and bringing in an Invento thereof upon

as attests Ira Addington Cler
24 July Anno 1679
Simon Bradstreet Esqr Govr
Edwd. Tyng Esqr ⎫
Joseph Dudley Esqr. ⎬ Assist
Humphry Davie Esqr. ⎭

ADDITIONAL WINSLOW HISTORY.

Being always ready to confess my ignorance that good may come, the reward is shown in the following record which, to my mind, has a possible development of very much history connected immediately with the Pilgrims, which I had not known before.

"Sir Herbert Pelham, who died 1676, married Penelope West, daughter of the third Lord De La Warr (of the new creation)."

This (Thomas West) third Lord De La Warr was Governor and Captain-General of Virginia, where he died 1618. His sister, Elizabeth West, was Sir Herbert Pelham's mother.

Mrs. Josiah Winslow's mother (Penelope West) was accordingly a first cousin of her own husband, Sir Herbert Pelham.

This Thomas West, third Lord De La Warr (Delaware) was the son of Thomas West, second Lord Delaware, the son of William West, first Lord De La Warr, who died 1595 (of the first creation).

There is a beautiful ancestry beyond all this, but sufficient has been given for present historical purposes, only it is well to know that it leads to the Pierreponts, the Hookers, the Collins, Edwards, Rogers, Burrs, Dwights, Saymours, etc., and my correspondent thinks Adam must have been a Hyde (!) claiming that everybody who is anybody in Connecticut and their descendants comes from Mr. Hyde, of Norwich, Conn.

A CERTAINTY.

The story seems a clear one, Thomas West, third Lord De La Warr, was one of the expedition with Somers and Gates to Virginia, of which he was afterward Governor and Captain-General. On one of these vessels went Stephen Hopkins and Edward Brewster, son of Elder William, who expected, and had paid his assessment, to be of the company.

There was no chance in this, and but for the shipwreck the Pilgrims would have had a sad deprivation in going without Steve Hopkins. Other non-conformists were of the company; who they were it behooves us to find out.

Elder William Brewster had been "frighted back into the low countries" by Carleton's persistent efforts to punish him for the publishing of religious works calculated to spread the spirit of religious freedom of thought and action.

Naturally, the daughter of Lord De La Warr knew of the various members of the expedition, and in later years easily fell into her husband's (Sir Herbert Pelham's) desire to cross the ocean and see for himself how affairs were progressing in the New World, and if any were kin judge of their prosperity.

Penelope Pelham's marriage to Josiah Winslow is a "twice-told tale;" still a poet's license may have been taken with some of the circumstances attending it, and born, though the Governor of New Plymouth was, in the land of his father's adoption, his stay in England with the first Governor of the name, while on one of his missions, was perhaps the beginning of the romance of his life.

MORE BREWSTER RECORDS.

Miss Emily Wilder Leavitt, of Boston, mindful of her obligations to the public, sends records which she secured in the town clerk's office, of Blandford, Mass., "300 miles above the house on Mt. Tom."

Blandford, Mass., Jenny Brewster, of Norwich, Mass., published her marriage intention with Jason Jones, of Blandford, February 20, 1797.

Moses Brewster, of Worthington, Mass., published April 20, 1842, to Jerusha Collins, of Blandford.

Dr. Joseph and Lorice Brewster, children born in Blandford: 1. Laura, March 10, 1788; 2. Venera, October 10, 1789; 3. Oliver, October 26, 1791; 4. Elizabeth, January 6, 1794; 5. Flarra, October 30, 1795.

Mr. Edward S. Beckwith, of Elkhorn, Wis., has contributed from his section, writing me: "I find in the United States census roll, town of Geneva, Walworth County, Wisconsin, June 1, 1860, the following Brewsters:

Deodat Brewster, aet. 71, born in Connecticut.

Louisa Brewster, aet. 71, born in Massachusetts.

Franklin Brewster, aet. 40, born in Vermont.

Laura Brewster, aet. 32, born in New York.

Mary Brewster, aet. 4, born in Wisconsin.

Ella Brewster, aet. 3, born in Wisconsin.

Eliza Brewster, aet. 1, born in Wisconsin.

The History of Walworth County, Wisconsin, has the following: Deodat Brewster died, Geneva, Wis., October 28, 1881, aet. 93; Lois (Louisa) Brewster died, Geneva, Wis., August, 1872, aet. 84; George F (ranklin). Brewster, born in Vermont February 27, 1820, married Laura, daughter of J. G. Palmer. Children—1. Eliza, 2. Frank, 3. Lulu M., 4. Grace W., 5. Fred.

In the Public Records of Connecticut, compiled by State Librarian Dr. Charles J. Hoadley, LL. D., are the following:

Vol. 1, p. 258, Receipts for money received through Col. Selah Hart from the following captive officers are found in Revolutionary War, XII., 130-181: Lieut. Benjamin Brewster, etc., page 13; Ebenezer Brewster to be captain in the (eight) battalions now ordered to be raised in this State, page 15; Elisha Brewster, Jr., appointed ensign; Capt. Jonathan Brewster, a prisoner in New York, page 59, also a justice, Vol. II., pp. 7 and 255. Vol. II. has Elijah Brewster, a captain, page 532; Elisha, a lieutenant, page 284. Ichabod Brewster owns land near Colchester, Vol. II., p. 336.

From Mrs. George F. Newcomb, of New Haven, Mr. S. Cleveland, town clerk at Preston, Conn.; Mr. L. E. Misher, of Norwich, Conn., and Carll A. Lewis, of Guilford, Conn., have come the same list of Brewsters gathered by Mr. Edward Cook, of Brewster's Neck. He says that in the Brewster cemetery at Brewster's Neck are buried Mr. Jonathan Brewster, son of Elder William, who came there from New London in 1650. He died in 1661, and his wife, Lucretia, who is also buried there, died in 1671. The foot stone that marked the grave of Jonathan Brewster is still in existence, and the letters on it can be distinctly seen. Other stones have the following inscriptions:

Here lies the body of Capt. Benjamin Brewster, who died April 14, 1710, aged 80.

Here lies the body of Mrs. Brewster, who died May 9, 1709. (Evidently the wife of the above.)

Here lies the body of Mr. Jonathan Brewster, who died November 20, 1704, aged 40.

In memory of Joseph Brewster, who died October 15, 1770, in the 73d year of his age.

Here lies the body of Mrs. Dorothy, wife of Mr. Joseph Brewster. She died April 30, 1779, in ye 77th year of her age.

In memory of Mrs. Sarah Brewster, wife of Capt. Jabez Brewster, who departed this life June the 18th, A. D. 1773, in the 23d year of her age.

In memory of Miss Mary, daughter of Jonathan Brewster and Lucy, his wife. She died Dec. 31, 1778, in ye 24th year of her age.

In memory of Capt. Jabez Brewster, who died May 12, 1802, in the 56th year of his age.

In memory of Miss Dolly Brewster, daughter of Capt. Jabez and Dolly Brewster, who died Nov. 11, 1810, in the 20th year of her age.

Lord, I commit my soul to Thee;
Accept the sacred trust,
Receive this nobler part of me
And watch my sleeping dust.

In memory of Mr. Pelatiah Brewster, who died March 28, 1812, in the 59th year of his age.

In memory of Mrs. Hannah Brewster, wife of Mr. Pelatiah Brewster, who died August 31, 1811, in the 57th year of her age.

In memory of Mr. Nathan Brewster, who died Aug. 30, 1817, aged 35.

The sweet remembrance of the just
Shall flourish, tho' they sleep in dust.

In memory of Mrs. Cynthia Brewster, wife of Mr. Nathan Brewster, who died Nov. 29, A. D. 1814, aged 30 years.

Tho' it may seem of little weight
Which of us goes before,
For surely we shall shortly meet
Never to part no more.

Mr. Cleveland further adds: "It is true that the son of Jonathan (2), Benjamin (3), is buried in Preston, and I do not think it is improbable that his mother Lucretia was.

"Benjamin, as you know, being the only surviving son of Jonathan, and his mother surviving her husband, would, I think, have been likely to have lived with him."

POSSESSIONS.

Why it is so much easier to reach the Brewster descendants than any other family is a mystery, but they respond promptly and willingly to any call for their history.

In this spirit Mr. E. B. Freeman, of New York, sent the following valuable information:

There is in the possession of his brother, William C. Freeman, of Owego, N. Y., a Brewster Bible, "printed in Edinburgh, England, A. D., 1663." From him I have its history.

"Mary Brewster, a direct descendant of Elder Brewster, married Silas Freeman some time in the year 1700."

This Bible was presented to her on her wedding day by her father and has passed through each generation of the Freeman family until it reached its present possessor.

A sister living in Wilkesbarre owns a pair of tramels, Mr. E. B. Freeman has a prayer book, and the family of the late Dr. S. D. Freeman, of Smethport, Pa., have a tea chest and silver buckles, all inherited from Elder Brewster.

HISTORICAL TANGLES—BENJAMIN FULLER PLACED.

Few courtesies extended to this department could be more acceptable to the public than the following, sent by Mrs. F. H. Lovell:

FULLER.

A great deal of research has been made by genealogists regarding the marriage of Benjamin Fuller (4), son of Samuel (3), of Samuel (2), of Edward (1), passenger on the Mayflower.

While studying quite a different line, the record of Benjamin Fuller's marriage has been discovered:

VITAL RECORD OF REHOBOTH.
James M. Arnold.

MARRIAGES AND INTENTIONS.
December 14, 1664.

Page 143—Jonathan Fuller and Elizabeth Willmot. (See note page 912.)

No record of birth, showing probably that both came from other places.

BIRTHS.

Page 613—Jonathan, 1665, son of Jonathan and Elizabeth Fuller. The first recorded Fuller born in Rehoboth.

Page 613—Gives a long line of Fullers from 1665 to 1700, no Benjamin, although the names of Samuel and Matthew appear, which seems to be conclusive that the Rehoboth and Barnstable, or Mayflower Fullers, were closely connected.

PROPRIETORS, NOT INHABITANTS OF REHOBOTH.

Page 917—Benjamin Fuller, February 7, 1689.

BIRTHS.

Page 613—Ezekiel, son of Benjamin and Mary ——, February 11, 1695-6.

DEATHS.

Page 825—Mary, wife of Ben (!), February 27, 1695-6.

No record of this marriage in Rehoboth, although the birth of the son and the death of the mother sixteen days after are recorded there.

INTENTIONS AND MARRIAGES.

Page 143—Benjamin Fuller and Judith Smith. Intention 1697. Married January 13, 1698-9.

BIRTHS.

Page 613—Amos, son of Benjamin and Judith Fuller, second wife, October 25, 1699.

The births of
1. Temperance, March 7, 1702.
2. Hannah, May 20, 1704.
3. John, December 25, 1706.
4. James, May 1, 1711,

are recorded in Barnstable.

DEATHS.

Page 825—Benjamin Fuller, January 11, 1711-2, showing that Benjamin Fuller returned to Rehoboth to die. James, the last child, was born eight months before he died, or four months afterward.

DEATHS.

Page 877—Judith, died November 26, 1753. Recorded in Rehoboth.

PARENTAGE OF JUDITH,
Wife of Benjamin Fuller.

Page 343—Daniell Smith and Ester Chickering, October 20, 1659.

Page 743—Daughter, Judith, born February 7, 1678.

DEATHS.

Page 876—Ester, wife of Daniell Smith, Esq., buried June 6, 1687.

Page 877—Daniell Smith, Esq., buried March 5, 1724.

Judith's mother died before her marriage, no record of her father, Daniell Smith, making a second marriage. Judith probably went to her home in Rehoboth, from Barnstable, with her four young children and sick husband to her father's, Daniell Smith, whose record of death does not occur until twelve years after.

There is no doubt, I think, that as the record of the birth of James, the last child, is in Barnstable, 1711, and the Rehoboth Records give 1711-12, as the date of Benjamin Fuller's death, that the year was 1712, and the child James was eight months old when Benjamin died.

There are more records to prove the intimacy and friendship of the Fuller and Smith families, but probably sufficient has been given.